Constitutional Law and the EU Balanced Budget Princip

AF675757

Exploring the balanced budget rule as an economic standard and as a legal principle, this book explains the context and content of the balanced budget rule and presents a critical appraisal of its impact on legal systems, political institutions and social values, and particularly an evaluation of its constitutionalization in the European and national legal systems.

Examining a range of perspectives on the balanced budget rule as a legal principle, a series of chapters investigate the feasibility and effectiveness of the balanced budget rule. The book considers the impact this may have on the separation of powers within the state, on democratic decision-making, on the European social model and on the protection of fundamental social rights within the European Union. It suggests that this impact goes beyond the ethical issue of the public debt considered as a burden placed on future generations, and beyond injunctions imposed by international financial institutions on national public finances. The transfiguration of fiscal discipline from an economic requirement into a legal rule demanding a balanced budget embodies a challenge to the political nature of the budgetary process while creating the flexibility needed in order to further fiscal federalism within the European Union.

This book argues that the balanced budget rule is nothing more than it has always been: an instrument for devising public policies in a rational manner, a tool for conceiving qualitative choices regarding the well-being of citizens.

Elena-Simina Tănăsescu is Professor of Constitutional Law at the University of Bucharest, Romania.

Eric Oliva is Professor of Public Finance at Aix-Marseille Université, France.

Routledge Research in EU Law

Available titles in this series include:

Centralized Enforcement, Legitimacy and Good Governance in the EU
Melanie Smith

EU External Relations and Systems of Governance
The CFSP, Euro-Mediterranean Partnership and Migration
Paul James Cardwell

The EU Social Market Economy and the Law
Theoretical Perspectives and Practical Challenges for the EU
Delia Ferri and Fulvio Cortese

Gender and the Court of Justice of the EU
Jessica Guth and Sanna Elfving

The EU and the Proliferation of Integration Principles under the Lisbon Treaty
Francesca Ippolito, Maria Eugenia Bartoloni, Massimo Condinanzi

Migration Law and the Externalization of Border Controls
European State Responsibility
Anna Liguori

Member States Interests and European Union Law
Revisiting the Foundations of Member State Obligations
Marton Varju

Constitutional Law and the EU Balanced Budget Principle
Elena-Simina Tănăsescu and Eric Oliva

https://www.routledge.com/Routledge-Research-in-EU-Law/book-series/ROUTEULAW

Constitutional Law and the EU Balanced Budget Principle

Edited by
Elena-Simina Tănăsescu and Eric Oliva

Routledge
Taylor & Francis Group
LONDON AND NEW YORK

First published 2022
by Routledge
2 Park Square, Milton Park, Abingdon, Oxon OX14 4RN

and by Routledge
52 Vanderbilt Avenue, New York, NY 10017

Routledge is an imprint of the Taylor & Francis Group, an informa business

© 2022 selection and editorial matter, Elena-Simina Tănăsescu and Eric Oliva; individual chapters, the contributors

The right of Elena-Simina Tănăsescu and Eric Oliva to be identified as the authors of the editorial material, and of the authors for their individual chapters, has been asserted in accordance with sections 77 and 78 of the Copyright, Designs and Patents Act 1988.

All rights reserved. No part of this book may be reprinted or reproduced or utilised in any form or by any electronic, mechanical, or other means, now known or hereafter invented, including photocopying and recording, or in any information storage or retrieval system, without permission in writing from the publishers.

Trademark notice: Product or corporate names may be trademarks or registered trademarks, and are used only for identification and explanation without intent to infringe.

British Library Cataloguing-in-Publication Data
A catalogue record for this book is available from the British Library

Library of Congress Cataloging-in-Publication Data
A catalog record has been requested for this book

ISBN: 978-1-138-74287-1 (hbk)
ISBN: 978-1-032-11958-8 (pbk)
ISBN: 978-1-315-18188-2 (ebk)

DOI: 10.4324/9781315181882

Typeset in Bembo
by Taylor & Francis Books

Contents

Illustrations

Figures

Table

Contributors

Daphne Akoumianaki is Doctor of Law of the University Paris 1 Panthéon-Sorbonne and member of the Athens Bar Association. She teaches at the Hellenic Open University and works as a Scientific Associate at the Scientific Service of the Hellenic Parliament.

Giulia Aravantinou Leonidi is a Postdoctoral Research Fellow in Comparative Public Law at the University of Rome 'La Sapienza'.

Cornel Ban is Professor of International Political Economy at Copenhagen Business School.

Michel Bouvier is Professor Emeritus, University Paris 1 Panthéon-Sorbonne, founder of the International Public Finance Foundation (FONDAFIP) and editor of *Revue française de Finances publiques.*

Simona Gherghina is Professor of Public Financial Law and Public Contracts at the University of Bucharest.

Bogdan Iancu is Associate Professor at the Faculty of Political Science, University of Bucharest.

George Katrougalos is Professor of Public Law at Democritus University of Thrace and currently a Member of the Hellenic Parliament for SYRIZA party and former Minister of Foreign Affairs of Greece.

Eric Oliva is Professor of Public Finance at Aix-Marseille Université.

Gilbert Orsoni is Professor Emeritus, Aix-Marseille Université, Honorary Director of the Center for Fiscal and Financial Studies, and Honorary President of the *Société française de finances publiques.*

Ralf P. Schenke is Professor of Public Law at the University of Wurzburg.

Thomas Stauffer holds a Ph.D. in Social Sciences and a Master's degree in Legal Studies from the University of St Gallen (Switzerland). Currently, he is a Programme Manager for public financial management with the Swiss federal government.

Elena-Simina Tănăsescu is Professor of Constitutional Law at the University of Bucharest.

Marc Verdussen is Professor of Constitutional Law at the University of Louvain (UCL) and Director of the Research Center on State and Constitution (CRECO-JUR I).

Balanced budget and/in the law

Eric Oliva and Elena-Simina Tănăsescu

What is a balanced budget?

A budget is said to be in balance if the income is equal to the expenditure. A budget is in imbalance when it is in deficit or in excess. The budget deficit is the negative balance between revenue and expenditure. The budget surplus is the positive balance between revenue and expenditure. These are technical terms, which do not have a negative or positive connotation. Budgetary deficit or surplus may be the result of public policies wisely carried out in order to achieve certain objectives, or the product of errors of assessment in the planning or execution of the respective budget. When it comes to public finances, it seems that economists, relying on common sense,[1] show a marked preference for a balanced budget – that is, for a state budget whose expenditure is equivalent to revenue,[2] a public deficit being considered an undesirable result, while surplus enjoys a positive connotation. Yet, while there seems to be a consensus that state budgets have a triple nature, being political action concealed in a legal act and shaping economic phenomena, in this respect the economic approach seems to take precedence.[3]

What makes balanced budgets so appealing to economists? In general, a balanced budget is considered desirable not only as an objective in itself, but

1 The balanced budget is a political, economic and legal principle, but above all it rests on a psychological foundation. See Michel Bouvier, 'Les représentations théoriques du principe d'équilibre, essai sur la vanité d'un principe' in Lucile Tallineau (ed.) *L'équilibre budgétaire* (PUAM Economica 1994), 23.

2 "With a balanced budget rule, any proposal for expenditure must be coupled with a proposal for taxation." See James M. Buchanan, Richard E. Wagner, 'The Political Biases of Keynesian Economics' in James M. Buchanan, Richard E. Wagner (eds) *Fiscal Responsibility in Constitutional Democracy* (Martinus Nijhoff 1978), 89.

3 In the vocabulary of the theory of systems, the performance of each of these three approaches depends on the relationship between them, i.e. on the interaction between the political, the legal and the economic and social systems. "While each system fulfils a function that is indispensable to society as a whole, it cannot directly influence, but only irritate the others." See Lars Viellechner, 'The Limits of Law (and Democracy) in the Euro Crisis: An Approach from Systems Theory' (2016) 17 (5) *German Law Journal* 750.

DOI: 10.4324/9781315181882-1

also because of one of its most important consequences, namely the stabilization of the economy that generates the stability of the national currency. Indeed, if public finances are balanced, the value of the monetary benchmark against which economic exchanges are carried out on the respective national market can remain constant, which makes possible the confidence of economic actors and improves the predictability of economic and financial exchanges. The correlation between a balanced budget and the health of the economy has been established by economists in a sufficiently clear manner.[4]

The penchant for balanced budgets has also permeated law and, from a legal point of view, budgetary discipline is achieved through fiscal rules.[5] Legal requirements for a balanced budget are often heralded as a panacea for fiscal deficits and/or public debt, but are they likely to succeed in their stated goal? A balanced budget is a legal effect pursued through legal standards which address a political will and an economic reality. It is not easy to cure a political appetite for spending that might lead to public debt through abstract legal norms.

Fiscal rules, like any legal norm, operate through a legal hypothesis that identifies a targeted social phenomenon, a disposition that imposes certain behaviour and a sanction that should be applied in case of non-compliance with the disposition of the norm. Although they aim for an economic reality and they translate political actions, fiscal rules operate in the legal arena through instruments specific to law.[6] In that sense, a balanced budget requires legal rules which impose the equivalence between available resources and disbursements envisaged by the state. The general logic behind this is that requiring public revenues to equal public expenditures through legal norms will automatically cause the above-mentioned equivalence in practice. But even if public debt is avoided as a matter of principle, unforeseen circumstances can give rise to situations where exceptions could be granted and expenditures may increase beyond predicted levels.[7]

4 Academic scholarship identified three main functions of state budget: redistribution of resources, allocation of resources and stabilization of the economy. In fiscal federations, the stabilization function should belong to the federal level, which should have a central instrument to support federate entities while monitoring their fiscal policies. See Richard A. Musgrave, 'Theories of fiscal federalism' (1969) 24 (4) *Public finance = Finances publiques* 521–536; Wallace E. Oates, *Fiscal federalism* (Harcourt Brace Jovanovich 1972).

5 James Buchanan remains famous for his "BBA", i.e. the requirement that a balanced-budget amendment should be appended to the Constitution. See Buchanan and Wagner (n 2).

6 Neil MacCormick, *Rhetoric and the Rule of Law: A Theory of Legal Reasoning* (OUP 2005).

7 This approach is based on the historical precedent set by the decision of the US Congress in 1790 to nationalize at federal level the debt accumulated by the federate states during the War of Independence. Alexander Hamilton, then minister of finance, argued that the debt was the price of liberty. However, it is worth mentioning that, from that moment until the Civil War (1860–1861), federate states incurred new and significant public debt, which made the US Congress adopt a 'no bailout' policy. Since then, federate states must present annual balanced budgets while bailout at federal level, similar to the one performed in 1790, is

Additionally, from the resources available to them, states can always count on loans, so borrowing[8] may also be considered public revenue. Can legal rules state that a budget is still to be considered as balanced when it includes a deficit? Or is it possible that a certain level and/or kind of debt is conceivable within a balanced budget (e.g. for financing investment that may produce future revenue or providing disaster relief)?[9] In other words, is there a so-called "golden rule" concerning public debt which can be accepted within the legal definition of a balanced budget? Furthermore, can this "golden rule" be predefined, including by assigning it a specific figure (say, 3%)? Finally, when can such a rule be made operational – that is, when can a budget be assessed as balanced: early in the planning process, during its execution or upon budget discharge? Annually or over several years? The concept of balanced budget is not easy to pin down from a technical point of view, which makes its legal definition difficult.

It is the technicality of the matter that makes the balanced budget a relative concept from a political perspective. Revenues and expenditures are determined in the political arena, where it is fairly easy to delay spending into the next fiscal year or to formally consider that legal rules (i.e. abstract norms) imposing a balanced budget provide actual (i.e. factual) revenues and expenditures in the budget. It is difficult to imagine a balanced budget requirement having a meaningful impact on the day-to-day operations of any legislator. The experience of the USA has shown that limiting sovereign debt through mandatory legal rules can be tricky: if Parliament could legally prevent itself from incurring debt, any such rule would be easily challenged whenever Parliament was able to produce a justification; should the Constitution demand a balanced budget, all difficulties related to the technical definition of the concept would be politically exploited.[10]

On the other hand, the political responsibility for budgetary decisions may appear diminished due to a certain dilution of the causal link between a specific political decision and the budgetary imbalance that may be noticed only later. In contemporary democracies, political cycles inherent to representative mandates are conducive to short-term deficits and a postponement of austerity into

excluded. See also Laurence Tribe, *American Constitutional Law*, third edition, vol. I (Foundation Press 2000), 730 ss.

8 According to Buchanan, public debt constitutes a burden to future taxpayers, a moral hazard that may induce decision-makers in current politics to incur excessive debt and reveal a deficit bias in fiscal policies, and that is the reason why this deficit bias should be restrained by constitutional rules.

9 Switzerland and Germany epitomize the two alternatives. Thus, unlike Switzerland, where revenue and expenditure have to be kept in balance at all times over an economic cycle, Germany considers its budget to be balanced while including public debt up to a certain ceiling (0.35% of GDP). Also see Thomas Biebricher, 'Neoliberalism and Law: The Case of the Constitutional Balanced-Budget Amendment' (2016) 17 (5) *German Law Journal* 835–856.

10 David J. Hebert, 'The Irrelevance of Balanced Budget Amendments' in Richard E. Wagner (ed.), *James M. Buchanan – A Theorist of Political Economy and Social Philosophy* (Palgrave Macmillan 2018), 169–186.

the future.[11] And since the possible negative consequences of budgetary imbalances are likely to occur rather late – compared to the moment when the political decisions were taken – their electoral impact may be considerably reduced.

Furthermore, it is the principle of the separation of powers that supports the idea that politically designated parliaments adopt budgets but, in the practice of most states, governments are the masters of budgets. It is the executives that shape and lead economic policy of the state through budgets, which are formally approved by parliaments but no longer democratically discussed in each and every detail.[12] Although constitutionalism equates with limiting political power through legal rules, governments and parliaments are politically free to decide upon public policies and, while following budgetary procedures as prescribed by legal rules or even pretending to obey the orthodoxy of the technically balanced budget, they may simply enjoy their sovereign decision-making power and end up with imbalanced budgets. Consequently, from a political point of view, a balanced budget may be merely an illusion.

Moreover, the balanced budget principle may deserve attention not only from an economic, legal or political perspective, but also from a moral one. Financial burdens resulting from excessive public debt threaten to be transferred to future generations. Thus, the debate on the balanced budget can be linked to the topic of intergenerational justice, and its impact on future generations has remained an issue ever since the label of "deficit bias"[13] was coined on political strategies such as those described above.

Despite these conceptual twists, legal standards requiring balanced budgets have now become the norm.[14] Imposed initially at international level, they have been translated into constitutional or legal rules especially after the Second World War.[15] Such fiscal rules may be substantive requirements referring to expenditure or debt, or procedural complications for an executive or legislature that would like to pass imbalanced budgets. Numerous states have fiscal rules constraining revenue

11 It is interesting to note that while the evidence regarding the deficit bias of parliamentary and proportional representation political systems seems inconclusive, direct democracy does display a lower deficit bias. See Lars P. Feld, 'The Quest for Fiscal Rules' in Wagner (n 10) 983.

12 Violeta Ruiz Almendral, 'A Myopic Economic Constitution? Controlling the Debt and the Deficit Without Fiscal Integration' in Marise Cremona, Bruno De Witte, Claire Kilpatrick (eds), *Constitutional Change Through Euro-Crisis Law* (2015) 12 EUI Working Paper Series, LAW 19.

13 James M. Buchanan and Richard E. Wagner, *Democracy in Deficit: The Political Legacy of Lord Keynes* (Academic Press 1977).

14 It may be useful to remember that legal standards imposing budgetary discipline are not a contemporary phenomenon. Constitutional constraints on taxing and/or spending have existed in practice since 1215 – see paragraph 12 of Magna Charta Libertatum – and were widely applied across the European continent from the 11th century.

15 Fred L. Morisson, 'Fiscal Rules: Legal Limits on Government Deficit and Debt' in Fred Morisson (ed.), *Fiscal Rules – Limits on Governmental Deficits and Debt* (Springer 2016), 10–15.

or expenditure, capping debt or calling for a balanced budget.[16] Notwithstanding the fact that it came as a consequence of an economic crisis, the EU budgetary constraints imposed on EU member states through the Treaty on Stability, Coordination and Governance (TSCG)[17] landed on a rather fertile soil.

"Never waste a good crisis"

Winston Churchill is famously credited with uttering these words towards the end of the Second World War as he was working on the creation of the United Nations. This is a quote used in a variety of situations and it could be easily applied to the numerous crises faced by the European Union in recent years: the euro-crisis, the migration crisis, the rule of law crisis, the COVID-19 crisis. Let us start chronologically.

The global economic and financial crisis that started in 2008–2009 was ignited by financial losses incurred primarily by the private banking sector in some countries outside the European Union (EU). This crisis triggered the intervention of states, including within the EU, resulting in an increase in sovereign debt which, in some cases, came close to sovereign default. By the time this domino effect reached the EU member states, the label "euro-crisis" had already been created.

However, the euro-crisis also had a more specific context. The Economic and Monetary Union (EMU) created in 1991 by the Treaty on the European Union (TEU) has been considered flawed from the start, due to a lack of convergence between a monetary union that falls under the exclusive competence of the EU and an economic union based on the decentralized structure of the EU. While coordination of economic policies among member states was loosely regulated in the original treaties,[18] the creation of the single European currency (Euro) required them to complete the internal market and to put in

16 For a systematic account of the use and design of fiscal rules covering national and supranational fiscal rules in 96 countries from 1985 to 2015, see Victor Lledó, Sung-wook Yoon, Xiangming Fang, Samba Mbaye and Young Kim, 'Fiscal Rules at a Glance' (2017) IMF Background Note, Washington 2017, and the 'Fiscal Rules Dataset 1985–2015', www.imf.org/external/datamapper/FiscalRules/map/map.htm

17 The Treaty on Stability, Coordination and Governance in the Economic and Monetary Union, also known as TSCG, was signed on 2 March 2012 by 25 member states of the European Union and stated in its preamble: "Bearing in mind that the need for governments to maintain sound and sustainable public finances and to prevent a government deficit becoming excessive is of an essential importance to safeguard the stability of the euro area as a whole, and accordingly requires the introduction of specific rules to address this need, including a balanced budget rule and an automatic mechanism to take corrective action." It includes a "Fiscal Compact" that includes a balanced budget rule which is deemed to be transposed by all signatory parties "by provisions of binding force and permanent character, preferably constitutional".

18 Article 6 of the Treaty Establishing the European Community obliged member states to "coordinate their respective economic policies to the extent necessary to attain the objectives of the Treaty".

place a robust system of coordination of their economies that would allow for economic convergence. In principle, the stability of any given currency depends on the balance of public finances supporting it. In the case of the European Union, in the long term, common fiscal rules and tight budgetary discipline have been considered building blocks of the economic union. Yet it is difficult for a common market using a single currency to coexist with sovereign national decisions on public spending, and therefore economic governance remained problematic in the absence of political governance.[19]

Despite such incomplete European fiscal federalism, in order to attain the economic stability necessary for the monetary union, a certain fiscal balance had to be maintained in accordance with the requirement that "Member States shall avoid excessive government deficits".[20] Thus, a Stability and Growth Pact (SGP) was devised at European level. The SGP is, however, not a specific source of EU law. Rather, it represents a set of rules designed to ensure that member states have sound public finances and that they coordinate their fiscal policies through the prevention of problematic evolutions of national fiscal policies and the correction of excessive public debt or excessive budget deficit. Initially a part the generic prohibition of excessive deficit, the SGP also included Protocol 12 to the Treaty Establishing the European Community, which detailed the excessive deficit procedure. The Pact also included two Council regulations,[21] the first regarding the surveillance of budgetary positions (preventive arm) and the second clarifying the implementation of the excessive deficit procedures (corrective arm). Later, a revision of Protocol 12 quantified the term "excessive" as 3% of gross domestic product (GDP) for the budget deficit and 60% of GDP for the public debt. It was the sovereign debt crisis caused by the global economic and financial crisis of 2008–2009 that compelled both member states and the supranational organization itself to respond and strengthen the SGP through the "Six-Pack"[22] adopted in 2011, the Treaty on

19 Christian Joerges, 'The Market without a State? The "Economic Constitution" of the European Community and the Rebirth of Regulatory Politics' (1997) 1 (19) *European Integration Online Papers*http://eiop.or.at/eiop/pdf/1997-019.pdf

20 Former article 104 Treaty Establishing the European Community, currently article 126 of the Treaty on the Functioning of the European Union (TFEU).

21 Council Regulation (EC) 1466/97 on the strengthening of the surveillance of budgetary positions and the surveillance and coordination of economic policies is known as the *preventive* arm of the SGP; Council Regulation (EC) 1467/97 on accelerating and clarifying the implementation of the Excessive Deficit Procedure is known as the *corrective* arm of the SGP.

22 Two regulations revising Council Regulation (EC) 1466/97 and Regulation (EC) 1467/97, as well as Regulation (EU) No 1173/2011 on the effective enforcement of budgetary surveillance in the euro area (the sanctions regulation); Regulation (EU) No 1174/2011 of 16 November 2011 on enforcement measures to correct excessive macroeconomic imbalances in the euro area; Regulation (EU) No 1176/2011 of 16 November 2011 on the prevention and correction of macroeconomic imbalances; Directive 2011/85/EU on requirements for budgetary frameworks of the Member States.

Stability, Coordination and Governance in the Economic and Monetary Union (TSCG) adopted in 2012, and the "Two-Pack"[23] adopted in 2013.

Like any sovereign debt crisis, the euro debt crisis also represented a crisis of confidence.[24] In order to fight it, member states had to internalize budgetary discipline under external monitoring. This meant, among other things, a rather strict capping of state deficit and debt coupled with what is defined by the International Monetary Fund (IMF) as "fiscal consolidation" – that is, austerity measures.[25] The focus of the revised SGP has been the budgetary procedure and the final macro-position of national budgets, while defining those requirements and establishing the monitoring mechanisms belonged with the supranational level. And the EU has managed to coordinate fiscal policies of member states through procedures rather than through funds for macro-economic adjustments. Although, in principle, budgetary discipline does not necessarily equate with austerity, due to the EU context and the peculiarities of the manner in which it has been accomplished, the simultaneous and coordinated undertaking of a balanced budget rule by so many states under the given economic circumstances has been perceived as problematic from a democratic perspective[26] and its impact on the European welfare system has been questioned.[27]

Indeed, in the absence of adequate EU legal instruments member states resorted to the intergovernmental method. Given the limited capacity of the EU to borrow, its own budget was unable to ensure the function of economic stabilization. Much attention has been given to the fact that the first instrument used in order to deal with a financial and economic crisis, the European Financial Stability Mechanism, was imagined as a special fund outside the scope of EU law and was designed to allow the European Commission to contract loans on financial markets and to transfer such loans to those member states in need of assistance, but only based on conditionalities defined in close coordi-

23 Regulation (EU) No 473/2013 of the European Parliament and of the Council of 21 May 2013 on common provisions for monitoring and assessing draft budgetary plans and ensuring the correction of excessive deficit of the Member States in the euro area; Regulation (EU) No 472/2013 of the European Parliament and of the Council of 21 May 2013 on the strengthening of economic and budgetary surveillance of Member States in the euro area experiencing or threatened with serious difficulties with respect to their financial stability.

24 Eric Oliva, 'Le rôle de la dette publique dans la crise des équilibres' in Eric Oliva, Natașa Danelciuc-Colodrovschi (eds), *Dettes, équilibres et Constitutions en Europe* (Institut Francophone pour la Justice et la Démocratie 2020), 32.

25 Kevin Farnsworth, Zoë Irving, 'Deciphering the International Monetary Fund's (IMFs) position on austerity: Incapacity, incoherence and instrumentality' (2018) 18 (2) *Global Social Policy* 119–142.

26 Thomas Akermann et al., Editorial comments 'Debt and democracy: United States then, Europe now?' (2012) 49 (6) *CMLR* 1833.

27 Anastasia Poulou, 'Financial assistance conditionality and human rights protection: What is the role of the EU Charter of Fundamental Rights? (2017) 54 (4) *CMLR* 991–1026.

nation with the IMF.[28] The same applies to its successor, the European Stability Mechanism,[29] which is, essentially, an international agreement between a group of member states who decided to act in a coordinated manner in an area where EU law does not have exclusive competence, but resolved to entrust existing EU institutions with the implementation of such an agreement instead of creating new implementation mechanisms.

However, it is the Treaty on Stability, Coordination and Governance in the Economic and Monetary Union, where the same intergovernmental logic has been applied, that is of particular significance here. Thus, in order to avoid excessive deficits and prevent and/or correct macroeconomic imbalances, 25[30] member states signed an intergovernmental treaty (TSCG), committing themselves to maintaining the "budgetary position of the general government" in an "annual structural balance" and to introducing "provisions of binding force and permanent character, preferably constitutional, or otherwise guaranteed to be fully respected and adhered to throughout the national budgetary processes". In other words, an international treaty outside the realm of EU law obliged the signatory parties to transpose a normatively effective balanced budget rule into their internal legal orders, preferably through amendments to their Constitutions, under the surveillance of EU institutions. In addition, the balanced budget rule enforced through the TSCG juridicized one of the possible meanings of the corresponding economic concept by allowing a budgetary deficit (the so-called "golden rule") but imposing a debt brake, while at the same time dispensing with the legal definition of the "structural deficit" thus accepted. The legal, economic and political complexity of the arrangement has not gone unnoticed,[31] especially since it has been considered from the perspective of an ongoing construction of an economic Constitution of Europe, at

28 Bruno de Witte, Ben Smulders, 'Chapter 6 – Sources of European Union Law' and Fabian Amtenbrink, 'Chapter 26 – Economic and Monetary Union' in Pieter Jan Kuijper, Fabian Amtenbrink, Deirdre Curtin, Bruno De Witte, Alison McDonnell, Stefaan Van den Bogaert (eds), *The Law of the European Union* (Wolters Kluwer 2018) 227–232 and 892–894, respectively.

29 EU law proved rather insufficient for the establishment of a rescue fund in order to preserve the stability of the euro area and, at the same time, allow donor member states to provide financial assistance to beneficiary member states based on the use of conditionalities, which justified the recourse to the intergovernmental method in the case of the European Stability Mechanism and of the addition of para.(3) to article 136 TFEU. The ECJ supported this approach by ruling that art.123 (1) TFEU does not refer to member states granting financial assistance to other member states, but refers only to the European Central Bank and to national banks. (C-370/12, *Pringle*, para.125) However, it also stated that member states are entitled, in areas which do not fall under the exclusive competence of EU law, to entrust tasks to EU institutions outside the framework of the Union. (C-370/12, *Pringle*, para.158).

30 All member states of the euro-zone and other member states willing to undertake fiscal constraints, except the Czech Republic and the UK. Croatia was not an EU member state in 2012.

31 Biebricher (n 9).

the expense of amendments to the constitutions of member states.[32] However, the consequences of the euro-crisis were so severe in some member states that budgetary discipline has been enforced as a one-size-fits-all measure. According to an evaluation performed by the European Commission in 2017,[33] all signatory parties to the TSCG have fulfilled their nominal obligation to transpose the balanced budget rule into national law within the time limit prescribed by article 3 paragraph (2) of the Fiscal Compact.

That being said, other crises followed in Europe and across the world. Some of these crises required further financial resources, placing their burden on the EU and on its member states. The migration and refugee crisis of 2014–2016 prompted the EU to resort to creative financing solutions in order to fund its external actions. The rule of law crisis of 2017–2018 revived the idea of conditionalities, this time applied not to special funds, outside the realm of EU law, but to the funds disbursed through the EU budget itself.[34] Finally, the COVID crisis of 2020–2021 has given the European fiscal integration an impetus that could not have been imagined before, by the creation of the "Next Generation EU" special fund. All these crises have made the European Commission realize that, "if macroeconomic stability is to be pursued via the EU budget, then this might require much bigger funds than may be obtained even from a successful expansion of own resources".[35] In addition, the EU has displayed a tendency towards the use of financial instruments "which are demand-driven and take the form, in particular, of loans and guarantees backed by the Union budget".[36]

"Pecunia nervus rerum"[37]

"Finances are the lifeblood of the republic," said Jean Bodin almost 500 years ago. This statement is as valid for the European Union as it is for the member

32 Leonard F.M. Besselink, Jan-Herman Reestman, Editorial: 'The Fiscal Compact and the European Constitutions: "Europe Speaking German"' (2012) 8 (1) *European Constitutional Law Review* 1–7.

33 Communication from the Commission, The Fiscal Compact: Taking Stock, C (2017) 1200 final; Report from the Commission presented under Article 8 of the Treaty on Stability, Coordination and Governance in the Economic and Monetary Union, C(2017) 1201 final.

34 According to the Proposal for a Regulation of the European Parliament and of the Council on the protection of the Union's budget in case of generalized deficiencies regarding the rule of law in the Member States COM/2018/324 final – 2018/0136, if a generalized rule of law deficiency were ascertained, the offending member state would face the suspension of payments and commitments, and a prohibition on concluding further commitments. The implementing act would be proposed by the Commission, and the Council would decide by reverse qualified majority voting.

35 Editorial comments: "Tinkering with European Monetary Union" (2018) 55 (3) *CMLR* 715.

36 Richard Crowe, 'The European Budgetary Galaxy' (2017) 13 (3) *European Constitutional Law Review* 446.

37 "Pecunia nervus rerum" (Finances are the lifeblood of the republic), Jean Bodin, *Six livres sur la République*, Paris, VI, 1583, 2.

states. The COVID pandemic had a major impact on public finances worldwide. The economic crisis that ensued, called "the COVID crisis", encouraged the EU to be creative again with regard to financial instruments.[38] It offered a window of opportunity for member states to deliver themselves of an important element of the budgetary discipline established during the euro-crisis, namely the balanced budget rule. At the same time, it prompted the EU to undertake debt and commit to the disbursement of an important amount of financial support to member states, under relatively soft conditions set by the European Commission, and in an amount greater than the funds made available in the aftermath of the euro-crisis. The COVID crisis appears to politicize at EU level what the euro-crisis has juridicized at the level of member states, namely fiscal policies. In a supranational context where economic governance remains inadequate, the COVID crisis created an opportunity for the use of instruments specific to fiscal federalism by authorizing the supranational level to balance the fiscal difficulties of member states of the EU.

Following the July 2020 European Council summit, while deciding upon the multiannual financial framework which represents the EU budget for 2021–2027, the member states have also agreed upon "Next generation EU", a fund designed to help them recover from the economic recession caused by the COVID pandemic. This is an achievement that could not have been expected in the absence of such an exceptional situation, which strengthens the process of European integration in the economic and fiscal areas beyond what could have been imagined, even in the aftermath of the euro-crisis.[39] Indeed, member states have agreed to allow the EU to incur debt, de facto accepting that they can collectively borrow money in order to spend almost 5% of the EU annual GDP over the next several years in order to raise spending by the EU itself and not by member states. The issue of a balanced budget at EU level, and of the necessary equivalence between expenditure and revenue at supranational level, has been deferred.

"Next generation EU" is a special fund, a temporary instrument that is reminiscent of previous experiments. In the same way as the European Financial Stability Mechanism, it allows the European Commission to borrow money from the financial markets in order to transfer funds to member states in need of assistance, but this time the debt is underwritten by the European Union and it is guaranteed by the EU budget. The EU is not yet a fiscal federation. The answer found by the

38 Circumventing the ruling in *Pringle*, according to which the "grant of financial assistance to a member state does not fall within monetary policy" (C-370/12, *Pringle*, para.57), in early 2020 the European Central Bank announced a Pandemic Emergency Purchase Programme, i.e. a temporary asset purchase programme meant to run until the end of 2020. It also allowed for temporary "longer-term refinancing operations" in order to provide immediate liquidity support to the Euro area financial system, announcing, however, that, once national economies have recovered, this type of fiscal support will be withdrawn.

39 Brigid Laffan and Alfredo de Feo, *EU Financing for Next Decade. Beyond the MFF 2021–2027 and the Next Generation EU*, European University Institute, 2020.

EU to the politically important issue of how to make sure that taxpayers in a member state will not be held responsible for the decisions taken in another member state, where they do not have legitimate representation, was to shift responsibility at supranational level and allow EU institutions to deal with balancing common fiscal actions and sovereign rights of member states. The distribution of funds will be made through a mix of grants and loans. Conditionalities based on "national recovery and resilience plans" and the commitments of member states to contribute to the "green and digital transitions" have been put in place. A relatively diluted conditionality, referring to respect for the rule of law, which reminds the regulation already proposed by the European Commission in 2018,[40] has also been appended, with some difficulty, to both the "Next generation EU" and the EU budget. Also relevant to this discussion is the fact that the special fund called "Next generation EU" applies to all member states, rather than just the euro-zone countries, as it is a general recovery plan and not an instrument for the rescue of the single currency.

Scholarship tends to overstate the potential of the EU budget to raise more of its own revenues,[41] in the event that member states will not agree to revise the existing system of the EU's own revenues and particularly to increase their national contributions.[42] On the one hand, this would indicate that the EU takes seriously the requirement of a balanced budget at supranational level, instead of imposing it on member states only.[43] On the other hand, this would mean that at least some fiscal powers would be transferred from the national level towards the EU, a step towards further integration similar to the creation of the euro in the absence of economic integration among member states.

All these arrangements resemble fiscal federalism, according to which monetary policy and the redistribution of wealth belong at the federal level, while federate entities must comply with budgetary discipline.[44] However, unlike the fiscal federalism of the United States, European fiscal federalism has evolved in the context of two economic crises that occurred within a short period of time and not as the result of a historical evolution over more than half a century. In addition, European fiscal federalism differs from United States fiscal federalism in that it combines a top-down approach to balanced budget rules for the member states with the absence of fiscal centralization at supranational level, coupled with the existence of a central bank and a complex

40 See *supra* (n 34).

41 Alicia Hinarejos, 'Next Generation EU: On the Agreement of a COVID-19 Recovery Package' (2020) 45 (4) *European Law Review* 2.

42 Currently, there are three types of own resources of the EU budget: duties and levies, value added tax and national contributions based on Gross National Income (GNI). The GNI-based contribution represents the most important source of the EU's own revenue in the EU budget.

43 As in any arrangement that is reminiscent even remotely of a federation, creating incentives for fiscal discipline remains a difficult challenge at all levels. Also see Jonathan A. Rodden, *Hamilton's Paradox: The Promise and Peril of Fiscal Federalism* (Cambridge University Press 2006).

44 See Musgrave (n 4).

situation in terms of currency, with the Euro being the common currency of only 19 out of 27 member states. For a comparison, the 1790 "Hamiltonian moment" in the United States came with a political compromise that allowed the federal level to transfer and centralize sources of revenues at the federate level, while a central bank was established only a century and a half later.[45] EU fiscal federalism is still evolving and it will take political will and further legal harmonization in order to perfect it, including from a democratic legitimacy perspective.

Irrespective of all these developments, in February 2020, EU member states also agreed on a different but related topic, namely to allow themselves to temporarily deviate from the preventive and the corrective arms of the Stability and Growth Pact (SGP), as developed in the aftermath of the euro-crisis, in order to be able to respond to the COVID pandemic through fiscal interventions. Specifically, the Council endorsed a Communication[46] from the Commission which allows member states a deviation from the medium-term budgetary objective and an extension of the deadline set under the excessive deficit procedure in order to correct their excessive deficits. This does not equate with a suspension of the SGP since member states are still bound by the budgetary discipline imposed on them by the supranational entity, but they may depart from the fiscal adjustment requirements under the preventive arm of the SGP in order to cope with the COVID crisis. The reaction of the EU to the COVID crisis has been rapid and significant. It has partially and temporarily alleviated the fiscal constraints imposed on member states, since medium-term budgetary objectives and caps for public debts and budget deficits were some of the main measures introduced by the EU after the global financial crisis of 2008–2009. The discontinuation of fiscal discipline at EU level may be considered an illustration of the relativity of the standard of the balanced budget. As we have seen, from a theoretical perspective, unforeseen circumstances may justify increased expenditures but this may not be considered budgetary deficit if such flexibility is built into the legal rules pertaining to the balanced budget. Although a continuation of the policy of fiscal discipline could have been expected, since the TSCG allows member states to escape this constraint if confronted with economic downturns, the EU decided to give preference to supranational integration instead of budgetary restraint.

At the EU level, it seems that the COVID crisis has precipitated an evolution toward an even more innovative outline of fiscal integration, which had already begun in 1992 with the creation of an original formula of economic governance in the absence of political governance. Indeed, it is interesting to note that, ten years after a major economic crisis and confronting another one derived from a health crisis, member states appear to agree on a different cure,

45 Otmar Issing, 'The COVID-19 crisis: A Hamiltonian moment for the European Union?' (2020) 23 (2) *International Finance* 340–347.

46 Communication from the Commission to the Council on the activation of the general escape clause of the Stability and Growth Pact, COM (2020) 123 final.

namely reversing the course of budgetary discipline at state level, but strengthening European fiscal integration by allowing budgetary deficits at EU level. An interesting paradox. Let us rewind.

The EU Fiscal Compact and the balanced budget rule

There is already a considerable body of literature on the Fiscal Compact and, more generally, on the rules of budgetary discipline within the European Union,[47] as well as on the balanced budget rule as accommodated in various constitutions across the world.[48] Likewise, the "collateral damage" caused by this evolution – in particular austerity measures and their impact on the constitutional protection of social rights – has also been extensively examined, especially in the aftermath of the euro-crisis.[49] Is there anything left to be said about the balanced budget rule or its legal embodiment in the Fiscal Compact ten years after its entry into force? We believe there remain aspects that have not yet been fully examined.

Practical relevance

On the one hand, a renewed analysis of the balanced budget rule enshrined in the Fiscal Compact is of significant practical relevance, given the objective set by the TSCG to incorporate its provisions into the EU legal framework. Article 16 of the TSCG stipulates the obligation to take the necessary steps for the incorporation of the legal substance of the treaty into the normative framework of the European Union, based on a five-year assessment of its implementation. Ten years later, neither the TSCG in its entirety nor the Fiscal Compact were transposed into EU law.

47 See e.g. Xenophon Contiades (ed.), *Constitutions in the Global Financial Crisis* (Ashgate 2013); Maurice Adams, Federico Fabbrini, Pierre Larouche (eds), *The Constitutionalization of European Budgetary Constraints* (Hart Publishing 2014); Tuori Kaarlos, Tuori Klaus, *The Eurozone Crisis. A Constitutional Analysis*, (Cambridge University Press 2014); Sergio Fabbrini, *Which European Union? Europe after the Euro Crisis* (Cambridge University Press 2015); (2016) 17 (5) *German Law Journal – Special Issue:* 'Democracy and Financial Order'; Francisco Balaguer Callejon, Miguel Azpitarte Sanchez, Enrique Guillen Lopez, Juan Francisco Sanchez Barillao (eds), *The Impact of the Economic Crisis on the EU Institutions and Member States* (Thomson Reuters Aranzadi, 2015); E. Oliva, Natașa Danelciuc-Colodrovschi (eds), *Dettes, équilibres et Constitutions en Europe* (Institut Francophone pour la Justice et la Démocratie 2020).

48 See e.g. Fred L. Morrison (ed.), *Fiscal Rules – Limits on Governmental Deficits and Debt* (Springer 2016); Tom Ginsburg, Mark D. Rosen, Georg Vanberg (eds), *Constitutions in Times of Financial Crisis* (Cambridge University Press 2019).

49 See e.g. Claire Kilpatrick, Bruno De Witte, 'Social Rights in Times of Crisis in the Eurozone: The Role of Fundamental Rights' Challenges' (2014) 05 *EUI Working Paper* LAW; Julia Iliopoulos-Strangas (ed.), *Soziale Grundrechte in den 'neuen' Mitgliedstaaten der Europaischen Union: Zugleich eine Einfuhrung in die Mitgliedstaatlichen Allgemeinen Grundrechts* (Nomos & Sakkoulas 2019).

The obligation pertaining to the incorporation of the TSCG into the EU legal framework could be interpreted as being incumbent on the member states in their capacity of masters of the treaties, or on the European institutions, particularly the European Commission in its capacity of guardian of the treaties. Member states have done nothing of the sort. In February 2017, the European Commission published two documents (a communication and a report),[50] which assessed not the implementation of the TSCG in its entirety but only three elements of the Fiscal Compact, namely the constitutionalization of the balanced budget rule, the constitutionalization of the so-called "corrective arm" of the Stability and Growth Pact, and the creation of national independent institutions in charge of monitoring compliance with TSCG requirements. Based on the examination of relevant national provisions and on consultations with the contracting parties, the Commission issued a Communication which concluded that all signatory states "have significantly adapted their national fiscal frameworks as a result of the Fiscal Compact requirements, in conjunction with Union legislation".[51] It also noted that, at that time, "the objectives of the TSCG could not be achieved within the Union legal order".[52] No further steps have since been taken in that direction. As a consequence, the budgetary discipline imposed by the TSCG remains outside the realm of EU law.[53] And while the internalization of the balanced budget rule by the contracting parties could have been subjected to the European Court of Justice (ECJ)[54] in the event that member states had not fulfilled their obligations, neither the ECJ nor the national courts were in the position to invoke, for instance, the direct applicability of the budgetary discipline imposed by the TSCG. This questions the effectiveness of the TSCG as a legal instrument.

Furthermore, the reality on the ground shows a clear distance between the restrained assessment made by the Commission in 2017 and "the budgetary position of the general government" of each signatory state over the period covered by that assessment or beyond. In fact, despite the adjustments undertaken by the national legal frameworks as a result of the Fiscal Compact

50 Communication from the Commission, The Fiscal Compact: Taking Stock, C (2017) 1200 final; Report from the Commission presented under Article 8 of the Treaty on Stability, Coordination and Governance in the Economic and Monetary Union, C(2017) 1201 final.

51 Ibidem.

52 Ibidem.

53 Regulation (EU) 473/2013 has incorporated part of the TSCG requirements into the EU legal framework, while in 2017 the Commission has put forward a Proposal for a Council Directive laying down provisions for strengthening fiscal responsibility and the medium-term budgetary orientation in the Member States COM/2017/0824 final – 2017/0335 (CNS).

54 According to article 8 TSCG, in the event that a contracting party fails to comply with article 3(2), the European Commission or other contracting parties could bring the issue before the ECJ. However, since all contracting parties have included the "golden rule" in their national legal systems within two years since the TSCG, this provision has not been enforced.

requirements, the budgetary practice of member states seems to evade such constraints. An overview of the compliance of the 27 member states with the deficit and debt criteria under Article 126(3) of the Treaty on the Functioning of the European Union (TFEU) between 2012 and 2017 shows that all signatory parties to the TSCG have been confronted with the opening of at least one excessive deficit procedure, although none has been brought before the ECJ. In 2020, the only ongoing excessive deficit procedure concerned Romania.[55] To take the example of Romania, the Council noted that two measures adopted in 2019 and scheduled to enter into force in late 2020 (a significant pension increase and the doubling of child allowance[56]) represent a high fiscal risk, which confirms the trend started in 2016, since when "Romania has systematically and repeatedly derogated from fiscal rules enshrined in the national fiscal framework, thereby rendering them largely ineffective".[57] This has not prevented the Romanian Parliament from enacting both measures into laws and the Constitutional Court from ruling that it has no jurisdiction upon articles 121 or 126 of the TFEU or upon the preventive arm of the SGP, and therefore these provisions are not relevant to the judicial review the Court performs.[58] Moreover, the Romanian Constitutional Court has unfailingly ruled that ordinary law,[59] which transposed the TSCG requirement on the balanced budget at national level, does not have constitutional status and therefore cannot constrain the future actions of Parliament, and hence it is not relevant to the judicial review the Court performs.[60] Thus, the prudent assessment made by the Commission in 2017 seems to be contradicted by the facts. A formal adaptation of the national fiscal framework does not necessarily mean substantive compliance with the requirement of the balanced budget rule and Romania is not the only member state in this situation. In fact, the judicial review of national fiscal constraints has contributed to the erosion, rather than the enhancement, of the EU balanced budget rule.[61] In this respect, the assessment carried out by the Commission in 2017 with regard to national

55 See https://ec.europa.eu/info/business-economy-euro/economic-and-fiscal-policy-coordination/eu-economic-governance-monitoring-prevention-correction/stability-and-growth-pact/corrective-arm-excessive-deficit-procedure/excessive-deficit-procedures-overview_en
56 Both measures have been stalled by the Parliament elected in December 2020.
57 Council Recommendation of 3 April 2020 with a view to bringing an end to the situation of an excessive government deficit in Romania (2020/C 116/01).
58 See especially Decision n°766/2016 regarding the remuneration of staff paid from public funds and decision n°127/2019 on the Law of the state budget for 2019.
59 Law n°69/2010 on fiscal responsibility as revised after the adoption of Law n°83/2012 for the ratification of the TSCG.
60 See e.g. Decision n°581/2016, Decision n°765/2016, Decision n°328/2017, Decision n°620/2016, Decision n°766/2016, Decision n°795/2016 or Decision n°795/2017 of the Romanian Constitutional Court.
61 Legal doctrine has been divided between scholars who considered the juridicization of the balanced budget rule a tool for the empowerment of courts and scholars who observed that courts rather protected fundamental rights instead of budgetary discipline. See e.g. Maurice Adams, Federico Fabbrini, Pierre Larouche

ownership over EU-induced budgetary discipline seems too generous and a renewed endeavour might be needed for the incorporation of the TSCG into the EU legal framework to remain a desired outcome.

Moreover, the context generated by the COVID pandemic has not been conducive to budgetary discipline. The consequences on the economic growth of the European Union have been clearly negative, with the Commission stating that "the fall in economic activity in 2020 could be comparable to the contraction of 2009",[62] the worst year of the euro-crisis. Such consequences will continue to unfold well beyond 2021. As member states had to adopt measures that contribute to substantially higher deficits than those envisaged by the SGP, the Commission has confirmed that the impact of such measures will be excluded when compliance with those requirements is reassessed. It is the TSCG that allows member states to deviate from their medium-term objective in the event of exceptional circumstances defined as

> [an] unusual event outside the control of the Contracting Party concerned which has a major impact on the financial position of the general government or to periods of severe economic downturn as set out in the revised Stability and Growth Pact, provided that the temporary deviation of the Contracting Party concerned does not endanger fiscal sustainability in the medium-term.[63]

In this sense, article 3 of the Fiscal Compact may be considered to support conflicting priorities: on the one hand, it requires member states to have balanced budgets; on the other hand, it allows them to escape this constraint if confronted with economic downturns. Compliance with these requirements will be assessed by the Commission but, while it is clear that the criteria and procedures provided by the preventive arm of the SGP will be used for the balanced budget, the Fiscal Compact is not clear with regard to the criteria that the Commission should use when a member state is confronted with "an unusual event" or with "a severe economic downturn". This high built-in flexibility may be another potential source of ineffectiveness of the TSCG as the escape clause seems to translate into a tautology: member states should have balanced budgets at all times except when they cannot have balanced budgets and it is for the European Commission to acknowledge that. Yet if the Commission does not accept that a member state is confronted with a specific problem, the TSCG makes no remedy available. But the reverse is also valid – namely, if a member state is confronted with "an unusual event" or with "a severe economic downturn" and cannot run a balanced budget, the Commission has no remedy available either. It looks as if, in the attempt to resolve a stringent economic crisis, the TSCG has

(eds) *The Constitutionalization of European Budgetary Constraints* (Hart Publishing 2014).

62 Communication from the Commission to the Council on the activation of the general escape clause of the Stability and Growth Pact, COM(2020) 123 final.

63 Article 3 paragraph 1 letter c) TSCG.

prevented member states and the Commission from dealing with other potential economic crises. If such a situation occurs with regard to one or more member states, it may have questionable consequences, whether for the "financial positions" of states concerned or for the legitimacy of the EU in imposing budgetary discipline, or for both. In any event, such conundrums would not support further fiscal integration. Rather, they would endanger European integration, while at the same time question its legitimacy and rationale. A renewed assessment of the TSCG and of the budgetary discipline it involves should take this reality into account.

In practice, the economic crisis generated by the COVID pandemic has been an external shock and an unusual adverse event with high economic impact, not just for one or a few member states of the European Union but for the entire world. Its implications did not bring to the forefront the economic and budgetary sovereignty of member states, or the criteria used by the Commission for the assessment of their compliance with the balanced budget rule. Rather, the pandemic has offered the EU the opportunity to become a common platform for the coordination of the economic response of all member states confronted with the COVID crisis. Since not only the TSCG but also the regulations included in the SGP comprise two types of clauses referring to both, the preventive and the corrective arm, and also facilitate the coordination of budgetary policies in times of severe economic downturn by allowing member states to deviate from the EU-imposed budgetary discipline, the European Commission resolved to make use of them in 2020.[64] The "unusual escape clause" refers to an unusual event outside the control of one or more member states which has a major impact on the financial position of the general government. The "general escape clause" addresses a situation of severe economic downturn faced by the euro area or by the Union as a whole. Although the Commission has briefly contemplated the first option, it has resorted to the later. This may have been a strategic choice, as it eludes the criteria needed for the assessment of "a major impact on the financial position of the general government"[65] of member states and, at the same time, it allows the Commission to act legitimately in order to address an economic downturn of the Union and absorb part of the economic shock at supranational level – that is, to enhance fiscal integration and European economic governance.

64 Specifically, for the preventive arm, Articles 5(1) and 9(1) of Regulation (EC) 1466/97 state that "in periods of severe economic downturn for the euro area or the Union as a whole, Member States may be allowed to depart temporarily from the adjustment path towards the medium-term budgetary objective, provided that this does not endanger fiscal sustainability in the medium term". For the corrective arm, Articles 3(5) and 5(2) of Regulation (EC) 1467/97 stipulate that in case of a severe economic downturn in the euro area or in the Union as a whole, the Council may also decide, on a recommendation from the Commission, to adopt a revised fiscal trajectory.

65 See the definition of "exceptional circumstances" in Article 3 paragraph 3 letter b) TSCG.

Although still short of fiscal federalism, the coordinated answer provided by the EU to the COVID crisis is reminiscent of macro stabilization at federal level coupled with budgetary discipline at federate level. Indeed, the Commission emphasized that "the general escape clause does not suspend the procedures of the Stability and Growth Pact"; it merely allows EU institutions to undertake the necessary policy coordination measures within the framework of the SGP, while departing from the budgetary requirements that would normally apply. Therefore, the balanced budget principle as enshrined in the TSCG is still enforceable, but the evaluations made by the Commission on the budgets of member states will allow states to exceed the deficit and the debt thresholds only in as much as they address the negative consequences of the COVID crisis.[66]

In conclusion, the balanced budget rule as provided by the Fiscal Compact remains a collective fiscal answer to a common fiscal issue of member states that the European Union still needs to address if it wants to achieve fiscal integration. In other words, if the EU budget is meant to ensure macroeconomic stability for the Union, it has to be matched by corresponding funds – far bigger than the funds available before these fiscal crises – and it has to secure the budgetary discipline of its contributors – that is, member states. The evaluation undertaken by the European Commission in 2017 remains partial and discreet, while the latest evolutions on the European stage require a renewed appraisal.

Renewed critical appraisal

On the other hand, the balanced budget rule set by the Fiscal Compact still deserves attention because, in hindsight, there are aspects that went unnoticed or remained underdiscussed during the period that followed the adoption of the TSCG. We have set ourselves the aim to provide not an explanation of the context and content of the balanced budget rule but a critical appraisal of its impact on legal systems, political institutions and social values. Construed as a complement to previous studies, ours is also an update with regard to the sway of the balanced budget rule on the actual fiscal life of member states and of the EU, including during the COVID crisis. Its authors are a mixture of academics, practitioners and experts in European law, finance and economics. The analysis is based on a comparative legal approach intersected with a political economy perspective and may be of interest both to legal scholars and practitioners. The following presentation of the structure of the book is not a summary, rather an appetizer in order to stimulate deeper insight into each individual contribution.

66 See the third paragraph of COM(2020) 123 final (n 61) which states explicitly: "The Commission and the Council have already clarified that the full flexibility available in the Stability and Growth Pact will be applied for the measures linked to the outbreak of COVID-19. […] This implies that the budgetary impact of the above-mentioned measures will be excluded when the Commission assesses compliance with the Stability and Growth Pact."

The first two chapters deal with the metamorphosis of an economic concept into a polysemic legal standard. The transformation of economic principles into normative realities of constitutional ambit and endowed with legal sanctions has been often alluded to and mostly criticized in legal studies, but it has not been closely dissected and, in particular, it has not been examined from a transdisciplinary viewpoint. At first glance, what could be simpler than a balanced budget, asks Gilbert Orsoni in the first part of this book, only to immediately answer that, contrary to simplistic appearances, the notion turns out to be polysemic. Being a document that traces the expenditures and revenues of public authorities, a balanced budget could imply a zero balance – that is, an arithmetic equality between expenses and incomes, an equilibrium. This design may seem to comfort both the economic and the legal approach, while also corresponding to a moral, practical and even anthropological principle, which guides one not to spend more than one's own available resources. However, this idyllic version of the balanced budget is not the one that has been juridicized, either at international or at supranational or national level. Moreover, it does not correspond to a compulsory economic theory or precept that would simply have to be transposed into legal language. On the contrary, Thomas Stauffer explains that choices made with regard to the legal concept of balanced budget are generally based on mainstream economic theories, while alternative solutions are always available. Thus, economic facts and related theories have to be understood when designing and implementing balanced budget rules. At the same time, simply imposing budgetary legal norms does not imply that a specific economic result will be reached. Identifying the "right formula" capable of maintaining a suitable level of growth in a given state implies using both economic and legal instruments that can be correlated but are not identical and cannot be swapped, either notionally or factually. Choices have to be made with regard to the economic concepts able to contribute to the achievement of a specific fiscal objective and normative instruments have to be selected in order to reach a specific legal effect. But just as there is not one single economic concept of balanced budget, there is not a universal set of legal rules pertaining to a balanced budget. Rather, pragmatically, budgetary rules have been designed in each state or at the level of EU in order to take into account realities and requirements suitable for specific contexts. If in pre-modern times a balanced budget meant that the king's treasury should suffice for his expenses, modern times make do with a budget in "structural quasi-equilibrium", as Gilbert Orsoni labels it – that is, a budget that may display some operating deficits or a budget that accommodates public debts incurred due to an "unusual adverse economic event", as Thomas Stauffer states. Combined, the first two chapters of this book demonstrate that the polysemy of the economic concept of balanced budget is different from the polysemy of the legal concept of balanced budget, but there are correlations between the two and these need to be taken into account when evaluating specific fiscal or budgetary policies. Bearing this in mind, a critique of the solution provided by the Fiscal Compact at EU level should start, or at least include, an argued critique of the underlying economics as well as of the legal tools used. Thomas Stauffer concludes that to the extent that the European legislator has enshrined certain economic theories in the Fiscal Compact, they have become part of the law bearing all its characteristics; to discount them for being merely economic theories exposes a lack of understanding of the relationship between legal norms and economic theories. From this theoretical and transdisciplinary perspective, the mere fact that the *application* of the Fiscal Compact leads to outcomes that are considered undesirable from a political, social, legal or even moral perspective does not address a valid critique to the concept of balanced budget. It rather deals with a factual consequence of the practical implementation of a specific economic and legal configuration of the concept of balanced budget. Although this seems to be the vantage point used in two other contributions to this book,[67] in fact they address the issue of the balanced budget rule imposed by the Fiscal Compact from the perspective of political institutions and social values. Thus, it is always necessary to keep in mind the difference between facts and norms and the statement of Hans Kelsen, according to whom the validity and the effectiveness of legal norms do not depend on their effects but solely on the validity of the legal system to which they belong.[68] Seen from this perspective, the balanced budget rule enshrined in the Fiscal Compact remains valid, although it may be convoluted and it is still challenged to the point that it has been discontinued upon a "severe economic downturn faced by the euro area or by the Union as a whole". The juxtaposition of the first two chapters in this book allows one to note that the generous idea of balance or equilibrium, when applied to public finance, allows for a multitude of approaches and that the balanced budget rule set by the Fiscal Compact is only one of its possible practical applications.

The second pair of chapters in this book use as a starting point the widespread idea that the balanced budget rule has been imposed by the EU on member states based on the template provided by the German experience. However, it is interesting to discuss why and how the German precedent came to enjoy this status, particularly since it was aware of the earlier practice of fiscal federalism in the United States of America and it has actually been inspired by a Swiss model. It is also stimulating to note that the constitutionalization of the balanced budget rule imposed on the signatory parties by the TSCG, inspired as it may be by the German precedent, was met with scepticism by other member states of the EU. Intriguingly, it is mainly member states that are intensely decentralized but stop short of federalism, such as Belgium, Italy and Spain, that have resorted to the revision of their Constitutions in order to transpose the balanced budget rule imposed by the Fiscal Compact. Unitary member states, such as Bulgaria, France, Greece and Romania, preferred to insert the balanced budget rule in laws and not in their Constitutions, thus limiting its impact at state level while, possibly, enhancing budgetary discipline at municipal level. It

67 See the contributions of George Katrougalos and Daphne Akoumianaki and of Julia Aravantinou Leonidi.

68 Hans Kelsen, *Théorie générale du droit et de l'État* (Bruylant – LGDJ 1997), 92.

is also true that some unitary EU member states, such as Poland, had followed the German model early and already had a balanced budget rule in their Constitution. From this, one could imply that rules specific to fiscal federalism prove useful for budgetary discipline in contexts where self-governance is firmly enshrined. This may have been the reason why the EU resorted to imposing a compulsory balanced budget rule on its member states. If that is the case, the Fiscal Compact would have a paradoxical Janus-like function: while furthering fiscal integration, it is also an indication of the large degree of autonomy that EU member states still enjoy with regard to taxing and fiscal policies. Thus, the initial flaw of the Economic and Monetary Union, with a centralized monetary union and a decentralized economic union, is highlighted once again. Moreover, this emphasizes the uniqueness of the yet-to-come EU fiscal federalism: an intergovernmental instrument outside the realm of EU legal framework made possible steps forward in the direction of fiscal integration. The impact of the Fiscal Compact on the EU has been widely discussed in the years following its adoption. The obligation imposed on member states to transpose the balanced budget rule preferably at constitutional level has also been extensively covered. However, the implications this had inside member states received less attention. Although neither of the two case studies presented in the book, Germany and Belgium, deals explicitly with fiscal federalism, the concept is implied in both analyses, which limit themselves only to the constitutional implications of the TSCG inside the respective states and do not go beyond the state level.

Ralph Schenke explains that the decision to limit public debt with a "debt brake" is better understood against the background of the history of German public debt law, which goes back to the Middle Ages. A brief incursion into its history allows the reader to understand the basic idea according to which, in Germany's federal states, initially public debt could only be justified by a special need that had occurred in the past, and to appreciate how this requirement managed to be metamorphosed in the Prussian Constitution into the idea of tolerance to a public debt that fulfils certain requirements, namely "it is used to finance a revenue-generating object, it is justified intergenerationally and corresponds to the pay-as-you-use principle". The postwar Constitution managed to instrumentalize public debt for purposes of economic management, which quickly made a "debt brake" necessary in order to implement counter-cyclical global governance. Successive reforms had further refined the economic concepts used and the legal instruments employed, but one of the constant features of German public debt rules has been their safeguard by the Constitution in order to prevent their change through a simple law and to make them compulsory for federated entities. The inherent hurdles of a constitutional revision and the legal and political entrenchments specific to federal Germany have always been considered a solid guarantee for the health of public finances. However, an in-depth analysis of the balanced budget rules in the German Basic Law and of their impact on the federal and federated levels does not necessarily end up with a cheerful conclusion. Ralph Schenke considers that the debt brake has limited spending aspirations although it has contributed to budget consolidation. This may have impaired growth opportunities but, overall, it has presumably increased the confidence of the capital markets in the performance and solvency of the German state. Thus, Germany reaped the benefits of its strict and enduring balanced budget rules, particularly during the COVID crisis, during which it has been able to finance itself on favourable terms. Moreover, the debt brake does not seem to seriously impede the policy of crisis management. Rather, the opposite question arises – that is, whether the exemption rules for crisis management leave too many loopholes open.

Marc Verdussen challenges not the balanced budget rule as such but the constraint that the Fiscal Compact imposes on signatory parties to internalize it at constitutional level or at least in provisions of binding force which are "guaranteed to be fully respected and adhered to throughout the national budgetary processes". The departure point is the three-dimensional dynamic existing inside the EU with regard to budgetary discipline, respectively the coordination of national public finances designed to allow for the creation of the euro, the accountability of EU member states which allow their public deficit to become "excessive", according to the EU definition, and the internalization by the signatory parties to the Fiscal Compact of a number of substantial budgetary constraints, including the "golden rule". The evaluation of the "golden rule" is done mainly using a grid based on basic notions of constitutional law, primarily the legitimacy of concrete restrictions on the budgetary powers of parliaments made in order to preserve their democratic power to shape affairs for the political body of the state in the long term. But the evaluation of the necessary constitutionalization of the "golden rule" is conducted from several positions: the validity, neutrality, relevance, appropriateness, and the effectiveness of such an approach. In other words, is it really necessary to constitutionalize a numerical threshold of the public debt and of the budget deficit in order to have the euro as a single currency? Marc Verdussen is convinced the answer is no. This is not only because the few examples of Constitutions that have been revised in order to stipulate a "golden rule" display a certain relativity of the effectiveness of this approach, but also because of the specific situation in his native Belgium, where the peculiarities of the federal arrangements brought forward an original solution to the conundrum, namely a convention between the federal authority, all federated entities, linguistic communities, regions and subordinate powers. The level of complexity of the Belgian federation cannot pass unnoticed, but the same is valid for the answer to a requirement concerning the constitutionalization of a budgetary constraint: in order to make it enforceable "throughout the national budgetary processes", Belgium took the view that it is better to internalize the rule at all levels where decisions on budgetary process are made, and since the rule is assumed by each and every level of such public authority, a convention among them would suffice. However, Marc Verdussen cautions that for such agreements have effect, they need to receive the consent of the legislator concerned. Thus, we get back to the point of departure: if the consent of the legislator that will see its budgetary powers limited has to be achieved in order to limit its discretionary powers, why constitutionalize the "golden rule"? This rather grim conclusion is reinforced by the institutional practice which shows that, despite the consent of all concerned legislators on the agreement thus devised, no consensus has been reached between the contracting parties since the entry into force of the above-mentioned cooperation agreement. Therefore, from its creation until 2020 no agreement on budgetary targets has been reached. The scepticism of the Belgian doctrine regarding the constitutionalization of the "golden rule" has been reinforced during the COVID pandemic of 2020–2021 when the European Commission and the Council have agreed that given the circumstances generated by the need to fight the economic consequences of the pandemic, "prudent medium-term fiscal positions" may be adopted.

The third part of the book is dedicated to the impact that the balanced budget rule enshrined in the Fiscal Compact has on the separation of powers inside EU member states but from insufficiently researched perspectives. Institutional and constitutional evaluations have flourished after the adoption of the TSCG just as European governance approaches have abounded. But a thorough analysis from the vantage point of representative democracy or local autonomy and the inherent tensions with technocratic institutions, as construed inside EU member states, have been less common.

Giulia Aravantinou Leonidi's analysis goes beyond the widely accepted ideas that budgetary constraints imposed from outside the state have contributed to the erosion of representative democracy inside the states concerned, and that the intergovernmental nature of economic reforms has deeply eroded the principle of representative democracy at the level of the European Union. The empowerment of governments and supranational institutions to the detriment of national parliaments, coupled with the weakness shown by elective assemblies in the implementation of the new budgetary constraints and procedures, represents one of the main arguments in the debate about the European Union. For a different perspective, it suffices to read the conclusion of the evaluation report issued by the European Commission five years after the adoption of the TSCG which states that the incorporation of the TSCG into the EU legal framework "would bring greater democratic accountability and legitimacy across the Union". To argue with this institutional approach, Giulia Aravantinou Leonidi develops an in-depth analysis of patterns of implementation of EU economic governance in Germany, Italy, Spain and Greece, and maintains that European fiscal integration has been pursued to the detriment of the principle of representative democracy. She concludes that, from a comparative perspective, the impact of budgetary constraints on national representative institutions relies on the role they play within the institutional architecture of each member state and fiscal centralization at EU level has increased asymmetries among national parliaments, fostering a gradual drain of authority from national legislatures toward supranational technocratic institutions.

Simona Gherghina addresses the impact of the EU-imposed balanced budget on the principle and practice of financial local autonomy. Following the incorporation of the balanced budget rule into national legislation, most EU member states have enforced additional limitations on local debt. Looking at several member states (such as Greece, Portugal, Ireland, Romania, Hungary, Latvia), Simona Gherghina observes that this translated into a reduction of transfers from central to local budgets coupled with a limitation of local public investment. These results have been achieved through a variety of fiscal discipline rules meant for local budgets such as legal requirements for balanced local budgets, debt brakes, suppression of local taxes or limitations of decision margins available to public authorities in respect of local tax rates, restructuring or reduction of transfers from central budgets, reinforcement of supervisory and control mechanism applicable to local budgets. In other EU member states (Italy, Austria, Spain, Denmark and the Netherlands) sanctions for local administrative units that fail to comply with the agreed objectives were imposed. Thus, the impact of successive fiscal austerity rules and procedures on local government has prompted questions regarding the existence of a real local autonomy in the EU member states. It is interesting to note that measures adopted at national level during the euro-crisis and aimed at reducing public deficits and debt continued to be applied and refined with regard to local government even after the end of the crisis irrespective of the principle of local autonomy. The conclusion is rather grim for local governments: EU balanced budget rules have reduced their margin of appreciation with regard to financial local autonomy. However, if the objective of sound public finances and the balanced budget rule imposed by the TSCG have not been made fully operational in the national legal system or have been only formally internalized, local financial autonomy tends to be greater and better protected. Paradoxically, although deprived of direct application, the balanced budget rule imposed by the TSCG is able to hamper local autonomy.

Bogdan Iancu deals with a niche topic, less often addressed than the impact of budgetary discipline on the legislative and/or executive powers of the state. The Fiscal Compact intends to prevent member states from adopting their budgets based on biased and unrealistic macroeconomic and budgetary forecasts, partially with the help of national independent institutions mandated to provide fiscal surveillance. Such "independent bodies", intended to enable *ex ante* (through technocratic opinions on the macroeconomic foundations of state budgets) and monitor *ex post* compliance with numerical fiscal rules (debt and deficit threshold among others) imposed by the Fiscal Compact, have already been required by Council Directive 2011/85/EU of 8 November 2011 on requirements for budgetary frameworks of the Member States. Bogdan Iancu draws parallels between this "language of legalized austerity" and similar situations – pertaining to the rule of law and the fight against corruption – where the EU expected that legal and institutional transplant would suffice to correct perceived dysfunctions. He resolves that representative democracy cannot remain immune to this type of approach. This conclusion refers only to the situation existing at the level of member states and does not encompass the state of democracy at European level, while the "economic constitution by instalments" created through the transformation of the Economic and Monetary Union after the "euro-crisis" is nothing but a waiting room for the future European federation as announced by the reaction of the European Union to the COVID crisis. Democracy is an issue to be considered not only in respect to member states but also with regard to the supranational entity.

Although only implicitly, the contribution of Bogdan Iancu also hints at another aspect, equally relevant to the discussion on the democratic character of a state budget and to the limitations imposed on it by technocratic rules such as the balanced budget, namely the fact that the management of public funds has become so complex in the modern state that the advent of agencies has been considered rather a blessing. The development of independent agencies outside traditional branches of government meant that they have escaped from the realm of political decisions made by representatives of the people and, thus, from the realm of the accountability mechanisms underlying representative democracy. This may have been beneficial, for instance, with regard to their budgetary autonomy, which translates into legislatures only being able to approve the overall budgets of independent agencies while the details of their budgetary execution are monitored mainly internally, by the agency itself. At the same time, the proliferation of agencies endowed with budgetary autonomy is an expression of a paradoxical reality: we still abide by the fiction that state budgets are debated and approved by parliaments because they democratically represent the people whereas, in fact, due to the increasing complexity of the allocation and control of public funds, state budgets have become documents difficult to manage and to discuss in public fora of debate, such as parliaments. Thus, the agencification brought with it a re-allocation of powers to decide upon the details of a state budget, with parliaments retaining decisions pertaining to the broad allocation of public funds and technocratic entities being granted the authority to choose their own budget within the overall allocation adopted by parliaments. In short, an important part of public funds is allocated and controlled outside the democratic institutions representing the will of the people. This evolution has no connection with the impetus provided by the European Union towards the creation of pockets of institutional autonomy. Rather, it is the result of a peculiar evolution of traditional political institutions and visions of the classic theory of separation of powers.

The final part of the book revisits the old rebuke of the balanced budget rule enshrined in the TSCG for not allowing the respect for fundamental rights, particularly social rights, and revisits the standards set by international financing institutions, particularly the IMF, which is the main engine behind the proclivity for budgetary constraints that are considered to engender fiscal austerity. Indeed, austerity measures associated with the balanced budget rule have often been criticized from the perspective of the protection that states have to grant to fundamental rights and particularly to social rights. Less common has been the reference to a decline of the constitutional autonomy of the state, to the point of becoming purely "nominal" in the face of contradicting supranational requirements. The last two chapters of the book have to be considered not as divergent or opposing approaches but as presenting different angles of the same conundrum, namely how to identify the "right formula" able to both maintain a suitable level of economic growth and cater for the needs of citizens in a functional democracy. Focusing on the protection of social rights, George Katrougalos and Daphne Akoumianaki consider whether international financing institutions are the best fora to establish constitutional rules for states in need of fiscal consolidation. From an entirely different viewpoint, Cornel Ban argues that between 2008 and 2012 the IMF was undergoing a doctrinal shift on fiscal policy and thus created "an interregnum in the realm of economic ideas", allowing for a mixture of "pre-crisis orthodoxy and the more 'Keynesian' overtures". Thus, during the euro-crisis the IMF loan conditionalities have been infused with the idea that fiscal consolidation has to be gradual and allow a lenient balance between revenue and spending measures. George Katrougalos and Daphne Akoumianaki examine the concept and the purposes of balanced budget rules and explain the connection between these rules and their implementation in national legal systems and the protection of fundamental rights. This chapter is most instructive, not only because of the comparative method used but also because, while having the case of Greece as focal point, it includes a wide variety of other case studies, providing examples from member states which are seldom mentioned in mainstream scholarship. It scrutinizes how EU law, especially the TSCG, affected the balance between the protection of fundamental social rights and budget discipline, particularly during times of crisis. And it concludes that since the balanced budget rules that followed the euro-crisis are still in force, albeit suspended at the level of EU due to the COVID-19 pandemic but fully operational at international level, a new balance between the economic and social dimensions in Europe is necessary in order to safeguard the protection of rights in times of multidimensional, health and economic crisis.

From a totally different viewpoint, Cornel Ban considers that the specific situation of Greece is not attributable to the IMF. Greece is deemed to be a state which has not managed to correct its macroeconomic imbalances upon the implementation of a first readjustment programme imposed by the IMF in a context where, even prior to the "Lehman Brothers" crisis, the IMF had tempered its emphasis on fiscal adjustment and seemed more attuned to social and economic development needs. Indeed, it is not habitual that the IMF is considered to have resorted to this type of "interregnum" of economic ideas prior to the "euro-crisis" even if further research is needed in order to determine whether this hybrid has actually travelled into the IMF loan conditionalities. But Cornel Ban argues that the IMF has made significant adaptive changes to the status quo that defined its pre-crisis policy. An earlier emphasis on maintaining states' credibility with financial markets remained the primary goal of policy, but this goal had to cohabit with greater acceptance of discretionary fiscal stimulus programmes. This recalibration can be explained, in part, by looking at the conceptual dynamics of academic macroeconomics, which brings us back to the point of departure and the interaction between economic and legal concepts. And all these are placed under a new light in the context of the COVID-19 pandemic and of the measures needed to manage this new economic crisis.

In the concluding chapter, Michel Bouvier reaches a troublesome, if somewhat expected, conclusion: budgetary issues are another word for political issues and the latest evolutions at EU level in the context of COVID-19 pandemic appear to point in the direction of much more than mere economic, budgetary or monetary coordination. Rather, they illustrate an attempt at financial federalism, which means political federalism expressed in other words. This should not come as a surprise to the sharp commentators of the supranational organization but it is remarkable that, in order to reach this point, the European integration process had to pass through the concept of "balanced budget", which it has used in its own manner, first as an instrument meant to discipline member states and later as a device allowing collective debt in order to counteract a collective threat. In other words, the European Union has followed the same path as any federal state would have followed with regard to its federated entities, which may be proof that the European Union is already acting as a federal entity despite not declaring itself as one. But at a more general level, Michel Bouvier concludes that the concept of "balanced budget" may be a source of "misunderstandings". Using as the starting point the concept of equilibrium, the notion of balance is part of an ancestral background that plays a reassuring role in social phenomena. However, in the realm of finance and for quite some time, a balanced budget has been portrayed as "the holy grail". Even today, balanced budgets continue to be presented as a stabilizing principle for society although the idea that imbalance can also be positive – if it is controlled – because it generates new energies which will eventually bring back balance, has been met with some acceptance, at least in the version proposed by Keynesian theories. Thus, there is, perhaps, no such thing as a "golden rule". In fact, if there is to be a "golden rule" in public finances, it should be the permanent return of policy makers to the source of their authority, namely citizens and their needs, because the budget of a public community expresses qualitative choices based on the current and future well-being of its citizens.

In that sense, a balanced budget is nothing more than what it has always been: an instrument for devising public policies in a rational manner. It should be respected as such and it should not be fetishized.

Bibliography

Adams M, Fabbrini F, Larouche P (eds), *The Constitutionalization of the European Budget Constraints* (Hart Publishing 2014)

Balaguer CJ, Azpitarte Sanchez M, Guillen Lopez E, Sanchez Barillao JF (eds.), *The Impact of the Economic Crisis on the EU Institutions and Member States* (Thomson Reuters Aranzadi, 2015)

Almendral VR, 'A Myopic Economic Constitution? Controlling the Debt and the Deficit Without Fiscal Integration', in Marise Cremona, Bruno De Witte, Claire Kilpatrick (eds), *Constitutional Change Through Euro-Crisis Law* (2015) 12 EUI Working Paper Series, LAW 19

Blanke H-J, Mangiameli S (eds), *The Treaty on European Union. A Commentary* (Springer 2013)

Bodin J, *Six livres sur la République, Paris, VI*, 1583

Bouvier M, 'Les représentations théoriques du principe d'équilibre, essai sur la vanité d'un principe' in Lucile Tallineau (ed.), *L'équilibre budgétaire* (PUAM Economica 1994)

Buchanan JM, Wagner RE (eds), *Fiscal Responsibility in Constitutional Democracy* (Martinus Nijhoff 1978)

Contiades X (ed.), *Constitutions in the Global Financial Crisis* (Ashgate 2013)

Iliopoulos-Strangas J (ed.), *Soziale Grundrechte in den 'neuen' Mitgliedstaaten der Europaischen Union: Zugleich eine Einfuhrung in die Mitgliedstaatlichen Allgemeinen Grundrechts* (Nomos & Sakkoulas 2019)

Kuijper PJ, Amtenbrink F, Curtin D, De Witte B, McDonnell A, Van den Bogaert S (eds), *The Law of the European Union* (Wolters Kluwer 2018)

Morisson F (ed.), *Fiscal Rules – Limits on Governmental Deficits and Debt, Global Studies in Comparative Law* (Springer 2016)

Oliva E, Danelciuc-Colodrovschi N (eds), *Dettes, équilibres et Constitutions en Europe* (Institut Francophone pour la Justice et la Démocratie 2020)

Rodden JA, *Hamilton's Paradox: The Promise and Peril of Fiscal Federalism* (Cambridge University Press 2006)

Sergio F, *Which European Union? Europe after the Euro Crisis* (Cambridge University Press 2015)

Sergio F (ed.), *Democracy and Federalism in the European Union and the United States: Exploring Post-National Governance* (Routledge 2005)

Tuori K, Tuori K, *The Eurozone Crisis: A Constitutional Analysis* (Cambridge University Press 2014)

Wagner RE (ed.), *James M. Buchanan – A Theorist of Political Economy and Social Philosophy* (Palgrave Macmillan 2018)

Part I

Balanced budget as normative and economic standard

1 Balanced budget as a substantive legal rule

Gilbert Orsoni

Introduction

In recent years, the old question of balanced budget has seen renewed interest, perhaps more of a political, rather than epistemological, nature. Indeed, under the pressure of events and of an austere economic and financial climate, a renewed approach has emerged from both juridicization endeavors and the development of a notion which one would be tempted to equate with a quasi-equilibrium, namely a (limited) structural deficit.

While we cannot rejoice in the fact that public finances under strain have caused the re-emergence or further development of certain concepts, the opportunity should not be missed to reclaim this field of research from both a legal semantic point of view and a perspective that could be described as "applied public finance" (when we refer, for example, to applied economics).

The budgetary principle of a balanced budget, often considered to be more of a political nature – that is, pertaining to economic policy[1] – has differentiated itself from the outset, at least at the level of public finances, from other budgetary principles that emerged in the 19th century. It should be noted here that for the "classic" scholars[2] this rule, no doubt obvious to them, did not need to be demonstrated and therefore was not developed in their treatises or manuals, whereas other legal principles were subject to significant developments. It could also be said that, insofar as it depends on phenomena completely outside the legal system (growth of the gross domestic product (GDP), political choices), the budgetary principle of a balanced budget does not belong primarily to the legal sphere. The active involvement of economists with this publication illustrates well that the economic dimension cannot be obscured.

1 We could also add psychologically or philosophically. On this topic, see the excellent contribution of Michel Bouvier, 'Les représentations théoriques du principe d'équilibre, essai sur la vanité d'un principe' in Lucile Tallineau (ed.), *L'équilibre budgétaire* (Economica 1984) 23.

2 In France, the classic period covers the period between 1814 (restoration of monarchy) and the beginning of 1930 (advent of Keynesian theories). It is characterised by a domination of liberal ideas, the limitation of state intervention in the economy, the quest for a balanced budget and mistrust of borrowing.

DOI: 10.4324/9781315181882-3

However, any social phenomenon, political decision or economic policy presumes the existence of legal norms and, therefore, the legal expert becomes inevitably involved, regardless of the precise degree of normativity that can be derived from it.

Yet it is necessary to determine what precisely we are referring to. Contrary to the view of "classic" authors, the balanced budget is a deceptively simple notion, hence the difficulties in its juridicization and, perhaps, the limitations of its juridicization, once it takes place. For example, one does not find any entry concerning the balanced budget in the excellent *Dictionary of Legal Culture* [3] or in the *Dalloz Lexicon of Legal Terms*, while one may find in there the "balance of the rights of the parties" and the "balance of the forces".[4] At the same time, concepts such as "overdraft" or "deficit" are included therein while the balanced budget lost its legal meaning after the disappearance, in 2006, of the distinction between total costs and variable costs following the adoption of the "LOLF".[5] However, the question that arises is: does the juridicization of the emerging structural quasi-equilibrium represent a deceptively convenient solution?

The balanced budget: a deceptively simple notion

At first glance, what could be simpler, one would argue, than a balanced budget? At least in appearance. Since the budget is a document that traces the expenditures and revenues of public bodies, its balance implies an arithmetic equality of both – that is, a zero balance.[6] This implies there should be no deficit, which would indicate that expenditure is higher than revenue, and no surplus, which would mean the reverse situation, namely revenue higher than the expenditure.

Nevertheless, contrary to simplistic appearances, the notion turns out to be polysemic, which contributes significantly (but it is not the only explanation) to its suitability for juridicization.[7]

A polysemic notion…

If the notion of balance is indeed polysemic France, along with other countries, has known several accepted meanings of the concept of a state balanced budget.

3 Denis Alland, Stéphane Rials (eds), *Dictionnaire de la culture juridique* (PUF 2003).

4 Serge Guinchard, Gabriel Montagnier (eds), *Lexique des termes juridiques* (15th ed. Dalloz 2005) 268.

5 Adopted in 2001 and implemented for the first time in 2006, the Organic Law on Finance Laws (LOLF – Loi organique relative aux lois de finances) has fundamentally changed the construction and monitoring of the French state budget.

6 In connection to which we could refer to the definition of zero given by its "discoverer" in the 7th century, the Indian astronomer and mathematician Brahmagupta (*in Brahma Sphuta Siddhanta*, 628), which consists of the "subtraction of a number from itself" or from an identical number.

7 And this despite the tendency of "juridicization" characteristic of the transformations of the law in the contemporary period. See Jacques Chevallier, *L'Etat post-moderne* (4th ed. LGDJ 2014) 108ff.

Thus, before the Organic Law on Finance Laws of August 1, 2001 (LOLF), and its full entry into force in 2006, the following meanings were in use:

1 Balance *above* or *below the line*, with the line separating total budgets (general budget, subsidiary budgets, total operating budgets in specified accounts) from temporary operations (special Treasury accounts).
2 One could also refer to a *strong* or a *weak* balance, depending on whether temporary operations were integrated.
3 Another meaning, which is still in force, refers to the *primary* balance, which leads to removing from the calculation the amount of interest on debt.
4 One can also differentiate the balance (if it exists) in the initial finance law from the balance (if it subsists) after the budget has been executed. From this follow *per a contrario*, even if the first term is no longer in use, the notions of impasse (estimated) and discovery (of execution).
5 Reference may also be made to the notion of *real balance*, used previously in the French law of local and regional authorities, which was subsequently clarified by the decentralization law of March 2, 1982[8] according to the following framework:

   - Balance of each section of the budget (even if surpluses are approved subsequently);
   - Accuracy of the budgetary forecasting;
   - Impossibility of borrowing for debt amortization purposes.

   With regard to the local budgetary balance, two complementary remarks should be made:

   - Local budgetary balance, which is a legal concept (subject to a penalty for lack of balance), is established by recording the loan as proceeds from the investment section;
   - The necessary congruity between the principles of balance and accuracy.

6 It is not possible today, when discussing the question of a budget in balance or in deficit, not to make reference to the budgetary discipline resulting from the European Treaties, which involves taking into account the balance of all public administrations and not just the state budget, an illustration of what can be described as the globalization of public financial systems. This implies using a specific terminology that is significant and relevant: *the need to finance* the public administration accounts to indicate an overall deficit situation, and *a funding capacity* when this situation turns out to be a surplus.

8 See Law n° 82-213 of March 2, 1982 on the rights and liberties of communes, departments and regions (Loi n° 82-213 relative aux droits et libertés des communes, des départements et des regions).

7 Finally, it is necessary to highlight the evolution of terms used in the first articles of the Ordinance of January 2, 1959 on public finance and, respectively, the Organic Law of August 1, 2001 on public finance. The 1959 Ordinance refers to "the economic and financial balance" determined by finance laws whereas the 2001 Organic Law uses the terms "budgetary and financial balance". This last expression should not be understood as the imposition of a strict budgetary balance, meaning a zero balance. Rather, it is a reference to the budgetary balance which compares the revenue and expenditure of the same budget (in France, the legal provisions on budgetary balance illustrate a situation of budgetary deficit).

Does this equate with an element that illustrates the difficulties with the juridicization of the concept of balance?

...Difficult to juridicize

1. The question that arises is, therefore, natural. While referring to the "classic" scholars of public finance, contemporary scholarship mentions the "dogma" of the balanced budget, which does not even need a special entry in the dictionaries. Yet why did classic authors not attempt to include the concept of a balanced budget in legal texts, at least not for the state budget?

The natural answer appears to come from observing a specific practice. We made a calculation that in France,[9] during the "classic" period, if the initial budgets were largely balanced (61 were balanced while 54 were not), this was the result of a calculation method, namely budgets that could not be funded other than by loans were qualified as "extraordinary". In fact, 82 budgets had a deficit in their execution while only 32 were balanced. The prevailing wisdom at the time meant that, while setting a "balance objective" (to use a more contemporary terminology), the awareness of the difficulties encountered in achieving it strongly discouraged the imposition of a legal obligation.[10]

As for the period that followed, during which the theories of Keynes were dominant, the prospect of a legally binding endeavor continued, of course, to be dismissed. Moreover, a similar approach was adopted in 1965 by the President of the Republic General de Gaulle. Having succeeded in submitting to the National Assembly for approval a balanced budget in 1965, his minister of economy and finance, Valéry Giscard d'Estaing, intended to amend the 1959 Ordinance on public finance in order to introduce a legal obligation of balanced budget for the state budget. But this would have only referred to the

9 Gilbert Orsoni, 'L'équilibre budgétaire, histoire d'une pratique' in Lucile Tallineau (ed.) *L'équilibre budgétaire* (Economica 1984) 6–7.

10 In any case, it is easier to enact rules relating to the presentation of the finance laws (unity, universality, specialty) or their periodicity (annual basis) than to their content (balance and sincerity).

financial operation of a final nature,[11] which would already have been a huge step. However, d'Estaing's proposal was dismissed by the President of the Republic, who felt that in this matter it was better not to make a commitment for the future and risk the failure to observe a standard that would have been initiated and adopted by himself.

2. While it cannot be questioned with regard to the state, the difficulty of the juridicization of the concept of balanced budget cannot be framed in the same manner for other public entities, whether local or regional authorities, or the European Union.

Local and regional authorities in France are obliged to submit and adopt their budgets in an effective balance. However, a small operating deficit is tolerated. This obligation was considered necessary, since the state does not have the obligation to reduce or close local deficits (although quite exceptionally it sometimes did). Moreover, local balanced budgets are achieved by taking into account loans as budgetary revenues in the investment section, which is something that cannot be done in the case of the state budget. This illustrates, once again, the diversity of definitions of a balanced budget. This could also be the true budgetary "golden rule", namely permitting the use of borrowing solely for financing future expenditure, this being the only way to justify demanding that future generations contribute to the burden of interest and the amortization of current loans.

As for the European Union, both the significance of its budget, essentially an intervention budget, and the fact that it mainly results from contributions paid by member states who cannot agree to contribute to "lost funds" justify the balanced budget principle. The EU budget must, therefore, be implemented without resorting to borrowing, with the sole exception of the "negative reserve",[12] which makes it possible to finance new expenses in anticipation of the savings to be realized during the financial year, this deficit having to be entered as expenditure in the next budget.

3. It follows that, for the state, the greatest difficulty in the juridicization of the concept of balanced budget is twofold: on the one hand, the balanced budget is mentioned in fundamental laws without, however, concrete consequences being perceived or attached to it; on the other hand, there seems to exist a will to constitutionalize the balanced (or quasi-balanced) budget.

First, there is the use of the term "balanced budget" with reference to the budgetary cash balance alone,[13] this expression having replaced the Keynesian terminology of "economic and financial balance" in the Ordinance of January 2, 1959 on public finance, and implying other relationships with the concept of balance (equilibrium) without necessarily requiring a strict balanced budget. In

11 Valéry Giscard d'Estaing, Séance Assemblé nationale, October 24 and November 25, 1964 (JO. Ass. nat., 1964) 3194 and 5636.

12 Cf. Céline Viessant, 'Les finances de l'Union européenne' in Gilbert Orsoni (ed.) *Les finances publiques en Europe* (Economica 2007) 490.

13 But we can always argue by explaining that the choice of this terminology is anything but innocent.

addition, to conform with European rules on budgetary discipline, the French fundamental law stipulates "an objective of balance" not only with regard to the state budget, but also concerning the public accounts of all "public administrations". Thus, according to article 34, final paragraph, of the French Constitution, as revised on July 23, 2008: "Planning laws … shall contribute to achieving the objective of balanced accounts for public administrations." But they are merely financial planning laws and objectives without a specified timeframe. This is a significantly softened version of the proposed constitutional law no 573 of January 9, 2008, which was intended to constitutionalize the balance of the operating budget, as it is the case for the rules in force at the level of local and regional authorities. This would have also involved a revision of the modalities of submission for approval of finance laws.

Second, and without answering for the time being the question whether the fundamental law is the relevant legislative level for the introduction of the balanced budget rule, in the European context of an increased budgetary discipline, one has to acknowledge a predisposition toward the introduction of a balanced (or quasi-balanced) budget at the constitutional level, together with observing the limit of 3% of GDP for public deficit.[14]

The German and Spanish examples are well known by now. As early as 1949, article 110 of the German Basic Law made reference to the balance of

14 This is not exactly the question dealt with in this too brief statement, but the existence of a constraint and of (potential) sanctions was a wholly new phenomenon and provided a legal framework for the observance, if not of the budgetary balance, at least of a limited deficit. We shall simply list, for illustrative purposes and without claiming to be exhaustive: the Stability and Growth Pact (Amsterdam, June 17, 1997), which already referred to the structural cash balance, the trajectory of the public finances, the procedures for excessive deficit (defined in the Council Regulation No 1467/97 of July 7, 1997, with fines provided therein); the *Six Pack*, five regulations and a directive entered into force on December 13, 2011, with a strengthened preventive component (European Semester for the Coordination of Economic Policies) and a repressive component, which, when the debt exceeds 60% of GDP, provides the implementation of the excessive deficit procedure when the State does not adjust 1/20 every year, over three years, the gap between its debt ratio and this level of 60% of GDP. Penalties may be imposed, with the exception of a qualified majority opposing such, for countries with an excessive deficit that do not comply with the Council's recommendations; the *Two Pack*, two new Council Regulations of May 23, 2013, further strengthening the supervision and penalizing excessive deficits more severely, the Commission having the capacity to request a revision of the plan submitted by the State; the *Treaty on Stability, Coordination and Governance* (TSCG) (see below) generalizing the technique of reverse qualified majority voting for the whole procedure, without, however, resorting to automatic corrections or sanctions. Beyond the numerical constraints aimed at approaching the situation of balance and the transposition into national law of the objectives set, institutions are set up (independent budget councils, which gave France the High Council of Public Finance) responsible for deciding on the seriousness and sincerity of the macroeconomic forecasts chosen by governments when constructing the budget for the financial year and other financial documents.

revenue and expenditure ("must be balanced"), although loans could be considered as budgetary revenue. However, in 1969 (Art. 115 (1)), a debt ceiling/loan threshold was fixed, while in 2006 the obligations related to budget discipline resulting from European Treaties were transposed into German law (Art.109, (5)). Finally, the revision of the Basic Law of July 29, 2009 further limits the use of loans, requires a status close to balance at both federal (2016) and *Länder* (2021) levels. With the exception of servicing the debt, the structural deficit should not exceed 0.35% of GDP at federal level in 2016 and at *Länder* level in 2020.

Furthermore, in 2010 Spain adopted the constitutional rule of a structural deficit not exceeding 0.4% of GDP by 2020, divided into 0.26% for the state and 0.14% for the autonomous communities.

Italy then followed suit, with its new article 81 introduced in the Constitution through the constitutional law of April 20, 2012 which states:

> The State shall balance the revenues and expenditure of its budget, taking account of the adverse and favorable phases of the economic cycle. No recourse shall be made to borrowing except for the purpose of taking account of the effects of the economic cycle or, subject to authorization by the two Houses approved by an absolute majority vote of their Members, in exceptional circumstances. Any law involving new or increased expenditure shall provide the resources to cover such expenditure. The content of the budget law, the fundamental rules and the criteria adopted to ensure balance between revenue and expenditure and the sustainability of general government debt shall be established by legislation approved by an absolute majority of the Members of each House in compliance with the principles established by constitutional law.[15]

These constitutional provisions requiring a balanced budget or a budget with a (very) limited deficit contain a reference to economic cycles, hence to their impact on budgetary cash balances. This necessarily leads to questioning the notion of structural balance (or structural deficit).

Structural balance, a deceptively convenient solution

The implications and requirements of a single market and, more importantly, of the prospect of replacing national currencies with a single currency have led, since the adoption of the Maastricht Treaty of 1992, to the establishment of convergence criteria. These rules were intended to allow member states that met those criteria to be qualified to join the Eurozone, if they chose to do so. Then, with a view to ensuring the sustainability of the euro, it was equally essential to maintain budgetary discipline between the member states in order

15 See the Constitution of the Italian Republic, article 81, www.cortecostituzionale.it/documenti/download/pdf/The_Constitution_of_the_Italian_Republic.pdf

to prevent excessive economic, financial and budgetary divergence from jeopardizing the new endeavor. However, the European economic and sovereign debt crisis which triggered debts and deficits resulted in the emergence of an additional level of fiscal discipline. Hence, the will to establish a "golden rule"[16] and to validate the concept of structural balance.

If the famous "golden rule" amounts to a (re)affirmation of the requirement of a balanced budget (although one may ask which balanced budget), the explicit reference to the "structural" dimension of the balance constitutes a supplementary aspect, at least in its expression,[17] and thus deserves further developments.

A notion which is difficult to grasp…

Undoubtedly, it is not a matter of confusing the economic or budgetary "structural balance" with the notion of "structural balance" which has been present since the 1950s in the field of social psychology and which refers to the structure of the links between two cognitive objects, between two values or between two individuals.[18]

Indeed, in response to the sometimes considerable increase in the debt of the member states after (for some, even before) the financial crisis of 2008, if we wanted to reverse this upward trend with a renewed budgetary prudence and because we wished to implement strict rules, it would be necessary to be aware, as the past few years have shown, that the effects of conjuncture might affect, if not annihilate, the efforts undertaken.

Moreover, the impact of the economic cycle had already been perceived, since recognized exceptional circumstances could temporarily exempt a state's budgets from the maximum deficits and debts provided by the Treaties.

Therefore, the terminology of "structural deficit" has been used ever since the prospect of a quasi-balance being reached by states in the medium term[19] has been evoked in the Treaty on Stability, Co-ordination and Governance of Economic and Monetary Union (TSCG). The "structural deficit" should not exceed 0.5% of the GDP of states concerned for all public administrations.

To restate the definition given by the then Minister of Economy of France and later European Commissioner for Economic and Monetary Affairs, Taxation and Customs, the notion of structural balance is intended to "remove from

16 On the "golden rule", see the colloquium organized at Lille, on March 27–28, 2014 and published in Numéro spécial 'La règle d'or des finances publiques en Europe' (2015) 1/2 *Gestion et Finances publiques.*

17 Even if the excessive deficit procedure is not indifferent to existing cyclical data.

18 Even if we could consider, by assimilation, that structural balance expresses the nature of the links between a given economic situation and the search for the best possible balance (cash balance) of the budget.

19 In fact, at the instigation of Germany, it was essentially a question of extending to the Union as a whole the rules which it had imposed on itself and of accelerating a movement which was still too reserved despite the few examples given above. Especially since France, which had not managed in 2011 to revise its Constitution in this sense, said that it too would adhere to this perspective in the medium term.

the public account balances the momentarily distorting effects of the hazards of the cycle, in other words, the gaps in economic growth".[20] That is, it was a matter of determining the real situation and the real figures in public accounts, excluding cyclical variations, which may indeed have temporary effects that appear to aggravate or improve the situation prevailing at a given moment. To give a telling and authentic example, the year (2010) when the Republic of Ireland had to rescue its banking system, the public deficit declared was 32% of the GDP. This crisis was temporary (although its consequences could not be erased at the stroke of a pen), but it did not reflect the deep and lasting reality of Ireland's public accounts.

Beyond this assertion, however, the clarity of the notion of structural balance is not necessarily obvious. No one will deny the weight of conjuncture its "distorting" effect on the budgetary and financial system of a country. However, at that time, the French Minister of Budget pointed out that the problem was that "the concept of structural balance refers to that of *potential growth*, that is, the growth which the country would have if the international crisis was not the one we have seen in recent years".[21]

What is "potential growth",[22] in fact? And is it really possible to determine what a non-hazardous budget in the cycle would be, knowing that there is always an element of volatility and that the question that arises is which hazards will be taken into account and which ones will not? Which seems, in essence, like a "random" exercise.

To express this phenomenon in a more academic manner, two authors wrote:

> The structural balance measures imperfectly the cyclical share of the public balance since it is based on an imperfect assessment of the position of the economy in the cycle and on the assumptions of average sensitivity to the various components of the public balance. In doing so, the structural balance in its traditional definition still contains at least part of a cyclical nature, in particular that related to fluctuations in the GDP elasticities of the various components of the public cash balance.[23]

20 Pierre Moscovici quoted in Marc Vignaud, 'Traité budgétaire européen: le PM joue les équilibristes', *Le Point* (September 26, 2012).

21 Jérôme Cahuzac quoted in Marc Vignaud, 'Traité budgétaire européen: le PM joue les équilibristes', *Le Point* (September 26, 2012).

22 Potential growth means "GDP growth resulting from the optimal use of factors of production and consistent with stable inflation". See Hélène Baudchon, 'Note de conjoncture' (BNP Paribas March 2014). Knowing that, as pointed out by Didier Migaud ('Reply to Eric Pichet' (2014) 48 *Droit fiscal* 45), the production gap and potential growth should not be mistaken for one another "in the calculation of the cyclical component of the deficit, it is the production gap that must be taken into account, that is, the gap between the level of actual GDP and that of potential GDP, and not the gap between actual growth and potential growth, which represents only the variation in this production gap".

23 Thibault Guyon and Stephane Sorbe, 'Solde structurel et effort structurel: vers une décomposition par sous-secteur des administrations publiques' (2009) 13 *Cahiers de la Direction générale du Trésor et de la politique économique* 4.

This difficulty may translate into differences of opinion as to the question of cash balance. As such, for the year 2011, the French structural deficit was evaluated by the European Commission at 4.1% of GDP and by the International Monetary Fund at 3.4%.

Such uncertainties do not, however, prohibit the setting of objectives in terms of structural deficit, or the correction of the budgets submitted to Parliament by imposing structural deficit requirements. The last difficulties of the presentation of the French public accounts in autumn 2014 illustrate it abundantly. Following the objections of the Commission, the 3.6 billion euro reduction in the funding needs of public authorities, leading to a structural deficit of 0.2% of GDP in 2015 compared to 0.5% of GDP in 2014, must be able to escape the Brussels attacks, whereas, after implementation, public deficits should represent only 4% of GDP instead of the 4.4% envisaged by the finance law for 2014 (this decrease resulting from a lower expenditure than had been envisaged).

...Has more theoretical than actual legal value

From the Maastricht Treaty to the Treaty on the Functioning of the European Union (Article 126 of TFEU and Protocol 12 on the excessive deficit procedure), the reference to the limitation of state deficit and debt concerned only a percentage of GDP without any other details. It was the TSCG which stipulated that structural deficit should not exceed 0.5% of GDP.[24] In addition, as noted above, Article 110 of the revised Basic German Law of 2009 refers to a structural deficit limited to 0.35% of GDP at federal level from 2016 and for the *Länder* from 2020, excluding debt service – that is, the primary cash balance. Hence the obligation for the states to include this new "golden rule" in their constitution or in another supra-legislative text. The TSCG uses the "constitutional preference" formula which, in the case of France, was reflected in the choice, validated by the Constitutional Council in its decision 2012-653 DC of August 9, 2012,[25] of an Organic Law on the planning and governance of public finances (no. 2012-1403 of December 17, 2012), and of Law no. 2012-1558 of December 31, 2012 on the planning of public finances for the years 2012–2017. This was followed by Law no. 2014-1653 of December 29,

24 More specifically, the TSCG considers that the balanced budget rule is observed when "the cumulative structural balance of public administrations corresponds to the country-specific medium-term objective (MTO) ... with an upper structural deficit limit of –0.5% of GDP" for the states whose debt is above 60% of GDP (and up to –1% for other countries). It also provides for the automatic triggering of corrections if significant deviations are observed in relation to the MTO and the trajectory suitable for its realization.

25 According to which it was established by the Council that the ratification of the Treaty on Stability, Coordination and Governance in Europe and its implementation, in particular the inclusion of its rule on balanced budgets in national law, did not require a revision of the Constitution.

2014, on the planning of public finances for the years 2014–2019 which corrected the over-optimistic forecasts of the previous public finance planning law. Finally, the provisions of Law no. 2018-32 of January 22, 2018 on the planning of public finances for the years 2018–2022 (currently in force) stipulates a structural balance of –0.8% for 2022, close to the 0.5% required, while public debt for 2022 is projected at 91.9% of GDP. However, the planned deficit reduction stipulated in the current law is now faced with the new context of the COVID-19 crisis, with the budget deficit exploding again and public debt expected to reach 130% of GDP.

Conclusion

In conclusion, France not only does not satisfy the trajectory intended to fulfill the objective of structural deficit contained in the programming law mentioned above as well in the other programming laws that have followed, but has only with difficulty managed to meet the 3% public deficit criterion, and that even before the COVID crisis had managed to plunge the country into a situation of serious public deficit.

Should we rejoice or worry?

The question cannot be asked as such. Notwithstanding the argument of an increasingly hypothetical budgetary sovereignty, it would be difficult to rejoice in a situation where, beyond the deficits that accumulate each year, the public debt continues to increase and is likely to reach alarming levels. But if we can only lament such circumstances and fear the consequences of a loss of confidence in the markets and the rising cost of loans that would follow, it will not come as a surprise to learn that the scope of the term "budgetary" is not reduced to simple accounting requirements. The diversity of circumstances must also be taken into account in order to find, sometimes on a narrow crest line, the genuine balance between the demands for a meaningful and reliable budget and the economic, political, sociological and even anthropological constraints. Such an approach could lead to the implementation of the "right formula", capable of maintaining a suitable level of growth[26] and managing, in a not too distant future, given the recent developments due to the COVID crisis, to launch the process of reducing public debt.

Bibliography

Alland D, Rials S (eds), *Dictionnaire de la culture juridique* (PUF 2003)
Baudchon H, 'Note de conjoncture' (March 2014) BNP Paribas
Chevallier J, *L'Etat post-moderne* (4th ed. LGDJ 2014)

26 Maintaining a suitable level of economic growth also needs to take into account an additional difficulty for states – that is, having to operate in an open and globalized economic environment that makes the scope of national measures more limited. Unless, of course, we seek a "change of the model", but that is another story. Quite hypothetical at the present time.

Guinchard S, Montagnier G (eds), *Lexique des termes juridiques* (15th ed. Dalloz 2005)

Guyon T, Sorbe S, 'Solde structurel et effort structurel: vers une décomposition par sous-secteur des administrations publiques' (2009) 13 *Cahiers de la Direction générale du Trésor et de la politique économique* 4

Tallineau L (ed.) *L'équilibre budgétaire* (Economica 1994)

Viessant C, 'Les finances de l'Union européenne' in Gilbert Orsoni (ed.) *Les finances publiques en Europe* (Economica 2007)

Numéro special 'La règle d'or des finances publiques en Europe' (2015) 1/2 *Gestion et Finances publiques*

2 Economic perspectives on budget balance

Thomas Stauffer[1]

Introduction

In pre-modern times to balance the budget was less about following a moral or legal precept or realising some economic theory, but rather a fact, in as much as there was money in the king's treasury or there was not. Later, a balanced budget, or, more specifically, not to spend more than you have as well as not to enter into debt, was a moral precept, and still is for many people.[2] In many cases to balance the budget became a legal obligation and today a great number of countries are bound by fiscal rules of different kinds.[3]

Such rules have also been agreed by 25 European Union member states in the Treaty on Stability, Coordination and Governance in the Economic and Monetary Union (TSCG), signed in March 2012: '[t]he budgetary position of [...] government shall be balanced'. Asking the proverbial man in the street what is required by this rule, he would probably say: simple enough, not to spend more than you have. But as we read on, we learn that this 'rule … shall be deemed to be respected if the annual structural balance of the general government is at its country-specific medium-term objective as defined in the revised Stability and Growth Pact with a lower limit of a structural deficit of 0.5 % of the gross domestic product at market prices'.[4] Not as simple as that, one may say.

1 The author is a Programme Manager for public financial management with the Swiss federal government; the opinions expressed here are solely his.
2 To illustrate this we may refer to an observation by Hugh Dalton (Chancellor of the Exchequer in the first British post-WWII government) according to which a balanced budget was 'not only … an unquestioned precept of finance, but … a moral precept as well. It is enunciated by orthodox financial experts with a cool puritanical pride', cited by Kurt Heinig, *Das Budget, Zweiter Band: Das Budgetwesen* (J.C.B. Mohr (Paul Siebeck) 1951) 97.
3 See Victor Lledó, Sungwook Yoon, Xiangming Fang, Samba Mbaye and Young Kim, 'Fiscal Rules at a Glance' (2017) IMF Background Note, Washington 2017, and the 'Fiscal Rules Dataset 1985–2015' www.imf.org/external/datamapper/FiscalRules/map/map.htm, accessed 24 December 2019.
4 Art 3 para 1 *Treaty on Stability, Coordination and Governance* (TSCG).

DOI: 10.4324/9781315181882-4

This book is primarily concerned with the impact of the balanced budget principle as expressed in the Fiscal Compact on constitutional issues such as the separation of powers, public governance in general and fundamental rights. Hence this chapter is addressed to constitutional scholars other than economists and deals with the question: what economic concept of balanced budget did the signatories to the TSCG agreed to? First, however, I would like to address in a somewhat cursory manner the question of how economic concepts relate to legal norms.

The use and misuse of economic concepts in law

There is an old and ongoing discussion on the nature and status of legal science. Often it is considered a social science on the account that law is a social phenomenon, influencing how individuals behave and society evolves. However, this approach blurs important methodological differences and fails to acknowledge the inherent normativity of the law. According to the view taken here, legal science, properly speaking, is hermeneutics in its primary meaning.[5] It aims at understanding and justifying norms by referring to other and in particular higher-level norms through the interpretation of legal text. This does in no way imply that, for example, economic facts and their study have no bearing on the law; on the contrary, to comprehend economic facts and related theories is absolutely necessary for understanding and applying budgetary norms.[6] It implies, however, that both economist and legal scholars must mutually understand the limitations of their respective approaches and the potential synergies to be realised.

On the one hand, the economist needs to understand that, for instance, the expression 'balanced budget' used in a legal sense does not necessarily correspond to the concept of balanced budget as he understands it. First, and I shall demonstrate this later, there is not one single economic concept of balanced budget. Second, and more importantly, once an economic concept has been included into a legal norm its meaning can no longer be determined by looking at economic theory (alone) but must be established through legal interpretation. To this economic theory may contribute as an ancillary science by explaining the balanced budget concept prevailing at the time of law-making or by demonstrating the impact of using a specific balanced budget concept on equity. However, economics cannot tell what the law is.

On the other hand, when determining through interpretation what the law is, legal scholars should examine seriously the underlying theories and concepts on their own terms. In this, they may want to heed the warning by the famous

5 There is a long history of and rich literature on the nature of law as a science in general and of legal hermeneutics in particular; for an overview, see Hubert Rottleuthner, 'Rechtswissenschaft als Sozialwissenschaft' and Matthias Jestaedt, 'Rechtswissenschaft als normative Disziplin', both in Eric Hilgendorf and Jan C. Joerden (eds), *Handbuch Rechtsphilosophie* (J.B. Metzler 2017).

6 Thomas Stauffer, *Instrumente des Haushaltsausgleichs, Ökonomische Analyse und Rechtliche Umsetzung* (Helbing & Lichtenhahn 2001) 6ff.

economist John M. Keynes addressed to practical men, 'who believe themselves to be quite exempt from any intellectual influences, [but] are usually the slaves of some defunct economist'[7], or the more recent observation that 'defunct economists – and their theories – are usually enslaved by those who do not fully understand them'.[8] Accordingly, legal scholars should not only search for and consider the best available economic guidance where appropriate, while recognising its limitations, but also disclose the methods or canon used in interpreting the balanced budget rules instituted by the Fiscal Compact.

Budget balances in accounting and statistics

In the end, all budget balances are based on what has been accounted for in books and ledgers. The way this is done is therefore of crucial importance for the understanding of the concept of budget balance, both in a normative and positive perspective. In this chapter we thus present a short outline of public sector accounting, its systems and standards, as well as government finance statistics with a view to the concept of budget balance.

Public sector accounting

Public sector accounting may be defined as the recording, classifying and aggregating of financial and economic data in such a way as to provide information about the government and other public entities controlled by it for accountability and decision-making purposes. This is a tentative, primarily descriptive definition, because unlike private sector accounting the theoretical basis of public sector accounting is still underdeveloped.[9] There are many ways for specifying and systematising budgetary information, and much of the confusion in discussing them stems from a lack of clarity regarding the objective pursued, namely managing the treasury, managing government and managing the economy. To these three objectives correspond, albeit somewhat loosely, cash accounting, accrual accounting and public financial statistics as outlined below.

Historically, modern public sector accounting may be traced back to the cameralistic method of accounting, which was developed in Sweden at the beginning of the 16th century. The cameralistic method became widely used after the Thirty Years War as part of mercantilist policies and dominant with its

7 John Maynard Keynes, *General Theory of Employment, Interest, and Money* (Macmillan and Co 1936) 383.

8 Lorenzo Bini Smaghi, Member of the Executive Board of the ECB, in a speech at the Master Programme in International Business and Economics, Università di Pavia, 24 February 2010, www.ecb.europa.eu/press/key/date/2010/html/sp100224.en.html, accessed 10 December 2020

9 See Andreas Bergmann, Sandro Fuchs and Christoph Schuler, 'A theoretical basis for public sector accrual accounting research: Current state and perspectives' (2019) 39 (8) *Public Money & Management* 560.

introduction in the Austro-Hungarian empire in 1815.[10] This system aimed first at recording all public revenues and expenditures and second to ensure permanent liquidity – that is, for the state to be able to pay all dues on time. From simple beginnings, the cameralistic system developed and differentiated into the modern systems of cash accounting,[11] which are still used by many governments, in the EU most notably Germany.

Cash accounting

At its most basic, cash accounting recognises a transaction when cash is received or paid. Accordingly, cash accounting aims at providing information about cash receipts, cash payments and cash balances necessary for assessing the capacity to cover cash requirements.[12] The simple cash balance approach compares current revenues (tax and non-tax) to the sum of current expenditures plus the acquisition of assets (real and financial). Thus, to balance the budget entails exactly matching cash payments to cash receipts (or vice versa) over the reporting period. In practice, this matching was often understood in a tautological manner, inasmuch as receipts and outlays do necessarily match in accounting, if also implicit and explicit credits count towards the determination of the budget balance.[13] However, in its appropriate form, the cash (budget) balance equals the difference between the sum of all payments minus all non-credit receipts. A refined form of the cash balance approach explicitly allows for credits by separating the budget in an ordinary and an extraordinary part, with credits considered extraordinary revenues and used for covering so-called extraordinary expenditures (e.g. investments or war costs); by declaring certain expenditures to be extraordinary, it is thus possible to maintain the fiction of a balanced budget.[14] More recently, the distinction between ordinary and extraordinary expenditures has found a new form in the one between current and capital account. The related approach to budget balancing posits that whereas current expenditures must be covered by current receipts, capital expenditures (i.e. investments) may be (partially) covered by borrowing if the net worth of the government remains positive (net-worth approach).[15]

10 For a general description of the cameralistic method of accounting and its origins, see Vassilios P. Filios, 'The Cameralistic Method of Accounting: A Historical Note' (1983) 10 *Journal of Business & Accounting* 443.
11 Heinig (n 2) 109ff.
12 International Public Sector Accounting Standards Board, *Financial Reporting under the Cash Basis of Accounting* (New York November 2017) 11.
13 For a historical overview of how states have faked their budget balance, notably during war times, see Heinig (n 2) 93ff.
14 Heinig (n 2) 100.
15 Net worth is calculated as total assets minus total liabilities. Cf. James L. Chan and Yunxiao Xu, 'Government Financial Reporting Standards and Practices' in Richard Allen, Richard Hemming and Barry H. Potter (eds), *The International Handbook of Public Financial Management* (Palgrave McMillian 2013) 767ff and in particular 773.

Despite these refinements and the possibility of establishing auxiliary accounts and providing statistical data, cash accounting has been falling out of favour because of its conceptual limitations, such as its ignorance of the intertemporal nature of economic entities and the paucity of information necessary for their management. With respect to budget balancing, the negative side-effects of balancing the cash budget on a yearly basis may be substantial. In particular, in a contracting economy achieving a balanced cash budget will require rigorous discipline, and restricting expenditures to given tax returns will emerge as the best fiscal policy.[16] This became fully apparent after World War I, whose five years of struggle pitted not only nations and armies but also economies against each other and thus greatly expanded the state's weight in and influence on the economy.[17] In the years after 1918, with the conventional justification for running deficits – namely the extraordinary nature of war – no longer available, governments started to reduce their expenditures in lock-step with shrinking revenues and set in motion a vicious circle of reductions in public expenditure, aggregate demand and tax revenues that led the world economy into the abyss of global depression of 1929–1933. There is a rich literature on the global depression and sometimes conflicting accounts on how fiscal and monetary policies contributed to it. In a nutshell, Keynes and his followers identify a contraction of aggregate demand due to reduced private investment in the private sector as a root cause and misguided fiscal policies aimed at maintaining the cash balance in public budgets as the driver of the depression. Monetarist economists, in particular Friedmann and Schwartz, take the view that monetary policy played an important part in deepening and prolonging the depression by severely contracting money supply and failing to act as lender of last resort.[18] However, there is also general agreement that public finances have macroeconomic implications, which need to be taken into account when making fiscal policies, and which may not be based on a simple cash balance for the government.

Accrual accounting

Accrual accounting, which has long been the standard approach in the private sector, answers at least to the conceptual limitations of cash accounting above, by not recording cash flows, but the accrual and decrement of value within a

16 A. Premchand, *Government Budgeting and Expenditures Controls: Theory and Practice* (International Monetary Fund 1983) 100.

17 Before World War I the weight of governments in the European economies was around 10% of GDP. At the end of the war it was much higher, at least for the warring countries, and continued to grow. In 1938, as a rule of thumb, the state's share in the economy was two to three times what it had been in 1913. See Ludger Lindlar, *Das mißverstandene Wirtschaftswunder* (*The misunderstood economic miracle*) (Mohr Siebeck 1997) 218.

18 Milton Friedman and Anna J. Schwartz, *A Monetary History of the United States 1867–1960* (Princeton University Press 1963).

given period. It recognises a transaction when the underlying economic event occurs and provides information not primarily about cash flows, but about the financial position and financial performance of an entity in the reporting period including assets, liabilities and net asset/equity. For example, a civil servant's salary will, under cash accounting, be debited entirely to the current account of the reporting period and impact fully on the budget balance. On the other hand, the payments for the construction of a road will be first recorded to the capital account and the depreciation (i.e. loss of value) spread over its service life by debiting the corresponding amounts in the current account of the reporting period. Whereas in cash accounting all outlays are thus made equal, in accrual accounting a payment may impact differently on the budget balance depending on its purpose. Accordingly, to balance the budget in an accrual perspective means to maintain the net asset position of the reporting entity, which is the sum of all value inflows minus all value outflows in the reporting period.

Public accounting standards

For the actual implementation of either cash or accrual accounting, standards are required, and in general these public accounting standards correspond to or at least aim for the International Public Sector Accounting Standards (IPSAS). IPSAS are developed by the Public Sector Accounting Standards Board (IPSASB), a body hosted by the International Federation of Accountants (IFAC) and funded by private and public sponsors. Whereas cash accounting is relatively simple and clear, accrual accounting is much more demanding and entails settling a great number of delimitation issues. It should thus be no surprise that there is one IPSAS standard for cash accounting[19] but more than 40 for accrual accounting.[20] Nevertheless, for the reasons stated in the previous chapter, we may observe an international trend towards accrual accounting, with most countries using mixed systems.[21] Accrual IPSAS are largely based on the private sector International Financial Reporting Standards (IFRS), while taking into account the specificities of the public sector, such as the prevalence of non-exchange transactions, the need to capture the service potential of an asset in the absence of cash flows or the requirement to report budget execution.[22]

19 International Public Sector Accounting Standards Board, *Financial Reporting under the Cash Basis of Accounting* (IFAC 2017).

20 International Public Sector Accounting Standards Board, *Handbook of International Public Sector Accounting Pronouncements* (IFAC 2020).

21 International Federation of Accountants, *International Standards: 2019 Global Status Report* (IFAC 2019), www.ifac.org/system/files/publications/files/IFAC-International-standards-2019-global-status-report.pdf, accessed 23 December 2019

22 For a general overview, see Ernst & Young, *A snapshot of GAAP differences between IPSAS and IFRS* (April 2013). For actual and detailed information, see www.ipsasb.org, accessed 10 December 2020.

Accounting systems and the standards that define them are not neutral from a policy perspective, but fulfilling their purpose of informing and instructing decisions they will necessarily frame the choice set and impact the decision-making process, even if it may be politically expedient to claim otherwise.[23] For example, it has been shown that the move towards accrual accounting by subnational governments in Germany has not impacted on their overall financial balance but that it has altered the structure of budgets, inasmuch as revenues from the sales of non-financial assets have decreased significantly. This is presented as an indication that in the past disinvestments have been used as one-off measures to respond to fiscal constraints.[24] On the other hand, changes to the accounting system may also be used to enable or enforce policy decisions already taken. For example, the link between New Public Management (NPM) and accrual accounting has always been obvious, as the objective of managing for results requires values to be accounted for.[25]

Government finance statistics

As stated before, cash and accrual accounting are instruments for managing respectively the treasury or all government entities connected by control, such as all units of a central government including public corporations, a subnational government and the entities controlled by it, or an independent social security unit. Any government account will therefore be both incomplete and misleading when our concern is the impact of public sector on the economy as a whole. For this purpose, the information provided by the different public accounts needs to be compiled and delimitated statistically. Such a specialised macroeconomic statistical framework, the Government Finance Statistics (GFS) framework, has been established by the IMF based on the global System of National Accounts (SNA 2008);[26] it is accrual-based and supports the development, implementation and assessment of fiscal policies with a view to achieving such goals as the stabilisation of the economy, the reallocation of resources and the redistribution of income. GFS aims at covering all entities that materially affect fiscal policies – that is, general government entities at every level including social security units as well as public corporations provided they are non-market producers.[27]

23 Enrico Bracci, Christopher Humphrey, Jodie Moll and Ileana Steccolini, 'Public sector accounting, accountability and austerity: More than balancing the books?' (2015) 28 (6) *Accounting, Auditing & Accountability Journal* 879.

24 Désirée I. Christofzik, 'Does accrual accounting alter fiscal policy decisions? Evidence from Germany' (2019) 60 *European Journal of Political Economy* 101.

25 Bracci et al. (n 23) 883ff.

26 European Commission, International Monetary Fund, Organisation for Economic Co-operation and Development, United Nations, World Bank, *System of National Accounts 2008* (2009), in particular 435ff.

27 *Government Finance Statistics Manual* (International Monetary Fund 2014).

GFS defines the fiscal balance (budget balance) of the general government as all its assets less liabilities in a given period of time (usually one year); a negative fiscal balance indicates a budget deficit, a positive fiscal balance, a surplus. Defined like this, fiscal balance is a stock measure, more akin to debt than deficit. However, by comparing the change in fiscal balance from one year to the next the corresponding flow measure (deficit) can be easily established. To determine fiscal balance in particular, two operations have to be performed: delimiting the scope of the general government and consolidating fiscal balances across the entities covered. Depending on how this is done, quite different outcomes may result, which are all equally correct but will have different policy implications if they are used indiscriminately.

The point above is illustrated by the matrix developed by Dippelsman et al., which presents the institutional coverage of gross debt together with the instruments through which this debt is contracted. Accordingly, Canada's general government debt in 2010 can be calculated at 67% or 104% of GDP solely depending on the scope of debt instruments included. Of this difference, 24% of GDP can be attributed to accounts payable and 13% to unfunded pension schemes (and similar instruments).[28] In order to be comparable across countries, coverage of gross debt should be as comprehensive as possible; that's why the authors propose general government with full instrument coverage (Government Level GL3/Debt instrument D4) as the indicator of government debt for international comparison. Whereas some countries already disseminate GL3/D4 data, many advanced economies, including the EU member states, publish GL3/D3 data.[29]

The accounting and statistical basis of the Fiscal Compact

The importance of accounting standards and how they are applied is a recurring topic of fiscal surveillance in the EU, with consecutive waves of fiscal restrictions imposed on national governments, followed by compliance with those rules achieved through one-off measures and creative accounting, and subsequently more detailed and specific rules in view of achieving the elusive objective of effective compliance.[30] This has been observed in the run-up to the Economic and Monetary Union[31] and again as a reaction to the economic downturn of the early 21st century. Whereas one-off measures, such as the sale of non-financial assets (e.g. privatisations) or tax amnesties, may have

28 Robert Dippelsman, Claudia Dziobek and Carlos A. Gutiérrez Mangas, 'What Lies Beneath: The Statistical Definition of Public Sector Debt' (SDN/12/09, International Monetary Fund 2012) 9ff.

29 Dippelsman et al. (n 28) 16.

30 This is, of course, not a peculiarity of the EU and accounting devices to create the illusion of a better fiscal position are being used by governments around the world. See Timothy I Irwin, *Accounting Devices and Fiscal Illusions* (2012) IMF Staff Discussion Note SDN/12/02.

31 See section 'Economic and Monetary Union (EMU)' below.

merits on their own, with the improvement of the accounted for fiscal position a secondary benefit, creative accounting serves no other purpose than to conceal the weakness of the underlying fiscal position. An incomplete inventory of such deficit gimmicks includes among others the exclusion of loss-making entities (e.g. hospitals) from general government or the Italian 'Eurotax'.[32] A whole class of gimmicks is based on the securitisation of existing or future assets or income flows, through which unrealised (and often uncertain) claims of the government are turned into cash payments by special-purpose vehicles (SPV). Similarly, a whole range of tricks have been used to push the gross public debt ratio towards or below the 60% threshold, without changing the government's net worth. Examples thereof have been the transfer of funds from central banks and public enterprises through the withdrawal of capital (e.g. gold sales) or extraordinary dividends. Other such instruments are the financing of public investments through Public Private Partnerships or the reduction of maintenance on non-financial public assets.[33]

For the EU the choice of accounting system has (once again) gained renewed interest in the context of the global financial crisis of 2009 and the ensuing sovereign debt crisis,[34] which highlighted the lack of and 'need for more rigorous, transparent and comparable reporting of fiscal data'.[35] This need translated into Art. 3(1) of the Council Directive 2011/85/EU (the Budgetary Frameworks Directive), which requires member states to 'have in place public accounting systems comprehensively and consistently covering all sub-sectors of general government and containing the information needed to generate accrual data with a view to preparing data based on the ESA … standard'.[36] In the meantime, some progress has been made in harmonising the treatment of various incidents across Public Sector Accounting (cash or accrual, depending on national regulations), Government Finance Statistics (Manual on Government Deficit and Debt[37]) and National Accounts (ESA 2010). Nevertheless

32 The Italian 'Eurotax' was a loan dressed up as a tax; i.e. the *Contributo Straordinario per l'Europa* was a supplementary progressive income tax levied in 1997 and refunded later: OECD, *Economic Surveys: Italy 1997* (OECD Publishing 1997) 65.

33 Vincent Koen and Paul van den Noord, *Fiscal Gimmickry in Europe: One-Off Measures and Creative Accounting* (2005) 417 OECD Economics Department Working Papers 6ff.

34 On public sector accounting in Europe, see Francesca Manes-Rossi, Sandra Cohen, Eugenio Caperchione and Isabel Brusca, 'Harmonizing public sector accounting in Europe: Thinking outside the box' [2016] *Public Money & Management* 189, in particular the overview in Table 1.

35 EPSAS Working Group (2017) *Guidance for the First Time Implementation of Accrual Accounting* EPSAS WG 16/11 rev 2.

36 The European system of national and regional accounts (ESA) is a standard for the compilation of national accounts, which is based on the SNA 2008 and includes specific requirements for EU Member States or countries within the European Statistical System; in the meantime the original ESA 95 has been replaced by EAS 2010.

37 Eurostat, Manual on Government Deficit and Debt. Implementation of ESA 2010 (2019 ed, Publications Office of the European Union).

important differences persist, and whereas ESA 2010 encourages the presentation of pension obligations as a memorandum item, the definition of debt used by the European Union's Excessive Deficit Procedure includes neither accounts payable nor pension schemes.[38]

From Bretton Woods to the Fiscal Compact

The Fiscal Compact designates Title III of the Treaty on Stability, Coordination and Governance in the Economic and Monetary Union[39] (TSCG) and commits the 19 Eurozone member states plus Bulgaria, Denmark and Romania to a set of fiscal rules and principles, among them a balanced budget rule and a concomitant debt brake rule.[40] The basis for these rules are to be found in the Stability and Growth Pact and ultimately in the Treaty on the Functioning of the European Union (TFEU).[41] Specifically, the notorious 3% of GDP deficit and 60% of GDP debt limits are defined in Protocol (No 12) on the Excessive Deficit Procedure[42] annexed to the TFEU. The two limits on government debt and deficit together with three other criteria on inflation, exchange rate stability and long-term interest rates were part of the Treaty of Maastricht on the European Union[43] (i.e. 'Maastricht Criteria') and defined the conditions for entering the final stage of the Economic and Monetary Union and adopting the euro as currency.[44]

European Monetary System (EMS)

Looking back, it was the collapse of the Bretton Woods system in 1971 that precipitated events, which ultimately lead to Economic and Monetary Union (EMU).[45] In March 1971 most members of the European Economic

38 Dippelsmann et al. (n 28).

39 The Treaty came into force on 1 January 2013 after ratification by 12 member states of the euro area. Also known as Fiscal Stability Treaty, in the meantime it has been ratified by all remaining members of the EU after the exit of the UK.

40 In addition, the TSCG includes provisions to promote the coordination of economic policy and to improve the governance of the euro area in general.

41 Specifically, art 121 TFEU on multilateral surveillance, art 126 TFEU on the Excessive Deficit Procedure (EDP) and art 136 TFEU on economic policy guidelines for the euro area to strengthen coordination and surveillance of budgetary discipline (OJ 2008/C 115).

42 Protocol (No 12) on the excessive deficit procedure [2008] OJ C115/279.

43 Treaty on European Union [1992] OJ C191/1.

44 Whereas the criteria on inflation, exchange rate and interest rates have been accepted as intuitive in principle, the fiscal criteria have been a point of contention from the beginning. See Willem Buiter, Giancarlo Corsetti and Nouriel Roubini, 'Excessive deficits: sense and nonsense in the Treaty of Maastricht' (1993) 8 (16) *Economic Policy* 58, the literature cited therein as well as the records of the panel discussion thereupon (90ff).

45 Hanspeter Scheller, *European Central Bank, History, Role and Functions* (European Central Bank 2004) 17.

Community (EEC) agreed to the creation of an economic and monetary reunion and, as a first step, to maintain their currencies' exchange rates in a narrow band (± 2.25%; the so-called 'snake in the tunnel').[46] In the absence of supporting institutions, this arrangement proved unsustainable and started to break down almost immediately, with only the German Mark as well as the Benelux currencies and the Danish krone remaining within the system.[47] A new attempt was made with the creation of the European Monetary System (EMS) in 1979, which initially included the idea of an Exchange Stabilisation Fund.[48] In the end, the EMS was composed of the European Exchange Rate Mechanism (ERM) with the European Currency Unit (ECU) as synthetic reference, a looser version of the snake (with a standard band of ± 2.25% and a wide band of ± 6% for certain countries), the extension of credit facilities and the creation of the European Monetary Cooperation Fund (EMCF), a precursor of the European Central Bank.[49]

Over the next 20 years, after some regular realignments (i.e. devaluations) against the German Mark in the early years, the EMS did work superficially, with stable exchange rates and a convergence of inflation rates. However, under the surface of the EMS, economic imbalances were accumulating and the less developed countries instead of catching up were further losing competitiveness. In the end, this led to the EMS crisis of 1992–1993 with the forced exit of the British pound and a broadening of the band to 15%.

Economic and Monetary Union (EMU)

In response and as part of the creation of the European Union (EU) through the Treaty of Maastricht, the Economic and Monetary Union (EMU) with the euro as common currency was formed.[50] Participation in the EMU is subject to fulfilling the so-called Maastricht Criteria, which in addition to sound and sustainable public finances are price stability, durability of convergence and exchange rate stability.[51] It's worth noting that at the time of the Maastricht Treaty, with respect to the fiscal criteria Germany, France, the UK and Luxembourg fulfilled the conditions for entering the EMU in 1991 and only France and Luxembourg did so in 1992. However, a longer-term analysis at this point in time revealed major differences among member countries, with

46 Resolution of the Council and of the Representatives of the Governments of the Member States of 22 March 1971 on the attainment by stages of economic and monetary union in the Community (OJ C28/1).

47 Scheller (n 45) 18.

48 Resolution of the European Council on the establishment of the European Monetary System (EMS) and related matters of 5 December 1978.

49 Harold James, 'The History of European Economic and Monetary Union' in Harald Badinger and Volker Nitsch (eds), *The Routledge Handbook of the Economics of European Integration* (Routledge 2016) 30ff.

50 On the history of the EMU, see ibid 32ff.

51 See Commission 'Report from the Commission to the European Parliament and the Council' Convergence Report COM (2018) 370 final 16ff.

both Italy and Greece needing major fiscal corrections to stabilise their debt ratio. Taking into account the much more stringent Maastricht Criteria of actually reducing the debt ratio to 60%, seven countries would have to undertake major adjustments to their fiscal policies, going in particular beyond the fulfilment of the 3% of GDP deficit criterion and being assessed as unrealistic for Belgium, Ireland, Italy and Greece.[52]

EMU an optimal currency area?

The conclusion of the Treaty of Maastricht was preceded by heated debates not only between politicians but even more so among economists on the preconditions for a monetary union, on whether the European Union and its member states actually met these conditions as well as on the design of such a monetary union. A point of departure for this discussion is the theory of optimal currency areas (OCA),[53] where optimal means economically efficient in general and capable of adaptation to exogenous shocks in particular. Accordingly, OCAs are marked by mobility of labour and capital as well as price and wage flexibility. To the extent that these conditions are not fully met, a risk-sharing mechanism and/or similar business cycles are also required.[54] Taking the United States of America as the obvious the point of reference for its size and development, the EU is not an OCA, and the question therefore rather is whether the euro zone is a good enough currency area, considering its institutional set-up and compared to other currency areas.[55]

Whereas mobility of capital in the euro zone is high, labour mobility is comparatively low due to linguistic and cultural barriers in particular; equally, prices of goods are relatively flexible, but wages are famously sticky; as a result, regional imbalances and exogenous shocks would require adapted monetary policies or (substantially greater) transfers.[56] A one-size-fits-all approach of monetary policy within the euro zone will therefore necessarily produce inefficient outcomes, which is lower GDP and higher unemployment. Nevertheless, monetary union as part of the teleology of 'an ever-closer Union' has been a more or less explicit objective of politicians, politics and policy since the Treaty of Rome. The supporting economic arguments and the proposed set-up have, however, changed over time. One set of arguments refers to the net economic benefits of a common currency. In this equation the benefits from

52 Buiter et al. (n 44) 64ff; see also their critical discussion of the Maastricht budgetary guidelines at the time of conception and in view of the transition period, ibid 72ff.

53 See the seminal paper by Robert A. Mundell, 'A theory of Optimum Currency Areas' (1961) 51 *American Economic Review* 657.

54 An ex-post analysis of the OCA criteria as drivers of the 2009 crisis shows that the classical trade-related criteria, like labour mobility, have been relatively extraneous, whereas the newer institutional criteria, like transfers, were much more relevant. See Charles Wyplosz, 'The Common Currency: More complicated than it seems' in Badinger and Nitsch (n 49) 103ff.

55 Kevin H. O'Rourke and Alan M. Taylor, 'Cross of Euros' (2013) 27 (3) *Journal of Economic Perspectives* 167, 177.

56 Ibid 175.

reduced transaction costs, greater price transparency and the elimination of exchange rate uncertainties are greater than the costs in terms of reduced macroeconomic room for manoeuvre.[57] Although these arguments are valid, it remains difficult to gauge their impact in terms of economic value or growth.

More instructive with regard to the Maastricht Criteria is the analysis of Ljnunberg and Ögren (2019) on the shifting economic reasoning in favour of monetary union and on how this argumentation has affected the design of the EMU: until the end of the 1970s the argument was framed in terms of preventing and off-setting economic imbalances by combining the alignment of monetary policies with strong elements of financial and fiscal solidarity, regional policy and economic integration.[58] By the late 1980s the worries for the management of inevitable imbalances in a monetary union were no longer seen as relevant and 'the disciplinary effect of a fixed exchange rate had instead become the main concern'. This was also a reflection of the rise of a monetarist economics, which considers money as a purely nominal phenomenon: accordingly, exchange rates in the long run are determined by the purchasing power parity theorem[59] and inflation is a function of monetary policy. Assuming rational expectations, the argument was that higher-inflation countries could borrow credibility and reduce inflation by renouncing their own monetary policy and foster growth and convergence by making their economic policy rule-bound. As a result, the Maastricht design of the EMU included a common currency (the euro), an independent central bank (the ECB) and no mechanism for supporting members in financial difficulties (no bail-out clause). Imbalances were considered less likely, due to rule-based economic policy as well as structural reforms. To the extent they would nevertheless arise, the expansion of structural funds would take care of them.[60]

Stability and Growth Pact (SGP)

In the transition period following the Treaty of Maastricht, the conditions for monetary union were put into place.[61] Among them was in particular the

57 See the comprehensive overview by Paul de Grauwe, *The Economics of Monetary Union* (13th ed., Oxford University Press 2020) 3ff, in particular 75ff.

58 Jonas Ljunberg and Anders Ögren, 'Discipline or external balance? The choice of international monetary systems in Europe' (2019) 190 Lund Papers in Economic History (Lund University, Department of Economic History 2019) 14ff.

59 The purchasing power parity theorem posits that a unit of currency should buy the same amount of goods anywhere, i.e. after having been exchanged in a different currency, even if in many instances it does not hold, especially in the short run (see Michael R. Pakko and Patricia S. Pollard, 'Burgernomics: A Big Mac™ Guide to Purchasing Power Parity' (2003) 85 (6) *Federal Reserve Bank of St. Louis Review* 9ff.

60 Ljunberg/Ögren (n 58) 20ff; on the general optimism regarding monetary union, see also Heather D. Gibson, Theodore Palivos and George S. Tavlas, 'The Crisis in the Euro Area: An Analytic Overview' (2014) 39 Journal of Macroeconomics 234.

61 Institutionally, by the creation of the European Monetary Institute (EMI; 1994) and later, from it, the ECB (1998). On the history of the euro and the ECB in particular, see Scheller (n 45) 15ff.

Stability and Growth Pact (SGP) of 1997 to monitor whether the members states respected the Maastricht Criteria, to provide recommendations for their fiscal policy and to bring them back in line through the Excessive Deficit Procedure (EDP) if they didn't.[62] Two years later the final stage of the EMU was ignited with 11 countries renouncing their currencies and independent monetary policy; others have followed since then.[63] This success was, however, bought at a price, inasmuch as a lot of accounting wizardry and looking the other way was necessary to get the selected 11 member states[64] into the EMU.[65]

In its original form the SGP in the eyes of many proved to be both unreasonable and impossible to enforce. It was considered unreasonable because it required fulfilment of the Maastricht Criteria without consideration of conjunctural variations in the real economy of individual countries,[66] and it was impossible to enforce because sanctions for breach of those criteria required the acquiescence of the deficient member states (at least for the large ones such as Germany and France).[67] In order to make the SGP less restrictive and thus more enforceable, the member states agreed in 2005 to reform the SGP.[68] This 'new' SGP has been considered clear progress with respect to the flexibility criterium; its overall evaluation against the Kopits/Symansky criteria for ideal fiscal rules[69] is, however, much less positive/unambiguous, as the reform obfuscated and weakened the link between budgetary medium-term objectives and the excessive deficit procedure.[70] In particular, the uniform limit to the structural deficit was replaced by a more tailored approach

62 Resolution of the European Council of 17 June 1997 on the Stability and Growth Pact [1997] OJ C236/1, as well as Council Regulation (EC) 1466/1997 of 7 July 1997 on the strengthening of the surveillance of budgetary positions and the surveillance and coordination of economic policies [1997] OJ L209/1, and Council Regulation (EC) 1467/1997 of 7 July 1997 on speeding up and clarifying the implementation of the excessive deficit procedure [1997] OJ L209/6.

63 Original members: Austria, Belgium, Finland, France, Germany, Ireland, Italy, Luxembourg, Netherlands, Portugal, Spain (1999); later members: Greece (2001), Slovenia (2007), Cyprus and Malta (2008), Slovenia (2009), Estonia (2011), Latvia (2014), Lithuania (2015).

64 Austria, Belgium, Finland, France, Germany, Ireland, Italy, Luxembourg, Netherlands, Portugal and Spain; Denmark and the United Kingdom were formally granted an opt-out from the obligation to join the Eurozone whereas Sweden remains outside based on the informal acceptance of a popular referendum by the EU.

65 See section 'The accounting and statistical basis of the Fiscal Compact' above.

66 Rui Henrique Alves and Oscar Affonso, 'The "New" Stability and Growth Pact: More Flexible, Less Stupid?' (2007) July/August *Intereconomics* 218, 220.

67 Willem H. Buiter, 'The "Sense and Nonsense of Maastricht" Revisited: What Have We Learned about Stabilization in EMU?' (2006) 44 (4) JCMS 689ff.

68 By Council Regulation (EC) 1056/2005 of 27 June 2005 amending Regulation (EC) No 1467/97 on speeding up and clarifying the implementation of the excessive deficit procedure [2005] OJ L174/5.

69 George Kopits and Steven Symansky, 'Fiscal policy rules' (1998) Occasional Paper 162 (International Monetary Fund 1998).

70 Alves and Afonso (n 66) 223ff.

that was less constricting for countries with 'low debt and high potential growth'. Whereas this may have been justified in terms of considering the specifics of individual countries, it was also much more technical and open to interpretation.[71,72]

In addition to the increased ordinary flexibility provided by the SGP by design, it also comprises extraordinary flexibility, on the one hand for unexpected adverse economic events with major negative consequences for government finances in one or more member states – the 'unusual events clause'[73] – and on the other hand the 'general escape clause' that provides for similar flexibility in the event that the whole EU or Euro area faces a severe downturn.[74] Whereas the application of the SGP including its built-in flexibility is, at least in theory, heavily conditioned on objectively verifiable economic indicators, the flexibility under the two clauses is not. In essence, breaches of the deficit limit may be excused as long as the respective member states are able to convince the EC and ultimately the European Council of their case. This is of particular concern in the application of the unusual events clause, where experience has shown that it is sufficient for member states to pretend to do almost anything, even if the underlying adverse economic events are under their control.

The SGP 2005 was successful inasmuch as it enabled the Eurozone to stay within the SGP's deficit limits, but it also covered the building up of economic and fiscal imbalances until by the end of 2009 the global financial crisis[75] had plunged a number of Eurozone members into de facto insolvency as they were unable to finance their debt or bail out systemically relevant banks in distress

71 For example, the distinction between deviations from plans mainly within and mainly outside the control of the government is not an exact science and is subject to methodological variations. See European Commission, 'Public Finances in EMU 2005' (2005) 3 *European Economy* 101ff.

72 Buiter (n 44) 690. For an assessment of the 2005 SGP against the Kopits and Symansky criteria of ideal fiscal rules, cf. Alves and Afonso (n 66). Their analysis points towards a clear increase in flexibility together with the probable emergence of new enforcement problems.

73 For example, in the case of Portugal, the 'unusual event clause' has been used by the EC to allow for a temporary deviation from the adjustment path towards the medium-term budgetary objective on the account that the wildfires of 2017 made necessary additional expenditures in relation to preventive measures to protect the national territory against wildfires (Council Recommendation on the 2019 National Reform Programme of Portugal and delivering a Council opinion on the 2019 Stability Programme of Portugal (COM(2019) 522 final), 3).

74 Arts 5(1), 6(3), 9(1) and 10(3) of Council Regulation (EC) 1466/97 of 7 July 1997 on the strengthening of the surveillance of budgetary positions and the surveillance and coordination of economic policies [1997] OJ L209/1 ('preventive arm') and arts 3(5) and 5(2) of Council Regulation (EC) 1467/97 of 7 July 1997 on speeding up and clarifying the implementation of the excessive deficit procedure OJ L209/6 ('corrective arm').

75 On the causes, effects and policy responses to this crisis, see Fritz Beuss, 'The Crisis in Retrospect' in Badinger and Nitsch (n 49) 331ff.

without outside help.[76] It became clear that the SGP of 2005 was not able to deliver on its promises, namely sustainable economic growth and macroeconomic stability.[77] Since then the reasons for this failure and the possible remedies to the flaws of the SGP have been discussed in innumerable publications. A mainstream view of the Eurozone crisis and its causes may be summarised as follows: the Eurozone (EZ) experienced a rapid and uncontrolled unwinding of economic imbalances. At the heart of these imbalances lay the preceding build-up of public and private debt in economically weaker EZ members, which was used to finance private investment into non-productive fixed assets (housing) and government consumption (public services and transfers). When the flow of capital from economically stronger EZ countries suddenly stopped due to the global economic and financial crisis, the capability to finance these foreign debts was put into question. This insecurity set in motion a vicious circle of loss of trust into the solvency of debtor countries, stability of their financial system and sustainability of their economies. With the European Central Bank explicitly forbidden to act as lender of last resort and the utter lack of a capable institutional infrastructure in the EMU, it proved impossible to prevent the EZ crisis from unfolding.[78]

Fiscal Compact

The policy response of the EU was a set of six regulations adopted in November 2011 ('Six Pack')[79] with the objective to (a) strengthen the surveillance of budgetary positions and to improve detection of macroeconomic

76 For a chronology of the crisis, see Mark Copelovitch, Jeffry Frieden, and Stefanie Walter, 'The Political Economy of the Euro Crisis' (2016) 49(7) *Comparative Political Studies* 811, 814 ss; see also Gibson et al. (n 60) 235ff.

77 For an overview of the macroeconomic position of EU and specifically Euro member states see Witold Wiliński, 'Changes in the fiscal policy of EU states after the 2008 crisis' (2019) 55 (1) *International Journal of Management and Economics* 52ff.

78 Richard Baldwin and Francesco Giavazzi, 'Introduction' in Richard Baldwin and Francesco Giavazzi (eds), *The Eurozone Crisis, A Consensus View of the Causes and a Few Possible Solutions* (CEPR Press 2015) 18ff.

79 Regulation (EU) 1173/2011 of the European Parliament and of the Council of 16 November 2011 on the effective enforcement of budgetary surveillance in the euro area [2011] OJ L306/1; Regulation (EU) 1174/2011 of the European Parliament and of the Council of 16 November 16 2011 on enforcement measures to correct excessive macroeconomic imbalances in the euro area [2011] OJ L306/8; Regulation (EU) 1175/2011 of the European Parliament and of the Council of 16 November 2011 amending the Regulation (EC) 1466/97 on the strengthening of the surveillance of budgetary positions and the surveillance and coordination of economic policies [2011] OJ L306/12; Regulation (EU) 1176/2011 of the European Parliament and of the Council of 16 November 2011 on the prevention and correction of macroeconomic imbalances [2011] OJ L306/25; Council Regulation (EU) 1177/2011 of 8 November 2011 amending Regulation (EC) 1467/97 on speeding up and clarifying the implementation of the excessive deficit procedure [2011] OJ L306/33; and Council Directive 2011/85/EU of 8 November 2011 on requirements for budgetary frameworks of the member states [2011] OJ L306/41.

imbalances, (b) prevent the build-up of unsustainable budgetary positions and macroeconomic imbalances and (c) enforce both the preventive and corrective parts of the Stability and Growth Pact as well as effectively correct excessive macroeconomic imbalances in the euro area through a system of sanctions.[80] In addition to these legislative changes and to prevent a repetition of two years of frantic financial diplomacy, costly emergency measures and 'unconventional' short-term fixes with dubious long-term effects, in March 2012 all EU member states except the Czech Republic and the UK agreed to the Treaty on Stability, Coordination and Governance in the Economic and Monetary Union (TSCG) and its Chapter III, which has become known as the Fiscal Compact.

Substantive elements of the Fiscal Compact

The Fiscal Compact is composed of four elements, namely (a) a mandatory balanced budget rule and (b) a debt reduction rule as well as (c) an enhanced excessive deficit procedure and (d) ex ante debt issuance reporting.[81] The obligation of member states to transpose its rules into national law, preferably at constitutional level, or the design of the automatic correction mechanism are being dealt with extensively in other contributions. Therefore, in the following we are exclusively concerned with the substantive rules of the Fiscal Compact – that is, the balanced budget rule and the debt reduction rule – while taking as a given the particular reference values for budget balance and debt. The values of 3% of GDP for deficit and 60% for debt are mutually consistent but seem to be somewhat arbitrary and contingent reflections of the average public investment rate among member states.[82]

Balanced budget rule

The mandatory balanced budget rule is without doubt the cornerstone of the Fiscal Compact. It is based on the SGP 2005 but modulates the country-specific objectives according to existing debt levels by requiring faster convergence for high-debt countries. As we will see, the balanced budget rule, despite its

80 This Six Pack was complemented in May 2013 with a so-called Two Pack of additional regulations aiming at further strengthening economic and budgetary surveillance (Regulation (EU) No 472/2013 of the European Parliament and of the Council of 21 May 2013 on the strengthening of economic and budgetary surveillance of Member States in the euro area experiencing or threatened with serious difficulties with respect to their financial stability [2013] OJ L140/1, and Regulation (EU) No 473/2013 of the European Parliament and of the Council of 21 May 2013 on common provisions for monitoring and assessing draft budgetary plans and ensuring the correction of excessive deficit of the Member States in the euro area [2013] OJ L140/11).

81 For a comprehensive overview of the Fiscal Compact, see European Commission, 'Vade Mecum on the Stability & Growth Pact' (2019) Institutional Paper 101 (2019 ed. Publications Office of the European Union).

82 Buiter et al. (n 44).

simplicity at first sight, is on the one hand exceedingly complicated in its construction and application, and on the other hand has still limited regard to the conjunctural cycle. In its basic form the balanced budget rule requires the 'budgetary position of the general government to be balanced or in surplus', which 'shall deemed to be respected if the annual structural balance [...] is at its country-specific medium-term objective as defined in the revised Stability and Growth Pact with a lower limit of the structural deficit of 0.5% of the gross domestic product at market prices'.[83] In addition, the actual or planned (nominal) deficit may not exceed 3% of GDP at market prices.[84]

General government

As stated before, 'general government' refers to all levels of government (central, state and local) including social security units as well as public corporations provided they are non-market producers. Accordingly, in order to be attributed to the general government, an institution has first to be government-controlled and second must not finance its operational activity by sales of goods and services at economically significant prices (i.e. it has to be 'non-market'); the third criterion of 'autonomy in decision-making' is mainly relevant when deciding on whether to consolidate one unit into another one or to apply the two other criteria to them separately. In keeping with the underlying ESA 2010 substance-over-form principle, these criteria are to be applied not in a formal or legal but in a functional manner.[85] The delimitation of general government is trivial with respect to administrative units and significant for corporations and not-for-profit organisations because of the substantive influence their financial position can have on the budgetary position of the government. It is particularly relevant for the treatment of pension institutions, which depending on the pension scheme involved will be considered part of general government or classified, for instance, as an insurance corporation. Unfunded defined benefit schemes will generally be considered government because the beneficiaries of such entitlements represent a burden on future budgets in the same way the contraction of loans implies a future stream of outlays. Otherwise, a fully funded defined contribution scheme will be considered outside of general government because the underlying risks are ultimately born by the beneficiaries.[86]

Annual structural balance

The notion of 'annual structural balance' refers to the nominal general government balance adjusted for the output gap in the reporting year, which in

83 Art 3 paras 2 and 3 TSCG.
84 Art 126 para 2 TFEU in connection with art 1 Protocol (No 12) on the Excessive Deficit Procedure.
85 See Eurostat (n 37) 11ff.
86 See ibid 45ff.

turn is calculated by comparing the actual to potential GDP in a given year – that is, the GDP that would be achieved if all resources in the economy were used at the level of their long-term potential. This potential cannot be observed but must be estimated and, like every estimation, it thus depends heavily on the methodological choices made. Due to cyclical movements in the economy, it is unlikely that actual GDP will equal potential GDP in any given year; however, there is the assumption built into the concept of potential GDP that the deviations will net out over the duration of the conjunctural cycle. If this assumption holds true and to the extent that the government balance effectively reflects the state of the economy, the nominal government balance over the conjunctural cycle will be (close to) zero; otherwise, the budget is in structural imbalance and the corresponding deficit or surplus may be calculated for every year.

The concept of structural balance and the rationale for limiting any structural deficit is easily understood. The devil is however, as always, in the detail, or more specifically in the way the output gap (and thus the admissible structural deficit) is calculated by the EC, which has been hotly debated by economists. We shall refrain from venturing into the technicalities of this discussion,[87] but instead present the basic criticisms and its policy implications under the SGP and specifically the Fiscal Compact. To start with the latter, its critics assert that the methodological choices underlying the EC's model lead to pro-cyclical limitations on national fiscal policy, in particular for those countries most in need of fiscal stimulus.

With its 'potential output model' (PO-model) as the engine for assessing fiscal policy and determining necessary corrective actions, the EU takes a middle stand between the statistical approach chosen by Switzerland[88] and

87 The more publicised criticism of the 'Campaign against Nonsense Output Gaps (CANOO)' of Robin Brooks and Greg Basile – www.iif.com/Publications/ID/3361/Global-Macro-Views-Campaign-against-Nonsense-Output-Gaps-CANOO, accessed 26 May 2020 – is based on Philipp Heimberger and Jakob Kapeller, 'The performativity of potential output: pro-cyclicality and path dependency in coordinating European fiscal policies' (2017) 24 (5) *Review of International Political Economy* 904 and Jakob Huber, Philipp Heimberger and Jakob Kapeller, 'From paradigms to policies: Economic models in the EU's fiscal regulation framework' (2020) 18 (2) *Socio-Economic Review* 337, which are also the foundation of the following presentation; a semi-official riposte was published by a group of EC officials in their personal capacity (Marco Buti, Nicolas Carnot, Atanas Hristov, Kieran Mc Morrow, Werner Roeger and Valerie Vandermeulen, 'Potential output and EU fiscal surveillance' (2019), https://voxeu.org/article/potential-output-and-eu-fiscal-surveillance, accessed 13 April 2020).

88 The expenditure ceiling is determined by multiplying the estimated revenues with a conjunctural factor, which relates the trend GNP to the estimated GNP; the trend GDP is extrapolated from the yearly GNP during past 24 years by applying a modified Hodrick–Prescott filter. See C. Colombier, F. Bodmer, P.A. Bruchez, A. Geier, T. Haniotis, M. Himmel and U. Plavec, 'Eine Neubewertung der Schuldenbremse' (2004) Working Paper 2/2004 (revised version, Eidg. Finanzverwaltung 2004).

the possible use of a more complicated macroeconomic model with explicit microeconomic foundations.[89] In line with neo-classical economic theory,[90] the PO-model uses a standard approach based on a Cobb–Douglas production function[91] and models the economy exclusively from the supply side. This has the advantage for policy makers of being relatively straightforward and giving unambiguous indications on the drivers of growth. On the other hand, the model in conjunction with the norms of the SGP creates pro-cyclical feedback loops, which both in boom and crisis move the economy closer towards the world represented by the PO-model. These feedback loops in turn are driven by the methodology used to determine the structural (i.e. natural) component of unemployment, which will fall in boom times and increase in crisis time. However, the smaller the cyclical component of a given unemployment rate, the smaller also the fiscal space for expansionary deficit financed public expenditure.

As a result, the PO-model contributes to positive feedback effects arising from the model's political application and triggers *a reinforcement of cyclical trends and developmental trajectories.* The reinforcement of cyclical trends arises from the model's impact on short-run fiscal policymaking as the PO-model promotes a pro-cyclical fiscal policy stance, which is most visible in the countries hit hardest by the crisis. A second instance of positive feedback is geared more towards long-term structural developments: the pro-cyclical policies and constraints imposed by the PO-model in conjunction with the Stability and Growth Pact make it much more difficult for crisis-ridden countries to change their current path of development as they lack policy space.[92]

To re-formulate this in terms of the balanced budget rule: the larger the past cyclical imbalances, the greater will be the share of the deficit identified as structural and potentially not permissible.

89 For example, a Dynamic Stochastic General Equilibrium (DSEG) model, like the one used by the EC for macroeconomic policy analysis and research (named QUEST) or those used by the IMF for the analysis of fiscal policy issues.

90 The neo-classical synthesis is the dominant theory and practice in today's (macro-) economics. Its building blocks are the price mechanism based on supply and demand, as well as three behavioural assumptions regarding economic actors, i.e. individuals and firms: rational preferences, maximisation of utility/profit and full information. See Olivier Jean Blanchard, 'Neoclassical Synthesis' in Steven N. Durlauf and Lawrence E. Blume (eds), *The New Palgrave Dictionary of Economics* (Palgrave Macmillan 2008), https://doi.org/10.1057/978-1-349-95121-5_1218-2. The fact that these assumptions do not always and/or fully hold in reality, as has been rightly noted by many critics of neoclassical economics, does in itself not imply that this approach is useless and any competing theory correct.

91 The Cobb–Douglas production function expresses total production as a function of labour and capital at a given level of technology. See Gregory Mankiw, *Macroeconomics* (9th ed. Macmillan 2019) 58.

92 Heimberger and Kappeler (n 87) 9.

Country-specific medium-term objective

The 'country-specific medium-term objective (MTO)' is part of the Stability and Growth Pact as revised in 2005. Whereas before the SGP merely required participating member states to maintain a budgetary position 'close to balance or in surplus', the post-2005 rules are more specific to the individual member states and their underlying economic situation. These country-specific MTO are calculated on the basis of respective structural balances and thus subject to the same criticisms as set out in the preceding chapter. Basically, the MTO is calculated based on the country-specific structural balance by adjusting for fiscal risk and by subtracting the effect of so-called one-off or other temporary measures. Deficit-generating measures are considered one-off when they do not change the underlying fiscal position of a country but merely bring existing commitments into the accounting area. The standard example for such a one-off-measure is to fully fund a public defined benefit pension scheme before spinning it off in a private defined contribution pension fund.[93]

According to Council Regulation (EC) 1466/97, it is up to the individual member state to calculate and adjust their (structural) MTO. In this however, they are constrained by a limit value of at least -1% of GDP, which is another way of stating that the adjusted structural deficit shall be equal to or smaller than 1% of GDP.[94] For those countries that are also signatories to the TSCG, the maximum deficit must not exceed 0.5% of GDP, except when their debt ratio is significantly below 60% of GDP and the risks to their long-term sustainability are skewed to the up-side. Within these margins, the MTO has to be set to a level that:

1. Provides for a sufficient safety margin against the cyclical fluctuations of the (nominal) government deficit breaching the 3% of GDP threshold;
2. Ensures sustainability or rapid progress towards sustainability by maintaining at or reducing debt ratios to prudent levels considering the likely impact of ageing populations;
3. Allows for fiscal space to respond to investment needs and unexpected expenses.

The economic rationale for a sufficient safety margin is to ensure the effectiveness of the automatic stabilisers, which have a countercyclical effect on the economy without discretionary changes to public policies. For example, in a downturn public expenditure for unemployment benefits will rise, while social contributions receipts will be lower, thus creating a fiscal stimulus equal to the combined differences from the structural reference point. Whether a country's

93 See section 'The accounting and statistical basis of the Fiscal Compact' above.

94 Technically, this rule also applies to ERM II countries, which have to keep their currencies' exchange rate in a narrow band towards the euro; currently Denmark is the only EMR II country (19 April 2020).

MTO is compliant with this condition depends on past output volatility as well as budgetary sensitivity to output fluctuations[95]: the greater the former and the larger the later, the smaller will be the structural deficit compatible with the objective of letting the automatic stabilisers work without breaching the 3% deficit threshold.[96] In practice this implies that small countries with an undiversified, export-based economy or countries with a highly developed social security system will have to set a more cautious MTO than their structural balance would otherwise dictate. Again, how those different factors affect the budgetary objectives and results is exceedingly complicated, despite, or perhaps because of, the scientifically rigorous methodology applied by the EC, rendering the whole exercise into a black box.

Whereas the first criterion for setting the MTO seeks to hedge against the impact of medium-term cyclical fluctuations, the second aims at factoring in one important and unquestionable long-term development: ageing populations. Demographics affect fiscal outcomes in many ways, most basically by the ratio of the active to the overall population. Its direct effects pertain on the expenditure side to the increased need for medical care of the old and the budgetary costs of pensions systems financed on a pay-as-you-go basis. On the revenue side, the reduction of labour as a main production factor and driver of GDP growth translates into lower direct tax revenues and social contributions. However, there are also indirect effects; for example, the dissaving by pensioners to finance ongoing consumption decreases the available capital in the economy and thus may depress output and concomitantly tax returns. As the overall effects of an ageing population on fiscal balance are difficult to gauge, the SGP takes only the expenditure side into account by calculating the MTO as the sum of the fiscal balance, which would stabilise public debt at 60%, to which a third of the present value of the projected increase in age-related expenditures is added; for countries with a debt above 60% of GDP the resulting MTO is topped up by a further 0.2%, respectively by 1.4% of GDP once the debt to GDP ratio attains 110%. Again, the statistical analysis and mathematical calculations used to determine the MTO, which will maintain at or reduce debt ratios to prudent levels considering the likely impact of ageing populations, is exceptionally complicated and the last underlying report of the Ageing Working Group (AWG) with the related economic and budgetary projections for the 28 EU member states (plus Norway as well as the European Union and the euro area as a whole) for the years 2013–2060 comes in at 424 pages.[97]

95 Output volatility is a measure for the amplitude of the conjunctural cycle, whereas budgetary sensitivity to it refers to whether the change in the fiscal position of the government in reaction to a 1% change in output is smaller, equal to or greater than 1%.

96 Stéphanie Riso and Christine Frayne, 'Vade mecum on the Stability and Growth Pact' (2013) *European Economy. Occasional Papers* 151 (European Commission Publications 2013) 20.

97 https://ec.europa.eu/economy_finance/publications/european_economy/2015/pdf/ee3_en.pdf, accessed on 3 May 2020.

The lower bound of the effective MTO is then set to be at least equal to both values calculated to ensure the proper working of automatic stabilisers and sustainability respectively, as well as to the lower bound of −1% of GDP in the case of euro area and ERM II member states. There is also a higher bound, inasmuch as the MTO should allow for fiscal space to respond to investment needs and unexpected expenses.[98]

Debt reduction rule

Although debt levels have always been part of the EU fiscal rules, in practice they were of little effect as soon as a country had become member of the EMU. With the 2005 reform of the SGP greater relevance was again attributed to this indicator of the sustainability of the budget position in the medium and long run.[99]

Conclusions

This chapter has been mostly descriptive, by selectively presenting some of the economic facts, theories and methods underpinning the Fiscal Compact and its application in practice. However, by doing so it also offers a vantage point from which two conclusions may be drawn in view of the Fiscal Compact's assessment from a legal perspective.

First, the rules of the Fiscal Compact and their application have developed over time in response to specific historical and political situations. Although they have been based on economic theory and analysis, the choices made in this respect have not been inevitable even if, unsurprisingly, they have leaned towards mainstream economics. Thus, a critique of the Fiscal Compact should start or at least include an argued critique of the underlying economics. The notion that the application of the Fiscal Compact leads to outcomes that are considered undesirable from a political, social or legal perspective is not such a critique. Equally, to the extent that the European legislator has enshrined certain economic theories in the Fiscal Compact, they have become part of the law; to discount them for being merely economic theories exposes a lack of understanding of the relationship between legal norms and economic theories.

Second, the construction over time of the Fiscal Compact has resulted in a monument to the lack of trust and common purpose within the EU. This is apparent from the excessive complexity and technicality of the EU's fiscal regulations, which is only thinly veiled by the brevity and simplicity of the respective rules at Treaty level. Methodological choices are made by committee, in which expert officials will veto any change at odds with their government's position. To ensure acceptance, the European Commission must

98 To our knowledge, there has been no case of a country's MTO being rejected for being excessively ambitious and lacking fiscal space.

99 Alves and Affonso (n 66) 223.

demonstrate rigorous equality of treatment, which results in a formalistic application of agreed procedures and norms; it also prevents making allowances for specific situations and economic facts not (sufficiently) captured by those regulations. It is thus obvious that the failure or at least limited success of the Fiscal Compact in terms of its own objectives can be traced back to economic theory pressed into service to correct problems outside of its scope.

Postscript: This chapter was largely written before the COVID-19 pandemic, whose impact in terms of the Fiscal Compact is still incalculable but will without doubt be enormous. Expected deficits will be higher, sometimes substantially higher than 3% for all member countries, and any progress achieved in the past few years to get within the 60% debt limit will be reversed for the years ahead.[100] With the activation of the general escape clause of the SGP, any remaining limits on deficit spending have been suspended and for all practical purposes abolished.[101]

Bibliography

Allen R, Hemming R, Potter BH (eds), *The International Handbook of Public Financial Management* (Palgrave McMillian 2013)

Badinger H, Volker N (eds), *The Routledge Handbook of the Economics of European Integration* (Routledge 2016)

Baldwin R, Giavazzi F (eds), *The Eurozone Crisis, A Consensus View of the Causes and a Few Possible Solutions* (CEPR Press 2015)

Bergmann A, Fuchs S, Schuler C, 'A theoretical basis for public sector accrual accounting research: Current state and perspectives' (2019) 39 (8) *Public Money & Management* 560

Bracci E, Humphrey C, Moll J, Steccolini I, 'Public sector accounting, accountability and austerity: More than balancing the books?' (2015) 28 (6) *Accounting, Auditing & Accountability Journal* 879

Buiter W, Corsetti G, Roubini N, 'Excessive deficits: sense and nonsense in the Treaty of Maastricht' (1993) 8 (16) *Economic Policy* 58

Christofzik DI, 'Does accrual accounting alter fiscal policy decisions? Evidence from Germany' (2019) 60 *European Journal of Political Economy* 101

Durlauf SN, Blume LE (eds), *The New Palgrave Dictionary of Economics* (Palgrave Macmillan 2008)

Eichengreen B, *Globalizing Capital: A History of the International Monetary System* (2nd ed. Princeton University Press 2008)

Filios VP, 'The Cameralistic Method of Accounting: A Historical Note' (1983) 10 *Journal of Business & Accounting* 443

Friedman M, Schwartz AJ, *A Monetary History of the United States 1867–1960* (Princeton University Press 1963)

100 'Policies for the Recovery' (2020) *Fiscal Monitor* (IMF 2020) 77ff.

101 Proposed by the Commission in Communication from the Commission to the Council on the activation of the general escape clause of the Stability and Growth Pact EC (COM(2020) 123 final), and agreed to by the Council (Press Release 173/20).

de Grauwe P, *The Economics of Monetary Union* (13th ed. Oxford University Press 2020)

Heimberger P, Kapeller J, 'The performativity of potential output: pro-cyclicality and path dependency in coordinating European fiscal policies' (2017) 24 (5) *Review of International Political Economy* 904

Heinig K, *Das Budget, Zweiter Band: Das Budgetwesen* (J.C.B. Mohr (Paul Siebeck) 1951)

Hilgendorf E, Joerden JC (eds), *Handbuch Rechtsphilosophie* (J.B. Metzler Publisher 2017)

Huber J, Heimberger P, Kapeller J, 'From paradigms to policies: Economic models in the EU's fiscal regulation framework' (2020) 18 (2) *Socio-Economic Review* 337

Keynes JM, *General Theory of Employment, Interest, and Money* (Macmillan and Co 1936)

Kopits G, Symansky S, 'Fiscal policy rules' (1998) Occasional Paper 162 (International Monetary Fund 1998)

Lindlar L, *Das mißverstandene Wirtschaftswunder* (Mohr Siebeck Publisher 1997)

Ljunberg J, Ögren A, 'Discipline or external balance? The choice of international monetary systems in Europe' (2019) 190 *Lund Papers in Economic History* (Lund University, Department of Economic History 2019) 14

Lledó V, Yoon S, Fang X, Mbaye S, KimY, 'Fiscal Rules at a Glance' (Background Note, IMF 2017)

Mankiw G, *Macroeconomics* (9th ed. Macmillan 2019)

Mundell RA, 'A theory of Optimum Currency Areas' (1961) 51 *American Economic Review* 657

O'Rourke KH, Taylor AM, 'Cross of Euros' (2013) 27 (3) *Journal of Economic Perspectives* 167

Pakko M, Pollard PS, 'Burgernomics: A Big Mac™ Guide to Purchasing Power Parity' (2003) 85 (6) *Federal Reserve Bank of St. Louis Review* 9

Premchand A, *Government Budgeting and Expenditures Controls: Theory and Practice* (IMF 1983)

Puechberg JM, *Einleitung zu einem verbeßerten Cameral-Rechnungs-Fuße, auf die Verwaltung einer Herrschaft angewandt* (Trattnern Wien 1762)

Scheller H, European Central Bank, History, Role and Functions (European Central Bank 2004) 17

Stauffer T, *Instrumente des Haushaltsausgleichs, Ökonomische Analyse und Rechtliche Umsetzung* (Helbing & Lichtenhahn 2001)

Part II

Balanced budget as constitutional rule

3 The German debt brake

Ralf P. Schenke

The so-called debt brake has been at the center of German public debt law since 2009. It has replaced the 'golden rule',[1] which had tied the maximum permissible level of debt in the federal budget to the investments entered in it, as stipulated in the previous version of Article 115 (1) (sentence 2, half-sentence 1 of the German Constitution), from 1 January 2011 onward.[2] According to the previous provision, a higher level of debt was also permissible in order to prevent a disruption to the overall economic equilibrium (previous version of Article 115 (1), sentence 2, half-sentence 2 of the German Constitution).

Before the debt brake came into force, Germany had reached a level of public debt often perceived as threatening.[3] In 2007, the total debt of the federal government, the states, and the municipalities amounted to about €1.5 trillion,[4] which corresponded to 64% of gross domestic product (GDP). The associated interest charges amounted to €38.7 billion – that is, 12% of all tax revenue was tied up in this way.[5] Far more serious was the continuous disregard for the Maastricht Criteria since 1999.[6] The national debt then reached its peak a year after the debt brake came into force, when a debt level of 82.4% of GDP was reached.

1 For more details, see A.III.
2 Henning Tappe, 'Die neue "Schuldenbremse" im Grundgesetz' (2009) 21 *Die öffentliche Verwaltung* 881–890 (882).
3 Deutsche Bundesbank, *Zur Reform des deutschen Haushaltsrechts. Monatsbericht Oktober 2007*, www.bundesbank.de/resource/blob/692644/c96fc26ed9d40067b8d0ba6ff4d6340a/mL/2007-10-haushaltsrechtsreform-data.pdf, accessed 20 January 2021.
4 Statistisches Bundesamt, *Schulden des Öffentlichen Gesamthaushalts 2018*, 14.
5 Institut der deutschen Wirtschaft, *Ein Tilgungsplan für Deutschlands Staatsschulden (A repayment plan for Germany's national debt)* 7.
6 Thomas Fuster, 'Fünf Antworten zum Maastricht-Vertrag', *Neue Züricher Zeitung*, 9 December 2016, www.nzz.ch/wirtschaft/europaeische-waehrungsunion-fuenf-antworten-zum-maastricht-vertrag-ld.133407, accessed 20 January 2021; Deutscher Bundestag – Wissenschaftliche Dienste, (WD-4-141/09) *Entwicklung der Staatsverschuldung von 1970 bis 2013*, 11, www.bundestag.de/resource/blob/409658/11b75e4dbbe9eff808baca0f1ea4ffc5/WD-4-141-09-pdf-data.pdf, accessed 20 January 2021.

DOI: 10.4324/9781315181882-6

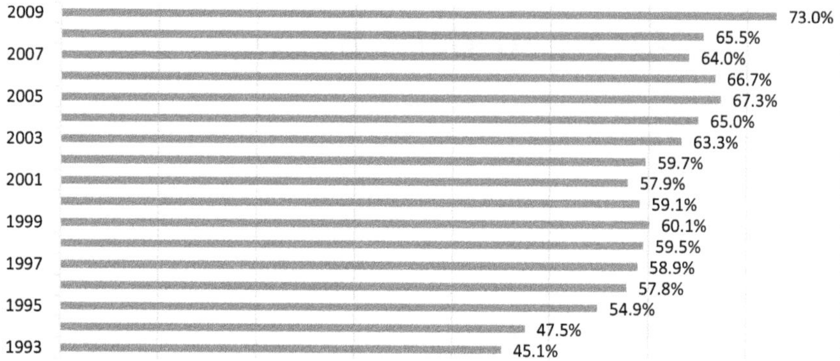

Figure 3.1 Debt of the general public budget in relation to gross domestic product (GDP) in Germany according to the Maastricht Treaty from 1993 to 2009
Source: The diagram is based on data from the German Federal Bank[7]

With the creation of the debt brake, the legislator wanted to meet the requirements of the European Stability and Growth Pact (Article 3 (2) (a) of the Council Regulation (EC) No. 1466/97) as amended in 2005, to present budgetary positions that are close to balance in the medium term. Compared with the previous 'golden rule', the debt brake sets much tighter limits on government debt. The *Länder* are in principle prohibited from incurring new public debt (Article 109, (3) sentence 1 of the Constitution). The federal government, on the other hand, is entitled to a margin of debt amounting to 0.35% of GDP (Article 115 (2) sentence 2 of the Constitution). However, these strict debt limits only apply under normal conditions. In the case of economic crises, natural disasters and unusual emergency situations, the debt brake allows for a higher debt level (Article 109 (3) sentence 2 of the Constitution). At federal level, the constitutional requirements are specified in Article 115 (2) of the Constitution as well as in the Law implementing Article 115 of the Constitution,[8] which came into force at the same time as the debt brake. Implementation at the *Länder* level, which is much more complex, will be addressed in detail later.

In addition to the material limitations of public debt, the new public debt law provides further institutional and procedural safeguards. This includes a Stability Council, which is responsible, among other things, for the continuous monitoring of the budgetary management of the Federation and the *Länder* (Article 109(a) of the Constitution). A statutory borrowing authorization that

7 Deutsche Bundesbank, *Zeitreihe* BBK01.BJ9959, www.bundesbank.de/dynamic/action/de/statistiken/zeitreihen-datenbanken/zeitreihen-datenbank/723452/723452?tsId=BBK01.BJ9959&listId=www_v27_web001_02a, accessed 20 January 2021.

8 Art. 115, Law accompanying the second reform of federalism (Federalism Reform II), Act of 10 August 2009.

disregards the requirements of the debt brake leads to the unconstitutionality of the budget.[9]

To subject budgetary policy to the strict requirements of Article 109 (3) and Article 115 (2) of the Constitution immediately after the debt brake came into force would have resulted in considerable budgetary distortions. In order to avoid this, while amending the Constitution, the legislator allowed the Federal Government and the *Länder* to deviate from the debt limits during a transitional phase. At federal level, the targets were to be met until the fiscal year 2016, while at the *Länder* level they did not need to be met until 2020. In addition, the financially weak *Länder* were granted consolidation assistance from federal funds, which was conditioned by a reduction in debt.

The debt levels of public budgets have decreased significantly by the end of 2019. The public debt ratio has slightly decreased to c. 61% of GDP, with the federal government now spending only €17.6 billion[10] annually on interest charges. This positive development is certainly a consequence of the historically low interest rate. Conversely, the previous sharp increase in public debt was largely due to one-off effects, such as the high cost of German unification.[11] However, the debt brake is also likely to have played its part in reducing the national debt.

Despite, or perhaps because of, these successes in budget consolidation, Germany is currently engaged in an intense debate on the need for a fundamental reform of the debt brake. One point of criticism is that the current debt brake leaves little room for emergency investments in the future, especially in the area of infrastructure. On the other hand, the proponents of the current regulation point out that a restrictive public debt policy is in the interest of future generations, who will no longer be held responsible for excessive spending policies. The discussion is thus decisively shaped by the topos of generational justice.[12] In Germany, however, there is also a specific federalist aspect. Within the Federal Republic, there are considerable economic disparities between the individual *Länder*. Resulting differences in tax power are largely offset by the federal financial equalization among the *Länder*. The recipient *Länder* are dependent on transfer payments from the donor *Länder*, which can provoke political resistance in the donor

9 Hanno Kube, 'Art. 115' in Theodor Maunz and Günter Dürig (eds) *Grundgesetz. Kommentar* (Beck-Online 2019), Art. 115 recital 229.

10 Bundestag, *Finanzplan des Bundes 2019 bis 2023* (*Federal financial plan 2019 to 2023*), document 19/11801, 38, https://dip21.bundestag.de/dip21/btd/19/118/1911801.pdf, accessed 20 January 2021.

11 Deutscher Bundestag – Wissenschaftliche Dienste, WD-4-141/09 (n 6) 6.

12 Council of Economic Experts, *Staatsverschuldung wirksam begrenzen: Expertise im Auftrag des Bundesministers für Wirtschaft und Technologie* (2007), 31; Hilde Neidhardt, *Staatsverschuldung und Verfassung: Geltungsanspruch, Kontrolle und Reform staatlicher Verschuldungsgrenzen* - Recht der nachhaltigen Entwicklung (vol. 5, Mohr Siebeck 2010) 7f; Christian Seiler, 'Konsolidierung der Staatsfinanzen mithilfe der neuen Schuldenregel' (2009) 64 (14) *Juristenzeitung* 721–728; Tappe (n 2) 882.

Länder. From an institutional economics point of view,[13] such a structure entails a double risk: in financially weak *Länder*, financial burdens resulting from excessive public debt threaten to be transferred to future generations (deficit bias).[14] Beyond that, an unbalanced financial equalization can also create an incentive to shift excessive government spending in the recipient *Länder* to the financially strong *Länder* at the expense of taxpayers.[15]

In this chapter, the focus will not be on such politico-economic considerations, but on the legal analysis of the debt brake. To this end, the history of the development of German public debt law, the emergence of the debt brake, its systematics and further budget development under the debt brake will be discussed first. The chapter concludes with an overview of the current reform debate and considerations on the general problem of constitutional public debt rules. The last part deals with the dramatic changes in the budget situation that resulted from the COVID-19 crisis.

A. Historical development of German public debt law

The decision taken to limit public debt with the help of the debt brake can only be understood against the background of the history of German public debt law.[16] Important milestones were the sovereign debt rules of the ancient Constitutions, the Constitution of the German Empire, the Weimar Reich Constitution and the various versions of the sovereign debt rule of the Constitution. However, this chapter will not use individual constitutional systems as a starting point but will take a different path. Rather, it is based on the central ideas of regulation that lie behind the various constitutional orders and which have often outlasted different epochs of German constitutional history.

I. Reservations of corporative/parliamentary approval

Ever since the early Constitutions, state borrowing has been tied to the approval of the estates or the people's representatives.[17] Historically, this

13 For an introduction to the institutional economics perspective of budget decisions, see Charles B. Blankart, *Öffentliche Finanzen in der Demokratie: Eine Einführung in die Finanzwissenschaft* (Franz Vahlen 2017) 92ff.

14 Ibid 269; fundamentally, James M. Buchanan and Richard E. Wagner, *Democracy in Deficit: The political legacy of Lord Keynes* (Academic Press 1977); for further evidence, see n 20.

15 Hans Pitlik and Günther Schmid, 'Zur politischen Ökonomie der föderalen Finanzbeziehungen in Deutschland' (2000) 49 (1) *Zeitschrift für Wirtschaftspolitik* 100–124.

16 Overview in Heiko Burret, 'Die deutsche Schuldenbremse als Allheilmittel – eine Analyse im historischen Kontext' (2013) 13 (2) *Journal für Generationengerechtigkeit* 48–65; Klaus Stern, *Das Staatsrecht der Bundesrepublik Deutschland – Klaus Stern, Das Staatsrecht der Bundesrepublik Deutschland, Bd. II: Staatsorgane, Staatsfunktionen, Finanz- und Haushaltsverfassung, Notstandsverfassung* (vol. II, Beck 1980), 1264ff.

17 Stern (n 16) 1272.

restriction is a response to the extensive public debt policy during absolutism and the criticism of contemporary finance, which almost entirely rejected debt.[18] The restriction of consent served to secure the corporative right to tax approval. This connection is obvious. Today's public debt is tomorrow's tax burden.[19] It is therefore necessary to prevent government expenditure from being financed by loans without parliamentary or corporative approval, the repayment of which then requires the levying of higher taxes.

In its purest form, this approach was implemented in the Constitution of the Grand Duchy of Baden of 1818, which explicitly stated: 'No loan can be validated without the consent of the estates.' There it was done without any material requirements for government debt policy. The only protection against excessive government debt was the consent of the estates. From today's point of view, such a purely procedural safeguard may seem insufficient. In order to increase their chances of being elected, politicians are only too willing to finance particular interests by increasing borrowing (so-called deficit bias).[20] One lasting merit of this regulatory model, however, is that it has democratized public debt policy. In subsequent periods of German constitutional history this parliamentary reservation has therefore been maintained with good reason.[21]

II. Justification of public debt by a special need

The constitutions of the North German Confederation (Art. 73) and the German Reich of 1871 (Art. 73) linked the admissibility of public debt to an 'extraordinary need'.[22] The Bavarian Constitution of 1818 already contained a similar formulation allowing for an 'increase in the national debt' in the event of an 'urgent and extraordinary' need of the state, which had to serve 'for the true benefit of the state' (Title VII, § 12 of the Constitutional Charter for the Kingdom of Bavaria). Such material limitations were an expression of increasing skepticism toward an excessive debt policy. Their regulatory power, however, was extremely limited. They were not able to stop a steadily growing public debt.[23] This is probably due to the lack of clarity and justiciability of the

18 Adam Smith, *An Inquiry into the Nature and Causes of the Wealth of Nations* (London: 1776), 711.

19 Tappe (n 2) 881.

20 Buchanan and Wagner (n 14); William D. Nordhaus, 'The Political Business Cycle' (1975) 42 (2) *The Review of Economic Studies* 169; Deutsche Bundesbank, *Zur Reform des deutschen Haushaltsrechts. Monatsbericht Oktober 2007* (n 3) 49. On the empirical validity of this thesis, see Clemens Fuest, Klaus Gründler, and Niklas Potrafke, 'Für eine nachhaltige Finanzpolitik mit der Schuldenbremse' (2019) 99 (5) *Wirtschaftsdienst* 307–313 (311f).

21 On the ratio of the parliamentary reservation, see e.g. Kube (n 9) recital 2.

22 'In cases of extraordinary need, the taking up of a bond and the assumption of a guarantee can be effected at the expense of the Federation by way of federal legislation.'

23 Burret (n 16).

rules. Ultimately, the requirement of an extraordinary necessity was limited to a mere burden of proof, without being able to substantially limit state borrowing.

III. The model of future-favorable public debt

Beginning with the Prussian Constitution, many of Germany's public debt rules can be traced back to the model of future-favorable public debt.[24] This also includes the Weimar Reich Constitution (Article 87), which only allowed state debt for 'promotional purposes'. The same approach was adopted in the original version of the German Constitution of 1949.[25] Thus, public debt is no longer rejected outright but made dependent on the purpose of the debt. If debt is used to finance a revenue-generating object, it is justified intergenerationally and corresponds to the pay-as-you-use principle. A debt barrier that takes this into account is often referred to as the 'golden rule of fiscal policy'.[26]

However, the object-related approach of debt rules has been criticized many times. In practice, this provision was also largely deprived of its effect by an extensive interpretation of the concept of 'advertising purposes'.[27] This criticism led to the new version of Article 115 of the Constitution, which came into force in 1967. At the time, Article 115 stipulated:

> (1) The raising of loans and the assumption of sureties, guarantees, or other warranties which may lead to expenditure in future financial years shall require an authorization by federal statute which is specific or specifiable in terms of amount. The income from loans may not exceed the sum of the investment expenditure entered in the budget …

With the principle of linking national debt to investments entered in the budget, the Constitution consistently followed the model of future-favorable public debt. To the extent that the public debt is matched by corresponding investments, there is at least a legitimate expectation that the return generated by investments can cover future debt service. This expectation was not met due to shortcomings in previous versions of Article 115. These issues will be discussed in more detail later.

24 Kube (n 9) recital 34.
25 Art. 115 of the Constitution of 1949 stipulates: 'Funds may only be obtained by means of credit in the event of extraordinary needs and, as a rule, only for expenditure for promotional purposes and only on the basis of a federal law. Credits and guarantees at the expense of the Federation, the effect of which extends beyond one accounting year, may only be granted on the basis of a federal law. The law must specify the amount of the loan or the scope of the obligation for which the Federation assumes liability.'
26 Tappe (n 2).
27 Stern (n 16) 1274.

IV. Instrumentalization of public debt for economic management

One facet of the basic idea of future-favorable public debt is its instrumentalization for purposes of economic management. The financial foundation of this concept goes back to John Maynard Keynes,[28] whose economic policy credo stands in sharp contrast to the classics. In Keynesian economic theory, aggregate demand plays a decisive role. Thus, in phases of economic downturn, both private consumption and demand for capital goods collapse, which can lead to a disastrous downward spiral if the effects are mutually reinforcing. As a remedy, Keynes proposes a concept which in Germany is referred to as *Globalsteuerung* (overall control), a term coined by former Finance Minister Karl Schiller.[29] According to this logic, the state has the responsibility to respond to a decline in private demand by increasing state demand, which could be financed by resorting to a policy of deficit spending. The interest and redemption burdens associated with a growing national debt are to be paid from additional tax revenues, which will increase once the crisis ends.

The concept of counter-cyclical global governance has been implemented in Germany through the above-mentioned revision of Article 115 Constitution. The new version of Article 115 (1) sentences 2 and 3, reads:

> The income from loans may not exceed the sum of the expenditure on investments entered in the budget; exceptions may be made only to avoid disturbance of the overall economic balance. Further details shall be regulated by federal statute.

According to Article 115 (1) sentence 2 half-sentence 2 of the Constitution, new debt exceeding the sum of investments was permissible in order to avert a disturbance of the overall economic balance. Article 115 of the Constitution was developed in the Act on the Promotion of Stability and Growth of the Economy (StabG) of 8 June 1967, which stipulates that the Federal Government and the *Länder* must take account of the requirements of macroeconomic equilibrium in adopting economic and financial policy measures. Such measures are to be taken in such a way which, within the framework of a market economy, contribute simultaneously to price stability, a high level of employment, and an external economic equilibrium

28 John Maynard Keynes, *The General Theory of Employment, Interest and Money* (Harcourt, Brace and Company 1936).

29 Karl Schiller, 'Zukunftsaufgaben der Industriegesellschaft' in Andrew Shonfield (ed.) *Geplanter Kapitalismus. Wirtschaftspolitik in Westeuropa und USA* (Kiepenheuer & Witsch 1968) XV; summing up the policy of global governance Deutscher Bundestag – Wissenschaftliche Dienste, (WD-3-130/09) *Konjunkturprogramme in der Geschichte der Bundesrepublik Deutschland: Einordnung und Bewertung der Globalsteuerung von 1967 bis 1982 (Economic stimulus programs in the history of the Federal Republic of Germany: Classification and evaluation of global control from 1967 to 1982*), www.bundestag.de/resource/blob/409658/11b75e4dbbe9eff808baca0f1ea4ffc5/WD-4-141-09-pdf-data.pdf, accessed 20 January 2021.

with steady and appropriate economic growth (§ 1 sentence 2 StabG). One expression of the concept of counter-cyclical global governance was the text of § 6 (2) StabG which stipulates that the federal government may determine that additional expenditure, including expenditure financed by loans, will be made in the event of a slowdown in general economic activity. If, however, the increase in demand exceeds the economic capacity, funds should be earmarked for additional debt repayments to the German Bundesbank or for allocations to an economic equalization reserve (§ 5 (2) StabG).

B. The path to legislating the debt brake

I. Deficiencies of the traditional public debt law

If the effectiveness of the public debt law in force before 2011 is measured by the level of public debt, the result is sobering. In fact, public debt rose steadily after 1970.[30] In the 38 years since Article 115 of the Constitution entered into force, net borrowing exceeded investment expenditure 16 times in total, up until 2007.[31] Because of the significantly higher interest burden at that time, the growing debt was also a noticeable burden on public budgets, which had to allocate considerable resources to debt service. In 1970, the national debt amounted to €64 billion[32] which, in relation to the GDP, corresponded to a debt ratio of 18%, while interest expenditure accounted for 4.5% of the federal budget.[33] In 1985, the debt level was €390 billion[34] and the debt ratio increased to 40%.[35] There were further significant increases as a result of German unification, which led to an increase of the debt ratio to 67% in 2005.[36]

30 At a glance, Deutscher Bundestag – Wissenschaftliche Dienste (WD-4-141/09) (n 6).
31 Karl Heinz Hausner and Silvia Simon, 'Die neue Schuldenregel in Deutschland und die Schuldenbremse der Schweiz: Wege zu nachhaltigen öffentlichen Finanzen?' (2009) 89 (4) *Wirtschaftsdienst* 265–271 (269).
32 Evaluation by the *Statistisches Bundesamt*, https://de.statista.com/statistik/daten/studie/154798/umfrage/deutsche-staatsverschuldung-seit-2003, accessed 20 January 2021; Deutscher Bundestag – Wissenschaftliche Dienste (n 6) 4f.
33 Ewald Nowotny, *Der Öffentliche Sektor – Formen und Entwicklung der öffentlichen Schuld* (Springer 1991), 289.
34 Evaluation by the *Statistisches Bundesamt* (n 32).
35 Jutta Hinrichs, *Die Verschuldung des Bundes 1962–2001*, Working paper 77 (2002) 10, www.kas.de/c/document_library/get_file?uuid=9fa bd90d-704c-3f37-8651-9682803df721&groupId=252038, accessed 20 January 2021; *Statista 2019*, Schulden des Öffentlichen Gesamthaushalts in Relation zum Bruttoinlandsprodukt (BIP) in Deutschland in den Jahren von 1950 bis 2018, https://de.statista.com/statistik/daten/studie/4783/umfrage/anteil-der-schulden-des-oeffentlichen-gesamthaushalts-am-bip, accessed 20 January 2021.
36 Deutsche Bundesbank, *Zeitreihe* BBK01.BJ9959 (n 7); Statistisches Bundesamt, *Schulden des öffentlichen Gesamthaushalts von 1950 bis 2018 (General government debt from 1950 to 2018)* (n 4), *Deutscher Bundestag – Wissenschaftliche Dienste* (n 6) 11.

The reasons for this increase were not only one-time effects, notably the disturbance of the German unification, but also structural deficiency in public debt law.[37] The credit rule in Article 115 (1) sentence 2 of the Constitution offered insufficient safeguards to realize its two basic concepts: the concept of counter-cyclical global governance and the concept of future-favorable public debt.

In phases of economic slowdown, the concept of counter-cyclical global governance deliberately accepts an increase in public debt. If it is not possible to fall back on reserves, new debt provides the fiscal authorities with the necessary leeway to compensate for declining private consumption and investment expenditure. This instrument has been widely used since 1967. However, the requirement to reduce existing government debt during phases of economic recovery was obviously not met. Instead, the debt ratio was kept constant at best. From the point of view of institutional economics, this is hardly surprising because debt reduction, which is bought at the price of expenditure cuts, forces unpopular cuts in government funding and support measures, and is therefore omitted (deficit bias).[38] If such cuts are not made because of the lack of binding rules on debt repayment,[39] debt is likely to increase when growth rates are weak.

The concept of a future-favorable public debt was ineffectively implemented by the public debt rules applicable until 2010. The key concept of investments was already one of the predetermined breaking points which, under normal conditions, limited the amount of net borrowing. The concept was criticized for being too broad and, thus, not guaranteeing that the 'investments' would be matched by financial returns. Furthermore, depreciation of tangible assets was not taken into account.[40] This should actually have restricted the scope of debt, because investments in the amount of depreciation alone can only secure the existing stock of productive assets. In addition, the government was able to freely dispose of revenues generated from the sale of assets. In particular, it was possible to spend such revenues purely consumptively.[41]

A further weakness of the traditional public debt rule was the exception clause of the earlier version of Article 115 (1) of the Constitution. In cases of macroeconomic imbalance, it allowed the standard limit of permissible net debt to be exceeded. This clause was used extensively with the approval of the Federal Constitutional Court. At first glance, the case law made high demands on this exception: it should only take effect 'if the macroeconomic equilibrium is significantly and continuously

37 Very instructive is the overview in Christian Magin, 'Die Wirkungslosigkeit der neuen Schuldenbremse' (2010) 90 (4) *Wirtschaftsdienst* 262–268 (263f).

38 See the evidence in note 20.

39 Tappe (n 2) 883.

40 Ibid 884.

41 Deutscher Bundestag/Bundesrat, *Die gemeinsame Kommission von Bundestag und Bundesrat zur Modernisierung der Bund-Länder-Finanzbeziehungen (The joint commission of the Bundestag and Bundesrat for the modernization of federal-state financial relations)* (2010), 7, www.bundesrat.de/SharedDocs/downloads/DE/sonstiges/Abschlussbericht-Foeko-II.pdf?__blob=publicationFile&v=1, accessed 20 January 2021.

disturbed or if there is an immediate threat of such a disturbance'.[42] In addition, increased borrowing had to be 'suitable in terms of volume, used to avert the disruption, and related to the prevention of disruption'.[43] The fact that these requirements remained practically ineffective was due to the scope for assessment and evaluation that the Federal Constitutional Court granted the budget-making legislator. This scope for assessment corresponded to a burden of proof on the legislator. In practice, the control exercised by the Federal Constitutional Court was limited to scrutinizing whether the assessment and evaluation presented by the legislator in the legislative procedure was justifiable. In a ruling made in 2007, the Federal Constitutional Court expressly rejected tightening this standard.[44] Even if the constitutional requirements had proven sufficiently controllable in the past, it was up to the 'government and parliament ... to make future-effective, risky decisions on the basis of expert advice concerning the assessment and forecast of macroeconomic development and the choice of adequate means of control, and to take political responsibility for their consequences'.

However, as became apparent, particularly in the course of coping with German unification, the public debt law in force at the time had another open boundary. According to Article 115 (2) of the Constitution, exceptions to the debt limitation pursuant to Article 115 (1) of the Constitution could be permitted by federal statute for special federal assets. This option had been used in a variety of ways. These included the special assets of the Federal Railway,[45] the Federal Post Office,[46] the equalization fund[47] and the European Recovery Program (ERP) special assets.[48] The fiscal significance of Article 115 (2) of the Constitution changed during the process of German unification. As a result, the German Unification Fund,[49] the Inheritance Redemption Fund[50] and the Compensation Fund[51] were established. At the end of the 1990s, the share of debt attributable to special assets accounted for more than half of the outstanding reported federal debt.[52]

In summary, the existing rules for limiting public debt showed considerable deficiencies. The lack of efficient sanction mechanisms was also detrimental to their effectiveness. As the German Council of Economic Experts rightly stated in its 2007 special report, even obvious violations could not be punished or could only be punished after a very long delay.[53]

42 BVerfGE 119, 96 (140).
43 Ibid.
44 BVerfGE 119, 96 (146).
45 § 31 Bundesbahngesetz; § 17 des Gesetzes zur Zusammenführung und Neugliederung der Bundeseisenbahnen.
46 § 22 Postverwaltungsgesetz; § 40 Postverfassungsgesetz.
47 § 7 (1) Lastenausgleichsgesetz (previous version).
48 § 10 (1) ERP-Verwaltungsgesetz (previous version).
49 § 5 (2) des Gesetzes über die Errichtung eines Fonds 'Deutsche Einheit'.
50 § 5 des Gesetzes über die Errichtung eines Erblastentilgungsfonds.
51 § 9 des Entschädigungsgesetzes.
52 Kube (n 9) recital 52.
53 Council of Economic Experts (n 12) 3.

II. The reform discussion

In view of ever-increasing debt, calls for a fundamental reform of the public debt law became more persistent. The reform debate received impetus from various directions. Apart from the Federalism Reform the European context should be mentioned first and foremost. In the Maastricht Treaty, Germany had committed to cap new debt at 3% of GDP and to limit its public debt ratio. According to Article 126 (1) TFEU in conjunction with the Protocol on Deficit Reduction, this may not exceed 60% of GDP. However, Germany had already reached this ratio in 2002 and was confronted with an excessive deficit procedure.

Additional pressure to act was added by the warning signs of the financial crisis, which became increasingly apparent from 2007.[54] The Federal Constitutional Court is also likely to have had some influence on the reform discussion. It had already called for reform of the public debt law in 1989. This was formulated even more clearly in a follow-up ruling made in 2007, according to which 'there is currently hardly any doubt about the need to revise the existing constitutional regulations'.[55] Such reminders are extremely unusual from the point of view of the separation of powers. The role of the Federal Constitutional Court is usually limited to securing the existing constitutional order. The reform debate was further boosted by similar appeals from the Council of Economic Experts, an influential body in Germany that assesses overall economic development.[56] In its annual report for 2005/2006 – which was quoted in the Federal Constitutional Court ruling – the Council had already pointed out the undesirable development of rising public debt.[57] In addition, a special report commissioned by the Federal Ministry of Economics and Technology in March 2007 also received wide attention. In this report, the Council of Economic Experts proposed that a new version of the debt rules in the Constitution be modeled after the Swiss debt brake.[58]

In Switzerland the new debt rules have been enshrined in Article 126 of the Swiss Federal Constitution since the end of 2001[59] and further developed in

54 See Deutscher Bundestag/Bundesrat (n 41) 51.

55 BVerfGE 119, 96 (141).

56 The Council of Economic Experts consists of five experts with specialist economic knowledge and experience who are appointed by the federal government and whose task is to advise the government by giving a periodic assessment of the overall economic development of the Federal Republic of Germany. The tasks and composition of the Council of Economic Experts are set out in the Act on the Establishment of a Council of Economic Experts (Act of 14 August 1962, last amended by Art. 249 Act of 31 August 2015).

57 Council of Economic Experts, *Die Chance nutzen – Reformen mutig voranbringen: Jahresgutachten 2005/06 (Seize the opportunity – courageously advance reforms: Annual Report 2005/06)* (Heenemann 2005).

58 Council of Economic Experts (n 12) 134.

59 Adopted in the referendum of the 2 December 2001 and in force since 2 December 2001 (Federal Decree of 22 June 2001, Federal Council Decree of 4 February 2002).

the Financial Budget Act. The core of the Swiss debt brake is to keep income and expenditure in balance in the long term. To this end, the maximum total expenditure to be authorized in the statement of estimates is limited by the estimated revenue, taking into account the economic situation. Public debt is thus controlled by using the expenditure approach.[60] In order to avoid pro-cyclical effects, estimated revenues are smoothed by means of a cyclical factor. In phases of recession, higher spending is possible, whereas in phases of economic boom, expenditure must lag behind revenue. However, the maximum amount resulting from Article 126 (2) of the Swiss Federal Constitution may be increased appropriately in case of extraordinary payment needs. This leaves room for maneuver, for example, to counteract natural disasters or severe recessions. A compensation account serves to ensure budgetary discipline. If the total expenditure shown in the national accounts exceeds the maximum amount according to paragraphs 2 and 3, the additional expenditure shall be compensated in subsequent years.

The model proposed by the German Council of Economic Experts was based on three modules, or building blocks, which were used to develop the existing public debt law.[61] In principle, the limitation of net borrowing by the amount of investment, and thus the concept of future-favorable public debt, should be maintained (Module 1). In contrast to the previous law, however, reductions in state assets, especially through write-offs or privatization, would have been taken into account. In Module 2, the Council of Economic Experts placed considerable faith in the Swiss debt brake, in which expenditure was to be linked to the cyclically adjusted development of regular revenues in the sense of a revenue-oriented expenditure policy. The technical implementation envisaged multiplying the revenues by an economic factor, which was the quotient of the production potential and GDP. Deviations were to be recorded in a virtual adjustment account. This update was the basis for Module 3, which was intended to supplement the revenue-oriented expenditure policy with sanction mechanisms.

III. Federalism Reform II

Since the basic public debt rules are enshrined in the Constitution, they cannot be changed by a simple law. Changing the Constitution is possible only under the requirements set out in detail in Article 79 of the Constitution. Particularly important in this context is Article 79 (3) Constitution, which stipulates that revising the Constitution requires the consent of two-thirds of the members of the *Bundestag* and two-thirds of the votes of the *Bundesrat.* The requirement of a qualified majority in the *Bundestag* and *Bundesrat* means that constitutional amendments are politically enforceable only if they are supported by a broad consensus that includes government and opposition. The search for the necessary compromises usually begins well before the actual legislative procedure is initiated.

60 Hausner and Simon (n 31) 267.
61 Council of Economic Experts (n 12) 3ff.

1. *Background and structure of the Federalism Reform II*

A good example of the agreements reached during the preparation of constitutional revision is the Federalism Reform II,[62] which introduced the debt brake. Thus, in December 2006, the *Bundestag* and the *Bundesrat* decided to establish a joint parliamentary commission, also known as Federalism Commission II, meant to draw up proposals for modernizing the financial relations between the Federation and the *Länder* in order to adapt them to the new economic conditions, especially in terms of growth and employment policy. The aim was to increase the self-reliance of municipalities and to ensure that they have adequate financial resources for their tasks. A more detailed description of the Commission's tasks was included in an open collection of topics listed in an annex. These issues included, under the heading of budgetary economics, the 'development of substantive criteria for admissible debt (introduction of debt limits and "debt brakes")'.

The constitutional background of this development was the long and growing conflict between financially strong and financially weak *Länder*. In the course of the financial equalization system set up under Article 107 of the Constitution, the financially strong *Länder* (so-called donor *Länder*) had and still have to make substantial transfer payments to the financially weak *Länder* (so-called recipient *Länder*). However, the donor *Länder* were only prepared to do this if the recipient *Länder* committed themselves to restrictive budgetary discipline in return.[63] To streamline the process, working groups were set up within the Commission, of which Working Group 1 was responsible for the further elaboration of the new public debt rule. It was supported by the Federal Ministry of Finance, which bundled the results of the consultation by elaborating those rules and including them in its own proposals.[64]

2. *The discussion process*

In the course of the Commission's consultation process, various concepts of a fundamental reorganization of the limits of public debt were discussed. An important preliminary decision was the question of whether the *Länder* should have the powers to determine their debt policy in the future. The price for the gain in autonomy would have been a limitation of the guarantee to help the *Länder* in case of financial crisis. Proponents of this model expected it to significantly strengthen the country's budgetary discipline. The *Länder* would then

62 The Federalism Reform II is closely related to the Federalism Reform I. This last one was adopted in 2005 and was intended, among other things, to contribute to separating financing responsibilities between the federal and federate (*Länder*) levels and to strengthen the legislative powers of the *Länder*. It was incorporated into the amendment of the Constitution that came into force in November 2006 (Act of 28 August 2006).

63 Deutscher Bundestag/Bundesrat (n 41) 98, 103.

64 See in particular Deutscher Bundestag/Bundesrat (n 41) Arbeitsgruppe 1. AG 1-07.

have been fully liable for their debts and would have been sanctioned in the form of poor conditions for borrowing on the capital market. There was no majority for such a radical break with the previous model of the federal state, which was based on solidarity. However, the continuation of the federal assistance was conditioned by the willingness of the recipient states to submit to federal debt rules.

A proposal to overcome the weaknesses of Article 115 of the Constitution outlined above by redefining the concept of investment as proposed by the Council of Economic Experts was also rejected. In this respect, the Commission could not agree on whether and to what extent expenditures related to education should be taken into account as investment. Moreover, any credit granted in order to finance investments bore the risk of softening the debt limitation.[65] In this regard, the Commission followed the example of the Swiss debt brake,[66] albeit tacitly. However, the Commission diverged from this by agreeing on a limited, new structural debt. The proposal to introduce a strict, absolute ban on new borrowing was therefore not accepted.

A clear majority in the Commission countered this with the view that financing state loans was useful in certain situations and could even be beneficial from an economic point of view.[67] For the necessary quantification, the Commission followed the close-to-balance approach of the European Stability and Growth Pact (SGP). The Commission still considered this standard to be met where new structural debt amounted to a maximum of 0.5% of GDP.[68] According to the Federal Ministry of Finance, this value was to be divided between the Federal Government and the *Länder* in such a way that the Federation was granted a structural debt of 0.35% and the *Länder* a structural debt of 0.15%. The fact that the *Länder* were deprived of this debt margin in the further course of the discussions is the result of a compromise with those members in the Commission who had rejected structural debt altogether. The fact that the Swiss regulation served as a model is also demonstrated by two other elements of the final draft of the legislative proposal which stipulate exceptions to the principle of material budgetary equalization. Thus, in order to avoid a procyclical effect of the debt brake, the scope for borrowing increases in times of downturn. The same applies in emergency situations. However, such extensions must then be accompanied by a binding repayment provision.

65 Deutscher Bundestag/Bundesrat (n 41) 78f.

66 A detailed comparison of the German and the Swiss debt brakes can be found at Hausner and Simon (n 31) 269.

67 Deutscher Bundestag/Bundesrat (n 41) 73.

68 Ibid 82. The value of 0.5% was also adopted by the Federal Government; see Bundesministerium der Finanzen, 'Deutsches Stabilitätsprogramm. Aktualisierung Dezember 2008' (German stability program. Update December 2008), 17, www.bundesfinanzministerium.de/Content/DE/Standardartikel/Themen/Oeffentliche_Finanzen/Deutsches_Stabilitaetsprogramm/deutsche-stabilitaetsprogramme-anlage05a.pdf?__blob=publicationFile&v=3, accessed 20 January 2021.

A consensus was also reached that both the Federal Government and the *Länder* had to be granted an appropriate transition period to adjust to the new, more restrictive debt rules. The suggestion by the Council of Economic Experts to secure the new debt rules institutionally and procedurally was only partially implemented. The Commission agreed on the establishment of a Stability Council, which is responsible for monitoring compliance with the debt rules. On the other hand, the proposed sanctions failed to pass due to resistance from the *Länder*. In the course of the legislative procedure, the proposals drawn up by the Commission for the reorganization of the public debt rules were incorporated, virtually unchanged, into the revision of the Constitution which came into force on 1 August 2009.[69]

C. Systematic description[70]

By adopting the debt brake, the legislator amending the Constitution has only partially broken new ground. The principle of substantive budgetary equilibrium – that is, the ban on borrowing in principle – is new. In partly deviating from this principle, on the other hand, the debt brake adopts traditional lines of earlier regulations and supplements them with procedural and institutional safeguards.

It is difficult to gain an overview of the debt brake because of the nature of the German legal system. Common principles applicable to the Federation and the *Länder* can be found in Article 109 (3) of the Constitution, while at the federal level these principles are already concretized in Article 115 (3) of the Constitution. Concretization at *Länder* level, however, is left to federate law. The substantive requirements for the *Länder* level are completed by the procedural safeguards of Article 109a of the Constitution. In order to facilitate a smooth transition to the new budget rules, transitional arrangements have been created in Article 143d of the Constitution.

I. The principle of material budgetary equilibrium

The key rule, and the actual innovation of the debt brake, is Article 109 (3) sentence 1 of the Constitution, which standardizes the principle that applies to both federal and federate budgets, namely that the budget is to be balanced without income from loans (so-called material budget equilibrium). The previously widely used, but also often criticized, option of setting up special funds with their own credit authorization (Article 115 (2) of the previous version of the Constitution) has been dropped for the federal level.

The obligation to balance the budget without loans applies only to the Federal Government and the *Länder*. Municipalities and social security funds are

69 Act of 29 July 2009. An English version of the German Constitution can be found at www.gesetze-im-internet.de/englisch_gg, accessed 20 January 2021.

70 The following explanations are based in part on Ralph Schenke, 'Art. 109' in Helge Sodan (ed.) *Grundgesetz* (Beck 2018), Art. 109.

not included as their indebtedness is regulated solely by the general rule of Article 109 (2) of the Constitution.[71] Thus, the Federal Government and the *Länder* jointly fulfill the obligations of the Federal Republic of Germany under European Union acts based on Article 126 TFEU to maintain budgetary discipline and, within this framework, take account of the requirements of macroeconomic equilibrium.

The use of the term credit is not fully congruent with that of Article 115 (1) of the Constitution.[72] In the case of Article 109 (3) sentence 1 of the Constitution, the net principle applies, which means that loans used for repayment or debt rescheduling are not taken into account.[73] Also not included are cash back-up loans, which are intended to guarantee sufficient liquidity in the short term.[74] Alternative forms of financing are subject to a legal reservation under Article 115 (1) of the Constitution ('other guarantees'). However, as will be discussed later in this chapter, they are in principle not covered by Article 109 (3) sentence 1 of the Constitution.[75]

The debt brake applies not only to the preparation but also to the implementation of the budget. From the perspective of legal theory, the Federal Constitutional Court assigns constitutional rank to Article 109 (3) sentence 1 of the Constitution, yet it states that this must be carefully balanced with other constitutional values and guarantees in accordance with the principle of practical concordance.[76] This wording could give the impression that Article 109 (3) sentence 1 of the Constitution is not to be classified as a rule, but merely as a principle in the sense of Dworkin's[77] theory of principles. In this case, the principle of material budgetary equilibrium could be weighed against other constitutional principles, such as the welfare state principle (Article 20 (1) of the Constitution) or the state goal of environmental protection (Article 20a of the Constitution). However, such an understanding would largely deprive the debt brake of its effect. Moreover, it is also contrary to the German legal system, which explicitly provides exceptions to the principle of material budgetary equilibrium. These would be superfluous if the debt brake could also be qualified by other constitutional principles. In addition, there would be a danger of failing to meet the requirements of the European Stability and Growth Pact and thus failing to achieve a key objective of the debt brake.

71 Hans D. Jarass, 'Art. 109' in Hans D. Jarass and Bodo Pieroth (eds) *Grundgesetz für die Bundesrepublik Deutschland. Kommentar* (Beck 2018), Art. 109 recital 12.

72 Schenke (n 70) recital 2.

73 Henning Tappe and Rainer Wernsmann, *Öffentliches Finanzrecht* (2nd edn, C.F. Müller 2019), recital 441; Henning Tappe, 'Wie passt die Schuldenbremse zur staatlichen Doppik?' (2010) 90 (4) *Wirtschaftsdienst* 269–271.

74 Ibid recital 441. But cf. Christian Mayer, 'Greift die neue Schuldenbremse?' (2011) 136 (2) *Archiv des öffentlichen Rechts* 266–322, 306ff.

75 Herrmann Pünder, 'Art. 115' in Karl Heinrich Friauf and Wolfram Höfling (eds) *Berliner Kommentar zum Grundgesetz* (Erich Schmidt Verlag 2019), Art. 115 recital 83; Tappe and Wernsmann (n 73) recitals 443ff; see also BVerfGE 129, 124 (182).

76 BVerfGE 140, 240 recital 108ff.

77 Ronald Dworkin, *Taking rights seriously: New impression with a reply to critics* (Duckworth 2005), 22ff.

It is therefore correct to assert that the debt brake is not open to any balancing.[78] Other constitutional requirements, such as the principle of an appropriate salary for civil servants (Article 33 (5) of the Constitution), may have to be rescinded if they could only be implemented at the cost of disregarding the debt brake.

II. Deviations

The full significance of the principle of material budgetary equilibrium of Article 109 (3) sentence 1 Constitution only becomes apparent when viewed in conjunction with other provisions which specify the basic rule in more detail and permit exceptions. A distinction is made in some cases between the federal and *Länder* levels.

1. Limited structural debt at federal level

In accordance with Article 109 (1) sentence 4 of the Constitution, at federal level, the principle of a balanced budget is still fulfilled if the income from loans does not exceed 0.35% of the nominal GDP under normal economic circumstances. This gives the federal government the option of limited structural borrowing. The reference value GDP is the sum of all goods produced and services rendered in the Federal Republic of Germany which are manufactured in Germany within one year and are not considered preliminary work.[79] In the explanatory materials, the legislator amending the Constitution expressed the expectation that the limited structural debt would provide an impetus for steady economic growth and sustainable development. However, this expectation is not legally enforceable, as borrowing is deliberately decoupled from the previous concept of investment, which was considered unsuitable. Thus, the revision of the Constitution grants the budget-making legislator a margin of confidence, while at the same time interpreting debt not as an undesirable development per se, but rather as a legitimate and sensible instrument of state financing. However, this concession does not go far enough for the critics of debt brakes.

2. Transitional provisions

Timewise, the transition from the old system of public debt law in Article 143d of the Constitution was cushioned by a system of graduated interim regulations. As a result, the debt brake only took full effect at federal level in the financial year 2016. At *Länder* level, the transitional period was extended until 31 December 2019. However, both federal and federate governments had already restructured their budgets from 2011 onwards, in such a way that they were able to comply with the debt brake when the transition periods expired.

78 See also Deutsche Bundesbank, *Die Schuldenbremse in Deutschland – Wesentliche Inhalte und deren Umsetzung (The debt brake in Germany – essential content and its implementation)* (2011), 17, https/2011-10-schuldenbremse-data.pdf, accessed 20 January 2021.

79 Jarass (n 71) recital 8.

3. *Counter-cyclical economic policy option*

Article 109 (3) sentence 2, 3 of the Constitution allows for a deviation from the principle of material budgetary equilibrium in order to pursue an anti-cyclical economic policy by means of increased borrowing. The exercise of this power is subject to further federal legislation. According to Article 109 (3) sentence 4 of the Constitution, details at the level of the *Länder* are left to their constitutional autonomy.

The basic idea behind the counter-cyclical economic policy made possible by Article 109 (3) sentence 2 half-sentence 1 of the Constitution is to stimulate economic activity during the downturn phase by increasing government spending financed by borrowing. During the upswing phase, national debt is to be reduced by increasing tax revenues and by decreasing government spending.[80]

According to the economic cycle clause, the debt brake ties in with the previous version of Article 109 (2) of the Constitution. This committed the budget-making legislator to the concept of counter-cyclical global governance. What is new here is that the debt brake contains provisions for a consistent implementation of the concept of counter-cyclical global governance even in upswing phases. A rule allowing additional cyclical deficits must be combined with a commitment to include cyclical surpluses in the upswing. In the medium to long term, increased borrowing in the downturn will thus be offset by surpluses in the upswing. In this way, the legislator amending the Constitution follows the example of the Swiss debt brake to a certain extent while, at the same time, mitigating the criticism of the previous regulation, which did not include any precautions to repay debt taken in downturns in phases of economic recovery.

4. *Emergency situations*

In addition to the cyclical clause, Article 109 (3) sentence 2 half-sentence 2 of the Constitution provides a further derogation for natural disasters or other exceptional emergency situations in order to guarantee the state's capacity to deal with the crisis. The concept of natural disaster corresponds to that of Article 35 (2) sentence 2, (3) of the Constitution. Natural disasters are severely damaging events which are demonstrably not caused by humans but by natural forces.[81] The historical genesis shows that the restrictive requirements for emergency situations in the sense of the regulations also apply to natural disasters – that is, the natural disaster must be exceptional, beyond the control of the state and must create a significant impairment on the budget. Examples of exceptional emergency situations are particularly serious accidents, but also events of 'positive historical significance' which, like German reunification, trigger considerable financial requirements. The explanatory materials also mention, as a further possible example of application, a

80 Bernd Scholl, 'Die Neuregelung der Verschuldungsregeln von Bund und Ländern in den Art.109 und 115 GG' (2010) 4 *Die öffentliche Verwaltung* 160, 164f.

81 Walter Georg Leisner, 'Art.35' in Helge Sodan (ed.) *Grundgesetz* (Beck, 2018), Art. 35 recital 5.

sudden impairment of economic processes to an extreme extent due to an exogenous shock, explicitly referring to the financial crisis that began in 2007.[82]

In order to ensure compensation for an increased need for credit, Article 109 (3) sentence 3 of the Constitution obliges the budget-making legislator to provide an increased net borrowing with a binding repayment schedule which regulates the repayment of borrowings above the standard limits.

III. Concretization of the debt brake at the federal level

At federal level, Article 109 (3) of the Constitution, which applies to both the federate and federal levels, is given concrete form by Article 115 (2) of the Constitution. First, it repeats the principle of material budgetary equilibrium. Then, the federal government is unconditionally granted a structural debt of 0.35% of GDP. Paragraph 2 sentence 3 of Article 115 ties in with the option opened up in Article 109 (3) sentence 2 half-sentence 1 of the Constitution to pursue a counter-cyclical economic policy and obliges the budget-making legislator to take economic developments into account when determining permissible borrowing.[83] The same principles are applied when deciding whether there is a deviation from normal circumstances and what is the significance of the requirement for symmetrical consideration of the budget in upswings and downturns.[84] The legislator enjoys limited discretion with regard to which of these principles can be reviewed and which is limited by a burden of justification in the legislative procedure.[85]

Article 115 (2) sentence 4 half-sentence 1 of the Constitution ensures that debt limitation cannot be undermined in the implementation of the budget. Thus, deviations of the actual borrowing from the value permitted under Article 115 (2) sentences 1–3 of the Constitution must be recorded in a control account. Deviations may be due in particular to the fact that the economic situation has developed differently from the way the budget was prepared. Therefore, in order to determine the actual structural borrowing, the cyclical margin of debt has to be recalculated on the basis of the actual development of GDP in the previous financial year and subtracted from total borrowing. If debts exceed the threshold of 1.5% of the nominal GDP, they must be reduced in accordance with the economic cycle. The possibility of reducing the control account even below the threshold remains unaffected.[86]

Article 115 (2) sentence 5 of the Constitution obliges the federal legislature to specify in more detail in an implementing law the constitutional requirements resulting from paragraph 2. The non-exhaustive list of issues to be regulated includes the adjustment of income and expenditure for financial transactions,[87] the

82 BT-Drs. 16/12410, 11, http://dipbt.bundestag.de/dip21/btd/16/124/1612410.pdf, accessed 20 January 2021.
83 Ibid 12.
84 Schenke (n 70) Art. 109 recital 13.
85 Jarass (n 71) recital 11 with reference to BVerfGE 79, 311 (344ff); 119, 96 (140).
86 Jarass (n 71) recital 12.
87 § 3 G 115. See BVerfGE 119, 96 (144). But cf. Henning Tappe, 'Haushaltsrechtliche Umsetzung der Artikel 109 und Artikel 115 GG n.F. in Bund und

procedure for calculating the upper limit of annual net borrowing, taking into account economic developments on the basis of a cyclical adjustment procedure, the credit limit in exceptional situations and the control and compensation of deviations of actual borrowing from the standard limit. The guidelines contained in Article 115 of the Constitution are binding on the budget-making legislator.[88]

Further exceptions to the principle of substantive budgetary equilibrium are permitted by Article 115 (2) sentence 6 of the Constitution in the listed exogenous emergency situations. The parliamentary decision necessary for the use of this exception in individual cases must be made with the majority of the members of the *Bundestag* (Article 121 of the Constitution) and can take the form of a legislative act. However, a separate parliamentary act is also conceivable, usually in connection with the adoption of the budget law, which allows borrowing beyond the regulatory limits.

IV. Institutional safeguards

In its decisions on the fiscal equalization scheme between the *Länder*, which were issued under the previous law, the Federal Constitutional Court had already pointed out the lack of procedural and substantive rules on how to deal with current and potential cases of financial recovery.[89] Article 109a of the Constitution attempts to address this weakness by establishing a new constitutional body called the Stability Council.[90]

The scope of the Stability Council is to establish a system of continuous control of the federal and *Länder* budgets.[91] The composition and tasks of the Stability Council are regulated by a federal law requiring the consent of the *Bundesrat*. The Stability Council Act (StabiRatG), which came into force in 2009,[92] is of indirect relevance for the interpretation of Article 109a of the Constitution since the legislator already had the draft in mind when amending the Constitution.[93]

The Stability Council is a joint body of the Federal Government and the *Länder* that fulfills a new joint task under financial constitutional law. The wording 'joint body' sets a guideline for its composition and suggests equal representation.[94] Apart

Ländern' in Christian Kastrop, Kastrop-Meister-Scheufelen-Sudhof, and Gisela Meister Scheufelen (eds) *Die neuen Schuldenregeln im Grundgesetz. Zur Fortentwicklung der bundesstaatlichen Finanzbeziehungen* (BWV Berliner Wiss.-Verlag 2010), 432–462, 436ff; Clemens Hetschko and Marius Thye, 'Die Bereinigung um finanzielle Transaktionen – Achillesferse der deutschen Schuldenbremse' (2012) 12 *Deutsches Verwaltungsblatt* 743–746.

88 Ekkehart Reimer, 'Art. 115' in Volker Epping, Christian Hillgruber, and Peter Axer (eds) *Grundgesetz. Kommentar* (C.H. Beck 2020), Art. 115 recital 49.

89 BVerfGE 86, 148 (266); 116, 327 (393).

90 Schenke (n 70) Art. 104a recital 4.

91 From the monographic literature, see Marius Thye, *Der Stabilitätsrat*, Dissertation, (vol. 15, Mohr Siebeck 2014).

92 Act of 10 August 2009, last amended by Act of 14 August 2017.

93 Ekkehart Reimer (n 88) Art. 109a recital 4.2.

94 Reimer (n 88) recital 14.

from that, Article 109a of the Constitution leaves the composition of the Stability Council to the discretion of the legislator. It is conceivable to establish ex officio memberships, elected memberships or to appoint changing representatives.[95] The Stability Council itself is not subject to instructions. However, the representatives of the federal government and of the *Länder* who belong to it – the Federal Minister of Finance, the Finance Ministers of the *Länder* and the Federal Minister for Economic Affairs and Energy – may be subject to binding instructions within the framework provided by the Constitution or by the constitutional law of the *Länder.* [96]

According to Article 109a (1) No. 2 of the Constitution, what is a budgetary emergency and under what conditions such an emergency is likely to occur is to be determined, in principle, by federal law. Furthermore, the criteria recognized by the Federal Constitutional Court in the context of Article 107 (3) of the Constitution can be used as indicators of a budgetary emergency.[97] It is possible to delegate the substantive requirements to the Stability Council itself if this is stipulated in the federal law passed in accordance with Article 109a (1) of the Constitution.[98] The Stability Council has adopted four key indicators: the structural balance, the debt financing ratio, the debt ratio and the interest tax ratio. The control mandate of the Stability Council includes the federal, *Länder* and municipal budgets,[99] social security[100] and other institutions for which a guarantor for liability (still) exists.[101]

5. *Avoiding budgetary emergencies (Paragraph 1)*

The system to be implemented in order to avoid budgetary emergencies should comprise four elements. The first stage is the permanent monitoring of federal and *Länder* (including municipal) budgets based on financial ratios determined by the Stability Council. The aim of this monitoring is to identify the risk of a budgetary emergency at a sufficiently early stage to allow for a successful response. If the risk of a budgetary emergency becomes apparent at the first stage, a comprehensive analysis of the budgetary situation of the public authority concerned must be carried out and, eventually, a rehabilitation program must be agreed with the Stability Council. The implementation of the rehabilitation program is also monitored by the Stability Council. In the event of violations, the Council cannot impose sanctions,[102] so the

95 Ibid recital 16.
96 Ibid recitals 19, 21.
97 Ibid recital 75; see also BVerfGE 86, 148 (258); Schenke (n 70) Art. 107 recital 13.
98 For a critical opinion, see Reimer (n 88) recital 75.
99 Ibid recital 73.
100 Gregor Kirchhof, 'Art. 109a' in Hermann von Mangoldt, Friedrich Klein, and Christian Starck (eds) *Grundgesetz. Kommentar* (C.H. Beck 2018) recital 11. For a different opinion, see Jarass (n 71) Art. 109a recital 3; for an obligation to observe, see Kube (n 9) Art. 109a recital 43.
101 Helmut Siekmann, 'Art. 109a' in Michael Sachs (ed.) *Grundgesetz. Kommentar* (C. H. Beck, 2018), recital 10.
102 Rolf Schmidt, 'Die neue Schuldenregel und die weiteren Finanzthemen der zweiten Föderalismusrefom', (2009) *Deutsches Verwaltungsblatt,* 1274–1288 (1284).

implementation of the rehabilitation program is to be determined through a political process alone.

6. *Monitoring of government borrowing (Paragraph 2)*

Article 109a (2) of the Constitution was inserted by the Federalism Reform III. It assigns monitoring tasks directly to the Stability Council, which must 'orient itself' toward the requirements and procedures of TFEU on budgetary discipline. From this it cannot be inferred that the audit mandate necessarily extends to the limits of state borrowing under European Union law.[103] It is true that, according to the explanatory documents, the responsibilities of the Stability Council are also expanded in view of Germany's obligation to comply with the requirements of the preventive arm of the European Stability and Growth Pact and the Treaty on Stability, Coordination and Governance in Economic and Monetary Union. However, the fact that Article 109a (2) of the Constitution is intended to serve EU legal requirements does not necessarily mean that there is a double audit mandate. This is contradicted not only by the wording 'orients itself', but also by the history of its origins, because the *Bundesrat* had expressly pointed out the differences between national and European debt rules, so that compliance with the national debt rule was not suited to ensure compliance with EU requirements.[104]

Article 109a (2) of the Constitution also represents a mere allocation of tasks[105] from which no sanctioning powers can be derived. The Stability Council is to be entrusted with the supervision of the reduction of structural financing deficits of the *Länder* that may use consolidation assistance.[106]

7. *Publicity (Paragraph 3)*

The obligation to publish the Stability Council's resolutions and the supporting consultation documents has a double function. On one hand, it allows for public pressure on budget-making legislators. On the other hand, it makes transparent the work of the Stability Council, so that the body can be monitored by the general public and experts.[107] A violation of the obligation to publish constitutes a violation of the constitutional freedom of information (Article 5 (1) sentence 1.2 of the Constitution).[108] However, the meetings of the Stability Council remain confidential.

103 But see G. Kirchhof (n 100) recital 16.
104 Deutscher Bundestag, BT-Drs. 18/11135, 30, http://dip21.bundestag.de/dip21/btd/18/111/1811135.pdf, accessed 21 January 2021.
105 Siekmann 'Art. 109a' (n 101) recital 25.
106 Schenke (n 70) Art. 143d recital 8.
107 Hans-Günter Henneke, 'Art. 109a' in Bruno Schmidt-Bleibtreu, Hans Hofmann, and Hans-Günter Henneke (eds) *Kommentar zum Grundgesetz* (Carl Heymanns Verlag 2018), recital 37.
108 See Reimer (n 88) recital 67.

V. Implementation of the debt brake at **Länder** *level*

According to Article 109 (3) of the Constitution, both the federal and the *Länder* deficits are included in the debt brake. In contrast to the federal level, the *Länder* cannot opt for structural debt. *Länder* are allowed to deviate from the principle of material budgetary equilibrium only to avert economic crises and in cases of exceptional need. The restrictive debt limit raises the question of whether the revision of the Constitution has observed the 'eternity clause' of Article 79 (3) of the Constitution, which warrants the federal state principle. Additionally, there is a discussion as to whether the debt brake should be anchored in *Länder* law. The majority of *Länder* have opted for an anchoring of the debt brake in *Länder* constitutional law, while some implement the debt brake exclusively in simple statutory law, although parts of the legal literature criticize the latter approach as unconstitutional.

8. Debt prohibition as an attack on the sovereignty of the Länder

Länder are hit much harder than federal government by the ban on taking on new structural debt because they can only finance themselves, to a limited extent, by levying their own taxes (i.e. local taxes on consumption and expenditure, as well as land transfer tax).[109] Income tax, corporate and sales taxes are federal taxes, whose revenue is shared equally with the *Länder*, but which *Länder* cannot autonomously increase. Against this background, it is understandable that constitutional objections were raised against the inclusion of the *Länder* in the debt brake.[110] The prevailing opinion rejects a violation of Article 79 (3) of the Constitution for convincing reasons. Article 79 (3) of the Constitution does not protect the budgetary autonomy of the *Länder* in a comprehensive sense, but only the core of the *Länder's* sovereignty. This is only violated if a minimum level of funding is withheld from the *Länder*. The current system of federal fiscal equalization, as described in Article 105ff. of the Constitution, is, however, far away from this.[111] This is all the more true since the debt brake does not postulate an absolute ban on indebtedness for the *Länder*, rather government debt remains permissible as an instrument of counter-cyclical global management and for averting emergency situations.[112]

9. Constitutional reservation on the implementation of the debt brake

At the end of the transitional period stipulated in Article 143d (1) of the Constitution, the *Länder* are directly bound by the principle of material budgetary equilibrium. Beginning on 1 January 2020, *Länder* budgets must be balanced in principle, without income from loans. The wording 'in principle' refers to the possibility of

109 Ralf P. Schenke, 'Aufgabenrechte Finanzverteilung' (2014) *Neue Juristische Wochenschrift* 2542–2546.
110 Deutscher Bundestag/Bundesrat (n 41) 134.
111 See also Kirchhof (n 100) recital 110ff.
112 Seiler (n 12) 728.

deviations from the debt prohibition in the economic cycle as well as to the prevention of extraordinary emergency situations.

According to Article 109 (3) sentence 2 of the Constitution, *Länder* 'may' provide for the above-mentioned exceptions and *Länder* regulate the detailed design of the debt brake within the framework of their constitutional powers. The use of the word 'may' does not give the *Länder* the option of waiving implementation. On the other hand, the *Länder* have the right to decide to what extent they wish to make use of the exceptions to the principle of substantive budgetary balance.

Between the entry into force of the debt brake on the 1 January 2011 and the expiry of the transition period on 1 January 2020, political views, particularly concerning budgets, have changed considerably.[113] The adoption of the debt brake was supported by a relatively broad party-political consensus, excluding only the party *Die Linke*. Meanwhile, the debt brake is met with opposition both from the party *Bündnis 90/Die Grünen*, but also from large parts of the *SPD* (*Sozialdemokratische Partei Deutschlands*), which is part of the current coalition government.[114] This caused a dilemma for the *Länder* in whose governments these parties are or were involved in the implementation of the debt brake and, perhaps, it also explains why the Land of Berlin in particular took a long time to pass *Land* legislation.[115] Its legislators did not want the enactment of the implementing regulations to be understood as their approval of an unpopular regulation and therefore postponed it as long as possible. Nevertheless, there was no alternative to this step, especially for opponents of the debt brake. Failure to implement it would have made the situation significantly worse. A *Land* that fails to provide more detailed regulations in accordance with Article 109 (3) sentence 4 of the Constitution remains subject to the debt brake but does not have the option of deviating from the principle of formal budgetary equilibrium. The *Länder* are allowed to do so only on the condition of a more detailed implementation. This path has now been taken by all *Länder*.

One facet of the debate on the pros and cons of the debt brake is the regulatory locus of the implementation on the *Länder*. Most of the *Länder* have included corresponding regulations in their constitutions, with the remaining states including the implementation in simple law only (Berlin, Baden-Württemberg, Lower Saxony, North Rhine-Westphalia, Saarland, Saxony-Anhalt, Thuringia). Parts of the legal literature have denied the

113 Exemplary David Böcking, 'Abkehr von der schwarzen Null: Warum die Schuldenregeln wackeln' in *Spiegel Online* (20 August 2019), www.spiegel.de/wirtschaft/soziales/schuldenbremse-und-schwarze-null-warum-sie-wackeln-a-1282596.html, accessed 21 January 2021

114 *AFP*, Zeit online, 8 December 2019, Walter-Borjans attackiert Schuldenbremse scharf, previously available at www.zeit.de/news/2019-12/08/walter-borjans-attackiert-schuldenbremse-scharf

115 See Markus Heintzen, 'Die Umsetzung der Schuldenbremse des Grundgesetzes unter besonderer Berücksichtigung von Bayern und Berlin' in Roland Ismer, Ekkehart Reimer, Alexander Rust, and Christian Waldhoff (eds) *Territorialität und Personalität. Festschrift für Moris Lehner zum 70. Geburtstag* (Dr. Otto Schmidt 2019) 533–546.

constitutional conformity of a regulation in simple *Länder* law.[116] However, the wording of Article 109 (3) sentence 5 Constitution ('within the scope of their constitutional powers') also allows for implementation by simple law. Nevertheless, it must be acknowledged that an implementation in simple *Länder* law excludes the possibility of asserting a violation of the debt brake before the constitutional courts of the *Länder*. It is therefore all the more important that the budgetary economy in these *Länder* is subject to effective control by the Stability Council. Another reason for this is that the implementation of the debt brake in the *Länder* varies widely.[117]

D. Empiricism of the debt brake

In 2010, the financial year preceding the entry into force of the debt brake, the debt ratio of Germany climbed beyond 80%, well above the Maastricht Criterion, which allows a debt ratio of only 60%. As can be seen from the following charts based on *Bundesbank* data the budget situation has eased significantly since then, with ca. 61% in 2019 and an estimated of only 55.6% for 2020.[118]

Figure 3.2 Debt of the general public budget in relation to gross domestic product (GDP) in Germany according to the Maastricht Treaty from 2009 to 2018
Source: Chart based on data from the German Federal Bank.[119]

116 Ulrich Palm, 'Art. 84' in Volker Haug (ed.) *Verfassung des Landes Baden-Württemberg. Handkommentar. NomosKommentar* (Nomos 2018), Art. 84 recital 24.

117 Deutscher Bundestag – Wissenschaftliche Dienste, (WD-4-092/19) *Umsetzung der Schuldenbremse in den Ländern (Implementation of the debt brake in the federal states)* (2019), www.bundestag.de/resource/blob/654168/cc4e18e68753c49fb8e31c20dee16988/WD-4-092-19_mitAnl-pdf-data.pdf, accessed 21 January 2021; Deutsche Bundesbank, *Zur Konjunkturbereinigung der Länder im Rahmen der Schuldenbremse (2017)*, www.bundesbank.de/resource/blob/693394/5db64ce881426c33a79f9f6cb145f74a/mL/2017-03-konjunkturbereinigung-data.pdf, accessed 21 January 2021.

118 Bundesbank, 'Monatsbericht – November 2019' 58, www.bundesbank.de/resource/blob/814802/e21a81a11308c4ace1bacad949a00eff/mL/2019-11-monatsbericht-data.pdf, accessed 21 January 2021.

119 Deutsche Bundesbank, *Zeitreihe BBK01.BJ9959* (n 7).

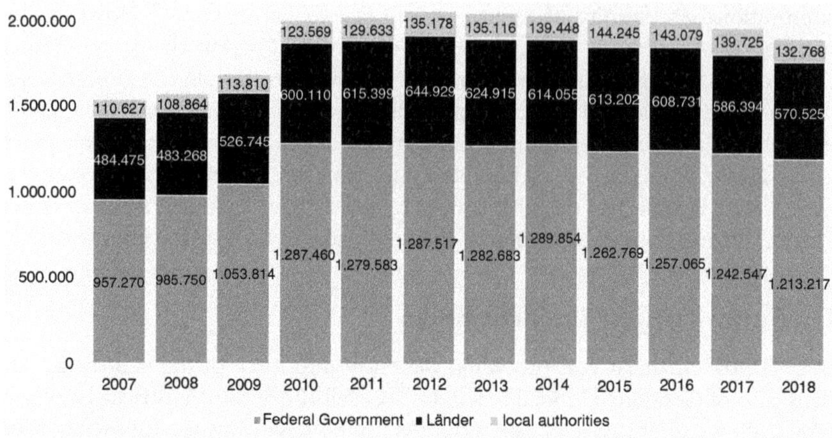

Figure 3.3 Amount of debt in the federal government, the *Länder* and the local authorities in Germany from 2007 to 2018 (in million euros)
Source: Chart based on data from the Federal Statistical Office.[120]

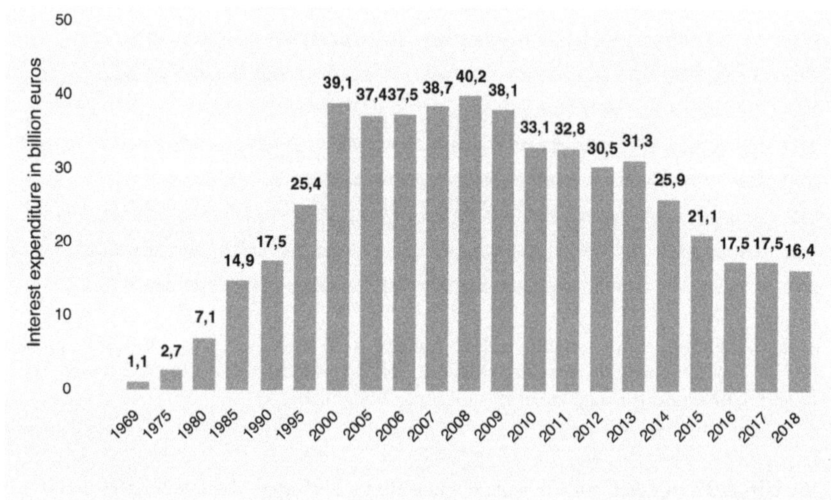

Figure 3.4 Federal interest expenditure from 1969 to 2018 (in billion euros)
Source: Chart based on the monthly report of the Federal Ministry of Finance, January 2019.[121]

120 Statistisches Bundesamt (Destatis), 'Schulden des Öffentlichen Gesamthaushalts – Fachserie 14 Reihe 5–2018' 14, www.destatis.de/DE/Themen/Staat/Oeffentliche-Finanzen/Schulden-Finanzvermoegen/Publikationen/Downloads-Schulden/schulden-oeffentlicher-haushalte-2140500187004.pdf?__blob=publicationFile, accessed 21 January 2021.

121 Monatsbericht des BMF, January 2019, www.bundesfinanzministerium.de/Monatsberichte/2019/01/Inhalte/Kapitel-6-Statistiken/6-1-08-gesamtuebersicht-entwicklung-bundeshaushalt.html, accessed 21 January 2021.

As the above figures demonstrate not only the federal government but also the *Länder* and the municipalities have benefited from this improvement.

This development was also clearly reflected in the decrease in interest charges. This is demonstrated by the figures for the federal budget shown in the chart above.

The fact that the debt brake has achieved its primary goal of consolidating state budgets is thus acknowledged even by its harshest critics.[122] However, its supporters also concede that the historically low interest rate played a significant role in this.[123]

E. Reform discussion and outlook

Regardless of its success in budget consolidation, the debt brake was, and still is, by no means, uncontroversial. On the tenth anniversary of its entry into force, its pros and cons have once again become the focus of economic and financial policy debate. The most recent annual report of the German Council of Economic Experts[124] as well as critical statements by renowned economists bear witness to this.[125] The discussion can be structured according to whether the debt brake is being called into question completely or only selective improvements are being demanded. The analysis below seeks to provide an independent assessment of the predominantly financial arguments.

I. Fundamental criticism

The main criticism of the debt brake remains that the goal of budget consolidation is achieved at the expense of urgently needed investments. This argument has already been put forward in the run-up to Federalism Reform II.[126] However, according to critics of the debt brake, it has gained further weight in view of recent economic policy developments. Here, reference is

122 Marcel Fratzscher, Alexander Kriwoluzky, and Claus Michelsen, 'Gut investierte Schulden sind eine Entlastung in der Zukunft' (2019) 99 (5) *Wirtschaftsdienst* 313–317.

123 Fuest, Gründler, and Potrafke (n 20) 308.

124 Council of Economic Experts, *JG 2019/20: Kapitel 5 – Die Schuldenbremse: Nachhaltig, Stabilisierend, Flexibel* 238ff, www.sachverstaendigenrat-wirtschaft.de/fileadmin/dateiablage/gutachten/jg201920/JG201920_05_Schulden.pdf, accessed 21 January 2021.

125 For criticism of the debt brake, see Peter Bofinger, 'Schuldenbremse: von der statischen "schwarzen Null" zur dynamischen "schwarzen Null"' (2019) 99 (5) *Wirtschaftsdienst* 321–324; Fratzscher, Kriwoluzky, and Michelsen (n 122); Michael Hüther, 'Alles hat seine Zeit, auch die Kreditaufnahme' (2019) 99 (5) *Wirtschaftsdienst* 317–321. For views in favor of the debt brake, see Lars P. Feld and Wolf Heinrich Reuter, 'Die Bewährungsprobe der Schuldenbremse hat gerade erst begonnen' (2019) 99 (5) *Wirtschaftsdienst* 324–329; Fuest, Gründler, and Potrafke (n 20).

126 Peter Bofinger and Gustav Horn, *Die Schuldenbremse gefährdet die gesamtwirtschaftliche Stabilität und die Zukunft unserer Kinder* (2009), www.boeckler.de/pdf/imk_appell_schuldenbremse.pdf, accessed 21 December 2021.

made, on the one hand, to the investment backlog in public infrastructure[127] and, on the other, to the historically low interest rates. Since the growth of GDP exceeded the nominal interest rate, the debt brake was not associated with a gain, but with an estrangement from the postulate of generational justice.[128] A relatively new argument is that the decline in the public debt ratio is associated with negative economic effects. As a consequence of the decrease in national debt, government bonds no longer constituted safe investment opportunities, which could encourage the formation of price bubbles.[129] As an alternative to the debt brake, many – including the Bundesbank – recommend a return to the golden rule.[130]

On the other hand, prominent critics of the debt brake are confronted by important voices from the world of finance who wish to maintain it. The advantage of the debt brake was the containment of political economic cycles. Attempts by incumbents to buy votes through election gifts were made more difficult and, therefore, the inefficient use of public funds was reduced.[131] The investment backlog was not so much due to the debt brake as to the fact that funds available for investment were not retrieved.[132] In addition, it had to be taken into account that a decrease in indebtedness would free up funds for investment, which had previously been spent on interest for debt service.[133] Since the debt brake guaranteed a sound budget policy, it was associated with a fall in refinancing costs on the financial markets.[134] The full exploitation of existing debt potential had to be prohibited because demographic change was associated with major budgetary risks.[135] In addition, Germany had to fulfill the role of an anchor of trust in the euro area. As long as Germany was not only able to bear its own national debt but was also available as a guarantor for joint rescue programs, greater confidence in the euro area as a whole would be maintained.[136]

II. Criticism inherent in the system

The discussion of individual issues surrounding the debt brake should be distinguished from the fundamental debate. The former is not a matter of questioning

127 Fratzscher, Kriwoluzky, and Michelsen (n 122) 315.

128 Hüther (n 125) 320.

129 Fratzscher, Kriwoluzky, and Michelsen (n 122) 314; Hüther (n 125) 320.

130 Bofinger (n 125) 322f; Hüther (n 125) 320; differentiating Deutsche Bundesbank, *Europäischer Stabilitäts- und Wachstumspakt: zu einzelnen Reformoptionen* (*European Stability and Growth Pact: on individual reform options*) (2019) 85ff, www.bundesbank.de/resource/blob/794134/a1ca9e65e4eb15f2d4274fc0c024ad02/mL/2019-04-wachstumspakt-data.pdf, accessed 21 December 2021.

131 Fuest, Gründler, and Potrafke (n 20) 312.

132 Ibid 308.

133 See already Deutscher Bundestag/Bundesrat (n 41) 88.

134 Feld and Reuter (n 125) 325.

135 Ibid 326.

136 Council of Economic Experts (n 124) recital 467.

the debt brake in principle, but of criticizing details. However, to the extent that possibilities for circumvention are addressed, their evaluation can hardly be separated from the fundamental question of whether the debt brake is supported or rejected as an excessive restriction on government debt. Anyone who is critical of the debt brake as a whole is more likely to see opportunities to circumvent it as a chance to break out of an excessively restrictive limit on public debt.

1. *Lack of precision of the debt brake*

As shown above, a key argument in favor of the introduction of the debt brake was the need to fulfill the requirements of the EU Stability and Growth Pact which, since 2005, has prescribed budgetary positions that are close to balance in the medium term. For Germany, this has been specified in the national stability pact to the effect that the close-to-balance approach is still met even if the public budget deficit amounts to 0.5% of GDP.

For various reasons, however, the EU requirements are not sufficiently implemented by the debt brake. First, the scope of the debt brake is limited to the federal budget and the budgets of the *Länder*. Independent legal entities are not included,[137] in particular municipalities and social insurance institutions. By contrast, the classification of the government sector under the rules of the European System of Accounts is much broader. Although there may be good reasons for this divergence for municipalities and social security institutions,[138] it cannot be denied that the debt brake is less precise in terms of meeting the European requirements.[139] This is all the more so as there is considerable scope for circumvention in the case of other independent legal entities.[140]

Second, there is reason to doubt the precision of the debt brake with regard to the adjustment of transactions.[141] According to Article 115 (3) sentence 4 of the Constitution, revenue and expenditure must be adjusted for financial transactions. The purpose of this provision is to prevent the sale of assets as a means to balance the budget. If government authorities dispose of valuable financial assets, this does not result in an increase in revenue relevant to the debt brake. However, it was probably not sufficiently considered that the provision requiring that revenue and expenditure must be adjusted for financial

137 See Georg Hermes, 'Juristische (Kurz-)Analysen zu ausgewählten Themen' in ADAC (ed.) *Reformmodelle für die Bundesfernstraßen. Eine institutionenökonomische Analyse unter Berücksichtigung (verfassungs-)rechtlicher Aspekte* (2016) 57, at 66.

138 The working paper presented by the Bundesministerium für Finanzen is convincing in this respect. See Deutscher Bundestag/Bundesrat (n 41) Arbeitsgruppe 1. AG 1-07, annex 2.

139 However, as the existing legal rules set strict limits on borrowing for social security funds and municipalities, the associated risks of disregarding European requirements are very limited, Deutsche Bundesbank, *Die Schuldenbremse in Deutschland – Wesentliche Inhalte und deren Umsetzung* (n 78) 17.

140 See, at a glance, Hermes (n 137) 67.

141 See for this 'partially double element', Tappe (n 73) 4; instructively, Deutsche Bundesbank (n 79) 30ff.

transactions also opens possibilities to extend the scope for debt. This is because the neutralization of financial transactions also makes it possible, for example, to acquire holdings and companies without the associated expenditure being included in the balance of income and expenditure. Loans granted by public authorities – for example, to private or public infrastructure companies – would also not be taken into account.[142]

The latter is a consequence of the lack of recording implicit debt. When public authorities accumulate liabilities that will only take effect in subsequent financial years, this limits the authority's room for maneuver. However, the debt brake relates solely to current expenditure. This fact is of considerable importance for the accounting treatment of public-private partnerships (PPP). Here, the current accounting rules may provide incentives to favor PPPs over traditional project implementation simply because PPP project costs are not accounted for as expenditure until later and are not affected by the debt brake.[143] On the other hand, the rules of the European Fiscal Compact are different. There, the decision is based on economic ownership, so that allocation to the contractor is only possible if the opportunities and risks have also been transferred to the contractor.[144] This is generally not the case with the models used in Germany.[145] In order to remedy the associated false incentives, the Scientific Advisory Board of the Federal Ministry of Finance has proposed that the accounting of PPP, in the context of the debt brake, should be based on the Eurostat treatment.[146]

2. *Cyclical adjustment*

The most recent annual report of the German Council of Economic Experts dedicates a large segment to questions of cyclical adjustment of the debt brake.[147] According to Article 115 (2) sentence 3 of the Constitution, in the event of economic developments deviating from normal circumstances, the effects on the budget in the upswing and downturn must be taken into account symmetrically. At federal level, the provision is *lex specialis* to the basic rule of

142 Critical regarding this issue, Deutsche Bundesbank (n 79) 32.

143 Bundesministerium der Finanzen, *Chancen und Risiken Öffentlich-Privater Partnerschaften: Gutachten des Wissenschaftlichen Beirats beim Bundesministerium der Finanzen (Opportunities and risks of public-private partnerships: Expert opinion of the Scientific Advisory Board at the Federal Ministry of Finance)* (2016) 29. See also Bundesministerium der Finanzen, *Kompendium zur Schuldenbremse des Bundes (Compendium on the federal debt brake)* (2015), 21 with the relativizing remark that the decision on the type of project must be made on the basis of economic feasibility studies, whereby the effects on the debt brake are not to be taken into account; on the other hand, see Deutsche Bundesbank (n 79) 32.

144 EC, *European System of Accounts: ESA 2010* (2014).

145 In detail, Nicolas Gatzke, *Public Private Partnerships und öffentliche Verschuldung* (2nd ed. Peter Lang 2011), 134ff.

146 Bundesministerium der Finanzen (n 143) 30.

147 Council of Economic Experts (n 124) recitals 496ff.

Article 109 (3) sentence 2 Constitution, according to which the inclusion of corresponding regulations is left to the discretion of the Federation and the *Länder*. As has been shown above, the debt brake follows its predecessor, 'golden rule', which allowed public debt to be instrumentalized for the purposes of economic management.

The idea behind this provision is understandable. Since a cooling of the economy will be reflected in reduced government revenues and, typically, in increased expenditures, budget balancing can only be achieved by limiting expenditures. The consequence would be a further drop in demand, which would exacerbate the crisis and thus have a pro-cyclical effect.[148]

The design of the debt brake at federal level prevents this by extending the scope for borrowing in the event of an emerging economic crisis and correspondingly restricting it in a phase of economic recovery.[149] The risk of a pro-cyclical effect can only be averted at the expense of accepting concessions in the consistent limitation of new borrowing. The legal policy findings based on this conclusion are, thus, contradictory because some authors deny the possibility of counter-cyclical economic policy in principle.[150] However, others argue that the economic impetus emanating from a widening of the scope for borrowing does not go far enough. This criticism emanates from the fact that the cyclical component extends the scope for debt only insofar as to secure the normal level. No economic initiatives can be adopted beyond severe economic crises covered by Article 109 (3) sentence 2 of the Constitution. It is also questionable, in terms of constitutional policy, that key decisions on the implementation of the economic adjustment have been outsourced to an ordinance.[151]

3. *Procedural weaknesses*

As shown above, the substantive requirements of the debt brake were meant to be safeguarded institutionally and procedurally through the establishment of the Stability Council (Article 109a Constitution). It remains to be seen to what extent this will be successful, especially vis-à-vis the *Länder*, which have only been fully subject to the debt brake since the beginning of 2020.[152]

The more detailed definition of the legal status of the Stability Council by the legislator gives rise to doubts about its effectiveness. The lack of independence of the Stability Council is particularly critical.[153] A body that has to

148 Deutsche Bundesbank (n 78) 33.

149 See Bundesministerium der Finanzen (n 143).

150 Kube (n 9) recital 154.

151 Seiler (n 12) 724f.

152 Critical of this is Deutsche Bundesbank, *Deutsche Schuldenbremse: zur Überwachung durch den Stabilitätsrat* (April 2019), www.bundesbank.de/de/publikationen/suche/deutsche-schuldenbremse-zur-ueberwachung-durch-den-stabilitaetsrat-794136, accessed 21 January 2021.

153 Ibid 96.

decide on the misconduct of its own members can hardly be expected to identify and clarify, without fear or favor, any undesirable developments.[154] This criticism is confirmed by the way in which the Stability Council has implemented the requirements for regular budgetary surveillance.[155] In this respect, a compendium adopted in December 2018 specifies that the decision on the publication of the results of the harmonized analytical system is optional, while the publication of the decision on the results of the debt brake is mandatory. There is no support for such a distinction in the wording of the law, which stipulates that the budget figures submitted and the Council conclusions are to be published (§ 3 (3) StabiRatG). The exclusion of such a sensitive assessment, which is based on the generally applicable indicators defined by the Stability Council, is hardly compatible with the purpose of the publication and the history of the statute's development. In this respect, the legislative materials state that the publication of reports and conclusions is a fundamental part of the procedure to ensure transparency.[156]

F. Constitutionalization of the public debt law – risks and side effects

The question of whether and under what conditions states should incur debt is primarily to be answered not by lawyers but by economists. If in this matter legal science expects clarity from finance, it will quickly be disappointed.[157] The assessments of legal and finance experts of the conditions under which states should incur debt are far apart. The views of two scholars of the early stages of the national economy, which are still topical, support this assertion. For *David Ricardo*, public debt is one of the most terrible scourges ever invented to plague the nation.[158]*Lorenz von Stein* formulates it quite differently. National debt is not an evil, but rather a moral duty: 'A state without national debt either does too little for its future or demands too much from its present.'[159]

154 It is true that according to § 1 (4) StabiRatG, the *Land* concerned is not entitled to vote on decisions affecting individual *Länder*. Nevertheless, this provision cannot prevent alliances from being formed. This applies all the more so since decisions are taken by the federal government and a majority of two-thirds of the *Länder* (§ 1 (4) sentence 1 StabiRatG).

155 Deutsche Bundesbank (n 152) 96.

156 BT-Drs. 16/12400, 18, http://dipbt.bundestag.de/dip21/btd/16/124/1612400.pdf, accessed 21 January 2021.

157 Lerke Osterloh, 'Staatsverschuldung als Rechtsproblem?: Kritisches zum Urteil des Zweiten Senats des BVerfG vom 18.4.1989' (1990) 43 (3) *Neue Juristische Wochenschrift* 145–152 (at 150).

158 David Ricardo, 'Funding System – An Article in the Supplement to the Fourth, Fifth and Sixth Editions of the Encyclopaedia Britannica, 1820' in Piero Sraffa (ed.) *The Works and Correspondence of David Ricardo. Volume IV* (CUP 1951), 143 (at 197).

159 Lorenz von Stein, *Lehrbuch der Finanzwissenschaft: - als Grundlage für Vorlesungen und Selbstudium, mit Vergleichung der Finanzsysteme und Finanzgesetze von England, Frankreich und Deutschland* (2nd ed. Brockhaus 1871) 666.

The debate on the German debt brake shows that finance is still far from a consensus on the legitimacy of public debt. As the Director of the Institute of German Economics, Michael Hüther, correctly argues, the debate sometimes exhibits 'theological traits'.[160] Similarly, *Peter Bofinger*, a long-standing member of the German Council of Economic Experts, speaks of an 'ideological fixation' that must be overcome.[161]

This assertion represents a call for restraint in constitutional law and constitutional politics. In Germany, people have long been accustomed to formulating political conflicts as constitutional issues which are decided by the Federal Constitutional Court in Karlsruhe with its rulings having binding force for the simple legislator. This concept of 'constitutionalization'[162] is clearly at odds with the idea of democratic self-determination and the ability of a political system to learn from, and adapt to, new problems in a process of trial and error.[163] In the area of public debt law, particular caution is required for the reasons given above. Restricting political room for maneuver with reference to a concept that is as controversial in the academic world as the debt brake would contradict the rules of political prudence.

The former Federal Constitutional Court judge *Lerke Osterloh* struck the heart of this issue in an article published in 1990: 'A [...] "responsible" public debt policy requires very complex considerations, and a large number of uncertain or controversial factors must be taken into account in these considerations.'[164] The expectation of being able to take account of all these imponderables by a simple formula seems unrealistic. If the constitutional legislator sets material limits on public debt, it must therefore be aware of the risks involved.[165]

These risks include tying future budget legislation to a state of financial knowledge that may become obsolete within a few years. Moreover, what was sensible under certain macroeconomic conditions may prove economically counterproductive under different circumstances. A pertinent example in this sense is the interest rate level. In 2009, the debt brake was primarily aimed at regaining room for maneuver that had been tied up by increased interest rates. In the current phase of low interest rates, this reason has become almost

160 Hüther (n 125) 318.

161 Bofinger (n 125) 324.

162 Fundamentally, Rainer Wahl, 'Der Vorrang der Verfassung und die Selbständigkeit des Gesetzesrechts' (1984) 7 *Neue Zeitschrift für Verwaltungsrecht* 401; Gunnar Folke Schuppert and Christian Bumke, *Die Konstitutionalisierung der Rechtsordnung: Überlegungen zum Verhältnis von verfassungsrechtlicher Ausstrahlungswirkung und Eigenständigkeit des 'einfachen' Rechts* (vol. 29, Nomos Verlagsgesellschaft 2000).

163 For a critique of the constitutionalization of security law, see Ralf P. Schenke, 'Konstitutionalisierung: Vorbild für die Europäisierung des Sicherheitsrechts?' in Dirk Heckmann, Ralf P. Schenke, and Gernot Sydow (eds) *Verfassungsstaatlichkeit im Wandel. Festschrift für Thomas Würtenberger zum 70. Geburtstag* (Duncker & Humblot 2013), 1079ff.

164 Osterloh (n 157) 150.

165 See also Neidhardt (n 12) 408ff.

obsolete. The Federation can borrow at zero or even negative interest rates. If the growth rates permanently exceed the interest rate, debt limits cannot be convincingly justified.[166]

Thus, there is much to be said about the assumption that the Constitution-changing legislator has missed its objective in its efforts to consolidate public finances. Reducing the deficit ratio from just over 80% to just over 60% in little more than eight years is an impressive achievement. However, the fact that even former advocates of the debt brake now almost unanimously advise against continuing this policy should be seriously considered. In the current macroeconomic situation, the risk of failing to invest in the future at the expense of future generations is very real. Conversely, the danger of an irresponsible shifting of the burden into the future is negligible, at least when the debt level is approaching 50% of GDP. A realistic policy option is therefore not another total revision of the public debt law, but a relaxation of the debt brake. This should be all the easier to achieve as the European guidelines leave sufficient room for maneuver.[167] If the debt level falls again after the COVID-19 crisis has been overcome, both the European Stability and Growth Pact and the European Fiscal Compact allow the debt margin to be extended to 1% of GDP.[168] To exhaust this scope for debt, a revision of Articles 109 (3) and 115 (2) of the Constitution could accommodate the critics of the debt brake without creating the danger of another 'breach of the dam'. The result would be a 'breathing' debt brake, which would not only take into account cyclical factors in determining the level of permissible debt, but also the overall level of debt.

G. Recent developments: fiscal policy and the COVID-19 crisis

This chapter was finalized before the Coronavirus pandemic. Current developments are dealt with in this section alone. This separation has the advantage of showing how much the view of budgetary constitutional law is shaped by current political, social, and economic developments and experiences.

I. The development and economic consequences of the fight against the COVID-19 pandemic

In principle, the Coronavirus crisis in Germany took a course similar to that in other Western European countries. In March 2020, after a rapid increase in the number of cases, the competent authorities ordered the closure of schools and almost all private and public institutions. In addition, extensive bans were

166 Council of Economic Experts (n 12) recital 35.

167 Christoph Gröpl, 'Einleitung' in Christoph Gröpl (ed.) *Bundeshaushaltsordnung, Landeshaushaltsordnungen. Staatliches Haushaltsrecht: Kommentar* (C.H. Beck 2019) recitals 63ff.

168 Article 2a, 5 Council Regulation (EC) no. 1466/97; Article 3 (1) (d) Treaty on Stability, Coordination and Governance in the Economic and Monetary Union; Council of Economic Experts (n 124) recital 446.

introduced on human contact in the private sector and the wearing of masks became mandatory in shops open to the public. Only grocery and drugstores remained open. These measures significantly reduced the spread of the virus. The restrictions were gradually eased at the end of April 2020. The Coronavirus crisis has led to an economic boom in some sectors (digital companies, logistics companies, online trade). In many other economic sectors (restaurants, retail, tourism, trade fairs) there was an abrupt shut-down of business activity and a dramatic loss in turnover. In macroeconomic terms, the gross national product is expected to fall by 5.8% in 2020 compared to the previous year, with correspondingly lower tax revenues.[169]

II. *Reactions from politicians and the budget legislator*

The state reacted to the decline in economic activity with a wide range of measures, some of which have placed considerable burdens on the federal and state governments' budgets. In order to avoid large-scale lay-offs, access to short-time work benefits was made easier and the duration of benefits was extended. Small businesses were supported by €40 billion in the form of subsidies. In addition, an economic stabilization fund was set up to enable the federal government to purchase shares in struggling companies.

The funds needed to implement these measures were included in two supplementary budgets. The first supplementary budget, approved by the *Bundestag* on 25 March 2020, provides for €122 billion, which increases the estimated federal expenditure to €484 billion.[170] The second supplementary budget, approved on 2 July 2020, provides for an additional €24 billion and serves as an 'economic stimulus and crisis management package'. It was adopted together with the second Corona Tax Assistance Act.[171] In addition to a further €25 billion allocated for extending aid to small and medium-sized companies, the second supplementary budget law primarily provides tax relief. Also, €3 billion was brought forward in investments and €2 billion in contributions to childcare facilities.

III. *Fiscal policy assessment*

In order to finance the two supplementary budgets the federal government had to take on considerable debt. The budget legislator has thus made a U-turn, which seems to call into question much of what has been achieved in terms of budget consolidation in recent years. Whether such a high level of new debt

169 A forecast of the Federal Government in the interim projection for 2020 is available at www.bmwi.de/Redaktion/DE/Dossier/wirtschaftliche-entwicklung.html, accessed 5 October 2020.

170 BT-Drs. 19/18100, 3 (at 5ff), https://dip21.bundestag.de/dip21/btd/19/181/1918100.pdf, accessed 21 January 2021.

171 BT-Drs. 19/20000, 5, https://dip21.bundestag.de/dip21/btd/19/200/1920000.pdf, accessed 21 January 2021.

was necessary remains politically controversial and was met with skepticism by the Federal Audit Office[172] and parts of the political opposition.[173] During the refugee crisis, the federal government has built up a large reserve fund which has now reached €48.2 billion. It is difficult to understand why new debt was taken on, instead of using this reserve.[174]

Other objections are related to the use of the funds raised. In large part, these loans are not used to finance additional expenditure directly related to the fight against the COVID-19 pandemic or to compensate for loss of revenue. Instead, they are used to finance general government tasks. In addition, more than €24 billion is not spent directly, but placed in reserves that are held as special assets outside the regular budget. It is currently not foreseeable when these funds will actually be spent.[175] The federal government justifies this policy by stating that the creation of the reserves makes it possible to react quickly and effectively to further developments.[176]

IV. Budgetary assessment

The efficiency and effectiveness of the response to the COVID-19 crisis, which the German Finance Minister described as 'bazooka' and 'kaboom',[177] can only be assessed in retrospect and with a time lag of several years. However, it is already clear that the budget legislator must deal with the constitutional objections that have been raised against the two supplementary budgets from the point of view of the debt brake.[178]

It remains open to discussion whether the COVID-19 crisis provides sufficient ground for derogating from the principle of substantive budgetary equilibrium. Article 109 (3) sentence 2 and Article 115 (2) sentence 6 of the Constitution refer to an exceptional emergency situation which is beyond the control of the state and seriously affects the state's financial status. Given the dramatic effects of the COVID-19 pandemic, there should be no doubt about the existence of an extraordinary emergency situation.[179] However, the

172 Bundesrechnungshof, Public Hearing of the Budget Committee of the German Bundestag on 29 June 2020.

173 BT-Drs. 19/18152, 2, https://dip21.bundestag.de/dip21/btd/19/181/1918152.pdf, accessed 21 January 2021.

174 Ibid.

175 Bundesrechnungshof, Public Hearing of the Budget Committee of the German Bundestag on 29 June 2020, 9.

176 Letter of the BMF on the draft for a Second Supplementary Budget Act of 15.6.2020, 6.

177 See Deutschlandfunk v. 5.6.2020: 'Wenn Politiker reden wie im Comic', www.deutschlandfunkkultur.de/lyrikerin-ueber-wumms-zitat-von-olaf-scholz-wenn-politiker.1008.de.html?dram:article_id=478051, accessed 9 October 2020.

178 Christoph Gröpl, 'Olafs "Wumms" in die multiple Verfassungswidrigkeit' (2020) 73 *Neue Juristische Wochenschrift* 2523–2528.

179 For its adoption by the Bundestag, cf. the resolutions BT-Drs. 19/18108, https://dip21.bundestag.de/dip21/btd/19/181/1918108.pdf and BT-Drs. 19/20128, https://dip21.bundestag.de/dip21/btd/19/201/1920128.pdf.

criterion of a significant deterioration of the financial situation should be questioned. According to the second supplementary budget, the total of unspent reserves amount to over €70 billion.[180] This means that an emergency situation can only be presumed if the situation is expected to deteriorate, which will require the reserves to be spent on crisis management in the near future. In this respect, however, the budget legislator will have to be granted a reasonable margin of discretion.

In this case, the question of the permissible level of debt must be answered. The wording of Article 109 (3) sentence 2 and Article 115 (2) sentence 6 of the Constitution leaves this undetermined. In contrast to the debt framework cycle, the legal text is silent on the scope of permissible debt and relies instead on procedural safeguards. The decision to exceed the existing borrowing limits requires a majority vote in the *Bundestag* and must be accompanied by a repayment schedule. Furthermore, according to Article 115 (2) sentence 8 of the Constitution, the repayment of loans taken out under sentence 6 must be made within a reasonable period of time. This systematic approach suggests that the determination of the level of debt should be regarded solely as a political responsibility. However, in view of the requirements of the European Stability and Growth Pact (Article 5 (1) subparagraph 10 Regulation (EC) No 1466/97), emergency situations must not be seen as a free pass for unlimited new borrowing but only as a permit for a higher level of debt in case of extraordinary events beyond the control of a state and only to the extent that the medium-term sustainability of public finances is not at risk.

Further limitations also result from the genesis of the debt brake. According to the explanatory memorandum of the law, the requirement of significant deterioration of the financial situation refers to financial needs for repairing the damage resulting from a natural disaster or the management of an extraordinary emergency situation. Thus, a causal link can be established between the borrowing and the event triggering it.[181] A breach of the debt rule seems justified only to the extent necessary to return to normality. However, not much has been gained from this requirement in the case of the COVID-19 crisis. While a causal link can be established comparatively easily in the case of natural disasters, it is difficult to determine the same causality in the case of an abrupt decrease in demand, such as that caused by the COVID-19 pandemic. If the state steps in as a buyer on a large scale, there is still a causal connection even if the impulses for economic growth are set in sectors not directly affected by the pandemic. The only imperative remaining is that the contribution of the additional expenditure financed by loans leads to a stabilization of the economy as a whole. Again, the budget legislator will have to be granted a wide margin of discretion.

180 Gröpl (n 178) 2527.
181 Gröpl (n 178) 2523.

V. Concluding remarks

Even a decade after its enactment, it is still too early to make a final assessment of the German debt brake. The debt brake has limited spending aspirations and thus contributed to budget consolidation. This may have impaired growth opportunities but, overall, it has presumably increased the confidence of the capital markets in the performance and solvency of the German state. Germany benefits from the debt brake, especially during the current crisis, because it can continue to finance itself on very favorable terms.[182] It cannot be claimed that the debt brake has created serious obstacles to a policy of crisis management. Rather, the question arises the other way around – that is, whether the exemption rules for crisis management leave too many loopholes open. In this extraordinary situation, the debt brake does not have a clearly defined debt limit. However, the budget legislator's discretion in its assessment and evaluation is not infinite: it is limited both by the European Stability and Growth Pact and by the requirement of a causal link between borrowing and the objective of combating the crisis. A debt-financed creation of reserves must therefore be an exception. It is to be hoped that during the course of the COVID-19 pandemic the build-up of reserves will prove to be a precautionary measure which, in retrospect, would not have been necessary.

Special thanks go to Ms. Jessica Flint for the translation of the article, to Ms. Larissa Kowalski for evaluating the statistical data and creating the diagrams, and to Ms. Meya Maniram, for reviewing the final section of this paper.

Bibliography

Blankart CB, *Öffentliche Finanzen in der Demokratie: Eine Einführung in die Finanzwissenschaft, 9. Aufl.* (Franz Vahlen 2017)

Bofinger P, 'Schuldenbremse: von der statischen "schwarzen Null" zur dynamischen "schwarzen Null"', (2019) 99 (5) *Wirtschaftsdienst* 321

Bofinger P and Horn G, 'Die Schuldenbremse gefährdet die gesamtwirtschaftliche Stabilität und die Zukunft unserer Kinder' (2009) www.boeckler.de/pdf/imk_appell_schuldenbremse.pdf, accessed 29 January 2021.

Buchanan JM and Wagner RE, *Democracy in deficit: The political legacy of Lord Keynes* (Academic Press 1977)

Dworkin R, *Taking rights seriously: New impression with a reply to critics* (Duckworth 2005)

Hausner KH and Simon S, 'Die neue Schuldenregel in Deutschland und die Schuldenbremse der Schweiz: Wege zu nachhaltigen öffentlichen Finanzen?' (2009) 89 (4) *Wirtschaftsdienst* 265

Henneke HG, 'Art. 109a' in Bruno Schmidt-Bleibtreu, Hans Hofmann, and Hans-Günter Henneke (eds) *Kommentar zum Grundgesetz* (Carl Heymanns Verlag 2018)

Hetschko C and Thye M, 'Die Bereinigung um finanzielle Transaktionen – Achillesferse der deutschen Schuldenbremse' (2012) *Deutsches Verwaltungsblatt* 743

182 Cf. Lars P. Feld et al., 'Rekordschulden gegen Corona-Folgen – waskann sich der Staat leisten?' (2020) 73 (8) *ifo Schnelldienst* (ifo Institut – Leibniz-Institut für Wirtschaftsforschung an der Universität München) 03–32 (at 5).

Jarass HD, 'Art. 109' in Hans D. Jarass and Bodo Pieroth (eds) *Grundgesetz für die Bundesrepublik Deutschland. Kommentar* (Beck 2018)

Keynes JM, *The General Theory of Employment, Interest and Money* (1936)

Kirchhof G, 'Art. 109a' in Hans D. Jarass and Bodo Pieroth (eds) *Grundgesetz für die Bundesrepublik Deutschland. Kommentar* (Beck 2018)

Kube H, 'Art. 115' in T Maunz and G Dürig (eds) *Grundgesetz. Kommentar* (Beck 2019)

Nordhaus WD, 'The Political Business Cycle' (1975) 42 (2) *The Review of Economic Studies* 169

Osterloh L, 'Staatsverschuldung als Rechtsproblem?: Kritisches zum Urteil des Zweiten Senats des BVerfG vom 18.4.1989' (1990) *Neue Juristische Wochenschrift* 145

Pünder H, 'Art. 115' in Karl Heinrich Friauf and Wolfram Höfling (eds) *Berliner Kommentar zum Grundgesetz* (Erich Schmidt Verlag 2019)

Reimer E, 'Art. 109a' in Volker Epping, Christian Hillgruber, and Peter Axer (eds) *Grundgesetz. Kommentar* (CH Beck 2020)

Ricardo D, 'Funding System – An Article in the Supplement to the Fourth, Fifth and Sixth Editions of the Encyclopaedia Britannica, 1820' in Piero Sraffa (ed.) *The Works and Correspondence of David Ricardo*. Volume IV (CUP 1951)

Schenke RP, 'Konstitutionalisierung: Vorbild für die Europäisierung des Sicherheitsrechts?' in Dirk Heckmann, Ralf P. Schenke, and Gernot Sydow (eds) *Verfassungsstaatlichkeit im Wandel. Festschrift für Thomas Würtenberger zum 70. Geburtstag* (Duncker & Humblot 2013)

Scholl B, 'Die Neuregelung der Verschuldungsregeln von Bund und Ländern in den Art. 109 und 115 GG' (2010) *Die öffentliche Verwaltung* 160

Schuppert GF and Bumke C, *Die Konstitutionalisierung der Rechtsordnung: Überlegungen zum Verhältnis von verfassungsrechtlicher Ausstrahlungswirkung und Eigenständigkeit des 'einfachen' Rechts, Band 29, Forum Rechtswissenschaft* (Nomos Verlagsgesellschaft 2000)

Siekmann, H, 'Art. 109a' in Michael Sachs (ed.) *Grundgesetz. Kommentar* (CH Beck 2018)

von Stein L, *Lehrbuch der Finanzwissenschaft: - als Grundlage für Vorlesungen und Selbstudium, mit Vergleichung der Finanzsysteme und Finanzgesetze von England, Frankreich und Deutschland* (2nd ed. Brockhaus 1871)

Stern K, *Das Staatsrecht der Bundesrepublik Deutschland, Bd. II: Staatsorgane, Staatsfunktionen, Finanz- und Haushaltsverfassung, Notstandsverfassung* (CH Beck 1980)

Tappe H, 'Die neue „Schuldenbremse" im Grundgesetz' (2009) *Die öffentliche Verwaltung* 881

Tappe H, 'Haushaltsrechtliche Umsetzung der Artikel 109 und Artikel 115 GG n.F. in Bund und Ländern' in Christian Kastrop, Gisela Meister-Scheufelen, and Margaretha Sudhof (eds) *Die neuen Schuldenregeln im Grundgesetz. Zur Fortentwicklung der bundesstaatlichen Finanzbeziehungen* (Berliner Wiss-Verl 2010)

Tappe H, 'Wie passt die Schuldenbremse zur staatlichen Doppik?' (2010) 4 *Wirtschaftsdienst* 90

Tappe H and Wernsmann R, *Öffentliches Finanzrecht* (2nd revised ed. CF Müller 2019)

Wahl R, 'Der Vorrang der Verfassung und die Selbständigkeit des Gesetzesrechts' (1984) *Neue Zeitschrift für Verwaltungsrecht* 401

4 The constitutional stakes of the Golden Rule

Marc Verdussen

On March 2, 2012, the Heads of State and Government of 25 Member States of the European Union signed the Treaty on Stability, Coordination and Governance (TSCG), more commonly referred to as the 'European Budget Pact'. It is an intergovernmental treaty that concerns the Eurozone states and the other signatory parties. According to Article 1 of the Treaty, its objective is

> to strengthen the economic pillar of the economic and monetary union by adopting a set of rules intended to foster budgetary discipline through a fiscal compact, to strengthen the coordination of their economic policies and to improve the governance of the euro area, thereby supporting the achievement of the European Union's objectives for sustainable growth, employment, competitiveness and social cohesion.

The Treaty contains a balanced budget rule ('Golden Rule') that is particularly intrusive for the signatory States, which not only have an obligation to transpose it, but also to do so through provisions of binding force and permanent character, preferably constitutional. The Treaty is therefore intended to have an impact on the constitutions of all signatory parties. This chapter focuses specifically on these constitutional issues.[1] The European consecration of the Golden Rule (I) and the national transposition of this rule (II) shall be successively studied.

1 Four studies were published on this topic by members of the Research Center on State and Constitution (CRECO-JUR I): Paul Dermine, 'La Belgique face à la règle d'or sur l'incorporation de l'article 3, § 1er, du Traité de stabilité, de coopération et de gouvernance au sein de l'ordre juridique belge' (2014) 21 *Revue belge de droit constitutionnel* 177–196; Paul Dermine, 'Le Traité de Stabilité, de Coopération et de gouvernance au sein de l'Union économique et monétaire et l'internalisation de la *Golden Rule* par les Etats membres de l'Union européenne' (2014 Supplement) *Romanian Journal of Comparative Law* 79–107; Celine Romainville, 'Autorité européenne, déséquilibres démocratiques et droits fondamentaux', paper presented at the 9th World Congress of the International Association of Constitutional Law, (Oslo, 12–16 June 2014); Marc Verdussen, Laurent Maniscalco, Stéphanie Wattier, 'La Cour constitutionnelle et l'équilibre des finances publique: Belgique' (2012) 28 *Annuaire international de justice constitutionnelle* 127–155.

DOI: 10.4324/9781315181882-7

I The European recognition of the Golden Rule

Having defined the Golden Rule and thus described its essential components (A), this chapter seeks to assess this rule (B).

A Definition of the Golden Rule

Faced with the most serious financial crisis in its history, the European Union needed to take a series of convergence measures with the Member States. The adoption of the Golden Rule is the result of an evolution that can be broken down into three successive dynamics: coordination, accountability, and internalization.

1 A dynamics for coordination

Originally, the Member States of the European Union wishing to accede to the euro committed themselves to shape the balance of their public finances in order to preserve a common balance so as to prevent the budget deficit of one or several Member States from leading to global destabilization. Since 1992, the Treaty on European Union, signed in Maastricht, has been concerned with the balance of public finances within the Member States. In its Article 104-C the Treaty obliges the Member States to avoid 'excessive government deficits'. To this end, the European Commission was tasked with overseeing 'the development of the budgetary situation and of the stock of government debt in the Member States with a view to identifying gross errors' and, in particular, to assess the 'compliance with budgetary discipline', on the basis of the criteria laid down in the same Article 104-C. These are the famous 'Maastricht criteria'.

Five years later, the Member States of the euro area adopted another instrument to coordinate their national budgetary policies and to avoid the appearance of excessive government deficits – that is, the Stability and Growth Pact.

However, the widespread ignorance of these two instruments by the state authorities and the acute financial crisis have forced the Member States to quickly take more radical initiatives, notably the European Financial Stabilization Mechanism and the European Financial Stability Facility.

2 A dynamics for accountability

Finding that the existing instruments were not satisfactory in terms of reducing the level of public indebtedness and taking into consideration the inadequacy of these instruments in the face of macroeconomic imbalances, the European Union wished to reinstate the budgetary discipline of the Member States and the supervision of their economic policies. At the European level, for example, the Council and the Parliament, which were seized by the Commission, agreed on six texts intended to reform the European economic governance. These six texts – five regulations and one directive – make up the so-called 'Six Pack'.

These regulations, which entered into force on December 13, 2011, provide that financial sanctions may be imposed on those Member States of the euro area which do not take appropriate measures to reduce their deficit. The Member States currently undergoing the excessive deficit procedure must comply with the specific recommendations addressed to them by the European Council. If a Member State of the euro area fails to comply with its obligations, the European Council may impose a financial penalty at the recommendation of the Commission, unless a qualified majority of Member States objects. The use of a qualified majority voting procedure makes the enforcement of rules much stricter. Financial sanctions are, in this perspective, more dissuasive than before.

3 A dynamics for internalization

On March 2, 2012, the Heads of State or Government of the various Member States of the European Union, with the exception of the United Kingdom and the Czech Republic, signed the Treaty on Stability, Coordination and Governance within the Economic and Monetary Union (TSCG). This is part of an institutional logic distinct from that prevailing in the Stability and Growth Pact. Indeed, since it intends to preserve the stability of the euro area, it concerns with 'priority' only the Member States of the euro area, unlike the Stability and Growth Pact, which covers all the Member States of the European Union. Having been ratified by 25 of the 27 Member States of the European Union, the TSCG is an intergovernmental treaty, formally outside the Community domain. Article 16 of this document stipulates, however, that

> within five years of the date of entry into force of the Treaty, based on an assessment of the experience with its implementation, the necessary steps shall be taken, in accordance with the Treaty on the European Union and the Treaty on the Functioning of the European Union, with the aim of incorporating the substantive provisions of the Treaty into the legal framework of the European Union.

Article 3 (1) of the TSCG[2] imposes on the participating States a number of substantial budgetary constraints, including the Golden Rule, which is

2 Article 3 (1) is worded as follows: 'The Contracting Parties shall apply the rules set out in this paragraph in addition and without prejudice to their obligations under European Union law:

(a) the budgetary position of the general government of a Contracting Party shall be balanced or in surplus;

(b) the rule under point (a) shall be deemed to be respected if the annual structural balance of the general government is at its country-specific medium-term objective, as defined in the revised Stability and Growth Pact, with a lower limit of a structural deficit of 0.5% of the gross domestic product at market prices. The Contracting Parties shall ensure rapid convergence towards their respective medium-term objective. The timeframe for such convergence will be proposed by the European Commission taking into consideration country-specific sustainability

undoubtedly at the heart of the Treaty.[3] This rule requires the Member States concerned to ensure that the budgetary position of all public administrations is in balance or surplus. To this end, the State must ensure, without resorting to borrowing, that public operating expenditure does not exceed the revenue it receives to finance these expenses. Ideally, therefore, the annual structural balance of public administrations cannot be in deficit. This constraint is, however, accompanied by two mitigating provisions. Thus, some degree of tolerance is allowed up to a maximum deficit of 0.5% of the gross domestic product (GDP). In addition, the Member State may invoke exceptional circumstances.

Article 3 (2) of the TSCG requires Member States to incorporate such substantive constraints into their national law, including the Golden Rule:

> The rules set out in paragraph 1 shall take effect in the national law of the Contracting Parties at the latest one year after the entry into force of this Treaty through provisions of binding force and permanent character, preferably constitutional, or otherwise guaranteed to be fully respected and adhered to throughout the national budgetary processes. The Contracting Parties shall put in place at national level the correction mechanism referred to in paragraph 1(e) on the basis of common principles to be proposed by the European Commission, concerning in particular the nature, size and time-frame of the corrective action to be undertaken, also in the case of exceptional circumstances, and the role and independence of the institutions responsible at national level for monitoring compliance with the rules set out in paragraph 1. Such correction mechanism shall fully respect the prerogatives of national Parliaments.

In Article 8, the TSCG secures the transposition mechanism of the Golden Rule into the domestic law of the Member States, providing that it can be scrutinized by the Court of Justice of the European Union. Paragraph 1

risks. Progress towards, and respect of, the medium-term objective shall be evaluated on the basis of an overall assessment with the structural balance as a reference, including an analysis of expenditure net of discretionary revenue measures, in line with the revised Stability and Growth Pact;

(c) the Contracting Parties may temporarily deviate from their respective medium-term objective or the adjustment path towards it only in exceptional circumstances, as defined in point (b) of paragraph 3;

(d) where the ratio of the general government debt to gross domestic product at market prices is significantly below 60% and where risks in terms of long-term sustainability of public finances are low, the lower limit of the medium-term objective specified under point (b) can reach a structural deficit of at most 1.0% of the gross domestic product at market prices;

(e) in the event of significant observed deviations from the medium-term objective or the adjustment path towards it, a correction mechanism shall be triggered automatically. The mechanism shall include the obligation of the Contracting Party concerned to implement measures to correct the deviations over a defined period of time.'

3 Paul Craig, 'The Stability, Coordination and Governance Treaty: Principle, Politics and Pragmatism' (2012) 37 *European Law Review* 235.

stipulates that 'the judgment of the Court of Justice shall be binding on the parties to the proceedings, which shall take the necessary measures to comply with the judgment within a period to be decided by the Court of Justice'. As regards the enforcement of the judgment of the Court of Justice, paragraph 2 provides that

> Where, on the basis of its own assessment or that of the European Commission, a Contracting Party considers that another Contracting Party has not taken the necessary measures to comply with the judgment of the Court of Justice referred to in paragraph 1, it may bring the case before the Court of Justice and request the imposition of financial sanctions following criteria established by the European Commission in the framework of Article 260 of the Treaty on the Functioning of the European Union. If the Court of Justice finds that the Contracting Party concerned has not complied with its judgment, it may impose on it a lump sum or a penalty payment appropriate in the circumstances and that shall not exceed 0.1% of its gross domestic product. The amounts imposed on a Contracting Party whose currency is the euro shall be payable to the European Stability Mechanism. In other cases, payments shall be made to the general budget of the European Union.

The TSCG came into force on January 1, 2013. The ratification of the treaty took place at very different paces for each State.

Internal constitutional constraints have sometimes delayed ratification. These include especially the procedures for the revision of the Constitution. In addition, appeals have been lodged with several constitutional courts. Decisions have been thus delivered, including a decision of the French Constitutional Council on August 9, 2012[4], a decision of the German Federal Constitutional Court on September 12, 2012,[5] and two judgments of the Austrian Constitutional Court on March 16, 2013[6] and October 3, 2013.[7] In Belgium, two

4 French Constitutional Council, 2012-653 DC, August 9, 2012. See Jean-Claude Bonichot, 'Le juge constitutionnel français et la 'règle d'or': réviser ou ne pas réviser la Constitution? That was the question' in Vincent Kronenberger, Maria Teresa d'Alessio and Valerio Placo (eds) *De Rome à Lisbonne: les juridictions de l'Union européenne à la croisée des Chemins – Mélanges en l'honneur de Paolo Mengozzi* (Bruylant 2013), 371–384; Eric Oliva, 'Le pacte de stabilité devant les juridictions constitutionnelles' (2012) 28 *Revue française de droit administratif* 1043–1054; Jérôme Roux, 'Le Conseil constitutionnel et le TSCG' (2012) 4 *Revue trimestrielle de droit européen* 855–876.

5 BVerfG, 2 BvR 1390/12, 12.9.2012. See Mattias Wendel, 'Judicial Restraint and the Return to Openness: The Decision of the German Federal Constitutional Court on the ESM and the Fiscal Treaty of 12 September 2012' (2013) 14 *German Law Journal* 21–52.

6 BVerfG, SV 2/12–18, 16.3.2013. See Claudia Mayer, 'ESM Treaty in Accordance with the Austrian Constitution' (2013) 7 *Vienna Journal on International Constitutional Law* 385–400.

7 BVerfG, SV 1/2013, 3.10.2013. See Christoph Schramek, 'European Fiscal Compact is Held to Be in Accordance with the Constitution' (2014) 8 *Vienna Journal on International Constitutional Law* 218–223.

actions for annulment were brought before the Constitutional Court. They were filed in 2014, notably by the Human Rights League.[8] In judgment No. 62/2016, delivered on April 28, 2016, the Court held that none of the applicants had the requisite interest in seeking the annulment of the law granting assent to the TSCG. The Court dismissed the appeals on that basis, without addressing the content of the request.

It is precisely institutional constraints specific to Belgium that explain why it was the last Member State to ratify the TSCG. It should be recalled here that the so-called 'mixed' international treaties – which deal with matters of both federal jurisdiction and matters within the competence of federated entities – require the approval of the eight parliamentary assemblies concerned, which is a source of certain delay.

B Evaluation of the Golden Rule

Many questions have been raised by the adoption of the Golden Rule. To order them to a certain degree, they are divided into five questions, which relate to the legitimacy, validity, neutrality, timeliness, and effectiveness of the rule.

1 The legitimacy of the Golden Rule

Is the Golden Rule legitimate? The question of the legitimacy of the Golden Rule is a question of its democratic legitimacy.

a. The democratic legitimacy of the Golden Rule establishment

The democratic legitimacy of the Golden Rule has been questioned because of the conditions for its adoption by the participating States and the conditions for its approval in national legal systems. At European level, the intergovernmental nature of the TSCG has removed it from any debate within the European Parliament. At national level, political realism has led the European States concerned to determine that the ratification of the TSCG was unavoidable, discouraging in advance any attempt at a comprehensive parliamentary debate. As for domestic constitutional courts, their decisions show that they did not obstruct the implementation of the TSCG, sometimes by using subtle intellectual and semantic contortions. In these circumstances, one may wonder whether the TSCG brings about a latent transformation of the European project into an 'executive federalism', which would soon become 'a paragon of post-democratic autocracy'.[9]

8 See Edgar Szoc, 'Droits économiques, sociaux et culturels: deuxième génération première importance' (February 2014) 69 *La Revue nouvelle* 18.

9 Jurgen Habermas, *La constitution de l'Europe* (Gallimard 2012), 14. See also Jurgen Habermas, 'The Crisis of the European Union in the Light of a Constitutionalization of International Law' (2012) 23 *European Journal of International Law* 348.

b. *The democratic legitimacy of the Golden Rule transposition*

The question of the democratic legitimacy of the Golden Rule also concerns – and perhaps most importantly – the limitation of the prerogatives it implies for national parliamentary assemblies. Is it not a surprising paradox? While the constitutionalization of budgetary principles represents the source of the concern about deferring budgetary decisions to the exclusive consideration of democratically elected parliamentary assemblies, the question here revolves around the issue of restricting this discretion.

This issue was examined by the German Federal Constitutional Court in a judgment on several appeals related to the ratification of the TSCG.[10] The essence of its justification lies in paragraph 224 of the Court's judgment:

> [I]t is not anti-democratic from the outset for the budget legislature to be bound by a particular budget and fiscal policy [...]. By putting into specific terms and objectively tightening the rules for borrowing by Federal and Länder governments (in particular Article 109-3 and 5, Article 109-a, Article 115 of the Basic Law new, Article 143-d-1 of the Basic Law), the constitution-amending legislature made it clear that a constitutional commitment on the part of the parliaments and thus a palpable restriction of their budgetary power to act may be necessary precisely in order to preserve the democratic power to shape affairs for the body politic in the long term [...]. Even if such a commitment restricts democratic legislative discretion in the present, it serves at the same time to guarantee it for the future.

The recital of the Karlsruhe judges derives from the idea that if the Golden Rule involves a step backward for the autonomy of parliaments, the aim is to better guarantee this autonomy in the future. To some extent, it is about stepping back in order to jump better. The position of the German judges refers to a crucial question: in the name of what imperative should the interests of the present generations be sacrificed for the benefit of the interests of future generations?

In so far as it limits the sovereignty of national parliamentary assemblies, the question that arises is: does the Golden Rule also pose a threat to political citizenship? In a self-respecting representative democracy, the right to vote cannot be reduced to the formal right of citizens to elect their representatives periodically. The right to vote is also the substantive right to influence the formation of political opinions and to have an impact on political decision-making.

2 *The validity of the Golden Rule*

Is the Golden Rule compatible with the so-called 'Europe' clause? This refers to the clause by which the Constitution empowers the legislator to transfer the shared exercise of sovereignty to international organizations.

10 See n 5.

The problem arose in Belgium with Article 34 of the Belgian Constitution, which read: 'The exercising of specific powers can be assigned by a treaty or by a law to institutions of public international law.' This provision was adopted in 1970 to circumvent the obstacle contained in Article 33 – which states that 'all powers emanate from the Nation' and 'are exercised in the manner laid down by the Constitution' – for the transfer of exercise of State powers, in particular constitutional powers, to an international authority.[11] The text of Article 34 of the Constitution 'has been drafted in very broad terms', so that 'it allows important, if not decisive, transfers of powers'.[12] However, two important limitations emerge from the wording of Article 34 of the Constitution. First, it is the 'exercising' of powers that can be transferred, not the enjoyment of these powers. It must be borne in mind that, under Article 33, which is one of the essential foundations of the Belgian constitutional system and which, for this reason, has remained unchanged since 1831, the sole source and the exclusive depositary of constitutional powers is the nation. It follows that any delegation of such powers to an international institution is necessarily reversible – for example, in the event of its disappearance. Then, only 'determined' powers can be transferred. During the parliamentary discussions, Senator Fernand Dehousse stressed that the State must know what it gives and the institution what it receives, because 'the degradation of the powers of the State is too severe, and the construction of international society too serious, for it to not be clearly expressed'.[13] The term 'specific' also means that there can be no question of transferring all the prerogatives and responsibilities attached to a state power, whether legislative, executive, or judicial, and that, by the force of circumstances, sovereignty could not be deprived of the exercise of all constitutional powers.

As Professor Francis Delperée wisely points out, if these limits 'should be erased in the name of the principles of fiscal governance, what would they still serve? In what institutional gear have we put, knowingly or not, the finger – or the arm?'[14] For, he continues,

> by taking control of the budgets, the European Union permeates not just the edges of national jurisdictions, but their very core. It does not just infiltrate surreptitiously but vigorously the policies pursued by the Member States and their components. It does not affect one or another of their fields of action. It affects them all and each one separately.[15]

Clearly, the Golden Rule empties Article 34 of its substance.

11 See Jacques Velu, *Droit public: Le statut des gouvernants* (Bruylant 1987), 84–90.

12 Francis Delpérée, 'Belgique' in Jean-Claude Masclet and Didier Maus (eds), *Les Constitutions nationales à l'épreuve de l'Europe* (La Documentation française 1993), 31.

13 *Parliamentary Documents*, Senate (1969–1970) 275/4.

14 Francis Delpérée, 'Les cordons de la bourse' (February 2012) *La Revue générale*.

15 Ibid. Also see Marc Dawson and Floris de Witte, 'Constitutional Balance in the EU after the Euro-Crisis' (2013) 76 *Modern Law Review* 826–827.

The question was posed to the Austrian Constitutional Court on the Treaty of July 11, 2011, establishing the European Stability Mechanism. In Austria, the 'Europe' clause appears in Article 9 of the Constitution and limits the possibility of transfer to 'specific' powers. In a ruling delivered on March 16, 2013, the Court rejected the argument by using a maximalist interpretation of Article 9 and by missing the opportunity to clarify what exactly should be understood by 'specific powers', which the Austrian doctrine has regretted.[16]

3 The neutrality of the Golden Rule

Does the Golden Rule interfere with the implementation of constitutional provisions? In any case, it is one or the other. Either the Golden Rule has been constitutionalized, and this is a problem of the intrinsic consistency of the constitutional text, or it has not been constitutionalized, and the question that arises then is that of its unconstitutionality.

The crux of the problem lies in the viability of the welfare state. Does not the limitation by the Golden Rule of the sovereignty of national parliamentary assemblies represent a potential hindrance to state policies on the redistribution of public resources? Constitutional provisions, more or less numerous according to the States, may be concerned. These are constitutional provisions which, such as Article 31§2 of the Spanish Constitution, require public expenditure to ensure 'an equitable allocation of public resources'. These are mainly constitutional provisions guaranteeing fundamental rights. To be precise, the Golden Rule is likely to weaken social, environmental, cultural, educational, or public health policies that are a concrete expression of economic, social, and cultural rights.

The risk of weakening is accentuated by the decision of the European Council of March 25, 2011, amending Article 136 of the Treaty on the Functioning of the European Union regarding a stability mechanism for those Member States whose currency is the euro.[17] This decision inserted a new paragraph 3, which stipulates that

> the Member States whose currency is the euro may establish a stability mechanism to be activated if indispensable to safeguard the stability of the euro area as a whole. The granting of any required financial assistance under the mechanism will be made subject to strict conditionality.

Of course, the Golden Rule does not directly prevent the legislator from pursuing policies aimed at guaranteeing economic, social, and cultural rights. But the legislator may be tempted to take refuge behind this rule in order to show an irresponsible attachment to the past in this matter.

16 Mayer (n 6) 396.
17 *Official Journal of the European Union*, April 6, 2011.

4 The appropriateness of the Golden Rule

Is the Golden Rule relevant? A rule is relevant if it is capable of achieving the objective, or objectives, which justified its adoption. However, many observers question the ability of the Golden Rule to bring about greater control over public finances in the euro area. Paul de Grauwe, Professor of Economics at the University of Louvain, said:

> It is now becoming increasingly clear that generalized austerity in the Eurozone will not pacify the financial markets. On the contrary, the increasing intensity with which budgetary austerity is applied will make the financial markets less rather than more confident that the sovereign debt crisis can be overcome. The reason is very simple, as is being increasingly recognized. When all Eurozone countries are forced to accept austerity at the same time, deflationary forces are set in motion that lower output and government revenues throughout the Eurozone. As a result, government budget deficits do not decline sufficiently to prevent the debt-to-GDP ratios from increasing, as the denominator in these ratios (GDP) goes down faster than the numerator (the debt level). Thus, the effect of generalized austerity is recession and more unsustainable levels of government debt. Generalized austerity undermines the confidence of financial markets, because it leads the Eurozone straight into a recession.[18]

In Belgium, a motion for a resolution was submitted to the House of Representatives, on May 9, 2012.[19] According to the authors of the motion:

> The demand for the budgetary golden rule, which requires respect for the balance of the annual budget of a State, in national constitutions or texts of similar scope, is a cosmetic argument, whose sole objective is to make believe the rigor and reassure the markets. This budgetary golden rule would only have the effect of enclosing the States in a heavy and counterproductive straitjacket. On the one hand, the entry into force of the Treaty will impose itself on the Contracting States like any other European treaty and will prevail over national laws in the hierarchy of standards. On the other hand, as such, this single budgetary golden rule will not offer a response to short-term or medium and long-term issues. Indeed, the threats that the financial markets impose on the States through a fall in the rating of their sovereign debt – and incidentally on (para) statutory bodies such as public interest organizations (PIOs), on the European Financial Stability Facility, on the banks and insurance companies holding these government securities, etc. – are mainly due to the lack of a prospect of

18 Paul de Grauwe, 'Who cares about the survival of the eurozone?' *CEPS Commentary* (November 16, 2011), http://aei.pitt.edu/32974/1/PDG_Who_cares_about_survival_of_eurozone.pdf

19 *Parliamentary Documents*, House of Representatives (2011–2012) 53-2180/1.

inclusive, intelligent and sustainable growth, synonymous with activities and jobs and, hence, tax revenues.

5 The effectiveness of the Golden Rule

The question of effectiveness is different from its relevance: 'How to make this rule binding when the Stability Pact was shamelessly flouted? Why would it be, even if it is included in the national law of the States, more mandatory than a European Treaty? And in case of non-compliance, what would the sanctions be?'[20] Clearly, the internalization of the Golden Rule can only be useful if it is effective as compliance with the rule must be subject to judicial review. The question of constitutional guarantees is a question of the sovereignty of each State and, for each of them, depends mainly on the legal nature of the norm internalizing the Golden Rule. That is the purpose of the second part of this text.

II The national transposition of the Golden Rule

The different Member States did not choose the same path in the transposition of the Golden Rule. Three options have been developed: constitutional (A), legislative (B), and contractual (C).

A The constitutional option

The constitutional option is certainly favored by the authors of the TSCG. It was followed by several States. But is it desirable?

1 The value of the constitutional option

Two issues are discussed here. Is the constitutional option mandatory? Is it relevant?

A. IS THE CONSTITUTIONAL OPTION MANDATORY?

The TSCG provides that the Golden Rule

> shall take effect in the national law of the Contracting Parties within one year after the entry into force of the Treaty through provisions of binding force and permanent character, preferably constitutional, or otherwise guaranteed to be fully respected and adhered to throughout the national budgetary processes.

20 Bernard Keppenne, 'La "Golden Rule", solution à la crise' (January 15, 2012) *La Libre Belgique*, www.lalibre.be/economie/entreprises-startup/la-regle-d-or-solution-a-la-crise-51b8e3a8e4b0de6db9c50a14

Two lessons emerge from this text, particularly from the term 'preferably constitutional'.

First, it is clear from the text that the granting of a constitutional basis to the Golden Rule is not binding on the Member States. The will of the authors of the TSCG is to impose on each State a transposition of the Golden Rule into an instrument sufficiently binding on the budgetary legislator. An obligation of constitutionalization would have been unprecedented within the framework of the European Union. When a State is obliged to revise its Constitution in order to comply with an obligation enacted or contracted within the framework of the European Union, especially to allow the ratification of an international treaty, it is not because a European or intergovernmental law requires it, but because of intrinsic constitutional constraints that lead the State to ensure harmonization of its constitutional text.[21]

Furthermore, we find in the same text a reference to the Constitution, and even a preference for the Constitution. This preference makes it possible to measure the place that the rule must occupy within a Member State. Indeed, the preference for the constitutional text is indicative of the willingness of the authors of the TSCG to consider the Golden Rule as, simultaneously fundamental, binding, and permanent within each Member State. The reason why the constitutional basis remains non-binding presumably lies in the will of the Member States to give a useful and binding effect to the Golden Rule at short notice without the constitutional rules, in particular those relating to the revision of the Constitution, representing a blockage for some Member States.

The non-binding nature of the constitutionalization of the Golden Rule results not only from the text and the political will of the TSCG participating States but also from the contingent nature of any Constitution. A Constitution is, by its nature, not intended to accommodate a rule such as the Golden Rule. There is no constitutional right by default. A Constitution does not have such content, or part of its content, which would naturally be constitutional, some provisions having a priori to be included in the Constitution. On the contrary, the constitutionalization of a principle or a rule is a judgment of value, of the order of the contingent, and not of the order of necessity. That is why it is difficult to say that a rule such as the Golden Rule must necessarily receive a constitutional basis. The constitutionalization of the Golden Rule raises questions for each State to decide. Does this rule reflect a fundamental social consensus? Does it respond to a profound and significant need for a society that lives in the long term? Or does it embody an ideological – notably economic – option which is not the responsibility of the constituent power but of the political majority in power or, what the Americans call, 'today's majority'[22]? In other words, is the choice of the society that conveys the Golden Rule the responsibility of the constituent power or of the legislator? This dilemma is beyond the competence of the European Union and is the sole responsibility of the States.

21 Victor Ferreres Comella, 'Amending the National Constitutions to Save the Euro: Is This the Right Strategy?' (2013) 48 *Texas International Law Journal* 229.

22 Laurence Tribe, *American Constitutional Law* (Foundation Press 2000), 18.

B. IS THE CONSTITUTIONAL OPTION APPROPRIATE?

This question must be well understood. Asked about the draft seeking to incorporate in the French Constitution the requirement for each new government to set a five-year structural deficit target at the beginning of the legislature, Dominique Rousseau observed that 'the purpose of the Constitution is to determine a framework within which public policies are conducted', but 'does not have to define its content'.[23] This argument has been adopted by those who oppose any undertaking to constitutionalize the Golden Rule. Rousseau's observation does not seem to be entirely relevant. By setting the framework for public policies, a Constitution inevitably determines part of their content. Any Constitution contains rules that substantially limit the autonomy of the legislature in the development of laws. Thus, the consecration by the constituent power of a fundamental right, whether civil or political, economic, social, or cultural, implies for the State, and especially for the legislature, the obligation to carry out positive and concrete actions in favor of a more effective protection of this right, or also the obligation, under certain conditions, not to regress in the protection of that right ('stand-still'). Like it or not, the Constitution is not limited to framing public policies. It also guides them.

This preliminary remark being made, it is a matter of questioning the strengths and limitations not only of the Golden Rule as such but also of the constitutionalization of this rule. These are different things, although it is not always easy to distinguish them clearly. In all States parties to the TSCG, this aspect was the subject of more or less detailed discussions, which mobilized parliamentarians, whether at the time of ratifying or at the time of giving effect to the TSCG, judges, especially constitutional judges and, of course, the doctrine. The answers to this question are very different from one State to another. Thus, while States like Germany, Italy, and Spain have carried out constitutional revisions, others, such as France and Belgium, have refused to do so.[24]

Indeed, there is no shortage of objections against the constitutionalization of the Golden Rule.

Constitutional symbolism. When one considers the constitutionalization of the Golden Rule, one cannot fail to notice that it is rich in symbolism on the meaning of 'living together'. The viability of a political community, or indeed of any social group, depends on the existence of a number of collective benchmarks. Today, the problem is that in Europe these benchmarks are increasingly linked to economic logic. The democratic space is dominated by economic discourse. Public policies are assessed mainly on the basis of economic parameters. Efficiency and performance have become the key words of political messages. This symbolism nurtures the apprehensions of the opponents of a constitutionalization of the Golden Rule. To constitutionalize the Golden

23 *Le Monde* (May 20, 2010), www.lemonde.fr/politique/article/2010/05/20/deficit-il-est-dangereux-d-inscrire-dans-la-constitution-une-obligation-qui-ne-pourra-pas-etre-tenue_1360813_823448.html

24 See *infra*.

Rule does not only mean to 'constitutionalize austerity',[25] but it is also a way to legitimize the transfer of economic logic to all aspects of society and to perpetuate the current divide between the partisans and the opponents of the 'economic whole', which profoundly divides contemporary societies.

Modern constitutionalism. As noted earlier in this chapter, many observers question the ability of the Golden Rule to lead to greater control over public finances in the euro area. Since the end of the Second World War, European constitutionalism has evolved in the direction of reinforcing the effectiveness of constitutional norms. Of course, the Constitution has always, in one way or another, provided models of conduct. It has always been meant to be observed by its recipients. In short, neither its normativity nor its compulsory character has ever been seriously challenged. On the other hand, for a long time there has been a lack of interest in the problem of the effectiveness of the Constitution – that is to say, knowing whether constitutional norms are generally obeyed or applied. This is where the modernity of constitutional law lies: in its 'jurisdictionalization' and its capacity to guarantee its effectiveness through judicial channels. If it were to prove that the Golden Rule was powerless to stabilize the Eurozone and promote growth, its constitutionalization would represent a regression in relation to this evolution of constitutionalism.

The rigidity of constitutional norms. The rigidity of constitutional texts is an element that has encouraged or compelled the States not to include the Golden Rule in their constitutions, which cannot be revised or cannot be revised within a reasonable period of time. In Belgium, strictly speaking, even had there been the political will to constitutionalize the budgetary Golden Rule, a revision of the Constitution in this sense would have been impossible.[26] Whether it is about inserting the Golden Rule in Title V of the Constitution ('On Finance'), or inserting in Title I*bis* of the Constitution ('On general political objectives of federal Belgium, the communities and the regions'), which is a new article, comparable to Article 7*bis*, [27] the declaration of the revision of the 2010 Constitution would not permit it in either case.[28]

25 Floris de Witte, 'EU Law, Politics, and the Social Question' (2013) 14 *German Law Journal* 589.

26 The revision of the Constitution is regulated by article 195 of the Constitution. According to this article, the federal legislative power can, in the legislative period, '*declare that there are reasons to revise such constitutional provision as it determines*'. Then, the two Houses – the House of Representatives and the Senate – 'are automatically dissolved' and elections are organized. After the elections, the new Houses '*make decisions, in common accord with the King, on the points submitted for revision*'. It is stated that the Houses can only debate provided at least two-thirds of the members who make up each House are present; and no change is adopted unless it is supported by at least two-thirds of the votes cast.

27 Art. 7*bis* of the Constitution: 'In the exercise of their respective competences, the Federal State, the Communities and the Regions pursue the objectives of sustainable development in its social, economic and environmental aspects, taking into account the solidarity between the generations.'

28 See *Parliamentary Documents*, Senate (2011–2012) 5-1499/1.

However, constitutional rigidity has another consequence, this time concerning the implementation of the Golden Rule. In Belgium, in an opinion issued on September 18, 2012, on the preliminary draft law approving the TSCG, the legislative section of the Council of State, while stressing that the constitutional option lies solely within the discretion of the constituent power, cautioned that:

> If we were to opt for an incorporation of the rules in question or at least their essential elements in the Constitution, [...] attention should be drawn to the fact that such precedent, by the rigidity which it entails, may make it more difficult to take into account the common principles which the European Commission must propose to the States under the second sentence of Article 3 (2) of the Treaty, on the basis of which the automatic correction mechanism referred to in that provision and in Article 3 (1) (e) must be introduced, taking into account in particular the possibility for these 'common principles' to change over time, particularly in the light of fluctuations in the economic context.[29]

The Council of State refers here to the common principles which should guide the States in determining the nature, extent, and timing of the measures to be implemented in order to correct any significant discrepancies found.

The relative effectiveness of a constitutionalization. At first glance, one may be tempted to think that the higher it climbs the hierarchy of norms, the more effective the Golden Rule will be in the national legal system. However, there are often pitfalls in the States concerned, which contribute to reducing the effectiveness of a constitutionalized Golden Rule.

There are, primarily, pitfalls linked to the particularities of constitutional litigation. In Belgium, for example, the constitutionality of budgetary legislative norms, as well as all norms having the force of law, falls within the exclusive competence of the Constitutional Court. However, the latter exercises a constitutional control which does not extend to the whole of the constitutional text. In its Title V on finance, only Articles 170 and 172 of the Constitution are among the standards of reference for constitutional judges. If the Golden Rule is included in the Constitution, Article 142 of the Constitution, which establishes the Constitutional Court and defines its powers, should therefore be revised in order to extend the Court's control to the observance of this rule. Otherwise, constitutionalization would be ineffective.

There is also a pitfall related to the jurisprudence of constitutional courts. What will happen when a constitutional court has to exercise control over the Golden Rule? In case of non-compliance, could it do anything other than entirely cancel the challenged budget? That would be a heavy responsibility, which would generate the greatest legal uncertainty. This is the reason why one would think that constitutional judges would decide on a very marginal

29 *Parliamentary Documents*, Senate (2012–2013) 5-1939/1, 53.

control. Moreover, a comparative examination of constitutional jurisprudence shows that, as a general rule, constitutional courts are very reluctant to extend their control to the heart of budgetary arrangements, especially in times of economic crisis, when the temptation of the 'judicial restraint' is even stronger.

Finally, there is a pitfall linked to the intergovernmental nature of the TSCG, which formally diverts from the EU law domain. To the extent that the TSCG does not extend to the provisions contained in it the mechanism for a preliminary ruling (under Article 267 of the TFEU), it is not possible for constitutional courts to refer to the Court of Justice of the European Union preliminary rulings on the interpretation of Article 3 (1) of the TSCG. Would it not be logical for a constitutional court notified with a dispute regarding the compatibility of a budget with the constitutional rule internalizing the Golden Rule, in the event of uncertainty as to its exact scope, to refer it to the Court of Justice?[30]

2 *The choice of the constitutional option*

Several States have opted for the constitutional option. Here, we consider the cases of Germany, Spain, and Italy. Germany is the paradigmatic example of a State that has opted for the constitutional way. It did so in 2009, without waiting to be bound by the TSCG.[31]

30 Comella (n 21) 240.

31 Article 109 of the German Constitution lays down the following rules:

(1) The Federation and the *Länder* shall be autonomous and independent of one another in the management of their respective budgets.

(2) The Federation and the *Länder* shall perform jointly the obligations of the Federal Republic of Germany resulting from legal acts of the European Community for the maintenance of budgetary discipline pursuant to Article 104 of the Treaty Establishing the European Community and shall, within this framework, give due regard to the requirements of overall economic equilibrium.

(3) The budgets of the Federation and the *Länder* shall in principle be balanced without revenue from credits. The Federation and *Länder* may introduce rules intended to take into account, symmetrically in times of upswing and downswing, the effects of market developments that deviate from normal conditions, as well as exceptions for natural disasters or unusual emergency situations beyond governmental control and substantially harmful to the state's financial capacity. For such exceptional regimes, a corresponding amortization plan must be adopted. Details for the budget of the Federation shall be governed by Article 115 with the proviso that the first sentence shall be deemed to be satisfied if revenue from credits does not exceed 0.35 percent in relation to the nominal gross domestic product. The *Länder* themselves shall regulate details for the budgets within the framework of their constitutional powers, the proviso being that the first sentence shall only be deemed to be satisfied if no revenue from credits is admitted.

(4) A federal law requiring the consent of the Bundesrat may establish principles applicable to both the Federation and the *Länder* governing budgetary law, the responsiveness of budgetary management to economic trends, and long-term financial planning.

(5) Sanctions imposed by the European Community on the basis of the provisions of Article 104 of the Treaty Establishing the European Community in the

In Spain, the Constitution was revised on September 27, 2011[32] due to an agreement between the Spanish Socialist Party, in power under the Zapatero Government, and the People's Party, then in opposition. The revision was subject to an urgent procedure that prevented any debate, whether among parliamentarians, citizens, or lawyers.[33] A new Article 135 was adopted.[34]

interest of maintaining budgetary discipline, shall be borne by the Federation and the *Länder* at a ratio of 65 to 35 percent. In solidarity, the *Länder* as a whole shall bear 35 percent of the charges incumbent on the *Länder* according to the number of their inhabitants; 65 percent of the charges incumbent on the *Länder* shall be borne by the *Länder* according to their degree of causation. Details shall be regulated by a federal law which shall require the consent of the Bundesrat.

32 *Boletin Oficial del Estado*, September 27, 2011, n° 233.

33 See Marc Carrillo, 'La Cour constitutionnelle et l'équilibre des finances publiques: Espagne' (2012) 28 *Annuaire international de justice constitutionnelle* 206–207.

34 The new Article 135 reads as follows:

1. All public administrations will conform to the principle of budgetary stability.

2. The State and the Self-governing Communities may not incur a structural deficit that exceeds the limits established by the European Union for their member states.

An Organic Act shall determine the maximum structural deficit the state and the Self-governing Communities may have, in relation to its gross domestic product. Local authorities must submit a balanced budget.

3. The State and the Self-governing Communities must be authorized by Act in order to issue Public Debt bonds or to contract loans.

Loans to meet payment on the interest and capital of the State's Public Debt shall always be deemed to be included in budget expenditure and their payment shall have absolute priority. These appropriations may not be subject to amendment or modification as long as they conform to the terms of issue.

The volume of public debt of all the public administrations in relation to the State's gross domestic product may not exceed the benchmark laid down by the Treaty on the Functioning of the European Union.

4. The limits of the structural deficit and public debt volume may be exceeded only in case of natural disasters, economic recession or extraordinary emergency situations that are beyond the control of the State and significantly impair either the financial situation or the economic or social sustainability of the State, as appreciated by an absolute majority of the members of the Congress of Deputies.

5. An Organic Act shall develop the principles referred to in this article, as well as participation in the respective procedures of the organs of institutional coordination between government fiscal policy and financial support. In any case, the Organic Act shall address:

a. The distribution of the limits of deficit and debt among the different public administrations, the exceptional circumstances to overcome them and the manner and time in which to correct the deviations on each other.

The methodology and procedure for calculating the structural deficit.

c. The responsibility of each public administration in case of breach of budgetary stability objectives.

6. The Self-governing Communities, in accordance with their respective laws and within the limits referred to in this article, shall take the appropriate procedures for effective implementation of the principle of stability in their rules and budgetary decisions.

In Italy, Constitutional Law No. 1 of April 20, 2012, introduced in the Constitution the budgetary balance rule ('pareggio di bilancio'),[35] through the hasty approval by a large majority of political forces.[36] A new Article 81 was adopted.[37] Italy's constitutional path is particularly problematic. Indeed, unlike most States using the European model of constitutional justice, in Italy individuals do not have the right to challenge directly the constitutionality of legislative norms through an action for annulment comparable to what exists in Germany, for example, as the Italian constituent power remains anxious about allowing purely abstract disputes before the Constitutional Court. As a result, there is no adequate control of compliance with the new Article 81 of the Constitution.[38]

B The legislative option

In France, according to Article 54 of the Constitution, the Constitutional Council is notified of the constitutionality of the TSCG. In its decision of August 9, 2012,[39] the Council opened the door to two possible solutions: a constitutional revision or the adoption of an organic law. But it considered that these solutions represent only one option of the alternatives offered by the provisions of Article 3 (2) of the TSCG. Indeed, according to the Constitutional Council:

> [U]nder the second alternative, the aforementioned provisions leave the States with the freedom to determine the provisions the full respect for and

35 *Gazzetta Ufficiale*, April 23, 2011, n° 95.

36 See Massimo Luciani, 'La Cour constitutionnelle et l'équilibre des finances publiques: Italie' (2012) 28 *Annuaire international de justice constitutionnelle* 346–347.

37 The new Article 135 reads as follows:

The State shall balance revenue and expenditure in its budget, taking account of the adverse and favorable phases of the economic cycle.

No recourse shall be made to borrowing except for the purpose of taking account of the effects of the economic cycle or, subject to authorization by the two Houses approved by an absolute majority vote of their Members, in exceptional circumstances.

Any law involving new or increased expenditure shall provide for the resources to cover such expenditure.

Each year the Houses shall pass a law approving the budget and the accounts submitted by the Government.

Provisional implementation of the budget shall not be allowed except by specific legislation and only for periods not exceeding four months in total.

The content of the budget law, the fundamental rules and the criteria adopted to ensure balance between revenue and expenditure and the sustainability of general government debt shall be established by legislation approved by an absolute majority of the Members of each House in compliance with the principles established with a constitutional law.

38 Tania Groppi, 'The Impact of the Financial Crisis on the Italian written Constitution' (2012) 4 *Italian Journal of Public Law* 13.

39 See n 4.

> adherence to which 'otherwise' guarantees that the rules on balanced public finances will take effect under national law; that in this case, adherence to the rules laid down in paragraph 1 of Article 3 will not be guaranteed by provisions 'of binding force'; that on the one hand, it is for the Member States to determine, for the purpose of ensuring that their commitment is respected, the provisions having the effect required under paragraph 2; that on the other hand, the Treaty stipulates that adherence to the rules laid down in paragraph 1 of Article 3 will not be guaranteed under national law by a provision that is hierarchically superior to legislation.
>
> (§ 22)

The Constitutional Council thus suggests that the Golden Rule should be transposed into the multi-annual Public Finance Act that would be framed by an organic law, which would limit itself to specifying, in compliance with the Constitution, the concepts to be used in the planning act.

In line with the decision of the Constitutional Council, the second alternative was preferred to the first. Thus, on December 27, 2012, an organic law on the planning and governance of public finances was adopted.[40] The solution ultimately adopted by the French authorities gave rise to various reactions on the part of the doctrine. Objections were raised to a part of it. Among other criticisms, it has been argued, on the one hand, that the reasoning of the Constitutional Council is based on an erroneously broad interpretation of Article 3 (2) of the TSCG and, on the other hand, the fact that the multi-annual planning acts have no legislative character.[41]

In Belgium, in its advisory opinion of September 18, 2012, the legislative section of the Council of State referred to the possibility of the adoption of a special law.[42] The special laws are federal statutes. They are hierarchically inferior to the Constitution, even if they are superior to ordinary laws. Indeed, they are voted by the House of Representatives and the Senate, which is not the case for all ordinary laws. In addition, special laws are voted under stricter conditions than those set for the adoption of ordinary laws: they require, in particular, a majority of votes in each linguistic group – the Dutch linguistic group and the French linguistic group –represented in each of the federal assemblies. The adoption of special acts is only necessary in cases expressly stipulated in the Constitution. In this case, the adoption of a special act would have involved the inclusion in the Constitution of a provision authorizing the special legislator to legislate in this matter.

40 *Journal officiel de la République française* (December 18, 2012). See Eric Oliva, 'La Cour constitutionnelle et l'équilibre des finances publiques: France' (2012) 28 *Annuaire international de justice constitutionnelle* 305–306.

41 Roux (n 4) 869–870.

42 See n 27, 53.

C The contractual option

In Belgium, discussions promptly took place at the House of Representatives and in the Senate. They were held, notably, within the House of Representatives Commission for Finance and Budget and within the Federal Advisory Committee on European Affairs, which is composed of members of the House of Representatives and the Senate.[43] It should be also noted that a motion for a resolution was tabled at the House of Representatives calling for the organization of a national consultation on the Treaty on Stability, Coordination and Governance in the Economic and Monetary Union.[44] However, such consultation is not authorized by the Belgian Constitution.

In a federal state like Belgium, the coordination of budgetary policies must be both 'fair and efficient, in order to distribute the effort adequately between entities, while making it possible to achieve the objectives established together with the European Commission' and 'sufficiently flexible to guarantee the fiscal and financial autonomy of the federated entities'.[45]

Prime Minister Elio Di Rupo said at first that

> the question of whether the transposition of this rule in Belgium will be done through constitutional revision or a special law, has yet to be examined and will be the object of a consultation with the communities and regions, according to internal procedures.[46]

In the end, the government has chosen the conventional path. It should be noted that, in matters requiring minimal harmonization, the federal government, the communities, and the regions 'may conclude cooperation agreements which concern, in particular, the joint establishment and management of common services and institutions, the joint exercise of their powers, or the development of joint initiatives'.[47] The agreements that relate to matters regulated by the legislator, as well as the agreements that may affect the federal community, a particular community, region, or individual citizens, have legal effect only after they have received the consent of the legislator concerned.

43 See *Parliamentary Documents*, House of Representatives (2011–2012) 53-2031/1 and Senate (2011–2012) 5-1460/1; *Parliamentary Documents*, House of Representatives (2011–2012) 53-2048/1; *Parliamentary Documents*, House of Representatives (2011–2012) 53-2102/1.

44 *Parliamentary Documents*, House of Representatives (2011–2012) 53-2105/1.

45 Benoît Bayenet, Marc Bourgeois, Maxime Uhoda, 'Les mécanismes de coordination des finances publiques en Belgique dans le cadre de la nouvelle gouvernance budgétaire européenne' (2013) 3 *Revue de fiscalité régionale et locale* 225.

46 *Parliamentary Documents*, House of Representatives (2011–2012) 53-2031/1; Senate (2011–2012) 5-1460/1, 7.

47 Art. 92*bis* § 1, al. 1, of the Special Institutional Reform Act of August 8, 1980; art. 42 of the Special Brussels Institutions Act of January 12, 1989; art. 55*bis* of the Institutional Reform Act for the German-speaking Community of December 31, 1983.

How did we get there?

In its advisory opinion of September 18, 2012, the legislative section of the Council of State stressed that the choice of the legal mechanism to guarantee 'full respect and strict observance' of the Golden Rule 'throughout the budgetary process', according to the terms of Article 3 (2) of the TSCG, 'depends to a large extent on the option to be made by the Belgian authorities'.[48] According to the advisory opinion, it is essential that the chosen mechanism is effective in achieving its objective in all 'public administrations' under the terms of Article 3 (2) of the TSCG – that is, 'in both the federal authority and the communities, regions, and subordinate powers'.[49] That being said, the Council of State appears to favor the conventional path, which has the advantage of greater flexibility than the other two options.

Thus, on November 29, 2013, the federal entity and the federated entities concluded a cooperation agreement to implement Article 3 (1) of the TSCG.[50] In this agreement, all parties undertake to include in their budgets the objective of balancing the accounts of public administration as provided by Article 3 of the TSCG (Article 2 (1)). The parties agreed that

> this rule is considered to be observed by Belgium if the annual structural balance of all public authorities reaches the mid-term objective or observes the convergence trajectory towards it, as defined in the Program of Stability, the lower limit being a structural deficit of 0.5% of the GDP.
>
> (Article 2 (2) para. 1)

Two easing measures are planned. On the one hand, 'this limit may [...] be raised to a structural deficit of up to 1% where the ratio of the government debt-to-GDP ratio is substantially less than 60% and long-term risks for the sustainability of public finances are weak' (Article 2 (2) para. 2). On the other hand, 'a temporary deviation from the mid-term objective or the adjustment path is only allowed in exceptional circumstances' (Article 2 (3)). It is also envisaged that 'the annual budgetary targets for all public authorities, defined in structural terms in accordance with the methods of the European Commission, shall be distributed in nominal and structural terms among the different levels of power of the whole of public authorities', while 'the nominal and structural setting of the individual budgetary objectives of the contracting parties and local authorities will be approved by a decision of the Concertation

48 See (n 28) 51.

49 Ibid.

50 *Moniteur belge*, January 16, 2014. Also see Eloïse Beauvironnet-Blot and Jean-François Boudet, 'Régionalisme belge et décentralisation française à l'épreuve du Pacte de stabilité et de croissance (PSC) réformé et du Traité sur la stabilité, la coordination et la gouvernance' (2015) 2 *Revue du Droit de l'Union européenne* 191–219; Dimitri Yernault, 'La dette publique dans le système constitutionnel et federal belge' in Fred Morrison (ed.) *Fiscal Rules – Limits on Governmental Deficits and Debt* (Springer 2016), 48.

Committee' (Article 2 (4)). As provided by the TSCG, correction mechanisms are organized (Article 4 (2)) and the High Council of Finance is responsible for assessing compliance with the commitments entered into by the parties to the cooperation agreement and, where appropriate, for ensuring the adoption and implementation of the corrective measures taken by the parties (Articles 4 (1) and (3)). Finally, the cooperation agreement states that 'a financial penalty imposed by the Council of the European Union for non-compliance with the budgetary commitments entered into shall be allocated, as appropriate, among the contracting parties in proportion to the deficiencies identified by the High Council of Finance'.

As a result of this cooperation agreement, the reactions of the various contracting parties were very different. Some, such as the Flemish Community, have not taken any further initiative related to the existing rules on the budgetary framework which were considered to be sufficient. Others, such as the Walloon Region, have opted for an amendment to the legislation on the budget. Others, such as the Brussels Region, preferred to settle the matter in the legislative act of assent to the cooperation agreement. This disparity is not surprising in a federal state where political majorities are not the same at all levels of power.[51]

The effectiveness of the formula adopted by Belgium depends on the combination of two conditions.

First, the effectiveness of the formula depends on the legal force granted to cooperation agreements, in particular to those agreements that have received legislative approval. It is essential that they are recognized as superior in authority to ordinary legislative standards. Admitting the argument that such an agreement would have merely legislative force, it 'would allow a partner to unilaterally shake off obligations it has entered into in a contractual framework'. Therefore, such an agreement 'must take precedence over the internal law of the various public authorities in the same way as the provisions of international law which have a direct effect on the domestic legal system take precedence over the provisions of domestic law'.[52] With regard to the implementation of the Golden Rule, this does not seem to have been seriously disputed.

Second, the effectiveness of the formula depends on the sanctions that may apply to legislators that fail to observe the terms of the cooperation agreement of November 29, 2013. In particular, whether the Constitutional Court could invalidate a budget law that does not observe the commitments stipulated in the cooperation agreement remains an open question because such a situation has not yet occurred. It is important to note that, even if they recognize a legislative value superior to ordinary laws, cooperation agreements are not part

51 On the implementation of the TSCG in Bruxelles law, see Bruno Lombaert and Marc Oswald, 'Les finances publiques régionales: l'autonomie sous pression européenne' in Pierre-Oliver de Broux, Bruno Lombaert and Dimitri Yernault (eds), *Le droit bruxellois. Un bilan après 25 ans d'application (1989–2014)* (Bruylant 2015), 227–235.

52 Marc Uyttendaele, *Trente leçons de droit constitutionnel* (Bruylant 2014), 959.

of the 'bloc de constitutionnalité' mobilized by the constitutional judges. However, the fact remains that, since 2014, the Constitutional Court has the jurisdiction to rule on applications for annulment and preliminary rulings when the alleged violation concerns Article 143 (1) of the Constitution according to which, in the exercise of their respective powers, the federal government and the federated communities 'act with respect for federal loyalty, in order to prevent conflicts of interest'.[53] The Constitutional Court did not wait for this reform to consider that federal loyalty implies an obligation 'not to disrupt the balance of the federal construction as a whole', so that this principle 'concerns more than the mere exercise of powers: it indicates the spirit in which it should be done'.[54] The federal loyalty stipulated in Article 143 (1) of the Constitution is just one example of such constitutional norms which, although drafted in imperative terms, have their normative density weakened by the use of a 'standard'.[55] The administrative and judicial authorities responsible for its application can only enjoy their broader margin of appreciation. The role of the Constitutional Court in determining the content of Article 143 (1) is now affirmed – 'ratified'[56] – officially by the special legislator. Let us hope that the Constitutional Court will see an incentive to draw from federal loyalty all the consequences that ought to be attached to it. Would lack of knowledge of the cooperation agreement of November 29, 2013, reflect, under certain conditions, a breach of federal loyalty[57] The effectiveness of the formula adopted by the Belgian authorities depends largely on this.

Céline Romainville wrote:

> [T]his agreement is a good example of a response to exogenous pressures in a context of important endogenous tensions. It develops an incompletely theorized agreement because it reaches an agreement on certain principles while leaving other issues undecided, such as enforcement in case one of the parties to the cooperation agreement does not comply with its terms[58]

In this respect, the solution devised in Belgium is typical of the underlying driving forces that are at play in Belgian federalism. Belgium enjoys another

53 Art. 1, 3°, and 26, § 1, 4°, of the Special act of January 6, 1989, on the Constitutional Court, added in 2014.

54 Belgian Constitutional Court, 119/2004, June 30, 2004, B.3.2; 124/2010, October 28, 2010, B.39.1; 7/2012, January 18, 2012, B.11.1.

55 Charles-Hubert Born and Marc Verdussen, 'Le soft law intraconstitutionnel' in Isabelle Hachez, Yves Cartuyvels, Hugues Dumont, Philippe Gérard, François Ost and Michel Van de Kerchove (eds), *Les sources du droit revisitées, vol. I – Normes internationales et constitutionnelles* (Presses de l'Université Saint-Louis 2012), 526–527.

56 *Parliamentary Documents*, Senate (2012–2013) 5-2232/5, 284.

57 See Paul Dermine, 'La loyauté fédérale et la sixième réforme de l'Etat: Essai d'interprétation' (2015) 2 *Administration publique* 39.

58 Celine Romainville, 'Dynamics of Belgian Plurinational Federalism: A Small State under Pressure' (2015) 38 *Boston College International and Comparative Law Review* 249.

particularity, of a political nature, likely to significantly complicate the implementation of its budgetary commitments: parliamentary majorities at federal level and those of the federated entities are not symmetrical and, sometimes, they are diametrically opposed. Such a situation, inherent in federalism, generates in Belgium a situation of perpetual confrontation between levels of power. Thus, in April 2015, the Federal Minister of Finance provided the regions with new tax data, which obliged them to correct their budgetary trajectories, only to find that the data transmitted were incorrect.

Nevertheless, according to the analysis of the Conseil Supérieur des Finances, in July 2020,[59] with the exception of the Belgian Stability Programme 2018–2021 on the trajectory to be followed by general government, no consensus has been reached between the contracting parties since the entry into force of the cooperation agreement and therefore no agreement on budgetary targets has been reached.

However, it must be noted that at the level of certain federated authorities, dissatisfaction with the European criteria for budgetary convergence is increasingly noticeable. Thus, on December 13, 2016, a motion for a resolution 'aimed at adapting European budgetary and accounting constraints to stimulate public investment' was tabled with the office of the Parliament of the Brussels-Capital Region. This proposal requests the Brussels Government to defend 'a revision of the European system of accounts to ensure that public authorities can spread over several financial years the investment expenditure which has strategic and economic added value'.

In conclusion, we find it useful to refer briefly to the health crisis triggered by Covid-19. On 20 May 2020, the Council of the European Union addressed a recommendation to Belgium 'on the 2020 National Reform Programme of Belgium and delivering a Council opinion on the 2020 Stability Programme of Belgium'.[60] The Council notes that

> in response to the COVID-19 pandemic, and as part of a coordinated Union approach, Belgium has adopted budgetary measures to increase the capacity of its health system, contain the pandemic, and provide relief to those individuals and sectors that have been particularly affected.
>
> (§14)

Some examples of these measures include a temporary federal unemployment benefit scheme, income compensation for the self-employed, federal provision for crisis-related expenditure, and various regional allowances for companies and sectoral subsidies. According to the 2020 Belgian Stability Programme, those budgetary measures amounted to 2.3% of GDP. The Council states that:

59 Conseil supérieur des finances, Section 'Besoin de financement des pouvoirs publics', Avis, Analyse des réalisations budgétaires récentes (July 2020) 116.

60 COM(2020) 501 final, https://ec.europa.eu/info/sites/info/files/2020-european-semester-csr-comm-recommendation-belgium_en.pdf, accessed 29 January 2021.

> Overall, the measures taken by Belgium are in line with the guidelines set out in the Commission Communication on a coordinated economic response to the COVID-19 outbreak. The full implementation of those measures, followed by a refocusing of fiscal policies towards achieving prudent medium-term fiscal positions when economic conditions allow, will contribute to preserving fiscal sustainability in the medium term.
>
> (§14)

However, as things stand at present (the pandemic is still ongoing), it is too early to accurately measure the budgetary impact of this crisis on public finances.

Bibliography

Bayenet B, Bourgeois M, Uhoda M, 'Les mécanismes de coordination des finances publiques en Belgique dans le cadre de la nouvelle gouvernance budgétaire européenne' (2013) 3 *Revue de fiscalité régionale et locale* 225

Beauvironnet-Blot E, Boudet JF, 'Régionalisme belge et décentralisation française à l'épreuve du Pacte de stabilité et de croissance (PSC) réformé et du Traité sur la stabilité, la coordination et la gouvernance' (2015) 2 *Revue du Droit de l'Union européenne* 191

Bonichot J-C, 'Le juge constitutionnel français et la "règle d'or": réviser ou ne pas réviser la Constitution? That was the question' in Vincent Kronenberger, Maria Teresa d'Alessio, Valerio Placo (eds), *De Rome à Lisbonne: les juridictions de l'Union européenne à la croisée des Chemins - Mélanges en l'honneur de Paolo Mengozzi* (Bruylant 2013) 371

Chiti E, Teixeira PG, 'The Constitutional Implications of the European Responses to the Financial and Public Debt Crisis' (2013) 50 *Common Market Law Review* 683

Craig P, 'The Stability, Coordination and Governance Treaty: Principle, Politics and Pragmatism' (2012) 37 *European Law Review* 231

Dawson M, de Witte F, 'Constitutional Balance in the EU after the Euro-Crisis' (2013) 76 *Modern Law Review* 826

Dermine P, 'La Belgique face à la règle d'or sur l'incorporation de l'article 3, § 1er, du Traité de stabilité, de coopération et de gouvernance au sein de l'ordre juridique belge ' (2014) 21 *Revue belge de droit constitutionnel* 177

Dermine P, 'La loyauté fédérale et la sixième réforme de l'Etat: Essai d'interprétation' (2015) 2 *Administration publique* 39

Dermine P, 'Le Traité de Stabilité, de Coopération et de gouvernance au sein de l'Union économique et monétaire et l'internalisation de la Golden Rule par les Etats membres de l'Union européenne' (2014 Supplement) *Romanian Journal of Comparative Law* 79

Fabbrini F, 'The Fiscal Compact, the "Golden Rule", and the Paradox of European Federalism' (2013) 36 *Boston College International & Comparative Law Review* 1

Ferreres Comella V, 'Amending the National Constitutions to Save the Euro: Is This the Right Strategy?' (2013) 48 *Texas International Law Journal* 223

Groppi T, 'The Impact of the Financial Crisis on the Italian written Constitution' (2012) 4 *Italian Journal of Public Law* 13

Habermas J, *La constitution de l'Europe* (Gallimard 2012)

Habermas J, 'The Crisis of the European Union in the Light of a Constitutionalization of International Law' (2012) 23 *European Journal of International Law* 335

Lombaert B, Oswald M, 'Les finances publiques régionales: l'autonomie sous pression européenne' in Pierre-Oliver de Broux, Bruno Lombaert and Dimitri Yernault (eds), *Le droit bruxellois. Un bilan après 25 ans d'application (1989–2014)* (Bruylant 2015)

Luciani M, 'La Cour constitutionnelle et l'équilibre des finances publiques: Italie' (2012) 28 *Annuaire international de justice constitutionnelle* 346

Mayer C, 'ESM Treaty in Accordance with the Austrian Constitution' (2013) 7 *Vienna Journal on International Constitutional Law* 385

Oliva E, 'La Cour constitutionnelle et l'équilibre des finances publiques: France' (2012) 28 *Annuaire international de justice constitutionnelle* 305

Oliva E, 'Le pacte de stabilité devant les juridictions constitutionnelles' (2012) 28 *Revue française de droit administratif* 1043

Romainville C, 'Dynamics of Belgian Plurinational Federalism: A Small State under Pressure' (2015) 38 *Boston College International and Comparative Law Review* 249

Roux J, 'Le Conseil constitutionnel et le TSCG' (2012) 4 *Revue trimestrielle de droit européen* 855

Schramek C, 'European Fiscal Compact is Held to be in Accordance with the Constitution' (2014) 8 *Vienna Journal on International Constitutional Law* 218

Verdussen M, Maniscalco L, Wattier S, 'La Cour constitutionnelle et l'équilibre des finances publique: Belgique' (2012) 28 *Annuaire international de justice constitutionnelle* 127–155

Wendel M, 'Judicial Restraint and the Return to Openness: The Decision of the German Federal Constitutional Court on the ESM and the Fiscal Treaty of 12 September 2012' (2013) 14 *German Law Journal* 21–52

de Witte F, 'EU Law, Politics, and the Social Question' (2013) 14 *German Law Journal* 589

Yernault D, 'La dette publique dans le système constitutionnel et federal belge' in Fred Morrison (ed.), *Fiscal Rules – Limits on Governmental Deficits and Debt* (Springer 2016)

Part III

Balanced budget and separation of powers

5 Balanced budget rule and representative democracy

A comparative analysis

Giulia Aravantinou Leonidi[1]

Introduction

In response to the 2008 financial crisis, recent reforms of the European Union's economic governance arrangements leading to the introduction and, in some cases, the constitutionalization of the balanced budget rule, have empowered governments and supranational institutions to the detriment of national parliaments. Representative democracy thus appears to be severely challenged both at national and at supranational levels, despite attempts to restore it by formally enhancing the role of national parliaments in the EU decision-making process. Contemporary scholarship has identified and examined a general trend described as "deparliamentarization",[2] a process structurally rooted in, and connected to, the loss of importance of parliamentary institutions. The decline of the role of elective assemblies has been particularly noticeable in the implementation of the new budgetary constraints. This raises some fundamental questions about the implementation of the principle of representative democracy in the European Union and its endurance during the process of crisis-related legislation and implementation. In order to assess the state of representative democracy in the context of the implementation of the new economic governance, this chapter first discusses the concepts of democracy and representative democracy and their application to the European Union. In addition, it examines the ways in which representative democracy is enshrined as a founding principle of the European Union in the Lisbon Treaty and the effects of the implementation of the European economic governance measures following the onset of the Eurozone crisis.

1 Special appreciation is due to Dr. Ilenia Bernardini, Policy Advisor of the European Parliament specializing in budgetary affairs for her help by providing insights as an expert staff member of a European institution.

2 John O'Brennan, Tapio Raunio, 'Introduction: Deparliamentarization and European Integration' in John O'Brennan, Tapio Raunio (eds), *National Parliaments within the Enlarged European Union, From 'Victims' of Integration to Competitive Actors?* (Routledge 2007), 1–26. See also Dieter Grimm, 'Il ruolo dei Parlamenti nazionali nell'Unione europea' in Fulco Lanchester (ed.), *Parlamenti nazionali e Unione Europea nella governance multilivello, atti del convegno Roma – Camera dei Deputati 12–13 maggio 2015* (Giuffrè 2016), 19–32.

DOI: 10.4324/9781315181882-9

In terms of methodology, my analysis draws on comparative law to identify lessons from the responses of four legal systems relevant to the implementation of the new economic governance. The empirical basis of the analysis consists of a comparative examination of the constitutionalization of budgetary constraints and the role played by national parliaments in the selected case studies. The conclusions of my analysis are derived from an assessment of the ways in which such reforms of the European Union's economic governance regime have empowered governments and supranational institutions to the detriment of national parliaments and that of representative democracy. The question of how to balance democratic legitimacy with the implementation of the Fiscal Compact is beyond the scope of this chapter. Nevertheless, this chapter seeks to contribute to the ongoing debate about the deepening of the European democratic deficit after the implementation of budget constraints.

In search of a European concept of representative democracy

Finding productive solutions to a fiscal crisis is a complicated endeavor for it involves fundamental issues that relate to the very essence of the concept of democracy and its relationship with debt control. Democracy is based on the Athenian meaning of the concept. According to the classic definition of Aristotle, democracy is "freedom and equality".[3] There are multiple ways of conceptualizing democracy and many different definitions of democracy have been proposed throughout the history of political thought: from Hobbes to Rousseau, from Locke to Stuart Mill. According to Bobbio, a democratic regime "is a set of procedural rules arriving at collective decisions in a way which accommodates and facilitates the fullest possible participation of interested parties".[4] A political system may therefore be considered legitimate when the people are sufficiently involved in the decision-making process or are adequately satisfied with the policy outcomes generated by the political system. In this perspective, democracy is a concept that does not concern only the States but can apply to any regime arriving at collective decisions as in the case of the European Union.

Robert Dahl sees democracy as a "twentieth-century phenomenon"[5] but it is in the twenty-first century that this concept is still evolving towards a new form of democracy, that of the European Union, whose borders are still blurry and undefined.[6]

It has been argued that one of the distinctive features of the European integration process is that "it takes place in a set of already existing representative democracies".[7] Arend Lijphart in his *Patterns of Democracy* maintains that the

3 Aristotle, *Pol.*, 1291 b, 34.
4 Norberto Bobbio, *The Future of Democracy: A Defence of the Rules of the Game* (University of Minnesota Press 1987).
5 Robert Dahl,*On Democracy* (Yale University Press 1998).
6 James Bohman, *Democracy Across Borders: From Demos to Demoi* (MIT 2007).
7 Erik Oddvar Eriksen, John Erik Fossum, *Rethinking Democracy and the European Union* (Routledge 2012).

most literal definition of representative democracy is government by the representatives of the people.[8] This paradigm has been subject to an unprecedented challenge by the economic crisis and its countermeasures.

Representative democracy is the main characteristic of contemporary democracies as the expression of the sovereign will of the *demos* that, through democratic elections, appoints its legitimate representatives. In the case of the European Union, one first distinction to be made is that there is no such demos, but many distinctive *demoi* which directly elect their representatives to the European Parliament, an institution which is still regarded as weak and uninfluential.[9]

In fact, although the European Parliament has gained further co-decision powers, its disconnection from the Commission, which does not represent the expression of a parliamentary majority, generates a wound at the very heart of representative democracy in Europe.

The Treaty of Lisbon strengthened the role of the European Parliament by recognizing its power to elect the President of the Commission on the basis of a proposal from the European Council and by taking into account the elections to the European Parliament (Article 17(7) TEU). The provision, which was applied for the first time in 2014, was intended to boost the democratic legitimacy of the EU decision-making process.[10]

Unfortunately, this attempt was not sufficient and the Lisbon Treaty was essentially a missed opportunity to further extend the European Parliament's powers in order to fill the democratic deficit gap.

8 In explaining the criteria for selecting the 36 democracies which build his theoretical argument, Lijphart fully accepts the eight criteria proposed by Robert A. Dahl in 1971 which define democracy as: the right to vote, the right to be elected, the right of political leaders to compete for support and votes, elections that are free and fair, freedom of association, freedom of expression, alternative sources of information and the dependence of institutions to make public choices on votes and on other expressions of preference. Arend Lijphart, *Patterns of Democracy: Government Forms and Performance in Thirty-Six Countries* (Yale University Press 1999).

9 The two main problems of parliamentarization are the lack of a demos and a weak European public sphere. Dieter Grimm, 'Il ruolo dei Parlamenti nazionali nell'Unione europea' in Fulco Lanchester (ed.), *Parlamenti nazionali e Unione Europea nella governance multilivello, atti del convegno Roma – Camera dei Deputati 12–13 maggio 2015* (Giuffrè 2016), 19–32.

10 As the process of European integration advanced, the demand for addressing the issues of democratic legitimacy also increased. The purpose of the wording of Article 17, paragraph 7 must be therefore interpreted as regarding the competence of the European Parliament. The President of the Commission is now "elected" and not "approved". The modifications introduced aim at establishing a meaningful relationship between people's will and the endorsement of the President of the Commission by the European Parliament which, in this way, increases the democratic legitimacy of the Commission in line with the principles of the parliamentary system.

The Eurozone crisis and the implementation of European economic governance have resulted in an increased marginalization of both the European Parliament and national parliaments, with preference being given to the intergovernmental method.[11] It has been in fact extensively acknowledged by scholarship that the intergovernmental nature of economic reforms has deeply eroded the principle of representative democracy in the European Union[12] by decreasing the quality of input and output legitimacy especially in States faced with the harshest bailout terms.

While the crisis has triggered exceptional measures implemented through exceptional means both at the EU and at the national level, it has also exposed the endemic weaknesses of the system. Such measures have sparked lively debates in national parliaments and electorates calling for new reforms to be implemented for the improvement of the functioning of European institutions.[13]

There are many ways in which a democracy can be organized as the EU case broadly demonstrates. The European Union structure is based on an extremely different model of representation than that of the nation-states. Consequently, representative democracy within the legal framework of the European Union must be subject to a careful revision which cannot be based on a model that applies exclusively to the State. The attempt to fill the democratic deficit by applying existing models may be considered inadequate, although during the past few years several prominent scholars have followed that theoretical path. One theoretical approach to addressing the democratic deficit proposed by a number of prominent scholars[14] is to fill such a democratic deficit through applying existing models. Such an approach, however, remains inadequate. In times of crisis, representative democracy has been constrained and has gone through severe limitations. The sovereign debt crisis and the consequent implementation of budgetary constraints applied to debtor States have led to a breach of the principles on which pluralist democracies are based. In this sense, risks of a further delegitimization of the EU have increased, especially where a Member State is placed under temporary receivership, as in the case of Greece.

Scholars have offered different solutions[15] among which is gaining credit the idea that the challenges faced by representative democracy can be effectively

11 On the intergovernmental method, see Paolo Ponzano, 'Méthode intergouvernementale ou méthode communautaire: une querelle sans intérêt?' (2011) 23 *Les Brefs the Notre Europe* 2–3; Sergio Fabbrini, 'Intergovernmentalism and Its Outcomes: The Implications of the Euro Crisis on the European Union' (2013) 1 *LUISS SoG Working Paper Series* 9–22.

12 Cristina Fasone, 'The Weakening of the European Parliament in the Framework of the New European Economic Governance', workshop *The Constitutional Architecture of the Economic Governance in the EU*, 23 Marzo 2012, EUI.

13 Simona Piattoni (ed.), *The European Union. Democratic Principles and Institutional Architectures in Times of Crisis* (Oxford University Press 2015). On the same position, see also Sergio Fabbrini, *Which European Union? Europe After the Euro Crisis* (Cambridge University Press 2015).

14 Simon Hix, *What's Wrong with the European Union and How to Fix It* (Polity Press 2008).

15 Federico Fabbrini, Ernst Hirsch Ballin, Han Somsen (eds), *What Form of Government for the European Union and the Eurozone?* (Hart Publishing 2015).

overcome by embracing a new notion of democracy in which both national parliaments and the European Parliament can play a key role.[16]

Representative democracy and the Treaties

At the time the European Economic Community was first established in 1957, the democratic nature of the community was not an issue of concern. Democratic accountability did not raise any serious concern as the community was based on functional expertise rather than on democratic participation. At the time, the European Parliament was indirectly elected and had only consultative powers. At this first stage of the European integration process, the democratic deficit issue was related exclusively to the lack of democratic control of the transfer of policy-making powers from the national to the European level. The redress found was to parliamentarize the European level by introducing in 1979 the direct election of the members of the European Parliament and by increasing its powers.

The Maastricht, Amsterdam and Nice Treaties extended the legislative powers of the European Parliament and democratic participation by introducing the co-decision procedure, the subsidiarity principle and European citizenship and by creating an advisory body, the Committee of the Regions. A tighter link between the Parliament and the Commission was also attempted by providing for the term of the Commission to coincide with that of the European Parliament.

The Constitutional Treaty – intended to create a consolidated constitution for the European Union – could not be ratified due to its rejection in national referendums and failed *de facto* to stimulate a debate on the constitutional settings of the Union. However, the Treaty of Lisbon provided for the first time a definition of the democratic principles shaping the European Union.

The Treaty of Lisbon, which entered into force on December 1, 2009, includes explicit provisions on democratic principles. Article 10 stipulates the right of citizens to participate effectively in the European Union's democratic life through direct representation in the European Parliament and that representative democracy is the founding principle of the EU. Such recognition does not give citizens new rights but it does have strong symbolic value as the Treaty on the European Union clearly describes a Union whose functioning is founded on the principle of representative democracy and determines that European institutions should maintain an open, transparent and regular dialogue with representative associations and civil society (Art. 11 n. 2).[17]

16 This position is discussed in Simona Piattoni, 'Is the EU a Representative Democracy? The Normative Debate and the Impact of the Euro Crisis' in Federico Fabbrini, Ernst Hirsch Ballin, Han Somsen (eds), *What Form of Government for the European Union and the Eurozone?* (Hart Publishing 2015), 133.

17 The EU governance model is a model where the traditional model of representative democracy no longer applies.

The Treaty of Lisbon has brought significant changes aimed at strengthening the powers of the European Parliament: the ordinary legislative procedure, in which the Parliament has the same powers as the Council, is extended to new policy areas; a greater role at the international level, such as the authority to approve international agreements in the areas covered by the ordinary legislative procedure; the strengthening of budgetary power by placing the Parliament on an equal footing with the Council in the procedure for adopting the EU's annual budget.

In response to national parliaments' persistent demands for more democratic legitimacy, the Lisbon Treaty has granted national parliaments new rights and powers in order to make the EU institutions more accountable.[18] The Lisbon Treaty determines that the role of national parliaments is to provide an active contribution to the good functioning of the Union through being comprehensively informed by the European institutions as well as through their involvement in the evaluation of the implementation mechanisms of EU policies (Article 12, paragraph c).

The Treaty of Lisbon aims to enhance the role of national parliaments which must henceforth ensure the proper application of the principle of subsidiarity. In this respect, they can intervene in the ordinary legislative procedure and have a right of referral to the Court of Justice of the EU.

The Lisbon Treaty has defined a new type of parliamentary democracy in which national parliaments substantially deviate from the standard role they are given in European parliamentary democracies.[19] Although the European Parliament has been strengthened, its role is still considerably weaker than that played by national parliaments.

The new European economic governance: the Fiscal Compact

The Fiscal Compact (FC) – that is, Title III of the Treaty on Stability, Coordination and Governance in the Economic and Monetary Union, also referred to as TSCG – is an intergovernmental treaty[20] introduced as a new, stricter version of the Stability and Growth Pact. Originally signed on March 2, 2012, by all Member States of the European Union, except for the Czech Republic,[21] the

18 Adam Cygan, *Accountability, Parliamentarism and Transparency in the EU – The Role of National Parliaments* (Edward Elgar 2013); Jean-Claude Piris, *The Lisbon Treaty – A Legal and Political Analysis* (Cambridge University Press 2010); Cesare Pinelli, 'Il deficit democratico europeo e le risposte del Trattato di Lisbona' (2008) 4 *Rassegna Parlamentare* 927.

19 Carina Sprungk, 'A New Type of Representative Democracy? Reconsidering the Role of National Parliaments in the European Union' (2013) 35 *Journal of European Integration* 547–563.

20 Bruno De Witte, 'Treaty Games –Law as Instrument and as Constraint in the Euro Crisis Policy' in Franklin Allen, Elena Carletti, Saverio Simonelli (eds), *Governance for the Eurozone: Integration or Disintegration?* (FIC Press 2012), 139.

21 The Czech government eventually expressed its commitment to join the treaty but the ratification has not yet occurred due to the three-fifths majority required by the Constitution.

United Kingdom[22] and Croatia,[23] it entered into force on January 1, 2013.[24] The Treaty was agreed outside the framework of EU law but was intended to be incorporated into it within five years (art. 16 FC). Regulation (EU) 473/2013 incorporated part of the TSCG requirements in the Union legal framework and a legislative proposal put forward by the European Commission on December 6, 2017, intended to make a step further in the same direction.

The Fiscal Compact was concluded as part of an overall strategy to tackle the sovereign debt crisis in the Eurozone by introducing a new constitutional architecture of economic governance. The tightening of budget policies through the constitutionalization of budget constraints has been considered a solution to the negative effects of the behavior of States in fiscal distress. Existing constraints on public finances were considered insufficient in the case of some Member States which failed to adopt any legal countermeasures, thus revealing the "European constitutional inadequacy".[25] Therefore, an explicit commitment of the States to intervene on their national fundamental charters or national normative frameworks was deemed necessary.[26]

The new European economic governance architecture introduced by the Fiscal Compact has two main characteristics: asymmetry and intergovernmentalism.

Asymmetry has been the result of the acceptance of differentiated integration as some provisions apply to all the contracting parties, while others apply only to the EU Member States adopting the euro as their national currency.[27]

The choice of an intergovernmental agreement rather than an amendment to EU Treaties was the result of the resistance by the United Kingdom to signing

22 The UK Prime Minister, David Cameron, vetoed the compact as an EU agreement, largely on the grounds that there was no guarantee that it would not affect the UK's financial services industry. For a narrative of the United Kingdom perspective on the Fiscal Compact, see Michael Gordon, 'The United Kingdom and the Fiscal Compact: Past and Future' (2014) 10 *European Constitutional Law Review* 28–53; Piet Eeckhout, 'The UK and European economic and monetary union governance' (2014) October *UCL policy briefing*; KarineTournier-Sol, Chris Gifford (eds), *The UK Challenge to Europeanization, The Persistence of British Euroscepticism* (Palgrave Macmillan 2015).

23 Croatia became the 28th Member State on July 1, 2013, but has not yet signed the treaty.

24 TSCG Article 14, paragraph 2: "This Treaty shall enter into force on 1 January 2013, provided that twelve Contracting Parties whose currency is the euro have deposited their instrument of ratification, or on the first day of the month following the deposit of the twelfth instrument of ratification by a Contracting Party whose currency is the euro, whichever is the earlier."

25 Nicola Lupo, 'La revisione costituzionale della disciplina di bilancio e il sistema delle fonti' in Vincenzo Lippolis, Nicola Lupo, Giulio M. Salerno, Gino Scaccia (eds), *Costituzione e pareggio di bilancio, Il Filangieri* (Jovene 2012) *Quaderno 2011.*

26 For insight on the evolution of the economic governance, see Alexandre De Streel, 'The evolution of the EU Economic Governance Since the Treaty of Maastricht: Un Unfinished Task' (2013) 20 *Maastricht Journal of European and Comparative Law*, 358.

27 Francis Snyder, 'Integration and Differentiation: Metaphor for European Union' in Paul Craig and Gráinne de Búrca (eds), *The Evolution of EU Law* (Oxford University Press 2011), 687–716.

any agreement aiming at strengthening the coordination and the control of national economic and fiscal policies and to introduce (preferably at constitutional level) the balanced budget clause into domestic legal systems. In terms of the international nature of the treaty, it has been extensively demonstrated that this choice is not a novelty.[28] The treaty defines a balanced budget as a general budget deficit not exceeding 3.0% of the gross domestic product (GDP), with a structural deficit not exceeding a country-specific Medium-Term budgetary Objective (MTO) which, at most, can be set to 0.5% of GDP for states with a debt-to-GDP ratio exceeding 60% or 1.0% of GDP for states with debt levels within the 60% limit. The country-specific MTOs are recalculated every third year and may be set at stricter levels compared to the maximum allowed by the Treaty. This rule is based upon the existing Stability and Growth Pact (SGP) deficit rule, where the concept of country-specific MTOs was integrated into the preventive arm of the pact in 2005, with an upper limit for structural deficits at 1.0% of GDP applying to all Eurozone and ERM-II member states.

The originality of the Fiscal Compact consisted in the introduction of a variable upper limit based on the debt level of the State. The key legal novelty introduced by the Fiscal Compact has been the obligation for the Member States to enact the so-called "golden rule" for a balanced budget through specific constitutional arrangements. The golden rule has profoundly affected the role parliaments play, not only in the budget process but as representative democratic institutions.

The implementation of the budgetary constraints estimated by the Fiscal Compact has been considered as an effective mechanism to control growing imbalances among national economies. However, the balance in European economic governance can be restored only within the framework of a Union with a common fiscal, economic, and social policy.[29]

The euro crisis has clearly shown that the EU is still far from being an economic and fiscal union but it is even further from being a political union. The economic and financial crisis of the Eurozone has shown a shortfall at European level, which affects not only the functioning of the Union's institutions but also compounds the progressive limitation of the representative democracy principle.[30] The Fiscal Compact represents a technocratic regime designed to

28 "In fact, there are numerous earlier examples of international treaties concluded between groups of Member States of the EU. They have concluded, ever since the 1950's, agreements in areas such as tax law, environmental protection, defense, culture and education." Bruno De Witte, 'Using International Law in the Euro Crisis Causes and Consequences', *ARENA Working Paper* 4/2013, www.sv.uio.no/arena/english/research/publications/arena-publications/workingpapers/workingpapers2013/wp4-13.pdf

29 Heinrich Enderlein, 'Solidarität in der Europäischen Union – Die ökonomische Perspektive' in Christian Callies (ed.), *Europäische Solidarität und nationale Identität* (Mohr & Siebeck 2013).

30 Nicolas de Sadeleer 'The new architecture of the European Economic Governance: a Leviathan or a flat-footed colossus?' (2012) 19 *Maastricht Journal of European and Comparative Law* 355. The author, after recalling how the new economic governance instruments are intended to strengthen the fiscal discipline of the

strengthen fiscal discipline in the Eurozone by legally binding Member States to implement budgetary constraints. As such, the constitutional architecture of the European economic governance has been so far characterized by an incremental centralization of power in the vertical relations between the Member States and the EU. The progressive loss of power experienced by representative institutions such as the European Parliament and national parliaments had three institutional consequences: (1) an increase of the strength of the decision-making power of the European Council whose role is no confined longer to a strategic function,[31] (2) the empowerment of the Economic and Financial Affairs Council (Ecofin) and the European Central Bank (ECB) and (3) the emergence of new institutions: the Eurogroup (formalized by the Lisbon Treaty in 2009) and the Euro-Summit.

The European Parliament from empowerment to marginalization

The new economic governance framework resulted in a continuing marginalization of the formal role of the European Parliament.[32] Following the entry into force of the Treaty of Lisbon, the empowerment of the European Parliament appeared to be a process that could not be undone.[33] The euro crisis and the challenge it poses to national fiscal sovereignty severely affected the European Parliament, prompting scholars to reconsider its role and the reversibility of its empowerment process.

During the drafting of the TSCG, the European Parliament expressed its concerns about the establishment of a purely intergovernmental coordination system of the economic and fiscal policy. These concerns were summarized on January 18, 2012, in a resolution strongly criticizing the draft of the Fiscal Compact.[34] Of particular concern was the intergovernmental nature of the

Member States, questions whether this hides "a deep-seated crisis of identity within the EU institutions which are simply at a loss about what to do, or should one see here a real desire to reinforce EMU, which recently fell victim to a congenital defect?"

31 François Foret, Yann-Sven Rittelmeyer (eds), *The European Council and European Governance: The Commanding Heights of the EU* (Routledge 2014). See also Petya Alexandrova, Marcello Carammia, Arco Timmermans, Sebastiaan Princen, 'EU High Politics: The Policy Agenda of the European Council, 1975–2010' in François Foret, Yann-Sven Rittelmeyer (eds), *The European Council and European Governance: The Commanding Heights of the EU* (Routledge 2014).

32 On the role of the European Parliament, see Cristina Fasone, 'European Economic Governance and Parliamentary Representation: What Place for the European Parliament?' (March 2014) 20 *European Law Journal* 164–185.

33 Berthold Rittberger, 'Institutionalizing Representative Democracy in the European Union: The Case of the European Parliament' (2012) 18 *Journal of Common Market Studies* 24–33.

34 See the Resolution of the European Parliament of 18 January 2012 on the Conclusions of the European Council of 8–9 December 2011 on a draft international agreement for the fiscal stability in the EU.

Treaty as the "community method" within the framework of the EU law was considered more suitable to address the balanced budget issues and create a true economic and fiscal union. Furthermore, the European Parliament called for an enhanced role for itself and for national parliaments in the coordination of economic governance.

The former President of the European Commission, José Manuel Barroso, in a speech delivered at the first European Parliamentary Week on the European Semester for Economic Policy Coordination, expressed his belief that

> Both the European Parliament and national parliaments play a crucial role... The European Union will remain a system of governance on multiple levels. So maximum democratic accountability must be provided at that level where the decision is taken, taking into account all levels where its impact will be felt. This also means... that one thing is crystal clear: democratic accountability and legitimacy within the European Union in the 21st century take place at national and at European level. And this should not be seen as a zero sum game. These are complementary concepts. The European Parliamentary Week is an expression of precisely this. The European semester must embody a strong parliamentary dimension. And it is obvious that many issues are at stake and decisions need to be prepared or be taken which involve both the European Parliament as much as national Parliaments, be it in budgetary, fiscal or macroeconomic terms.[35]

Barroso's intervention highlights the need for more effective democratic accountability within the European Union and the key role that the European Parliament may have.[36]

Representative democracy in the constitutionalization of budgetary constraints: a comparative overview

From a comparative perspective, the impact of the introduction of the budgetary constraints on the role of representative institutions relies mostly on the

35 Speech by President Barroso at the European Parliamentary Week on the European Semester for Economic Policy Coordination, 30 January 2013: "[W]e are willing to engage with the national parliaments. I want to underline that national parliaments retain their full rights in the national budgetary processes. The Commission does not have a veto, does not have the right to change the draft national budgets. But we can discuss this together. And this is important because it's the way that we can deepen this sense of economic governance at European level."

36 Ingolf Pernice, Mattias Wendel, Lars S. Otto, Kristin Bettge, Martin Mlynarski and Michael Schwarz, in *A Democratic Solution to the Crisis: Reform Steps Towards a Democratically Based Economic and Financial Constitution for Europe* (Nomos, 2012) at 115–137, maintain: "Any solution, also demanded on the principle of democracy, must therefore guarantee the representation of European interests in national fiscal policy decision-making processes and institutionalize these in law."

role played by representative institutions within the institutional architecture of each Member state and on the involvement of parliaments in EU affairs.[37]

The limited role of elective assemblies in the implementation of the new budgetary constraints and of the budgetary procedures is one of the main arguments in the debate regarding the European Union. This weakness has been expressed at the domestic level by the extensive use of emergency legislation (decree-laws) in order to implement European economic governance measures without the "uncertainty" of a democratic parliamentary debate.[38] The weakness of democratic control in European economic governance has profoundly eroded the principle of representative democracy in the European Union, as it has been widely acknowledged by scholars and policy makers alike.

Addressing the constitutionalization of budgetary constraints in the European Union requires a comparative analysis of representative case studies with different legal systems. The cases selected for this purpose are Italy, Germany, Spain and Greece.

These cases have been selected based on the following methodological criteria: they are all parliamentary systems; their participation in the EU affairs is markedly asymmetric; they face varying degrees of economic stability and fiscal constraints, ranging from Germany as the country leading the reform of the EU economic governance, to Greece which suffered from the most evident limitations of its financial sovereignty because of the extremely harsh austerity measures.

The analysis of the constitutionalization of budgetary constraints in the selected EU Member States reveals how the new economic governance has led to a significant shift of power from the national to the EU level. This shift of power has been perceived as problematic because the budget process is a fundamental attribute of national sovereignty and is expressed through the action of legislative assemblies. The constitutionalization of the budget balance clause was recommended as a "preference" by the final version of the Fiscal Compact, but it was not imposed. The majority of Member States refrained from making recourse to a constitutional amendment especially in the absence of parliamentary support. For example, in the case of France, Italy, Spain or Portugal. attempts to call for referendums (a constitutional possibility) failed repeatedly, a clear demonstration of the detachment of the economic governance process from the democratic circuit.

37 In this sense, recent research, drawing on comparative studies and specialist literature on the EU activities of national parliaments has defined five ideal types of parliamentary participation to EU decision-making: policy shaper, government watchdog, public forum, EU expert, European player. In this chapter I take account of this additional ranking based on detailed comparative empirical data on parliamentary activities. See Olivier Rozenberg, Claudia Hefftler, 'Introduction' in Claudia Hefftler, Christine Neuhold, Olivier Rozenberg, Julie Smith (eds), *The Palgrave Handbook of National Parliaments and the European Union* (Palgrave Macmillan 2015), 27–35.

38 *Contra* the position expressed by Scagliusi and Huber, according to whom the role of the European Parliament in the new economic governance is strengthened. See Marco Scagliusi, Stephan Huber, *Evaluating EU Economic Governance Elements for the debate on the 'Six-Pack' and 'Two-Pack'* (January 2015)'

Germany: the watchdog of parliamentary democracy

Germany was the first country to introduce, in 2009, a series of relevant amendments to its Basic Law in the context of a broader constitutional reform. The amendments to the Grundgesetz were enacted in June 2009 and are incorporated in the *Gesetz und Anderung des Grundgesetzes.*[39]

The German constitutional reform anticipated the budgetary constraints and the economic policy choices enshrined in the Fiscal Compact.

The ratification of the Treaty was not immediate as it was necessary to wait for the Constitutional Court to issue its fundamental decision on September 12, 2012. The Court's decision stated the constitutional legitimacy of the laws ratifying the Treaty and introduced a number of conditions in order to preserve the principle of representative democracy,[40] also known as the "watchdog of parliamentary democracy".[41] It is worth noting here that the German government needed a qualified majority of two-thirds to ratify the Fiscal Compact, which was treated as a constitutional amendment to the Basic Law.

The participation of the Bundestag in the euro-national procedures for the implementation of the economic governance measures has been strengthened thanks to the action of the German Constitutional Court.[42] The reasoning of the Court builds on an interpretation of Art. 38.1 GG, on the right to vote for the Bundestag as a "right to democracy". This article has been interpreted by the judges in conjunction with Art. 20.2 GG, which identifies the source of the state's authority as the people through democratic elections, and Art. 79.3 GG, also known as the eternity clause, which upholds the democratic principle as part of the German constitutional identity.

Germany has been the only case in which constitutional court decisions have acted as a counterbalance to the loss of parliamentary powers.[43] Although other

39 Gesetz und Anderung des Grundgesetzes Article 91c,d, Article 104b, Article 109, Article.109 a, Article, 115, Article. 143d.

40 The Bundesverfassungsgericht's decision aimed to guarantee the Bundestag's role. Among the Italian scholars, for a first comment, see Paolo Ridola,*Karlusruhe locuta causa finita? Il Bundersverfasssungsgericht, il fondo Salva Stati e gli incerti destini della democrazia federalista in Europa* (2012) 18, www.federalismi.it, 6. Also see Luisa Cassetti, 'Il "Sì, ma" del Tribunale costituzionale federale tedesco sulla ratifica del Trattato di Lisbona tra passato e futuro dell'integrazione europea' (2009) 14, www.federalismi.it; Raffaele Bifulco, 'Il custode della democrazia parlamentare – Nota a prima lettura alla sentenza del Tribunale costituzionale federale tedesco del 7 settembre 2011 sui meccanismi europei di stabilità finanziaria' (2011) 3, www.rivistaaic.it

41 For comments on this decision, see Antjevon Ungern-Sternberg, 'Parliaments – Figleaf or Heartbeat of Democracy? German Federal Constitutional Court (Judgment of 7 September 2011 – European Rescue Package)' (2012) 8 *European Constitutional Law Review* 304.

42 Ingolf Pernice, 'Domestic Courts, Constitutional Constraints and European Democracy: What Solution for the Crisis?' in Maurice Adams, Federico Fabbrini, Pierre Larouche (eds), *The Constitutionalization of European Budgetary Constraints* (Hart Publishing 2014), 297–318.

43 Oliver Höing, 'Differentiation of Parliamentary Powers: The German Constitutional Court and the German Bundestag within the Financial Crisis' in Marta

constitutional courts have been active, no other constitutional court has contributed to the empowerment of its national parliament to the extent the German Bundesverfassungsgericht has.[44] Other courts either remained neutral or disempowered their parliaments, as in the case of Spain.

Italy: normalizing "emergency" and disempowering Parliament

The incorporation of the balanced budget principle in the Italian Constitution has been the most significant outcome in terms of the impact of the Eurozone crisis on the Italian legal order. It profoundly redefined the contribution of the legislature to public budgeting. Although the formal procedure has been followed, according to the provisions of Art. 138 of the Italian Constitution,[45] Italian scholarship has unanimously pointed out the severe time constraints placed on the constitutional reform, which left no space for parliamentary debate to take place. This resulted in amendments to the constitutional bill being either rejected or never becoming the object of an effective debate.

The lack of parliamentary debate negatively affected the passage of this relevant constitutional reform, leaving several legal and political questions still pending. As Italy formally entered a recession in the first quarter of 2012, on April 20, the Italian Parliament enacted Constitutional Law No. 1/2012 to increase the commitment to stabilize public finances in accordance with the constraints imposed by the Europlus Pact, the Six Pack and the Fiscal Compact.[46] The law, which came

Cartabia, Nicola Lupo, Andrea Simoncini (eds), *Democracy and Subsidiarity in the EU: National Parliaments, Regions and Civil Society in the Decision-Making Process* (il Mulino 2013), 255–280.

44 The German Constitutional Court has issued four decisions on the European economic governance: BVerfG, 7 September 2011; BVerfG, 28 February 2012; BVerfG, 30 June 2012; BVerfG, 12 September 2012. For a contribution to the debate on the empowerment or disempowerment of national parliaments, see Aleksandra Maatsch, 'Empowered or Disempowered? The Role of National Parliaments during the Reform of European Economic Governance' (December 2015) 10 *MPIfG Discussion Paper* 15/10 Max-Planck-Institut für Gesellschaftsforschung, Köln, 1–25. *Contra* Fasone, observed that rulings of national or supreme courts have actually fostered national parliaments' control functions: Cristina Fasone, 'Eurozone, non-Eurozone and "troubled asymmetries" among national parliaments in the EU: Why and to what extent this is of concern' (2014) 6 *Perspectives on Federalism* 1–41.

45 Article 138 of the Italian Constitution states: "Laws amending the Constitution and other constitutional laws shall be adopted by each House after two successive debates at intervals within a period of three months, and shall be approved by an absolute majority of the members of each House in the second voting. Said laws are submitted to a popular referendum when, within three months of their publication, such request is made by one-fifth of the members of a House or five hundred thousand voters or five Regional Councils. The law submitted to referendum shall not be promulgated if not approved by a majority of valid votes. A referendum shall not be held if the law has been approved in the second voting by each of the Houses by a majority of two-thirds of the members."

46 Constitutional law no. 1/2012 is known as the "balanced budget law". Among the vast specialist literature, see Graziella Della Torre (ed.), *Dalla crisi economica al*

into force in January 2014, modifies Art. 81 of the Italian Constitution through the introduction of specific rules designed to guarantee a progressive balance between revenue and expenditure.[47]

In Italy, policy making has been centralized, as the 2012 constitutional amendment and the extensive recourse to decree-laws – a legal instrument that the executive can use in "extraordinary cases of necessity and urgency" according to Article 77 of the Italian Constitution – broadly show how the implementation of euro-crisis law has taken budgetary powers away from the representative assembly.[48] The Italian case demonstrates how legal measures adopted at the domestic level, within the framework of the reform of the economic governance in the EU, have considerably jeopardized parliamentary prerogatives, shifting power from the representative arena to the executive.[49]

pareggio di bilancio: prospettive, percorsi e responsabilità, Atti del LVIII Convegno di Studi, Varenna Villa Monastero, 20–22 settembre 2012, (Giuffrè 2013); Francesco Bilancia, 'Note critiche sul c.d. pareggio di bilancio', www.rivistaaic.it; Antonio Brancasi, 'L'introduzione del principio del c.d. pareggio di bilancio: un esempio di revisione affrettata della Costituzione' (2012) 1 *Quaderni costituzionali* 108; Renzo Dickman, 'Le regole della governance economica europea e il pareggio di bilancio in Costituzione' (2012) 4, www.federalismi.it, 43; Rita Perez, 'Dal bilancio in pareggio all'equilibrio tra entrate e spese', (2012) 18 *Giornale di Diritto Amministrativo* 929.

47 According to Art. 81§1 of the Italian Constitution "The State shall balance revenue and expenditure in its budget, taking account of the adverse and favorable phases of the economic cycle. No recourse shall be made to borrowing except for the purpose of taking account of the effects of the economic cycle or, subject to authorization by the two Houses approved by an absolute majority vote of their Members, in exceptional circumstances. Any law involving new or increased expenditure shall provide for the resources to cover such expenditure. Each year the Houses shall pass a law approving the budget and the accounts submitted by the Government. Provisional implementation of the budget shall not be allowed except by specific legislation and only for periods not exceeding four months in total. The content of the budget law, the fundamental rules and the criteria adopted to ensure balance between revenue and expenditure and the sustainability of general government debt shall be established by legislation approved by an absolute majority of the Members of each House in compliance with the principles established with a constitutional law."

48 Cristina Fasone, 'Taking Budgetary Powers Away from National Parliaments? On Parliamentary Prerogatives in the Eurozone Crisis' (2015) *EUI Department of Law Research Paper* No. 2015/37.

49 Allen Schick, 'Can National Legislatures Regain an Effective Voice in Budget Policy?' (2002) 1 (3) *OECD Journal on Budgeting* 15–42; Paul Posner, Chung-Keun Park, 'Role of the Legislature in the Budget Process: Recent Trends and Innovations' (2007) 7 (3) *OECD Journal of Budgeting* 1–26. See also Violeta Ruiz Almendral, 'A Myopic Economic Constitution? Controlling the Debt and the Deficit Without Fiscal Integration' in Marise Cremona, Bruno De Witte, Claire Kilpatrick (eds), *Constitutional Change Through Euro-Crisis Law,* (2015/12) EUI Working Paper Series LAW, 18.

Spain: abdicating democracy to the benefit of the markets

Along with Italy, Spain has been among the first Member States to constitutionalize the balanced budget clause,[50] motivated by the German example and under pressure due to an unprecedented speculative attack on the financial markets. European institutions encouraged Madrid to quickly proceed with the constitutional revision to restore its credibility and preserve its national financial interests in international markets.[51]

The agreement between the two main Spanish parties, *Partido Popular* and the Socialist Party,[52] allowed for the constitutional amendment bill to be passed[53] and published in the Official Journal just over a month after the submission of the government's proposal. This was achieved through a simplified revision procedure stipulated in Article 167 of the Constitution with a supermajority of three-fifths but without the need to call for a popular referendum because both parliamentary chambers refrained from making such a request within the 15-day term set out by the Constitution.[54] The decision to follow the simplified revision procedure was supported by the Constitutional Court's decision on the *recurso de amparo* filed by the representatives of the parliamentary group *Esquerra Republicana-Izquierda Unida-Iniciativa per Catalunyay verds.* The *Tribunal Constitucional* decided not to engage with the matters brought to its attention and ruled the appeal inadmissible.[55] The Court's decision and the constitutional reform have been strongly criticized by constitutional scholars for the use of fast-track procedures and the lack of an open and transparent parliamentary debate.[56] Many have argued that the Spanish constitutional reform

50 Francisco Balaguer Callejon, 'Crisis economica y crisis constitucional en Europa' (2013) 98 *Revista espanola de derecho constitucional* 91–107.

51 Violeta Ruiz Almendral, 'The Spanish Legal Framework for Curbing the Public Debt and the Deficit' (2013) 9 *European Constitutional Law Review* 189–204.

52 Spanish scholarship has called this agreement a "Pacto de Estado". For this definition and further comments, see Augusto Aguilar Calajorro, 'El impacto de la crisis economica en Espana: el renacimiento de la politica frente a la economia' in Francisco Balaguer Callejon, Miguel Azpitarte Sanchez, Enrique Guillen Lopez, Juan Francisco Sanchez Barillao (eds), *The Impact of the Economic Crisis on the EU Institutions and Member States* (Thomson Reuters Aranzadi 2015), 161–185.

53 According to the new text of Article 135, "All Public Administrations shall adapt their actions to the principle of budgetary stability".

54 In Spain, a referendum on a constitutional amendment passed by the Cortes Generales can be requested by one-tenth of the members of either House within 15 days after its passage (Art. 167§3 Constitution of Spain).

55 Auto de inadmision del recurso de amparo ATC 9/2012, January 13, 2012.

56 For comments on the Spanish constitutionalisation of the balanced budget clause see Laura Frosina, 'La costituzionalizzazione dei vincoli europei di bilancio' in Francisco Balaguer Callejon, Miguel Azpitarte Sanchez, Enrique Guillen Lopez, Juan Francisco Sanchez Barillao (eds), *The Impact of the Economic Crisis on the EU Institutions and Member States* (Thomson Reuters Aranzadi 2015), 489–525; Augusto Aguilar Calajorro, 'El impacto de la crisis economica en Espana: el renacimiento de la politica frente a la economia' in Francisco Balaguer Callejon, Miguel Azpitarte

has been delivered against the democratic principle and with disregard to the protection of the welfare state (Art. 1 CE).[57]

Greece: in the shadow of austerity

Greece has become the symbol of the economic crisis.[58] Notwithstanding the strong pressures to amend the Constitution coming from the European institutions, the balanced budget rule has not been constitutionalized by the Greek lawmakers. The rigidity of the Greek Constitution (GC) and the specific provisions related to its revision process (Article 110)[59] have been considered an obstacle to the introduction of a constitutional amendment.[60] Instead, the

Sanchez, Enrique Guillen Lopez, Juan Francisco Sanchez Barillao (eds), *The Impact of the Economic Crisis on the EU Institutions and Member States*, 161–185.

57 Critical on the reform, Gregorio Camara Villar, 'La reforma del articulo 135 CE' (2011) 93 *Revista Espanola de Derecho Constitucional* 159.

58 Xenophon Contiades, Ioannis Tassopoulos, 'The Impact of the Financial Crisis on the Greek Constitution' in Xenophon Contiades (ed.), *Constitutions in the Global Financial Crisis* (Ashgate 2013), 195; Giulia Aravantinou Leonidi, 'L'impatto della crisi sull'ordinamento costituzionale della Repubblica di Grecia' in Francisco Balaguer Callejon, Miguel Azpitarte Sanchez, Enrique Guillen Lopez, Juan Francisco Sanchez Barillao (eds), *The Impact of the Economic Crisis on the EU Institutions and Member States*, 335–377.

59 According to Art. 110 of the Greek Constitution:

1. The provisions of the Constitution shall be subject to revision with the exception of those which determine the form of government as a Parliamentary Republic and those of Articles 2 paragraph 1, 4 paragraphs 1, 4 and 7, 5 paragraphs 1 and 3, 13 paragraph 1, and 26.

2. The need for revision of the Constitution shall be ascertained by a resolution of Parliament adopted, on the proposal of not less than fifty Members of Parliament, by a three-fifths majority of the total number of its members in two ballots, held at least one month apart. This resolution shall define specifically the provisions to be revised.

3. Upon a resolution by Parliament on the revision of the Constitution, the next Parliament shall, in the course of its opening session, decide on the provisions to be revised by an absolute majority of the total number of its members.

4. Should a proposal for revision of the Constitution receive the majority of the votes of the total number of members but not the three-fifths majority specified in paragraph 2, the next Parliament may, in its opening session, decide on the provisions to be revised by a three-fifths majority of the total number of its members.

5. Every duly voted revision of provisions of the Constitution shall be published in the Government Gazette within ten days of its adoption by Parliament and shall come into force through a special parliamentary resolution.

6. Revision of the Constitution is not permitted before the lapse of five years from the completion of a previous revision.

60 On constitutional revision in the Greek context, see Xenophon Contiades, *The Revision of the Constitution, I. Methodological keystones* (Sakkoulas 2000); Kostas Mavrias, *Transition démocratique et changement constitutionnel en Europe du sud Espagne - Grèce – Portugal* (Sakkoulas 1997); Ioannis Varvitsiotis, 'Constitutional questions. Proposals for the Constitutional Revision' in Xenophon Contiades (ed.), *Five Years after the Constitutional Revision of 2001* (Sakkoulas 2006), 973.

ratification of the Fiscal Compact in Greece was part of a more general draft bill, which also contained the amendment of TFEU and the ratification of the European Stability Mechanism (ESM) treaty.[61] Law 4063/2012 was passed through ordinary parliamentary procedure according to Article 70 GC[62] and no fast-track procedure was followed, even though substantial legal problems were raised and extensively discussed[63] because of the implementation of the Balanced Budget Rule and the Fiscal Compact.

Because Greece had already committed to international obligations by signing the *Memoranda of Understanding* determining the conditions of the loan agreements with Greece, and because the *Medium-term budgetary frameworks* required it anyway, according to the Stability and Growth Pact, no further parliamentary debate concerning the Fiscal Compact took place. Although the implementation of the new economic governance was approved through the ordinary legislative procedure, the participation of the *Boulì ton Ellinon* in the economic governance reforms was significantly limited and partly overshadowed by the public debate over the State's commitment to the terms of the international loan agreements.[64]

Concluding remarks

This analysis demonstrates that, despite being more active in debating fiscal policies, Southern European States have been considerably more disempowered than the Northern European States. Southern European parliaments

61 The practice of mergers was extensively adopted in Greece where the members of parliament had one vote to approve the following reforms: the establishment of the European Stability Mechanism (ESM), the reform of the Article 136(3) and the ratification of the Fiscal Compact.

62 The constitutional basis for this procedure is vested in Article28 of the GC "The generally recognized rules of international law, as well as international conventions as of the time they are sanctioned by statute and become operative according to their respective conditions, shall be an integral part of domestic Greek law and shall prevail over any contrary provision of the law. The rules of international law and of international conventions shall be applicable to aliens only under the condition of reciprocity." An interpretive statement added with the constitutional reform of 2001 declares: "Article 28 is the basis for the participation of the Country in the procedures of European integration."

63 See the parliamentary debates of 28 March 2012, Πρακτικά Βουλής (Ολομέλεια), Συνεδρίαση ΡΙΣΤ, Τετάρτη, 28 Μαρτίου 2012, p. 8022. The constitutionalization of the balanced budget rule has fostered a lively debate among scholars. For the academic debate, see Lina Papadopoulou, 'Can Constitutional Rules, Even if "Golden", Tame Greek Public Debt?' in Maurice Adams, Federico Fabbrini, Pierre Larouche (eds), *The Constitutionalization of European Budgetary Constraints*, 223.

64 On August 19, 2015, the European Commission signed a Memorandum of Understanding (MoU) with Greece following approval by the ESM Board of Governors for further stability support accompanied by a third economic adjustment program. This agreement is the third in line since 2010, when Greece first entered a financial aid program to address economic imbalances.

experienced tighter constraints to their powers in comparison with the national parliaments of Northern European Member States.

The comparative overview of the selected case studies also shows that the ratification procedures of the Fiscal Compact varied significantly across states. In Italy, Spain, and Greece, voting on particular anti-crisis measures was either eliminated or exercised with little or no plenary debate, primarily because of the political fears related to the possibility of an uncertain outcome of an extended parliamentary debate. Among the case studies selected, Greece has been the only country not to constitutionalize the golden rule, notwithstanding its peculiar position among the EU Member States because of the unbearable burden of its public debt and the overall critical situation of its public finances. Greek parliamentary sovereignty, already challenged by the commitment to loan agreements which were approved by fast-track parliamentary procedures and which imposed unprecedented austerity measures, was further affected as Parliament once again acquiesced to the Fiscal Compact and introduced a number of changes to parliamentary procedure.

The debate over the democratic principles of the EU is rather complex as it concerns matters that are of fundamental importance to the future of the EU and its integration process. It also raises the critical question of whether the integration process has produced long-lasting de-democratizing side-effects. This debate has been particularly consistent in emphasizing the need for institutional reforms to improve democratic legitimacy and to restore a constitutional balance.[65]

As has been argued in this chapter, the economic crisis that started in 2009 has raised important questions about several aspects of representative democracy, both at the national and the European level. The financial state of emergency in which a group of Member States have been progressively drowning since 2009, has led to a greater centralization of power for the benefit of executive powers[66] and at the cost of the erosion of the role of national legislatures. As it has been frequently argued, centralization may conceal some considerable dangers despite being seen as the inevitable solution during a

65 Ingolf Pernice, Mattias Wendel, Lars S. Otto, Kristin Bettge, Martin Mlynarski, Michael Schwarz, *A Democratic Solution to the Crisis: Reform Steps Towards a Democratically Based Economic and Financial Constitution for Europe* (Nomos 2012), 115–137; Sergio Fabbrini, *Which European Union? Europe after the Euro Crisis* (Cambridge University Press 2015); Federico Fabbrini, *What Form of Government for the European Union and the Eurozone?* (Hart Publishing 2015).

66 Heirich Enderlein, *Nationale Wirtschaftspolitik in der europäischen Währungsunion* (Campus, 2014); Fritz W. Scharpf, 'The Costs of Non-Disintegration: The Case of the European Monetary Union' in Annegret Eppler, Henrik Scheller (eds), *Zur Konzeptionalisierung europäischer Desintegration: Zug- und Gegenkräfte im europäischen Integrationsprozess* (Nomos, 2013), 165–184; Fritz W. Scharpf, 'Die Finanzkrise als Krise der ökonomischen und rechtlichen Überintegration' in Claudio Franzius, Franz C. Mayer, Jürgen Neyer (eds), *Grenzen der europäischen Integration* (Nomos 2014), 51–60.

crisis.[67] In this perspective, calls for the preservation of an influential role of national legislatures in budgetary policies must be considered as legitimate.

The implementation of the Fiscal Compact has increased asymmetries among national Parliaments fostering a gradual drain of authority from national legislatures and favoring a "two-speed" Europe in which a certain group of Member States proceed to further steps of integration through devising their own institutional mechanisms.[68] The recent health crisis due to the COVID-19 pandemic, which triggered lockdowns in the majority of EU Member States and has seriously threatened the economy, has imposed an acceleration in the process of rethinking the tools of the economic governance of the Eurozone started in the last decade, with a significant change of step. As Europe remains confronted at all levels of government with unprecedented challenges, the budgetary rules remain in the background, while priority is given to enhancing principles of solidarity and subsidiarity to help steer the economy and prevent social disruption. However, it is too soon to say if measures undertaken to deal adequately with COVID-19 crisis, departing from the budgetary requirements that would normally apply under the European fiscal framework,[69] will bring to an end an era of fiscal rectitude that began during the Eurozone economic crisis. If things return as they were, the perspective of a true political union would be definitely abandoned.

A new democratic deficit emerged from the new European economic governance framework. This revival of the democratic deficit was due not only to the removal of budgetary powers from national parliaments, whose prerogatives have been seriously jeopardized by the legal measures adopted within the framework of the reform of economic governance in the EU.[70] Rather, a key element for the progressive widening of the democratic gap is given by the convergence or divergence among the Member States on specific binding measures or economic policy issues. This assertion relates primarily to politics and could be resolved at the political level, in the political forum provided by the European Parliament.

Since the onset of the economic crisis, the political debate has largely moved outside parliamentary chambers. The role of the European Parliament is crucial

67 Ken Kollman, *Perils of Centralisation: Lessons from Church, State and Corporation* (Cambridge University Press 2014).

68 Cristina Fasone, 'Taking budgetary powers away from national parliaments? On parliamentary prerogatives in the Eurozone crisis', EUI Department of Law Research Paper No. 2015/37.

69 See the Statement of EU Ministers of Finance on the Stability and Growth Pact in light of the COVID-19 crisis at www.consilium.europa.eu/en/press/press-releases/2020/03/23/statement-of-eu-ministers-of-finance-on-the-stability-and-growth-pa ct-in-light-of-the-covid-19-crisis

70 Miguel Poiares Maduro, 'A New Governance for the European Union and the Euro: Democracy and Justice' (2012) 11 *RSCAS Policy Paper* EUI, 6; Ben Crum, 'Saving the Euro at the Cost of Democracy?' (2013) 51 (4) *Journal of Common Market Studies* 614–630; Kaarlos Tuori, Klaus Tuori,*The Eurozone Crisis: A Constitutional Analysis* (Cambridge University Press 2014), 195.

in the return of the political debate to representative institutions. For this reason, a well-considered reform of the European Parliament should be considered. Regular and structured cooperation between the European Parliament and national Parliaments would be more effective in resolving conflicts through public debate rather than negotiations carried out without democratic scrutiny behind the close doors of non-elected institutions. An opportunity for national parliaments to play a more active role in the architecture of the new economic governance is offered by the newly established Interparliamentary Conference on Stability, Economic Coordination and Governance in the European Union, where national parliaments can exchange opinions and exercise collective oversight.

The lack of accountability for decisions on economic policy, taken primarily by the European Commission and by intergovernmental institutions, together with the progressive marginalization of representative institutions, have also triggered demands for new forms of citizens' participation, such as referendums.[71] These instruments may partly compensate for the loss of democratic accountability by allowing citizens to have a say on the austerity measures adopted under the Fiscal Compact and the ESM Treaty. Such measures have not yet been fully understood by the public because they are still perceived as destructive and disconnected from the democratic circuit. However, direct democracy does not represent a viable solution and cannot replace in any way representative democracy.

The EU system of governance continues to be perceived as remote and unresponsive,[72] notwithstanding the recent change of step in order to respond to the health emergency, and the implementation of the new economic governance measures during the euro crisis has compounded this perception.[73]

As Jürgen Habermas has pointed out, European politics must respond with deeper democratic integration to the political challenges ahead.[74] This will not

71 On the Greek referendum, see Giulia Aravantinou Leonidi, 'La sfida di Atene all'Europa dell'austerità: il referendum del 5 luglio 2015' (2015) 14 *Federalismi* 1–28; Giorgio Grasso, 'Il referendum greco e la questione democratica nella (ri)costruzione del soggetto politico europeo' (July 2015) *Osservatorio AIC* 1–11, www.osservatorioaic.it

72 Nicole Scicluna, 'Politicization without Democratization: How the European Crisis is Transforming EU law and Politics' (2014) 12 *International Journal of Constitutional Law* 545.

73 As Mair observed, governments in bailout states were therefore no longer recognized by their voters as "governments by the people" but rather "governments against the people". See Peter Mair,*Smaghi vs. the parties: Representative government and institutional constraint*, Paper prepared for the Conference on *Democracy in Straightjackets: Politics in an Age of Permanent Austerity*, Ringberg Castle, Munich, Germany, 23–26 March 2011.

74 These challenges are categorized by Habermas: "They concern (a) the imbalance in power relations that has developed within the Union, (b) the threat to the political culture in many countries of our post-imperialist Europe, (c) the disintegration of the achievements of the welfare state, and (d) Europe's failure to live up to its role in world politics." Jurgen Habermas, 'Democracy in Europe: Why the Development of the European Union into a Transnational Democracy is Necessary and

be possible without transferring additional sovereignty rights to the European level, which in turn requires an institutional reform that strengthens the European Parliament.

In recent years, European integration has been pursued to the detriment of representative democracy. It is now imperative to embark on a careful rethinking of the role of democratic participation and accountability in the European Union to prevent representative institutions, both at the national and the European levels, from becoming merely influential bodies within an institutional system governed by economic diktats rather than by democratic debate. Therefore, representative democracy should return to the center of scholarly concern and provide new proposals for the future shape that democracy should take within the European Union in order to guarantee its survival.

Bibliography

Adams M, Fabbrini F, Larouche P (eds), *The Constitutionalization of European Budgetary Constraints* (Hart Publishing 2014)

Alexandrova P, Carammia M, Timmermans A, Princen S, 'EU High Politics: The Policy Agenda of the European Council, 1975–2010' in François Foret, Yann-Sven Rittelmeyer (eds), *The European Council and European Governance: The Commanding Heights of the EU* (Routledge 2014)

Alonso S, Keane J, Merkel W, *The Future of Representative Democracy* (Cambridge University Press 2011)

Aravantinou Leonidi G, 'La sfida di Atene all'Europa dell'austerità: il referendum del 5 luglio 2015' (2015) 14 *Federalismi* 1–28.

Auel K, Höing O, 'Parliaments in the Euro Crisis: Can the Losers of Integration Still Fight Back?' (2014) LII (6) *Journal of Common Market Studies* 1184–1193.

Auel K, Raunio T, 'Introduction: Connecting with the electorate? Parliamentary communication in EU affairs' (2014) 20 (1) *Journal of Legislative Studies* 1–12.

Balaguer Callejon F, Azpitarte Sanchez M, Guillen Lopez E, Sanchez Barillao JF (eds), *The Impact of the Economic Crisis on the EU Institutions and Member States* (Thomson Reuters Aranzadi 2015)

Balaguer Callejon F, 'Crisis economica y crisis constitucional en Europa' (2013) 98 *Revista espanola de derecho constitucional* 91–107.

Bellamy R, 'An ever closer union among the peoples of Europe': Republican intergovernmentalism and *demoi*cratic representation within the EU (2013) 35 (5) *Journal of European Integration* 499–516.

Bellamy R, Kröger S, 'Domesticating the democratic deficit? The role of national parliaments and parties in the EU's system of governance' (2014) 67 (2) *Parliamentary Affairs* 437–457.

Blanke H-J, Mangiameli S (eds), *The Treaty on European Union: A Commentary* (Springer 2013)

How it is Possible' (December 2014) 13 *ARENA Working Paper* 3. Also see Jurgen Habermas, *The Crisis of the European Union: A Response* (Polity Press 2012).

Bobbio N, *The Future of Democracy: A Defence of the Rules of the Game* (University of Minnesota Press 1987)

Bohman J, *Democracy Across Borders: From Demos to Demoi* (MIT Press 2007)

Callies C (ed.), *Europäische Solidarität und nationale Identität* (Mohr & Siebeck 2013)

Contiades X, Tassopoulos I, 'The Impact of the Financial Crisis on the Greek Constitution', in Xenophon Contiades (ed.), *Constitutions in the Global Financial Crisis* (Ashgate, 2013) 195

Cooper I, 'Bicameral or tricameral? National parliaments and representative democracy in the European Union' (2013) 35 (5) *Journal of European Integration* 531–546.

Curtin D, 'The constitutional structure of the Union: A Europe of bits and pieces' (1993) XXX (1) *Common Market Law Review* 17–69.

Cygan A, *Accountability, Parliamentarism and Transparency in the EU: The Role of National Parliaments* (Edward Elgar 2013)

Dahl R, *On Democracy* (Yale University Press 1998)

Della Torre G (ed.), *Dalla crisi economica al pareggio di bilancio: prospettive, percorsi e responsabilità, Atti del LVIII Convegno di Studi*, Varenna Villa Monastero, 20–22 settembre 2012 (Giuffrè 2013)

Fulco L (ed.), *Parlamenti nazionali e Unione Europea nella governance multilivello, atti del convegno Roma – Camera dei Deputati 12–13 maggio 2015* (Giuffrè 2016)

Enderlein H, *Nationale Wirtschaftspolitik in der europäischen Währungsunion* (Campus 2014)

Eriksen EO, Fossum JE, *Rethinking Democracy and the European Union* (Routledge 2012)

Kröger S (ed.), *Political Representation in the European Union: Still Democratic in Times of Crisis?* (Routledge 2014)

Fabbrini S (ed.), *Democracy and Federalism in the European Union and the United States: Exploring Post-National Governance* (Routledge 2005)

Fabbrini S, *Which European Union? Europe after the Euro Crisis* (Cambridge University Press 2015)

Fasone C, 'European Economic Governance and Parliamentary Representation: What Place for the European Parliament?' (2014) 20 (2) *European Law Journal* 164–185.

Fasone C, 'Eurozone, non-Eurozone and "troubled asymmetries" among national parliaments in the EU. Why and to what extent this is of concern' (2014) 6 (3) *Perspectives on Federalism* 1–41.

Foret F, Rittelmeyer Y-S (eds), *The European Council and European Governance. The Commanding Heights of the EU* (Routledge 2014)

Fossum JE, 'The structure of EU representation and the crisis' in Sandra Kröger (ed.), *Political Representation in the European Union: Still Democratic in Times of Crisis?* (Routledge 2014)

Gordon M, 'The United Kingdom and the Fiscal Compact: Past and Future' (2014) 10 *European Constitutional Law Review* 28–53.

Griglio E, Lupo N, 'Parliamentary Democracy and the Eurozone Crisis' (2012) I (2) *Law and Economics Yearly Review* 313–372.

Griglio E, Lupo N, 'Towards an asymmetric European Union, without an asymmetric European Parliament' (2014) 20 *SOG Working Papers*.

Hefftler C, Neuhold C, Rozenberg O, Smith J (eds), *The Palgrave Handbook of National Parliaments and the European Union* (Palgrave Macmillan 2015)

Héritier A, Moury C, *Institutional Rule Three: The Parliament and the Investiture of the Commission, Explaining Institutional Change in Europe* (Oxford University Press 2007)

Höing O, 'Differentiation of Parliamentary Powers: The German Constitutional Court and the German Bundestag within the Financial Crisis' in Marta Cartabia, Nicola Lupo,

Andrea Simoncini (eds), *Democracy and Subsidiarity in the EU: National Parliaments, Regions and Civil Society in the Decision-Making Process* (il Mulino 2013) 255–280.

Lijphart A, *Patterns of Democracy: Government Forms and Performance in Thirty-Six Countries* (Yale University Press 1999)

Lindseth PL, *Power and Legitimacy: Reconciling Europe and the Nation State* (Oxford University Press 2010)

Lupo N, 'La revisione costituzionale della disciplina di bilancio e il sistema delle fonti', in *Il Filangeri, Quaderno 2011* (Jovene 2012)

Maatsch A, 'Are we all Austerians now? An analysis of national parliamentary parties' positioning on anti-crisis measures in the eurozone' (2014) 21 (1) *Journal of European Public Policy* 96–115.

Matthijs M, 'Mediterranean blues: The crisis in Southern Europe' (2014) 25 (1) *Journal of Democracy* 101–115.

Mavrias K, *Transition démocratique et changement constitutionnel en Europe du sud Espagne – Grèce – Portugal* (Sakkoulas 1997)

O'Brennan J, Raunio T (eds), *National Parliaments within the Enlarged European Union, From 'Victims' of Integration to Competitive Actors?* (Routledge 2007)

Pernice I, Wendel M, Otto LS, Bettge K, Mlynarski M, Schwarz M (eds), *A Democratic Solution to the Crisis: Reform Steps Towards a Democratically Based Economic and Financial Constitution for Europe* (Nomos 2012)

Piattoni S, (ed.), *The European Union. Democratic Principles and Institutional Architectures in Times of Crisis* (Oxford University Press 2015)

Pinelli C, *La giurisprudenza costituzionale tedesca e le nuove asimmetrie fra i poteri dei parlamenti nazionali dell'eurozona*, www.costituzionalismo.it, 25 March 2014.

Piris J-C, *The Future of Europe: Towards a Two-speed EU?* (Cambridge University Press 2012)

Pitkin H, *The Concept of Representation* (University of California Press 1967)

Puntscher Riekmann S, Wydra D, 'Representation in the European State of Emergency: Parliaments against Governments?' (2013) 35 (5) *Journal of European Integration* 565–582.

Rittberger B, *Building Europe's Parliament: Democratic Representation Beyond the Nation State* (Oxford University Press 2005)

Rodrik D, *The Globalization Paradox Democracy and the Future of the World Economy* (W. W. Norton & Company, 2011)

Ruiz Almendral V, 'A Myopic Economic Constitution? Controlling the Debt and the Deficit Without Fiscal Integration' in Marise Cremona, Bruno De Witte, Claire Kilpatrick (eds), *Constitutional Change Through Euro-Crisis Law*, EUI Working Paper Series, LAW 2015/12.

Ruiz Almendral V, 'The Spanish Legal Framework for Curbing the Public Debt and the Deficit' (2013) 9 (2) *European Constitutional Law Review* 189–204.

Scagliusi M, Huber S, Policy Performance Appraisal Unit, EPRS, 'Evaluating EU Economic Governance Elements for the debate on the "Six-Pack" and "Two-Pack"' (January 2015). www.europarl.europa.eu/RegData/etudes/BRIE/2015/536374/EPRS_BRI(2015)536374_REV1_EN.pdf

Scharpf FW, 'Die Finanzkrise als Krise der ökonomischen und rechtlichen Überintegration' in Claudio Franzius, Franz C Mayer, Jürgen Neyer (eds), *Grenzen der europäischen Integration* (Nomos 2014) 51–60.

Sprungk C, 'A New Type of Representative Democracy? Reconsidering the Role of National Parliaments in the European Union' (2013) 35 (5) *Journal of European Integration* 547–563.

Tuori K, Tuori K, *The Eurozone Crisis. A Constitutional Analysis* (Cambridge University Press 2014)

Winzen T, 'European integration and national parliamentary oversight institution' (2013) 14 (2) *European Union Politics* 297–323.

6 Financial local autonomy

A tale of balanced budgets and vertical separation of financial power

Simona Gherghina

Introduction

Among the multiple legislative changes brought to the legal architecture of the EU member states by the 2008–2013 global financial and economic crisis, a special place has to be reserved for those concerning the distribution of financial powers between central and local public authorities. The budgetary constraints enforced during the crisis and the sustained efforts made by member states to ensure compliance with the fiscal discipline rules enacted at the EU level revealed the fragility of the financial dependence of local communities on state budgets. Despite the principle of local autonomy, stated by many constitutions, and further detailed in the European Charter of Local Self-Government to include a financial autonomy element, the fiscal discipline rules aimed at balancing the public budgets had a significant impact on the balance of local budgets as well as on the ability of local authorities to receive funds from central budgets. All the various channels for state funding of local budgets, although seemingly complex and designed to cover as many of the multiple scenarios of local activities as possible, have been affected by the sharp reductions in central budgets, further to the enactment of the laws aimed at imposing fiscal discipline.

The direct and visible impact of successive fiscal austerity rules and procedures on the transfers of funds from central government to local administrations has prompted further questions regarding the existence of real local autonomy in the EU member states. A generally accepted principle for more than half a century,[1] the modern idea of self-government as a corollary of decentralized public administration made its way to national constitutions and, in Europe, to a multilateral treaty that seeks to impose international standards in the relationship between central and local governments.[2] The European Charter of

1 X. Cabannes, 'L'autonomie financière des collectivités territoriales après les récentes lois financières. Une adolescence difficile ou déjà une vieille lune?' (2018) 4 *AJDA* 720ff; M. Bouvier, M.-C. Esclassan, J.-P. Lassale, *Finances publiques* (15th ed. LGDJ lextenso 2016), 777–795.

2 C.M.G. Himsworth, *The European Charter of Local Self-Government: A Treaty for Local Democracy* (Edinburgh University Press 2015), 5–6.

DOI: 10.4324/9781315181882-10

Local Self-Government, ratified by the EU member states,[3] provides a detailed map of the building blocks of local autonomy, including the financial autonomy of local governments as defined by specific criteria. Although the criteria for a reasonable degree of financial autonomy were agreed upon following lengthy and protracted negotiations,[4] once inserted into the Charter and the national regulations, they consolidated the general acceptance of local financial autonomy.[5]

Indeed, the various national solutions designed to ensure the financial autonomy of local governments did not rule out transfers from central government and have followed common patterns for putting in place both permanent and temporary channels for such transfers. Alongside permanent sources of funds directly accessible to local authorities, such as certain local taxes, revenues from properties owned by local communities, local services, local public undertakings, and a limited access to loans, the national regulations usually created permanent mechanisms for reallocation to local budgets of income taxes collected in the central budgets, for re-balancing local budgets facing structural low incomes from regular sources, via reallocation of VAT income from central budgets as well as other transfer mechanisms allowing for financing or otherwise compensating specific expenditure of local governments from the central budgets.[6]

During the "golden years" of local autonomy[7] before the onset of the financial crisis, these transfer mechanisms that allowed local governments to exercise their autonomy while relying on constant inflows from the central budgets, justified as they were by the objective reasons of such mechanisms, grew in details and complexity. The financial support of local governments by the central government accounted for both the interdependence between the two levels and an economic approach to self-government, which took into account the close dependence of some local sources for central budget revenues on the action or inaction of local governments.

Overall, despite differences in the national design[8] of the financial component of local autonomy, it developed a pattern of tripartite structure, mostly mirrored by the outline in Article 9 of the European Charter of Local Self-Government of the basic elements of such financial independence: (i) direct access by local authorities to their own resources, as well as the power, within certain limits, to determine its amplitude, (ii) financial equalization mechanisms, meant to correct the inequities derived from the uneven access to potential sources of finance from the first category (own

3 The Charter was opened for signature in 1985 and was ratified by all Council of Europe 47 member states.
4 Ibid 60–62.
5 E. Oliva, *Finances publiques* (3rd ed. Sirey 2015), 88–90.
6 S. Damarey, *Droit public financier* (Dalloz 2018), 590–598.
7 Bouvier, Esclassan, Lassale (n 1) 777–787; Himsworth (n 2) 14–29.
8 M.-C. Steckel Assouere, 'Le partage des compétences financières entre les États et leurs collectivités territoriales dans les Constitutions des vingt-sept pays membres de l'Union européenne' (2013) 121 *RFFP* 63ff.

resources), and (iii) access to borrowing, at least for capital investments.[9] One way or another, these three major sources of funds are available to local budgets in all states that have accepted local autonomy as a principle of their internal organization, irrespective of the details of the complicated structure developed for its application. Needless to say, the formal legal procedures and guarantees for the enactment of this tripartite financing structure did not prevent the common complaint voiced by local governments concerning the insufficiency of the financing available from these sources to ensure the proper discharge of their legal duties. As a consequence, even before the onset of the 2008 financial crisis, the model of financial independence as a basic element of self-government was under a constant pressure, which resulted in a permanent adjustment of the details related to each of its three main components. Most likely, central governments were rarely in the position to secure an amount of financing that was adequately proportional with the needs of local governments, especially if one considers that any negative variations in the first source (own resources) shall always determine a request for increasing the amounts available under financial equalization mechanisms – that is, transferred from the central budget.

This fragile balance of financial power between central and local governments, defined for the most part by the distribution of tax sources, was seriously affected by the financial crisis, which reduced in a significant manner the tax income and the access to borrowing for both central and local budgets. During the early years of the crisis, the sharp decline in tax income had, in turn, reduced the sources for further transfers from the central to local budgets and concomitantly left local governments with a wider gap in their overall financing sources. With lower amounts collected from local taxes, mainly due to taxes and income taxes redirected from the central budget being directly affected by the economic downturn, as well as confronted with limited chances of borrowing at reasonable costs, local governments asked central governments for additional transfers of funds. Thus, the emphasis placed on central governments as a last resort financing source has not only collided with the fiscal discipline rules that central governments were compelled to put in place successively but, moreover, led to the reshaping of the idea of local autonomy.

The effects generated by the various legal solutions enacted at the EU level during the euro-crisis, further adapted for effective application in each of the different national legal systems of the member states, concomitantly hit each of the three sources that supported the financial independence of local governments. The fiscal discipline rules proved to have the most significant impact, namely (i) the fiscal rules, both numeric and procedural, (ii) the judicial review of fiscal rules and (iii) the independent fiscal monitoring institutions, established to independently assess compliance with the budgetary discipline rules.[10] The

9 A. Baudu, 'La réforme fiscale locale: une autonomie fiscale au point mort?' (2020) 6 *RFDA* 999ff; Damarey (n 6) 570–577.

10 National fiscal rules were also divided into three interrelated categories, to include procedural, numeric and institutional rules, the rules pertaining to the functioning

effectiveness of such rules, both uniform at EU level and specific at national level, as well as the mechanisms available for their enforcement – that is, judicial review and the independent fiscal monitoring institutions – proved to be to a significant extent dependent upon political will.[11] Consequently, the political dimension of local autonomy and of the ensuing relationship between central and local governments played a role in the reshaping of the financial structure of self-government. This influence subjected local autonomy to a major resilience test, which measured whether the overall transfers of much-needed funds from central to local budgets were based on objective, transparent criteria, as required by the European Charter of Local Self-Government, or whether the exceptional crisis measures shifted the prevalence to rather subjective, less criteria-based, if not plainly discretionary, transfers. The result of such a resilience test, namely the effects on the local financial autonomy of the changes in the financing structure of local budgets, decided at the central level, is further analyzed.

No insulation from the national turmoil

There is no doubt that local autonomy did not shield local communities or the local authorities from the turbulent changes imposed by the euro-crisis. As EU member states had to face severe financing difficulties, the older concerns about sustainability of public finances proved their relevance in parallel with the acknowledgment of the weaknesses of the mechanism included in the Maastricht Treaty for the purpose of achieving such sustainability. Within the new framework for the economic governance of the European Union stipulated in the Maastricht Treaty, fiscal discipline was essential for allowing the European Central Bank to maintain price stability as its primary objective.[12] Failure of the fiscal discipline mechanism developed prior to the crisis by the Stability and Growth Pact on a coordination basis provided by the Maastricht Treaty, as part of an asymmetric Economic and Monetary Union,[13] to prevent the financing difficulties of the member states, including of those in the euro-area, reopened the discussions on

of the independent fiscal institutions being the main part of the institutional rules. For an analysis of these three categories of fiscal rules, see M. Antoš, 'Fiscal Stability Rules in Central European Constitutions' in M. Adams, F. Fabbrini, P. Larouche (eds), *The Constitutionalization of European Budgetary Constraints* (Hart Publishing 2014), 209–210.

11 R. Streinz, 'The Limits of Legal Regulation: Will the Treaty on Stability, Coordination and Governance in the Economic and Monetary Union Have a Real Legal Effect?' in W.-G. Ringe, P. Huber (eds), *Legal Challenges in the Global Financial Crisis* (Hart Publishing 2014), 243.

12 For further explanations of the role of fiscal rules in the Maastricht architecture, see the European Fiscal Board, *Assessment of EU Fiscal Rules*, August 2019, 9–10, available at https://ec.europa.eu/info/sites/info/files/2019-09-10-assessment-of-eu-fiscal-rules_en.pdf

13 A. Hinarejos, *The Euro Area Crisis in Constitutional Perspective* (Oxford University Press 2015), 3–10.

the effectiveness of such fiscal rules that led to a new structure of the economic governance in the EU.

The normative limitations of the various elements of the use of public funds, such as public expenditure, public deficit, public debt or public revenues,[14] generally referred to as "fiscal rules", although generally accepted as legal instruments for preventing the accrual of high public debt as well as of unsustainable public deficits, are not a constant in national legal systems. Moreover, strong criticism was concentrated on their suitability, namely on their presumed effect of reducing economic growth.[15] More than a decade ago, the economic and financial crisis erupted and affected the EU member states, albeit with different intensities. Generally, at the EU level, the responses to the crisis were mainly twofold: (i) the strengthening of the preventive safeguards against fiscal and macro-economic imbalances, by adopting regulations that became an intrinsic part of what was called the "euro-crisis law",[16] and (ii) the creation of common instruments of financial assistance aimed at helping those EU countries that had come under severe pressure on financial markets. For non-euro countries,[17] the existing EU balance of payments assistance mechanism, as regulated by Art. 143 TFEU and further detailed by Regulation 332/2002, remained available.[18]

For those countries that have received financial assistance, the loan conditionality prompted the adoption of specific fiscal responsibility rules, such as rules on expenditure ceilings and procedural rules for preparing and amending

14 For an overview of the evolution in time and geographic spread of the various fiscal rules, see V. Lledó, S. Yoon, X. Fang, S. Mbaye, Y. Kim, *Fiscal Rules at a Glance* (International Monetary Fund 2017), www.imf.org/external/datamapper/FiscalRules/Fiscal%20Rules%20at%20a%20Glance%20-%20Background%20Paper.pdf

15 V. Ruiz Almendral, 'The European Fiscal Consolidation Legal Framework: Its Impact on National Fiscal Constitutions and Parliamentary Democracy' in T. Beukers, B. de Witte, C. Kilpatrick (eds), *Constitutional Change Through Euro-crisis Law* (Cambridge University Press 2017), 28–29.

16 T. Beukers, B. de Witte, C. Kilpatrick (eds), *Constitutional Change Through Euro-crisis Law* (Cambridge University Press 2017).

17 Hungary in 2008, Latvia from 2008 to 2012 and Romania from 2008 to 2015 had access to the balance of payments EU financial assistance. The emergency financial assistance was granted jointly by the European Union, the International Monetary Fund and the World Bank (the International Bank for Reconstruction and Development) and was made available subject to strict conditions. In the case of Latvia, the EU financial assistance was accompanied by bilateral loans made by Sweden, Denmark and Estonia. For Hungary, see Z. Szente, 'Breaking and Making Constitutional Rules: The Constitutional Effects of the Financial Crisis in Hungary' in X. Contiades (ed.), *Constitutions in the Global Financial Crisis. A Comparative Analysis* (Ashgate 2013), 245–261; for Latvia, see R. Balodis, J. Pleps, 'Financial Crisis and the Constitutions in Latvia' in X. Contiades (ed.), ibid 117–140; and for Romania, see E.S. Tănăsescu, S. Gherghina, 'Limitations on Government Debt and Deficits in Romania' in F.L. Morrison (ed.), *Fiscal Rules – Limits on Governmental Deficits and Debt* (Springer 2016), 247–248.

18 Council Regulation (EC) No 332/2002 of 18 February 2002 establishing a facility providing medium-term financial assistance for Member States' balances of payments, Official Journal L 053, 23/02/2002.

the draft budget during the parliamentary approval procedure, as well as the application of various measures aimed at curbing the public deficit and debt by means of various expenditure cuts.

The new regulations adopted at the EU level as the crisis unfolded, either as part of EU law (Six Pack,[19] Two Pack[20]) or as inter-governmental treaties (the ESM Treaty,[21] the Treaty on Stability, Cooperation and Governance in the Economic and Monetary Union[22] or the Fiscal Compact[23]) as well as soft-law instruments (such as the Euro Plus Pact in 2011) were thus accompanied, for certain EU member states, by specific rules and measures provided in the Memorandums of Understanding attached to the loans granted under the financial assistance mechanisms. Both sets of regulations – general (EU level) and national (MoUs) – shared the common objective of improving the sustainability of public finances and fiscal responsibility, including by ensuring that the balanced budget rule is included in national regulations. In this process, a significant role was reserved for the national ownership of such fiscal rules,[24] which was deemed to be able to give a signal to the financial markets holding a symbolic power similar to the initially envisaged amendment to the TFEU

19 A package including six Regulations and a Directive, adopted in 2011 – Directive 2011/85 on requirements for budgetary frameworks of the Member States, Regulation 1173/2011 on the effective enforcement of budgetary surveillance in the euro area, Regulation 1174/2011 on the prevention and correction of macroeconomic imbalances, Regulation 1175/2011 amending Council Regulation 1466/97 on the strengthening of the surveillance of budgetary policies and the surveillance and co-ordination of economic policies, Regulation 1176/2011 on the prevention and correction of macroeconomic imbalances, Regulation 1177/2011 amending Regulation 1467/97 on speeding up and clarifying the implementation of the Excessive Deficit Procedure (OJ 2011 L 301).

20 A package including two Regulations applicable to euro-area states, adopted in 2013 – Regulation (EU) no. 472/2013 of the European Parliament and of the Council of 21 May 2013 on the strengthening of economic and budgetary surveillance of Member States in the euro area experiencing or threatened with serious difficulties with respect to their financial stability and Regulation (EU) no. 473/2013 of the European Parliament and of the Council of 21 May 2013 on common provisions for monitoring and assessing draft budgetary plans and ensuring the correction of excessive deficit of the Member States in the euro area (OJ 2013 L 140).

21 Treaty establishing the European Stability Mechanism, signed on 2 February 2012.

22 Also named the Fiscal Compact Treaty. Signed on 2 March 2012 by the 17 euro-area states at that time and eight no-euro-area states, it entered into force on 1 January 2013.

23 Fiscal Compact refers to the provisions in Title III of the Treaty on Stability, Cooperation and Governance in the Economic and Monetary Union, concerning the balanced budget rule and its ancillary monitoring mechanisms. While all member states, except for the UK and the Czech Republic, have ratified the TSCG, only the eurozone states, Bulgaria, Denmark and Romania have ratified its Title III – the Fiscal Compact.

24 A. de Streel, 'EU Fiscal Governance and the Effectiveness of its Reform' in M. Adams, F. Fabbrini, P. Larouche (eds), *The Constitutionalization of European Budgetary Constraints* (Hart Publishing 2014), 97.

to include the same fiscal rules, but it failed to obtain acceptance by all member states.[25]

In the EU member states that have adopted the Fiscal Compact, the transposition of the balanced budget rule into their national legal systems followed different paths, reflecting the diversity of national budgetary settings, thus taking advantage of the margin given by the Fiscal Compact to customize national provisions to the specific institutional and budgetary framework of each state. The emphasis on the acceptance of the balanced budget rule at the national level in a *binding* and *permanent* manner[26] and the subsequent design of the legal mechanisms aimed at ensuring its application (such as the automatic correction mechanism and the opinions of the national independent fiscal institutions) led to a variety of national implementation solutions.[27]

In assessing the transposition of the balanced budget rule into the national legal systems, the Commission reached an optimistic conclusion which found the signatory parties to be compliant, based not only on facts but also on "non-legal" arguments, such as "formal and public commitments given by Contracting Parties that the national legal framework will be applied in line with the requirements of the TSCG",[28] or on procedural constraints applicable to the adoption of annual budgetary laws, which were deemed to rule out the possibility of departing from the balanced budget rule requirements.[29]

However tolerant and optimistic the Commission may have been when accepting that all member states which ratified the Fiscal Compact have included both the numerical and the procedural rules (correction mechanism and

25 V. Ruiz Almendral, 'The European Fiscal Consolidation Legal Framework: Its Impact on National Fiscal Constitutions and Parliamentary Democracy' in T. Beukers, B. de Witte, C. Kilpatrick (eds), *Constitutional Change Through Euro-crisis Law* (Cambridge University Press 2017), 39–47. Communication from the Commission, 'The Fiscal Compact: Taking Stock', C (2017) 1200 final, 4.

26 According to Article 3(2) in Title III of TSCG, "The rules set out in paragraph 1 shall take effect in the national law of the Contracting Parties at the latest one year after the entry into force of this Treaty through provisions of binding force and permanent character, preferably constitutional, or otherwise guaranteed to be fully respected and adhered to throughout the national budgetary processes. The Contracting Parties shall put in place at national level the correction mechanism referred to in paragraph 1(e) on the basis of common principles to be proposed by the European Commission, concerning in particular the nature, size and time-frame of the corrective action to be undertaken, also in the case of exceptional circumstances, and the role and independence of the institutions responsible at national level for monitoring compliance with the rules set out in paragraph 1. Such correction mechanism shall fully respect the prerogatives of national Parliaments."

27 An outline of these national solutions is provided in the *Report from the Commission presented under Article 8 of the Treaty on Stability, Coordination and Governance in the Economic and Monetary Union*, C(2017) 1201 final.

28 *Report from the Commission presented under Article 8 of the Treaty on Stability, Coordination and Governance in the Economic and Monetary Union*, C(2017) 1201 final, para 3.1, p. 4. Alongside Romania, Cyprus, Denmark, France and Netherlands also made such commitments.

29 *Report from the Commission presented under Article 8 of the Treaty on Stability, Coordination and Governance in the Economic and Monetary Union*, C(2017) 1201 final, para 3.1, p. 4, as concerns Bulgaria.

monitoring by an independent fiscal institution) in the national legal systems in a manner generally precluding deviations in budget laws, the foundation of such an assumption is ill-judged, at least in those cases in which it considers political commitments. For obvious reasons, such commitments cannot be effective in legal terms, and the possibility to deviate from the rules upon adoption or rectification of annual budget laws will be open at all times. On the other hand – for example, in the case of the Romanian legal system – the insertion of the balanced budget rules into an ordinary law was the only option available in the absence of a constitutional revision. As the limited domain of organic laws, determined by Article 73 of the Romanian Constitution, does not include fiscal or financial (budgetary) rules, an organic law providing such rules could not be passed.[30]

Some of the fiscal rules included in national regulations as part of the conditionality attached to the financial assistance programs did not entirely mirror those existing at EU level, thus raising the issue of their compliance with the EU law, especially concerning their impact on social rights.[31] The decisions of the constitutional courts in those states, establishing a certain degree of protection of social rights, are now the subject of extensive research regarding the relationship between the fiscal rules and the budgetary measures adopted as part of the sovereign debt programs, and the national constitutional settings and further envisaged constitutional reforms. Yet, in the aftermath of the euro-crisis, it remains to be seen whether the detailed framework of fiscal rules developed in the national legal systems from complementary sources, combining the general rules included in the EU law with the specific rules, addressing the particular situation of the states that were subject to financial assistance programs, will be maintained as such or will be further amended, to become a constant part of the fiscal discipline rules applicable outside the crisis. It is worth emphasizing here that most of the rules adopted during the financial and sovereign debt crisis that are still in place passed one or more judicial tests before national courts,[32] including constitutional courts,[33] as well as before the European Court of Justice.[34]

30 E.S. Tănăsescu, S. Gherghina, 'Limitations on Government Debt and Deficits in Romania' in Morrison (n 17) 247–248.

31 C. Kilpatrick, 'Constitutions, Social Rights and Sovereign Debt States in Europe: A Challenging New Area of Constitutional Inquiry' in T. Beukers, B. de Witte, C. Kilpatrick (eds), *Constitutional Change Through Euro-crisis Law* (Cambridge University Press 2017), 279–326.

32 J.-H. Reestman, 'Legitimacy through Adjudication: The ESM Treaty and the Fiscal Compact before the National Courts' in T. Beukers, B. de Witte, C. Kilpatrick (eds), *Constitutional Change Through Euro-crisis Law* (Cambridge University Press 2017), 243–278.

33 For an overview of consistent case law of constitutional courts in Latvia and Romania in relation to the expenditure cut measures during the crisis, see R. Balodis, J. Pleps, 'Financial Crisis and the Constitutions in Latvia' in X. Contiades (ed.), *Constitutions in the Global Financial Crisis. A Comparative Analysis* (Ashgate 2013), 121–128; and particularly, S. Gherghina, E.S. Tănăsescu, 'Roumanie. La Cour constitutionnelle et l'équilibre des finances publiques', (2012) 28 Annuaire international de justice constitutionnelle 415–424.

34 A. Hinarejos, *The Euro Area Crisis in Constitutional Perspective* (Oxford University Press 2015), 121–154, F. Fabbrini, *Economic Governance in Europe. Comparative Paradoxes and Constitutional Challenges* (Oxford University Press 2016), 63–114.

Thus, the negative effects of the financial crisis on the budgetary position of these countries had been tackled by specifically designed fiscal rules addressing the challenges faced by their respective public budgets. Of course, such fiscal rules were not new. However, they were not considered explicitly in budgetary practice, nor were they implicitly derived from the general deficit and debt limits in the TFEU and the Stability and Growth Pact. These rules included specific measures aimed at reducing specific expenditure (e.g. the interdiction to cumulate pensions and salaries in the public sector above a certain threshold, the reduction of personnel expenditure, cuts in public sector salaries and pensions, the reorganization of public institutions and public pensions or public sector salaries schemes). They also included more general rules addressing certain budgetary operations, such as the interdiction to transfer the expenditure allowed in the public budgets for investment to current expenditure allowances, the interdiction to increase personnel expenditure within a six-month period prior to general parliamentary elections, the interdiction to rectify state budgets more than twice a year, except for an exceptional worsening of the macro-economic conditions during the first semester,[35] etc.

The specific measures aimed at reducing the public deficit and debt could not ignore the financial relationship between central and local budgets, especially as regards the various financial equalization mechanisms, as they constantly drew significant amounts from the central budget. The scarcity of available financing revealed the weaknesses of the vertical distribution of financial powers and occasionally even placed central and local authorities in almost antagonistic positions, where they were seeking funds from the same pool – either income tax revenues (as they are most often subject to partial reallocation to local budgets of the community they were sourced from after their collection to central budget) or loans (considering in addition the preference usually given by banks to state borrowing due to the general credit provision rules under the prudential supervision regulations).

From this perspective, the three main elements of the financing structure of local budgets were affected to various degrees during the financial crisis, while some of the adjustments made to these elements remained in place. Moreover, the impact of the various changes made to the financing of local budgets, as part of the overall objective of reducing public deficits and debt, may be considered to have acted as a resilience test. The ability of the local authorities to perform their duties in a proper manner and, for most part, to continuously ensure the operation of local public services, despite the sharp reduction of

35 Such rules were included in Romania in Law no. 69/2010 on fiscal-budgetary responsibility, adopted as part of the fiscal consolidation program that was a condition for disbursements under the 2009 loan package granted by the EU according to the balance of payments regulation, the International Monetary Fund, the International Bank for Reconstruction and Development and the European Bank for Reconstruction and Development. S. Gherghina, E.S. Tănăsescu, 'Roumanie. La Cour constitutionnelle et l'équilibre des finances publiques', (2012) 28 Annuaire international de justice constitutionnelle 409–430.

some of or even all their available financing sources, could be seen as a fair indicator of the financial viability of local autonomy and, from a legal perspective, of the effectiveness of the legal mechanism designed to allow for it.

The general financing structure of local administrative units

Throughout the crisis and in the better times that followed, the common standard for the financial element of local autonomy in the EU member states continued to be the principles stated in Article 9 of the Charter ("Financial resources of local authorities") aimed at ensuring that decentralized local governments are adequately funded, as may be required for the proper fulfillment of their responsibilities. In general terms, the principles included in Article 9 articulate four different aspects of the financial relationship between central and local budgets, all four being ascribed as criteria for assessing the financial independence of local governments. Nevertheless, such independence should be read as an absence of a complete dependency on transfers of funds and decisions related thereto made by the central government. This is precisely the issue against which the impact of the financial crisis on local autonomy is to be assessed, particularly in terms of the resilience test mentioned above, by measuring the degree of financial independence of the local administrative units after the consolidation of the changes in their financing structures.

First, local authorities should have access to "adequate financial resources of their own", which are yet to be determined on a relative scale, "within national economy policy",[36] and "be commensurate with the responsibilities provided for by the constitution and the law".[37] The local authorities should decide freely on the administration of (at least) their own resources. This idea, of ensuring direct and permanent financing sources for local budgets, to be directly accessed and used by local authorities according to general rules on public budgeting and spending, is meant to provide autonomy through the separation of specific financing pools not accessible to the central government. The most evident source of financing for local budgets is directly related to the recognition in the national legal system of the ownership by local communities, the income from such owned assets being a constant source of funds for local budgets (rents, concession fees, dividends paid by local public undertakings, etc.), although not of equal significance in all cases.

As this specific source of funds is dependent upon the economic cycle, it may be easily wiped off during economic downturns. Generally, being a source that derives from the exploitation by local authorities of the ownership rights of the local community, national regulations do not provide specific compensation mechanisms to trigger a transfer of replacement funds from central budgets

36 Article 9 para 1 of the Charter: "Local authorities shall be entitled, within national economic policy, to adequate financial resources of their own, of which they may dispose freely within the framework of their powers."

37 Article 9 para 2 of the Charter: "Local authorities' financial resources shall be commensurate with the responsibilities provided for by the constitution and the law."

in case of loss of income from ownership due to adverse economic conditions. However, the fragility of this financing source and its partial or total unavailability, especially for smaller communities, requires the identification by law of additional financial sources that could ensure the adequacy of local authorities' own financial resources in relation to their responsibilities. This additional source, generally accepted in all member states, is local taxation – that is, taxation imposed and directed by law to local budgets. While local taxes are approved by law, they are payable directly to local budgets and, if allowed at the constitutional level, local authorities may establish specific taxes within the limits provided by law, thus ensuring in both cases full compliance with the constitutional principle of legality of taxation.

From an idealistic perspective on local autonomy, local ownership and local taxation should be the main financing sources for local authorities, having the capacity to a certain extent to ensure those resources that are adequate for their tasks. Yet, even in the absence of a financial crisis, the traditional line of division of financial power[38] that separated central from local governments upon the advent of the administrative decentralization movement in the 1970s was drawn on the already existing lines separating central ownership and taxation from local ownership and taxation, which were obviously not at all in favor of local communities. Local taxes and other charges directed by law to local budgets could not be compared in any way to those reserved for the central budgets. As the recognition of such structural asymmetry and, thus, of the insufficiency of these two "basic" financing sources was unavoidable, most states added a new taxation component, this time identified as a part of the centrally collected income tax and not as a specific source that is directly available only to local authorities. Thus, a much more productive tax, although collected at the central level, is partially redirected to local budgets, based on certain criteria provided by law. In most cases, the transfer of such amounts from the central to local budgets is automatic, on a regular (monthly) basis, and local authorities may freely dispose of these funds, once in local hands.

Although the financing of local budgets was much improved by the combined sources thus available – ownership, local taxation and transfer of part of locally generated[39] income tax – they all remain dependent on the economic cycle. Moreover, the legal mechanism that ensures both the taxation of income and the transfer from the central to the local budgets is entirely controlled by the central government – that is, it may be amended at any time. Local taxation is also established by law and may be further amended at the

38 Oliva (n 5) 86–90.

39 Locally generated means that the identification of the local community that is the recipient of income tax redirected from the central budget is related either to the fiscal residence of the taxpayer (the person who is the debtor of the payment obligation in the terms of applicable tax law), or to the fiscal residence of the natural person obtaining a taxable income, provided, of course, that in all cases such fiscal residence is in the reference state.

central level. This weakness became evident during the financial crisis, when the need to swiftly reduce public deficits opened the possibility for central authorities to consider reducing such transfers or adding supplementary conditions for them.

Second, at least a part of the financial resources of local budgets derives from sources that local authorities can control, within the limits set by law. Such control is mostly ensured by the recognized power of local authorities to determine local tax rates or amounts of charges due to local budgets within certain limits.[40] In addition, while the law may permit tax exemptions and the power of local authorities to decide on granting additional local tax exemptions, again within the limits set by law, central government may amend the law to include additional mandatory exemptions, thus affecting the financing source of the local budget. In most cases, the financial crisis did not affect the control exercised by local authorities over local tax rates and exemptions, although it revealed its rigid character inasmuch as the limits allowed by law for the decision of local authorities to increase taxation rates proved to be insufficient and difficult to amend.

Third, grants or transfers from the state budget to local communities should be in place, especially with the aim to "correct the effects of the unequal distribution of potential sources of finance"; they should not "diminish the discretion local authorities may exercise within their own sphere of responsibility"[41] and, as much as possible, should "not be earmarked for the financing of specific projects".[42] This amounts to accepting that the compatibility of financial equalization mechanisms with the local autonomy principle depends upon the lack of direction from the central authorities regarding the management of the transferred funds. At this point, the emphasis shifts from the independent access of local authorities to sources of financing and control thereof, to the independent management of the funds received from the state budgets. Fiscal autonomy is thus completed by autonomy in the management of funds,[43] both consolidating the financial element of local autonomy. The benchmark for the degree of autonomy of local authorities as concerns the management of the transferred funds should be that applicable for their own funds.

40 Article 9 para 3 of the Charter: "Part at least of the financial resources of local authorities shall derive from local taxes and charges of which, within the limits of statute, they have the power to determine the rate."

41 Article 9 para 5 of the Charter: "The protection of financially weaker local authorities calls for the institution of financial equalization procedures or equivalent measures which are designed to correct the effects of the unequal distribution of potential sources of finance and of the financial burden they must support. Such procedures or measures shall not diminish the discretion local authorities may exercise within their own sphere of responsibility."

42 Article 9 para 7 of the Charter: "As far as possible, grants to local authorities shall not be earmarked for the financing of specific projects. The provision of grants shall not remove the basic freedom of local authorities to exercise policy discretion within their own jurisdiction."

43 Bouvier, Esclassan, Lassale (n 1) 786–787.

The autonomy of local authorities in funds management was not significantly affected by the fiscal discipline rules enacted during the financial crisis, except for certain limitations imposed to prevent the accumulation of arrears in local budgets or any other similar increase of unpaid obligations.

Fourth, in addition to the various financing sources allowed mainly for current expenditure, local authorities should have access to loan financing for local capital investment.[44] In certain states (Germany, Romania), local administrative units may borrow for treasury (cash-flow) temporary needs and for refinancing existing loans of public guarantees.

Constant and temporary changes in the local financial autonomy

While provisions concerning the autonomy of local administrative units are included in the constitutions of most EU countries, constitutional references to their financial autonomy are far fewer.[45] In addition, all EU states have ratified the European Charter of Local Self-Government; therefore, its provisions concerning the financial autonomy of local administrative units should have been applied in the national legal systems, either by way of direct effects or by transposition.[46]

Depending on the constitutional limits of the local autonomy, the measures adopted by the member states for reducing public deficit and debt, either under the EU regulations, the Fiscal Compact, and/or the MoUs attached to the financial assistance programs (such as Greece, Portugal, Ireland, Romania, Hungary, Latvia), had impacted the financing of local budgets. In most cases, the primary aims of these measures were to reduce the amount of both transfers from the central to the local budgets and local debt, with the subsequent result of reducing expenditure of local budgets. Needless to say, such attempts did not remain unchallenged by local authorities,[47] which relied on the local autonomy principle and interpreted it as a general guarantee against any interference of central government with the revenues and expenditure of local budgets. Although not fully supported by the courts, this general approach, which confuses local financial autonomy with fiscal autonomy and funds management

44 Article 9 para 7 of the Charter: "For the purpose of borrowing for capital investment, local authorities shall have access to the national capital market within the limits of the law."

45 French Constitution (Art. 72), Spanish Constitution (Art. 142), Italian Constitution (Art. 119), Austrian Constitution (Art. 116), Croatian Constitution (Art. 138), Greek Constitution (Art. 102).

46 For an analysis of the reception of the Charter in the national systems as well as of its shortcomings, see Himsworth (n 2) 143–168.

47 See for Portugal, C. Nunes Silva, 'The Economic Adjustment Program Impact on Local Government Reform in Portugal' in C. Nunes Silva, J. Buček (eds), *Fiscal Austerity and Innovation in Local Governance in Europe* (Ashgate 2014), 44; for Belgium, D. Yernault, 'La dette publique dans le système constitutionnel et fédéral belge' in Morrison (n 17) 68, 74–75.

autonomy, opened an important debate[48] concerning the identification of the current extent and meaning of local financial autonomy.

The transformation of the elements of local financial autonomy under the pressure of crisis regulations was not uniform across the EU member states[49] as it accounted for different national settings as well as for differences in the financial pressure that prompted such regulations. However, certain common patterns may be identified, such as the enactment of fiscal discipline rules for the local budgets alongside a renewed emphasis on the requirement for a balanced budget, the application of debt brakes, the suppression of certain local taxes or the limitation of decision margins available to public authorities in respect of local tax rates, the restructuring or even direct reduction of transfers from central budgets, and the reinforcement of the supervisory and control mechanism applicable to local budgets. In addition, under some of the MoUs attached to the financial assistance programs (for Portugal and Greece, but not Ireland[50]), a reduction in local expenditure was envisaged by reorganization of the local governance, for optimizing allocation of responsibilities. Some[51] MoUs have also included requirements concerning the reorganization of public undertakings controlled by municipalities, which were generating constant losses for the local budgets. In 2011, the application of the Securities Market Programme bond-buying scheme in Italy, aiming to support its presence on the financial markets, was preceded by the European Central Bank's strong suggestion to reorganize (i.e. merge or otherwise abolish) intermediate levels of local government, such as provinces. The suggestion was accepted and the provinces were transformed, via emergency regulations, into public entities entrusted with the coordination of municipalities.[52] Such regulations were further challenged before the Italian Constitutional Court on grounds of local autonomy, and the Court held them to be unconstitutional on grounds of the inappropriateness of emergency regulations for a major reform of the local administration.[53]

The overall austerity measures adopted at state level concerning the limitation of deficit and debt in local budgets were focused on a general requirement of balanced budget, rather than on debt brakes, as well as on the limitation of transfers from central budgets, instead of interventions concerning the local

48 A. Baudu, 'La réforme fiscale locale: une autonomie fiscale au point mort?' (2020) *RFDA* 999ff; X. Cabannes, 'L'autonomie financière des collectivités territoriales après les récentes lois financières. Une adolescence difficile ou déjà une vieille lune?' (2018) 4 *AJDA* 720ff; Bouvier, Esclassan, Lassale (n 1) 793–795.

49 V. Ruiz Almendral, 'A Myopic Economic Constitution? Controlling the Debt and the Deficit Without fiscal Integration' (2015) 12 EUI Working Papers, Law, 22–23.

50 Nunes Silva (n 47) 36, 38–41.

51 Greece, Romania, Portugal.

52 L. Pierdominici, 'Constitutional Change through Emergency Decrees: The Abolition of Provinces in Italy' in T. Beukers, B. de Witte, C. Kilpatrick (eds), *Constitutional Change Through Euro-crisis Law* (Cambridge University Press 2017), 217–229.

53 Decision of the Italian Constitutional Court no. 220 of 19 July 2013.

budgets' own revenues from taxation and property. Contrary to the effects of the balanced budget rule at the national level, where a certain limited deficit is acceptable, for local budgets the required balance usually excludes deficits[54] and is limited to either equal revenues and expenditure or higher revenues (whereby in both cases revenues include loans for capital investments or for refinancing and, in some cases, treasury loans[55]).

As most national regulations already required local budgets to be adopted in balance, the crisis regulations have merely restated this obligation and reinforced the supervisory mechanism of compliance thereto. At the same time, the stricter conditions enforced both for transfers from central budgets and local borrowing made it more difficult for local authorities to rely on available financing sources for any deficit that may have "happened" to occur during the budget execution.[56] Local authorities were thus directed towards ensuring a better administration of their own revenues from local taxation and property as well as from the automatic transfers from central budgets in the form of redirected income tax. For most cases, borrowing was not only limited in value and subjected to strict conditions, including administrative approvals to be obtained from central authorities, but also available only for very few purposes – investments and refinancing of existing loans. Where law transferred administrative functions or responsibilities from the state to local authorities, appropriate funds for related costs had to be transferred to the local budget.

54 For Belgium, Yernault (n 47) 67; for the Czech Republic, where certain exceptions allow that a local budget is approved with a deficit, H. Marková, M. Kopecký, R. Suchánek, 'The Process of Budgeting and Issues of Indebtness in the Czech Republic' in Morrison (n 17) 94–95, for Greece, A. Tsevas, 'Limitations on Government Debt and deficits in Greece' in Morrison (n 17) 164, for Italy, E. Mostacci, 'From the Ideological Neutrality to the Neoclassical Inspiration: The Evolution of the Italian Constitutional Law of Public Debt and Deficit' in Morrison (n 17) 198, for France, A. Baudu, *Droit des finances publiques* (Dalloz 2018), 678–681, for the UK, T. Prosser, 'Limitations on Government Debt and deficits in the United Kingdom' in Morrison (n 17) 315; for Sweden, Damarey (n 6) 624. Since 2020, German regions are not allowed to adopt a budget in deficit; see Schenke, Chapter 3 in this book.

55 H. Pünder, 'Objects and Procedures of Budgetary Planning amd Limits to Borrowing ('Debt Brake') in the Federal Republic of Germany' in Morrison (n 17) 125–126, E.S. Tănăsescu, S. Gherghina, 'Limitations on Government Debt and Deficits in Romania' in Morrison (n 17) 260–261.

56 In the absence of a legal mechanism for ensuring a sound assessment of budget revenues upon the drafting of the budget projections, the balanced budget requirement may be forcibly met by an "optimistic" revenue overestimation. This leads most often to execution deficits, as the real revenues will not suffice for the planned expenditure. In Romania, for example, local authorities facing such contact with a much less favourable than estimated situation turn to central government for additional transfers. The most negative effect of such tolerated practice is the persistence of a grey area of discretionary, often politically justified, grants and loans from central budgets to local authorities. By seeking such type of subjective advantages, the local authorities are actively contributing to the undermining of financial local autonomy.

The fiscal discipline rules provided in national regulations or MoUs became equally applicable at the local level to the overall budget. Yet fiscal discipline did not go beyond the general requirement of a balanced local budget – that is, into the details of actual expenditure planned and incurred by local authorities. They continued to exercise their autonomy of funds management, provided that such management did not result in a local budget deficit. However, the combined pressure exercised by the reduction in grants and other transfers from state budgets, and in local taxes and charges influenced by the economic downturn during the crisis, has forced local authorities to limit their expenditures to those related to core functions and essential public services.

Consequently, alternative options were considered to ensure the adequacy of overall financing sources of local budgets, especially of ordinary sources such as local taxation, property revenues and regular transfers from state budgets. Among these were the increase of the local taxation base by eliminating exemptions, such as in Portugal,[57] and, more generally, the restructuring of the financial equalization mechanisms. Allowing for conditional transfers from the state budgets, the equalization mechanisms became more complicated as states sought to ensure that the limited amounts allocated at the central level for such transfers are proportional with the financial status of the recipients and also efficiently used at the local level. Beside the regular calculation of the equalization transfers, based on the combined criteria of (i) area of the local administrative unit (as an indicator of costs) and (ii) amounts generated from certain taxes (as an indicator of potential revenues), additional mechanisms were developed during the crisis. These ranged from an attempt to guarantee a minimal, basic, local budget, via regulation of minimal standard costs for public services, based on calculation per capita (e.g. Romania[58]) to allocation of exceptional transfers from state budgets designated to overcome local financial difficulties under certain conditions (Spain[59]).

These tailored solutions were further refined and resulted in specific national solutions for organizing the transfers from the central to local budgets. Their initial, short-term, aim to ensure both compliance with the deficit and debt limits at the central level and an efficient use of the funds was replaced, once the crisis was surpassed, by a more permanent objective of ensuring the cooperation and coordination between central and local authorities to achieve compliance

57 Nunes Silva (n 47) 35.

58 Under the minimal standard costs mechanism, a specific cost of essential public services is calculated per capita, usually for each type of local administrative unit, to be further used for assessing a minimal local budget for each such category of local communities. In case the estimated (budgeted) annual revenues of the local budget are lower than the minimal budget, taking into consideration the efforts made by the local authorities to collect any due revenues, the balance shall be transferred from the state budget. This type of safety net, at least for small and medium-sized local administrative units, was applied in Romania starting from 2015.

59 V. Ruiz Almendral, A. Cuenca, 'Budgetary stability in the autonomous regions: beyond constitutional reform' (2014) 3 (4) *Spanish Economic and Financial Outlook* 58–59.

with the applicable fiscal discipline rules. An additional, more comprehensive, coordination mechanism was created in France by the law concerning the public finance program for 2018–2022, based on contracts signed by the government with selected local administrative units.[60] The aim pursued by the cooperation based on such contracts is to consolidate the ability of local units to ensure sufficient of their own resources as well as to structure their contribution to the reduction of public expenditure and of public deficits. As the contract stipulates for each local administrative unit specific objectives for the evolution of current (functioning) expenses for the term of the contract as well as for the improvement of its financing needs, the financial penalty for failure to comply with contractual obligations is to be determined according to a formula and collected from the revenues generated by certain local taxes.[61] Although criticized as a serious coup against local financial autonomy, the French Conseil Constitutionnel upheld such a mandatory contracting mechanism. While recognizing that the limits imposed by the contract as well as its mandatory character and attached penalties may be deemed to have an adverse effect on the financial autonomy of local administrative units, such an adverse effect is not as grave as breaching articles 72 and 72-2 of the Constitution.[62] In reaching this conclusion, the Court considered the aim pursued by the contractual mechanism, namely ensuring compliance with the balanced budget objective stated in Article 34 of the Constitution. Furthermore, the Court assessed the proportionality of the restriction imposed on financial autonomy and considered the legal guarantees provided for this latter principle. Based on this legal rationale, the Court upheld the mechanism as a proportionate and legitimate restriction on financial local autonomy.

Similar mechanisms allowing for the cooperation between central and local governments, with the common objective of ensuring sound budgetary practices and including sanctions for the local administrative units that fail to comply with the agreed objectives, were adopted in Italy, Austria, Spain, Denmark and the Netherlands.[63]

Such transformations and the variety in the national solutions that were adopted represent a good indicator of the central role played by grants and loans offered by central government to local administrative units. Despite its variations due to the pressures imposed by the financial crisis, the mechanism of such transfers cannot be excluded from the financing structure available to local governments as part of their autonomy. This remains true not only for those

60 For 2018–2022, 322 local administrative units have signed such coordination contracts, being selected on criteria related to their financial status, namely current (functioning) expenditure higher than 60 million euros in the reference year (2016). Damarey (n 6) 580.

61 É. Douat, 'La contractualisation entre l'État et les collectivités territoriales: disparition ou évolution?' (2020) 6 *RFDA* 989ff; Cabannes (n 48) 720ff; Oliva (n 5) 95–96.

62 Ibid.

63 Damarey (n 6) 581–582.

states where such a mechanism is stated at the constitutional level,[64] but also for those that have implemented it in their public finance legislation, in most cases based on the principle provided by the Charter.

Most EU countries have enforced additional limitations on local debt, either by specific, detailed rules concerning the total amount of debt available on an annual basis for all local units, such as in Germany[65] or Romania,[66] or, in some cases, by specific debt brakes and financial conditions for borrowing. The supervision of the compliance with such limits, including of the intricate calculations supposed by these cumulative limitations, has been entrusted to central bodies. In certain cases, where the law or the case law have acknowledged that any loan or guarantee undertaken by local authorities in breach of such imperative limitations shall be *ultra vires* and thus null and void, certain "safe harbor" measures may be in place to protect lenders.[67]

As local public debt is generally limited to capital investments, during the crisis some central governments have compensated for the lack of available financing for such local investment by either creating national programs that provided additional financing topping the capital expenditure from local budgets (such as in Romania or Slovakia or France) or granted loans for such investments via specialized agencies, such as the Public Works Loan Board in the UK[68] or Agence France Locale in France.[69] However, special loans were also granted from central budgets to local administrative units, mostly to solve liquidity issues and avoid accumulation of overdue payments (Romania, Spain).

Most of the strict control mechanisms applied to local public debt during the crisis are still in place and it seems unlikely that this exceptional source of revenues for the local budget will be returned to the wider discretion of local authorities as long as the local public debt continues to be counted as part of the national public debt. If at the height of the crisis the no-bailout rule was relaxed in some cases by the creation of exceptional bailout mechanisms, such as in Spain for the autonomous regions,[70]

64 An overview of Euro area states in V. Ruiz Almendral, 'The European Fiscal Consolidation Legal Framework: Its Impact on National Fiscal Constitutions and Parliamentary Democracy' in Beukers, de Witte, Kilpatrick (n 52) 39–47.

65 For a detailed presentation, see Schenke, Chapter 3, in this book; Pünder (n 55) 125–132.

66 The Romanian Law on fiscal responsibility, adopted in 2010 pursuant to the MoU attached to the financial assistance received under the Council Regulation (EC) No 332/2002 of 18 February 2002 establishing a facility providing medium-term financial assistance for Member States' balances of payments, has added a second local debt ceiling to the one already existing. Under this double ceiling, a local administrative unit may undertake debt to a certain limit calculated in relation to a three-year ratio of own revenues, provided that it also stays below the national annual ceiling established for the total outstanding local debt.

67 Prosser (n 54) 316.

68 Ibid.

69 M. Bouvier, Esclassan, Lassale (n 1) 856–859.

70 V. Ruiz Almendral, A. Cuenca, 'Budgetary stability in the autonomous regions: beyond constitutional reform' (2014) 3 (4) *Spanish Economic and Financial Outlook* 58–59.

these are exceptions as in most cases the rule has continued to apply; most likely, the exceptional bailout schemes will cease to exist[71] once their aim is achieved and the exceptional context that justified them disappears.

The current pandemic crisis and the apparent reverse of the public deficit and debt limits it caused throughout 2020, and most likely through 2021, have not affected the financing structure of the local budgets. The decline in revenues from their own sources, such as local taxes and charges, local property revenues, redirected income tax or other shared taxes (transferred from the state budget), has been compensated for mostly through the equalization mechanisms and other available transfers from central budgets.[72] Local borrowing played no role in the financing of local budgets during this period, as the existing limitations made it unavailable for the, most often, current expenses imposed by the pandemic. Where new functions were assigned to local authorities, such as healthcare, education or prevention measures, the existing mechanisms should have ensured transfers from the state budget of adequate financing. Here, it should be noted the continuous validity of the financial provisions in Article 9 of the Charter, which proved their adequacy during both the global financial crisis and the pandemic crisis.

However, the resilience test applied by the crisis to local financial autonomy resulted in a pragmatic narrowing of its scope. The various measures adopted during the crisis and further maintained after it ended shifted the emphasis within the financial structure of the local budgets from their own resources to those transferred from central budgets. In the absence of fiscal autonomy of local administrative units, denied in most if not all EU member states, the financial local autonomy is concentrated in the autonomy of funds management. Such relative autonomy was further narrowed by the supervisory mechanisms developed at the central state level for ensuring compliance with the fiscal discipline rules.

Concluding remarks

After more than seven years of implementation at national level of the most important fiscal rules designed at the EU level for the purpose of overcoming the negative effects of the financial crisis and for ensuring the sustainability of public finances, the national practices developed by the member states prove the diversity allowed by the EU minimal standard rules. Based on both the differences among national legal systems and the political will to fully accept and apply the uniform fiscal rules, such diversity reveals the variety of national legal solutions for the implementation of the fiscal rules and for the mechanisms aimed at ensuring compliance with them.

71 Ibid 61.

72 M. Lascombe, V. Dussart, 'Des conséquences de la crise du covid-19 sur les finances publiques locales' (2020) *RFDA* 986ff.

Altogether, the measures adopted at the national level during the crisis and aimed at reducing public deficits and debt continued to be applied and refined even after the end the crisis. Financial local autonomy was reshaped by the limitations it suffered and is to be further assessed in relation to the public interest objective of maintaining sound public finances, pursuant to Article 126 TFEU, as well as to the constitutional provisions concerning a similar objective, as applicable in certain EU member states. Accordingly, the interpretation and application of the principle of financial local autonomy will depend on the national approaches to the balanced budget rule. This is to say that those countries that have inserted this rule at the constitutional level, or have otherwise complied with the obligation undertaken under the Fiscal Compact and have thus acquired national ownership of the rule, will most likely interpret the financial local autonomy in relation to the overall objective of budgetary discipline, accepting proportional limitations to such autonomy, subject to appropriate safeguards. On the other hand, where the Treaty objective of sound public finances and the balanced budget rule in the Fiscal Compact did not become an operational part of the national legal system and, while formally transposed, are largely ignored by both institutional practice and jurisprudence, the local financial autonomy will be interpreted in relation to the constitutional provisions in this respect, if at all.

Bibliography

Antoš M, 'Fiscal Stability Rules in Central European Constitutions' in M Adams, F Fabbrini, P Larouche (eds), *The Constitutionalization of European Budgetary Constraints* (Hart Publishing 2014)

Balodis R, Pleps J, 'Financial Crisis and the Constitutions in Latvia' in X Contiades (ed.), *Constitutions in the Global Financial Crisis. A Comparative Analysis* (Ashgate 2013)

Baudu A, *Droit des finances publiques* (Dalloz 2018)

Baudu A, 'La réforme fiscale locale: une autonomie fiscale au point mort?' (2020) 6 *RFDA*

Beukers T, de Witte B, Kilpatrick C (eds), *Constitutional Change Through Euro-crisis Law* (Cambridge University Press 2017)

Bouvier M, Esclassan M-C, Lassale J-P, *Finances publiques* (15th ed. LGDJ lextenso 2016)

Cabannes X, 'L'autonomie financière des collectivités territoriales après les récentes lois financières. Une adolescence difficile ou déjà une vieille lune?' (2018) 4 *AJDA*

Damarey S, *Droit public financier* (Dalloz 2018)

Douat É, 'La contractualisation entre l'État et les collectivités territoriales: disparition ou évolution?' (2020) 6 *RFDA*

Fabbrini F, *Economic Governance in Europe: Comparative Paradoxes and Constitutional Challenges* (Oxford University Press 2016)

Gherghina S, Tănăsescu ES, *Roumanie. La Cour constitutionnelle et l'équilibre des finances publiques* (Economica, Presses Universitaires d'Aix-Marseille 2013)

Himsworth, CMG, *The European Charter of Local Self-Government: A Treaty for Local Democracy* (Edinburgh University Press 2015)

Hinarejos A, *The Euro Area Crisis in Constitutional Perspective* (Oxford University Press 2015)

Kilpatrick C, 'Constitutions, Social Rights and Sovereign Debt States in Europe: A Challenging New Area of Constitutional Inquiry' in T Beukers, B de Witte, C Kilpatrick (eds), *Constitutional Change Through Euro-crisis Law* (Cambridge University Press 2017)

Lascombe M, Dussart V, 'Des conséquences de la crise du covid-19 sur les finances publiques locales' (2020) 6 *RFDA*

Lledó V, Yoon S, Fang X, Mbaye S, Kim Y, *Fiscal Rules at a Glance* (International Monetary Fund 2017)

Marková H, Kopecký M, Suchánek R, 'The Process of Budgeting and Issues of Indebtedness in the Czech Republic' in FL Morrison (ed.), *Fiscal Rules – Limits on Governmental Deficits and Debt* (Springer 2016)

Mostacci E 'From the Ideological Neutrality to the Neoclassical Inspiration: The Evolution of the Italian Constitutional Law of Public Debt and Deficit' in FL Morrison (ed.), *Fiscal Rules – Limits on Governmental Deficits and Debt* (Springer 2016)

Nunes Silva C, 'The Economic Adjustment Program Impact on Local Government Reform in Portugal' in C Nunes Silva, J Buček (eds), *Fiscal Austerity and Innovation in Local Governance in Europe* (Ashgate 2014)

Oliva E, *Finances publiques* (3rd ed. Sirey 2015)

Pierdominici L, 'Constitutional Change through Emergency Decrees: The Abolition of Provinces in Italy' in T Beukers, B de Witte, C Kilpatrick (eds), *Constitutional Change Through Euro-crisis Law* (Cambridge University Press 2017)

Prosser T, 'Limitations on Government Debt and Deficits in the United Kingdom' in FL Morrison (ed.), *Fiscal Rules – Limits on Governmental Deficits and Debt* (Springer 2016)

Pünder H, 'Objects and Procedures of Budgetary Planning and Limits to Borrowing ("Debt Brake") in the Federal Republic of Germany' in FL Morrison (ed.), *Fiscal Rules – Limits on Governmental Deficits and Debt* (Springer 2016)

Reestman J-H, 'Legitimacy through Adjudication: The ESM Treaty and the Fiscal Compact before the National Courts' in T Beukers, B de Witte, C Kilpatrick (eds), *Constitutional Change Through Euro-crisis Law* (Cambridge University Press 2017)

Ruiz Almendral V, 'A Myopic Economic Constitution? Controlling the Debt and the Deficit Without Fiscal Integration' (2015) 12 EUI Working Papers, Law

Ruiz Almendral V, 'The European Fiscal Consolidation Legal Framework: Its Impact on National Fiscal Constitutions and Parliamentary Democracy' in T Beukers, B de Witte, C Kilpatrick (eds), *Constitutional Change Through Euro-crisis Law* (Cambridge University Press 2017)

Ruiz Almendral V, Cuenca A, 'Budgetary stability in the autonomous regions: beyond constitutional reform' (2014) 3 (4) *Spanish Economic and Financial Outlook*

Steckel Assouere, M-C, 'Le partage des compétences financières entre les États et leurs collectivités territoriales dans les Constitutions des vingt-sept pays membres de l'Union européenne' (2013) 121 *RFFP*

de Streel A, 'EU Fiscal Governance and the Effectiveness of its Reform' in M Adams, F Fabbrini, P Larouche (eds), *The Constitutionalization of European Budgetary Constraints* (Hart Publishing 2014)

Streinz R, 'The Limits of Legal Regulation: Will the Treaty on Stability, Coordination and Governance in the Economic and Monetary Union Have a Real Legal Effect?' in W-G Ringe, P Huber (eds), *Legal Challenges in the Global Financial Crisis* (Hart Publishing 2014)

Szente Z, 'Breaking and Making Constitutional Rules: The Constitutional Effects of the Financial Crisis in Hungary' in X Contiades (ed.), *Constitutions in the Global Financial Crisis. A Comparative Analysis* (Ashgate 2013)

Tănăsescu ES, Gherghina S, 'Limitations on Government Debt and Deficits in Romania' in FL Morrison (ed.), *Fiscal Rules – Limits on Governmental Deficits and Debt* (Springer 2016)
Tsevas A, 'Limitations on Government Debt and Deficits in Greece' in FL Morrison (ed.), *Fiscal Rules – Limits on Governmental Deficits and Debt* (Springer 2016)
Yernault D, 'La dette publique dans le système constitutionnel et fédéral belge' in FL Morrison (ed.), *Fiscal Rules – Limits on Governmental Deficits and Debt* (Springer 2016)

7 Balanced budget rule and the transversality of agencies

Bogdan Iancu

Transversality of agencies in the constitutional state and in the European Constitutional Area

This chapter addresses the broader implications of institutional engineering in the context of the Fiscal Compact[1] and its surrounding legal and ideological environments. Budgets are unlikely to be balanced if some sanction or constraint is not placed on the adopting parliament and, by implication, on the government that drafts the budget bill. The Fiscal Compact, soundly enough in principle, entrusts domestic policing of its substantive rules to a technocratic autonomous body but, somewhat paradoxically, also provides that the correction mechanism implemented by this 'transversal' agency should fully respect the prerogatives of the parliament. I will briefly examine this antinomy by first addressing the constitutional issues related to agencification within the nation state. The first part of the argument also reviews an emerging international consensus on governance models embedded in policy solutions that rely on unelected bodies. Such models have been, for the most part, promoted in unstable, peripheral systems but reverse conformities are also appearing. The second section reviews the place of independent fiscal institutions (IFIs) in the Fiscal Compact. The chapter concludes with a brief discussion on germane patterns of agencification.

The place that should be occupied by autonomous agencies in the constitutional state has been contested from the very beginning. In the jurisdiction of the origin of 'independent agencies', the United States, autonomy from the classic branches of power was reconciled with inherited constitutional frameworks of reference via a play on concepts, namely by qualifying the powers exercised by such bodies as 'quasi-' (legislative, executive, judicial). According

1 The Treaty on Stability, Coordination and Governance in the Economic and Monetary Union (TSCG) or the Fiscal Stability Treaty, is an intergovernmental treaty meant to "strengthen the economic pillar of the economic and monetary union" and to introduce stricter rules on budgetary discipline within the Member States of the European Union. The treaty is divided into six titles, three of them (III–V) containing rules regarding fiscal discipline, coordination and governance. Title III is entitled "Fiscal Compact".

DOI: 10.4324/9781315181882-11

to the famous 1935 judgment of the United States Supreme Court in the case of *Humphrey's Executor v. United States*, [2] the intermingling of 'prefixed' functions – quasi-legislative and quasi-judicial – in the statutory powers of the Federal Trade Commission and the expert, apolitical character of the commission justified the constitutional in-betweenness of the institution and thus the fact that it was not formally assigned to either the legislative or the executive branch. At the practical level, this reasoning gave constitutional imprimatur to a novelty and reconciled the New Deal power imponderables but, from a doctrinal/normative perspective, the nominalist escape has been unpersuasive ever since. As Justice Jackson would point out later:

> Administrative agencies have been called quasi-legislative, quasi-executive or quasi-judicial, as the occasion required, in order to validate their functions within the separation-of-powers scheme of the Constitution. The mere retreat to the qualifying 'quasi' is implicit with confession that all recognized classifications have broken down, and 'quasi' is a smooth cover which we draw over our confusion as we might use a counterpane to conceal a disordered bed.[3]

Even though practices in the jurisdiction of origin have later revealed a slow retreat from the initial infatuation with counter-majoritarian 'expertise' and a partial return to classical frameworks and traditional normative references, agencification elsewhere has proceeded in a linear progression during the late twentieth century and the beginning of the twenty-first.[4]

This trend has been noticed by political science and public law comparativists since the early 2000s. In 2000, Bruce Ackerman drew attention to the agencification phenomenon as one of the factors indicating a more general need to rethink the inherited separation-of-powers paradigm.[5] In addition, a study by Frank Vibert on the proliferation of independent bodies in constitutional jurisdictions speaks, tellingly, of a *The Rise of the Unelected.*[6] Global taxonomies are generally hard to establish due to the lack of a common functional denominator: the uses and functions of such autonomous bodies vary widely,

2 295 US 602 (1935)

3 FTC v. Ruberoid Co., 343 US 470, at 487–488 (Jackson, J., dissenting).

4 For a comparative analysis of these processes and their relative implications, see Bogdan Iancu, 'Government and governance: The constitutional politics of institutional neutrality', in Bogdan Iancu and Elena-Simina Tănăsescu (eds) *Governance and Constitutionalism: Law, Politics, and Institutional Neutrality* (Routledge 2019) 11–31.

5 Bruce Ackerman, 'The New Separation of Powers, (2000) 113 (3) *Harv. L. Rev.* 633–729. I discuss in more detail the general implications of agencification in constitutional law and constitutional politics in Bogdan Iancu, "Government and governance: The constitutional politics of institutional neutrality", Bogdan Iancu and Elena-Simina Tănăsescu (eds) *Governance and Constitutionalism: Law, Politics, and Institutional Neutrality* (Routledge 2019), 11–31.

6 Frank Vibert, *The Rise of the Unelected: Democracy and the New Separation of Powers* (Cambridge University Press 2007).

from regulatory commissions proper to ombudsmen, to watchdog organizations of various kinds and human rights tribunals. Accommodating the autonomy of such agencies within national constitutional systems varies even at the terminological level, from the French *autorités administratives indépendentes* to the Romanian *autonomous administrative authorities* and the British *quasi-autonomous non-governmental organizations* (QUANGOs). The phenomenon as such, that is the proliferation of bodies which fall to various degrees outside the traditional political branches of government, and therefore escape the direct sweep of majoritarian political decisions, is undeniable. Whether by consensus or by acquiescence, this trend towards a proliferation of pockets of institutional autonomy is often presented, explicitly or implicitly, as a positive development.[7] From a normative standpoint, however, independence from politics is not an unqualified benefit and should therefore be the end result of complex and cautious trade-offs. In the logic of *trias politica*, the only pocket of independence from politics was represented by courts. Furthermore, even in the case of the judiciary, autonomy was very carefully circumscribed by reference to the paramount value that was to be served by independence (judicial impartiality, including vis-à-vis the state) and the premise that adjudication is in essence neutral and thus unproblematic (a belief the canonical expression of which was Montesquieu's 'mouthpiece' metaphor). To be sure, distance from direct majoritarian control has produced proven benefits in some other fields as well (central banks are often used as a paradigmatic example; constitutional courts are another). But outside textbook examples like courts and central banks, patterns of counter-majoritarian institutionalization are fraught with their own set of ambiguities and pitfalls, such as opaqueness, the possibility of capture, or tunnel vision. Therefore, whereas institutional autonomy from politics may be beneficial in certain settings and for certain purposes, the current drive towards innovation through agencification is also fraught with perplexities and perils.

Within the European Union as such, the impetus towards creating pockets of institutional autonomy distinct from traditional political institutions is distributed unevenly. In regard to older member states, few explicit conditionalities in this direction may be identified. A notable exception is represented by autonomous data protection supervisory bodies. In newer

7 See, for example, Ackerman (n 5). But cf. András Sajó, Renáta Uitz, *The Constitution of Freedom: An Introduction to Legal Constitutionalism* (Oxford University Press 2017), 159ff. The authors are deeply ambivalent about this *novum*, conceding that independent agencies may serve as *veto points*, in an age when traditional checks have been practically overrun by changes in context (generating e.g. executive dominance). At the same time, they emphasize numerous caveats, such as the possibility of capture by interests, the potential for veiled and thus unaccountable politicization, and a lack of consensus on which functions should/could be exercised by agencies: "In short, establishing an independent institution to perform a particular governmental function is a matter of choice: the same governmental tasks can be performed by different, yet equally plausible, arrangements" (p.161).

member states, the situation is different due to the requirement to adopt the *acquis* in all its dimensions, including political conditionalities, prior to accession, and also because this process is monitored by the Commission as the 'master of conditionalities'.[8] Although in the indeterminate, somewhat Byzantine constitutional framework of the EC/EU the European Commission is designated as the 'executive branch', the Commission itself was designed as an independent agency of sorts.[9] The need for ensuring and enforcing neutrality is after all the very reason why Commissioners, once appointed, *neither seek nor take instructions*, either from 'their' governments or from any other entity.[10] As such, the European Commission still evinces all the benefits of autonomy in the exercise of functions that require distance from a political, 'transmission belt' administration paradigm[11] (infringement actions, competition enforcement, data-gathering and statistical skills). By the same token, the Commission's dominant institutional features also predetermine the shortcomings and limitations deriving from the overuse or misuse of this institutional form. In this latter respect, the more the Commission is dragged out of its bureaucratic comfort zone and transformed into a quasi-political executive, in clumsy mimicry of national arrangements, the more tensions and logical cacophonies are bound to appear. The ill-fated post-Lisbon experiment with *Spitzenkandidaten* in 2014 and its rapid demise in 2019 are telling developments in this respect.[12]

The bureaucratic limitations of the Commission have generated novel forms of counter-majoritarian institution-building in newer members states, notably in the areas of judicial organization and anticorruption. The 'Judicial-council Euro-model' promoted by the Commission in all new member states is a case in point. With the exception of the Czech Republic, all continental (post-

8 See also, Jacques Ziller, 'Agencification as European Union Acquis', in Bogdan Iancu and Elena-Simina Tănăsescu (eds) *Governance and Constitutionalism: Law, Politics, and Institutional Neutrality* (Routledge 2019) 64–79.

9 This is essentially the core of the Peter L. Lindseth's argument, reiterated in ever more sophisticated forms since his landmark article on 'Democratic Legitimacy and the Administrative Character of Supranationalism: The Example of the European Community', (1999) 99 *Columbia Law Review* 628–738. Giandomenico Majone makes, from a different angle, a similar point in his influential early volume on the European Community as a regulatory quasi-state (with neutral institutions, primarily the Commission, at its core), *Regulating Europe* (Routledge 1996).

10 Art. 17 (3) TEU: "The members of the Commission shall be chosen on the ground of their general competence and European commitment from persons whose independence is beyond doubt. In carrying out its responsibilities, the Commission shall be completely independent. Without prejudice to Article 18(2), the members of the Commission shall neither seek nor take instructions from any Government or other institution, body, office or entity."

11 Richard B. Stewart, 'The Reformation of American Administrative Law' (June 1975) 88 (8) *Harv. L. Rev.* 1667–1813

12 I develop this line of argument in 'Changed Vocabularies: A Few Semantic Ambiguities of Network Constitutionalism', Chapter 11, in Iulia Motoc, Krzysztof Wojtyczek, Paulo Pinto de Albuquerque (eds), *New Developments in Constitutional Law: Essays in Honour of András Sajó* (Eleven International Publishing 2018) 191–212.

communist) states that have joined the EU after 2004 have adopted judicial councils corresponding to the 'good practice model' advocated by the Commission and its partner institutions in the Council of Europe, thus accepting the premise that judicial independence is best served by judicial self-government. However, whereas the international good practice had originated in a national blueprint (the Italian CSM),[13] this form of grand-scale constitutional engineering modeled after a national idiosyncratic institution is difficult to justify, even *prima facie*, in other settings. In practice, such reforms have already backfired, producing different effects from those envisioned by international promoters.[14] Furthermore, hasty or poor institutional engineering, once it becomes widespread, will generate unintended consequences, such as reverse conformities. Paradoxically, once a sufficient number of countries have adopted a certain model, the enforced conformity is capable of generating path dependencies and ratchet effects within the "common constitutional area".[15] In a globalized legal world, the boundaries between center and periphery are blurred and this tendency is exponentially potentialized in tight-knit, integrated spaces like the European Union or the Council of Europe. Otherwise, and more bluntly put, the habit of disposing of normative 'garbage' at the periphery will produce externalities which will reflect back to the center.[16] For example, whereas judicial independence (at least in the minimalist understanding of irremovability – that is, security of tenure) is an unquestionable, foundational value of liberal constitutionalism, in the field of prosecutorial forms of organization the accepted degree of autonomy is much more qualified. Yet years of insistence on prosecutorial independence for the purpose of generating reforms in liminal jurisdictions have already created expectations which have, in turn, been translated into jurisdictional standards, now applicable to mature Western

13 Simone Benvenuti, Davide Paris, 'Judicial Self-Government in Italy-Merits, Limits and the Reality of an Export Model' (2018)19 (7) *German Law Journal* (*Special Issue-Judicial Self-Government in Europe*) 1641–1670. "No doubt, the CSM is a successful Italian export product. Introduced by the 1948 Italian Constitution as the first of its kind, it served as a model for the new democratic constitutions of Greece, Portugal, Spain first, and then, under the pressure of the European institutions, for the constitutions of the newly established democracies in Central and Eastern Europe" (at 1642).

14 See Michal Bobek, David Kosař, 'Global Solutions, Local Damages: A Critical Study in Judicial Councils in Central and Eastern Europe' (2014) 15 (7) *German Law Journal* 1257–1292. With emphasis on the Western Balkans, see also Denis Preshova, Ivan Damjanovski, Zoran Nechev, 'The Effectiveness of the "European Model" of Judicial Independence in the Western Balkans: Judicial Councils as a Solution or a New Cause of Concern for Judicial Reforms' (2017) 1 *CLEER Papers* available at www.asser.nl/media/3475/cleer17-1_web.pdf

15 I develop this argument in Bogdan Iancu, 'Status Quo Hegemony? Conflicting Narratives about the "Rule of Law' *VerfBlog* 6 October 2020, https://verfassungsblog.de/status-quo-hegemony

16 See Marcelo Neves, 'Die Staaten im Zentrum und die Staaten an der Peripherie: Einige Probleme mit Niklas Luhmanns Auffassung von den Staaten der Weltgesellschaft' (2006) 12 (2 S) *Soziale Systeme* 247–273.

democracies.[17] Likewise, the fixation on 'corruption' as a master-key to conditionalities and thus on specific anticorruption reforms promoted in Romania, Bulgaria, Croatia, and the current candidate countries in the Western Balkans has resulted in an understanding of the rule of law centered on anticorruption as one of its primary pillars. This newer definition and therefore its practical implications are now applicable to all 27 Member States, in the framework of the revamped Rule of Law Mechanism.[18]

An overarching peril lies ensconced in the tendency to macromanage majoritarian democracy, limiting the reach of classic (traditional) representative politics and thus the scope of policy change brought about by electoral replacements of political majorities. It has been appositely pointed out in this respect that one of the primary causes for the current tidal wave of 'populism' in the peripheral states of the EU can be found in the pre-accession insistence, primarily by the Commission and its favored interlocutors in the accession states, on skewed, disproportionately counter-majoritarian institutional solutions: *chassez la politique, elle revient au galop* (and, one may add, with a populist vengeance).[19] The experimentation with independent fiscal institutions in the Fiscal Compact is another pertinent example of wider tendencies towards agencification. Such tendencies result partly from contextual complexity and irresolution (an inability to generate effective change at the interface between national and supranational constitutionalism) but they are also epiphenomenal manifestations of deep-seated, underlying discomforts with majoritarian politics.

Agencification and the Fiscal Compact: ambiguity, contingencies, unforeseen consequences

The correction mechanism of the Treaty on Stability, Coordination and Governance in the Economic and Monetary Union (hereinafter Fiscal Compact) is a revolutionary instrument in more than one respect. The Fiscal Compact was adopted in correlation with, and as a complement to, the Treaty establishing the European Stability Mechanism (ESM).[20] As neither of these solutions to the sovereign debt crisis could be entrenched in primary EU law, a second-best option was chosen: to conclude the two conventions as international law

17 Judgments in Joined Cases C-508/18 OG (Public Prosecutor's office of Lübeck) and C-82/19 PPU PI (Public Prosecutor's office of Zwickau) and in Case C-509/18 PF (Prosecutor General of Lithuania).

18 *See* the Commission's 2020 Rule of Law Report, COM(2020) 580 final, available at https://eur-lex.europa.eu/legal-content/EN/TXT/HTML/?uri=CELEX:52020DC0580&from=EN

19 Kosař David, Baroš Jiří, Dufek Pavel, 'The Twin Challenges to Separation of Powers in Central Europe: Technocratic Governance and Populism' (2019) 15 (1) *European Constitutional Law Review* 427.

20 According to ESM Treaty recital (5), the granting of financial assistance within the ESM is conditional upon ratification of the TSCG and, after the expiration of the transposition period of the Fiscal Compact, on compliance with the requirements of Art. 3(2) TSCG.

instruments which address EU shortcomings and import into their institutional framework European Union institutions.[21] The tribulations of accommodating the ESM and the Fiscal Compact with the general framework of European Union law, generated by the impossibility of reaching an agreement on amending the constitutive treaties, have already been extensively discussed in the literature. Unlike the ESM Treaty, which clashes primarily with EU law limitations on non-redressability, the Fiscal Compact presupposes significant tensions with domestic constitutional law.

Title III of the Treaty requires (Art. 3) all signatories to abide, as a rule, by budgets either balanced or in surplus and to gradually reduce their structural budget deficits to 0.5% of the gross domestic product at market prices, should their public debt go over the 60% of the GDP threshold and at most 1% in the event that the country's public debt is significantly lower. Should public debt exceed the convergence threshold, it must be reduced by a twentieth (5% of the surplus) every year, until the 60% maximum reference value is met (Art. 4). These are binding provisions, which prima facie allow the government and the parliament very little room for maneuver in drafting and adopting the budget law. At the level of 'international' law, sanctions may be imposed by the ECJ for failing to implement the treaty in national law, namely, a lump sum of 0.1% of the country's GDP. These sanctions refer solely to transposition – that is, the failure to write these rules into national legislation.

In the logic of Art. 3, the monitoring of the correction mechanism necessitated by the "golden rule" (i.e. a debt brake procedure) falls within the purview of an independent body– namely, a fiscal or budgetary council, or a similar type of dedicated agency. The functioning of the correction mechanism as such would thus depend on the way in which this neutral, apolitical fiscal/budgetary watchdog would be able to bring parliament to book in the eventuality of majoritarian budgetary profligacies.

At this juncture, certain perplexities arise. The treaty pithily provides that while such agency should be fully independent in monitoring the correction mechanism, this mechanism must *fully respect the prerogatives of national parliaments*. The implications of this formulation are not clear since, for the mechanism to function at all, a form of sanction should exist – for example, a procedural brake on the adoption of the budget law – perhaps reinforced by a ricochet possibility to dissolve the parliament. In other words, one cannot have both an unfettered parliament and an effective and limited budgetary procedure. This is not the only oxymoronic formulation in the treaty: it is equally unclear, for instance, judging from the qualification "preferably constitutional", what other types of national legislative provisions could be "permanent and binding". The alternative option, as indicated in the formulation "or otherwise guaranteed to be fully respected and adhered to throughout the national

21 Paul Craig, '*Pringle* and Use of EU Institutions outside the EU Legal Framework: Foundations, Procedure and Substance' (2013) 9 (2) *Eur. Const. L. Rev.* 263–284.

budgetary processes" does little to dispel such reservations.[22] The ambiguity concerning the role of independent institutions in monitoring the operative provisions of the Fiscal Compact has resulted in significant variations across national systems. For example, in the case of the Netherlands, compliance is monitored by the Advisory Division of the Council of State; although the Dutch *Raad van State* is functionally autonomous from the government, it is not an independent fiscal authority. Similarly, in Romania, the comply or explain procedure involves the Fiscal Council (*Consiliul Fiscal*). This body enjoys, by design, a small degree of functional autonomy ensured primarily through the common mechanism of diversifying somewhat the board-nominating stakeholders. The five members of the Fiscal Council are appointed by Parliament for a single, fixed term of nine years, upon nominations made by the Romanian Academy, the Academy of Economic Studies (ASE) of Bucharest, the National Bank of Romania, the Romanian Banking Institute, and the Romanian Banking Association. The selection of nominating institutions is somewhat perplexing. For instance, the Romanian Banking Institute is a subordinate research structure of the National Bank, whereas the Academy of Economic Studies is a public university among many. The Fiscal Council is peculiarly grafted onto the Romanian Academy (it uses its secretarial services, for instance), a setting somewhat analogous to that of the network of research institutes under the Academy's tutorship. Aside from these design peculiarities and its weak powers, the Fiscal Council does not formally qualify as an 'independent agency' ('autonomous administrative authority') under Romanian constitutional law.[23]

At the other end of the spectrum from the prevalent soft implementation (functional, relative autonomy of the implementing administrative body, 'explain or comply' correction mechanism) would be a solution involving hard implementation through constitutional entrenchment of oversight by a powerful fiscal watchdog and a correction mechanism 'with teeth' vis-à-vis the legislature.[24]

22 As a result, a clear majority of the parties have not entrenched the mechanism in their constitutions. Romania has, for example, ratified the TSCG using the regular, default instrument of treaty ratification, an ordinary law (L. 83/14.06.2012, M.Of. nr. 410/20.06.2012). A special ratification procedure is provided in the case of EU constitutive treaties, which requires a law passed by a two-thirds majority in a joint session of both houses of Parliament but the TSCG is not formally an EU treaty. The option of amending the Constitution in order to entrench the 'golden rule' (balanced budget), debt brake provisions, and a correction mechanism was not even considered.

23 According to the Constitution (Art. 117 (3)), autonomous administrative authorities may be established outside the executive hierarchy by organic legislation. Conversely, the Fiscal Council was set up by an ordinary law, L. 69/2010 on fiscal and budgetary responsibility.

24 Árpád Kovács, 'The Fiscal Council in the Hungarian Fundamental Law-Sketch on the Development of the Institution and the European Union Practice' (2016) 3 *Public Finance Quarterly* 312–330, at 319. "In the majority of the countries of the European Union an attention-provoking, advisory type, macro-analytical, technical forecasting (projecting) work without direct consequences tends to be more

This is, roughly, the Hungarian model. It should be noted, however, that this comparative reference does not concern the formal treaty obligations of this country. Hungary is a party to the Treaty but not bound by the operative rules on fiscal and budgetary discipline in titles III and IV.

Hungary established a Fiscal (Budget) Council under IMF pressure, in 2008. The Fiscal Council, whose initial creation was driven by external conditionality, was subsequently enshrined in a revamped form in the Hungarian Constitution of 2011. It consists of a three-member board, namely, its Chairman, appointed for a six-year term by the president of the Republic, the President of the National Bank of Hungary, and the President of the State Audit Office. The latter is elected with a two-thirds majority by the National Assembly, to a staggering twelve-year term of office. The New Fundamental Law of Hungary explicitly commits to an austere philosophy congruent with the Stability and Growth Pact and its elaborated version, the Fiscal Compact, namely, to "balanced, transparent and sustainable budget management" as an expression of transgenerational fairness (Art. N (1) in the "Foundations" section of the constitution). This general principle is rendered operative by a specific limitation on the government and parliament. As long as government debt exceeds half of the gross domestic product, no budget law may be adopted that is not attuned to the reduction of the ratio until the 50% reference limit is reached (note the GDP percentage, which is much more ambitious than that established by EMU convergence criteria). According to Art. 36 (5), "As long as government debt exceeds half of the total gross domestic product, the National Assembly may only adopt an Act on the central budget which provides for a reduction of the ratio of government debt to the total gross domestic product." The Fiscal Council has a veto right over the budget law, which may not be voted at the third reading should the Council object on the grounds that the draft is not in compliance with the constitutional phased debt reduction requirement.[25]

At the practical level, the Hungarian IFI seems to have remained, for the time being, and in spite of its formal powers, a "paper tiger". Due to the lack of resources (insufficient staff, primarily) and in view of the conflicting incentives of its board members, it cannot scrutinize adequately the parliament and fulfill its constitutional task.[26] Nonetheless, this weakness is by and large

typical [...] The 'Hungarian arrangement', with its direct public law mandate connected to the current (annual) budgeting process and the related responsibilities no doubt *represents an extreme point, and transcends the practice prevailing in the majority of European Union countries*" (emphasis added, references omitted).

25 For a comparison between the Hungarian Fiscal Council and other IFIs, see Lászlo Jánkovics, Monika Sherwood, 'Independent Fiscal Institutions in the EU Member States: The Early Years' (2017) 067 *EU Commission Discussion Paper* at https://ec.europa.eu/info/publications/economy-finance/independent-fiscal-institutions-eu-member-states-early-years_en

26 For a nuanced analysis, see Attila Vincze, 'Regulatory Bodies in an Illiberal Democracy', in Bogdan Iancu and Elena-Simina Tănăsescu (eds) *Governance and Constitutionalism: Law, Politics, and Institutional Neutrality* (Routledge 2019) 128–130. For example, Vincze (at 129) argues that "The new Budget Council

contingent upon the current political situation in Hungary, where the same party has held a comfortable supermajority for the better part of a decade. Should the context change, one can easily imagine a pre-electorally reinforced, institutionally refurbished Council, packed with long-term appointees of the outgoing majority and being used in a different context as a thorn in the side of a future parliamentary majority. The institution is constitutionally entrenched and its organic legislation falls in the domain of cardinal laws (Art. 44 (5), Hungarian Constitution); if rendered effective, it would be difficult to dislodge by means of ordinary majoritarian politics.[27]

One may draw some tentative inferences from the above. The ambivalence in the Fiscal Compact ('constitutional or otherwise'; corrective mechanism supervised by an IFI but fully observant of parliamentary prerogatives) is indicative of irresolution in the face of the task at hand. In the quantitative, austerity-driven logic of the 'golden rule', a Hungarian-style institution would be the natural conclusion but neither the drafters of the treaty nor national authorities, at the point of implementation, were committed to following the inherent logic of the endeavor to its end. This may follow in a future elaboration, just as the Fiscal Compact steps on the trail opened by the Stability and Growth Pact. Conversely, the perils of logical consistency are easily noticeable in this brief analysis of the Hungarian framework.

Conclusion: correlations, causations and creative institutional design in post-crisis 'new governance'

The more general impact of a balanced budget rule on agencification writ large would differ across jurisdictions. For the time being, the vague formulations in the Treaty have resulted in incomplete and incoherent implementation (a variety of transposition modalities, weak enforcement, no common understanding of institutional autonomy). The relative lack of incentives for seeking harmonization (for instance, by way of more robust oversight by the Commission and/or recourse to the ECJ) has rendered practices tentative and,

according to the Fundamental Law has three members; however, it is endowed with no staff of its own whatsoever, and therefore the members cannot make use of institutional expertise and manpower, a lack which hampers the conclusiveness of any findings [...] The president of the Budget Council, as mentioned, has no institutional staff to rely on, does not know more about the budget than anybody else and, therefore, cannot check whether taxes, expenditure growth and further estimates are probable and therefore whether public finances meet with the requirement of sustainability."

27 In the Hungarian system, cardinal laws are infra-constitutional laws. They are similar, in the sense that they form an intermediate category in between constitutional and ordinary legislation, to the category of 'organic laws' in the constitutional systems of Romania, France, Spain. Hungarian Cardinal Acts are, however, adopted with a more demanding qualified majority (two-thirds majorities of the MPs present, unlike constitutional amendments, which require two-thirds majorities in relation to the total number of National Assembly members).

consequently, more precise conclusions concerning such practices speculative. It should be noted, however, that the language of legalized austerity is part of a more general discourse, joined at the hip with other discourses, notably rule of law ideologies[28] and anticorruption as a *passe-partout* solution to general dysfunctions. Anticorruption has been used by the Commission, more timidly in the pre-accession evaluation of the 2004 new member states, then more energetically in the preparation for the 2007 and 2013 enlargements. The two countries that joined in 2007, Romania and Bulgaria, are subject to post-accession monitoring almost exclusively focused on anticorruption. Such policies are predicated upon implementation by agencification. By focusing on corruption as a source of all evils and on anticorruption as a panacea for peripheral jurisdictions, the Commission, as the 'master of conditionalities', has itself joined a more inclusive transnational bandwagon. To wit, in Ukraine the IMF has made funds conditional upon anticorruption reforms predicated upon the creation of ingenious agencification patterns. Thus, Ukraine has created a set of anticorruption courts fully autonomous from the regular judiciary.[29] This novelty was given the green light by the Venice Commission, also in the name of more effective anticorruption but, on a closer look, it presents not a few problematic implications, since an autonomous anticorruption court is in effect an *accountability meta-agency*.[30] The IMF expresses, in turn, an even wider consensus at the level of structural rule of law conditionality, reflecting conformities expressed by the translation of ostensibly normative language into the mock-quantification paradigm of anticorruption rankings.[31] More precisely, rule of law conditionalities, the rule of law being understood here as anticorruption policies backed by innovative judicial enforcement paradigms, are perceived as flip-sides of economic structural adjustments (with emphasis on liminal areas). To wit, in perfect correlation with the austerity packages, the 2011 Commission Report on Fighting Corruption in the EU floated a 5% GDP loss to corruption at the level of the Union.[32] This figure was mentioned

28 See generally, on rule of law ideologies, including the overlaps between anticorruption and austerity economics, Stephen Humphreys, *Theatre of the Rule of Law: Transnational Legal Intervention in Theory and Practice* (Cambridge University Press 2011).

29 I discuss Ukrainian reforms in comparison with Romanian anticorruption/judiciary reforms, with a focus on Venice Commission opinions, in Bogdan Iancu, 'Quod licet Jovi non licet bovi? The Venice Commission as Norm Entrepreneur' (2019) 11 (1) *Hague Journal on the Rule of Law* 189–221.

30 Cf. on accountability agencies and their ingenious design patterns, Elena-Simina Tănăsescu, 'The Impact of National Accountability Agencies on the EU', in Bogdan Iancu and Elena-Simina Tănăsescu (eds) *Governance and Constitutionalism: Law, Politics, and Institutional Neutrality* (Routledge 2019), 85–96.

31 See Mila Versteeg, Tom Ginsburg, 'Measuring the Rule of Law: A Comparison of Indicators' (Winter 2017) 42 (1) *Law & Social Inquiry* 100–137. The authors demonstrate that rule of law indicators, irrespective of how they are normatively defined, correlate saliently only with the Transparency International Corruption Perception Index.

32 COM(2011) 308 final, available at https://eur-lex.europa.eu/LexUriServ/LexUriServ.do?uri=COM:2011:0308:FIN:EN:PDF

in the Report with the suave footnote admission that it resulted from an extrapolation at the EU level from aggregated guesstimates concerning the global costs of corruption, compiled from a variety of sources (including a variety of institutions and NGOs, ranging from the UN to Transparency International and the International Chamber of Commerce). The text of the report as such presents *the extrapolation of the extrapolation* almost as a hard fact, emphasizing with urgency that "[it] is unacceptable that an estimated **120 billion Euros per year,** or one percent of the EU GDP, is lost to corruption"[33] (emphasis in original). How the Commission has reached this figure and the percentage reference is not readily apparent given that the only reference is to an aggregated estimate of a 5% loss at the global level. One may, however, imagine that the fraction was also reached through 'creative accounting', namely by relating the global percentage guesstimate of corruption costs to perception index differentials – CPI (Corruption Perceptions Index) and BPI (Bribe Payers Index) rankings – between the EU as a whole and the rest of the world. Once a figure is cited, however, it may be cross-referenced and circulated in future studies and reports as a fact, with (re) circulation within homogenous institutional and expert pool settings enhancing, in turn, credibility. For example, in a recent EP Green Party report, the methodology of which is unexplained, in the absence of corruption, "each [newborn Romanian] baby could receive more than (sic) 203.000 EUR!" at birth.[34]

Also pertinent to the general argument of this chapter is the proposal made by the Commission, in its 2020 Rule of Law Communication, to 'open' national parliaments widely to "meaningful" consultations with "stakeholders", experts, and civil society and also to "engage" the citizens in the legislative process, thus rendering parliamentarism more inclusive and legislation more "evidence-based".[35] To be sure, nothing in principle advocates against parliaments using, at their discretion, expertise and consultations with 'outside parties' in their committee work. However, it is hard to understand how such proposals could be formalized and entrenched in hybrid procedures (which seems to be the practical implication), without affecting the core majoritarian logic of representative democracy and the backbone of accountability mechanisms and structures of justification underlying it.

Correlation is certainly not causation but one may safely predict that balanced budget conformities and future agencification drives resulting from such conformities will coexist in symbiotic harmony with counter-majoritarian solutions resulting from germane ideologies centered on the rule of law and anticorruption.

Bibliography

Ackerman B, 'The New Separation of Powers' (2000) 113 (3) *Harvard Law Review* 633

Benvenuti S, Paris D, 'Judicial Self-Government in Italy: Merits, Limits and the Reality of an Export Model' (2018) 19 (7) *German Law Journal* 1641

33 Ibid. at 3.

34 www.greens-efa.eu/files/doc/docs/e46449daadbfebc325a0b408bbf5ab1d.pdf

35 COM(2020) 580 final (see the discussion at pages 21–22).

Bobek M, Kosař D, 'Global Solutions, Local Damages: A Critical Study in Judicial Councils in Central and Eastern Europe' (2014) 15 (7) *German Law Journal* 1257

Craig P, '*Pringle* and Use of EU Institutions outside the EU Legal Framework: Foundations, Procedure and Substance' (2013) 9 (2) *European Constitutional Law Review* 263

Humphreys S, *Theatre of the Rule of Law: Transnational Legal Intervention in Theory and Practice* (CUP 2011)

Iancu B, Tănăsescu ES (eds), *Governance and Constitutionalism: Law, Politics, and Institutional Neutrality* (Routledge 2018)

Iancu B, 'Changed Vocabularies: A Few Semantic Ambiguities of Network Constitutionalism', in Iulia Motoc, Krzysztof Wojtyczek, Paulo Pinto de Albuquerque (eds), *New Developments in Constitutional Law: Essays in Honour of András Sajó* (Eleven International Publishing 2018) 191

Iancu B, 'Quod licet Jovi non licet bovi? The Venice Commission as Norm Entrepreneur' (2019) 11 (1) *Hague Journal on the Rule of Law* 189

Iancu B, 'Status Quo Hegemony? Conflicting Narratives about the "Rule of Law"', VerfBlog, 6 October 2020, https://verfassungsblog.de/status-quo-hegemony

Kosař D, Baroš J, Dufek P, 'The Twin Challenges to Separation of Powers in Central Europe: Technocratic Governance and Populism' (2019) 15 *European Constitutional Law Review* 427

Kovács Á, 'The Fiscal Council in the Hungarian Fundamental Law-Sketch on the Development of the Institution and the European Union Practice' (2016) 3 *Public Finance Quarterly* 312

Lindseth P, 'Democratic Legitimacy and the Administrative Character of Supranationalism: The Example of the European Community' (1999) 99 *Columbia Law Review* 628

Majone G, *Regulating Europe* (Routledge 1996)

Neves M, 'Die Staaten im Zentrum und die Staaten an der Peripherie: Einige Probleme mit Niklas Luhmanns Auffassung von den Staaten der Weltgesellschaft' (2006) 12 (2, S) *Soziale Systeme* 247

Sajó A, Uitz R, *The Constitution of Freedom: An Introduction to Legal Constitutionalism* (OUP 2017)

Stewart, RB, 'The Reformation of American Administrative Law' (1975) 88 (8) *Harvard Law Review* 1667

Vibert F, *The Rise of the Unelected: Democracy and the New Separation of Power* (CUP 2007)

Part IV

Balanced budget, governance and fundamental rights

8 Rules of budgetary discipline and protection of rights

George Katrougalos and Daphne Akoumianaki

The financial power of the state has always been interwoven with political power although, traditionally, constitutions do not reveal much about this connection. However, budget law has been the cornerstone of the liberal state since the end of the 18th century, notably through rules concerning the democratic control and transparency of public finance. Some of these rules entered constitutions from the very beginning, in the form of procedural standards aiming to achieve parliamentary control of public funds or even of the necessary balance between public revenues and expenses. The 20th century has seen a true transfiguration of the public financial system of the state due to the impact of, and responses to, several major economic crises, especially from the perspective of economic theories. Their hold on the public financial law of the state has not been negligible. At constitutional level, this translates, *inter alia*, into the addition of substantive rules concerning the management of public finance, and into the legislative introduction of a certain idea of budgetary discipline, mainly by advancing the concept of the balanced budget to the level of legal principle.

In fact, the balanced budget, as a legal postulate, has made a comeback mainly with the global financial crisis of 2008, followed by the economic crisis. In Greece, for example, the crisis lasted a decade and involved three financial support programs.[1] The last of these programs concluded successfully on 20 August 2018. In July 2018, the Commission adopted a decision to activate the enhanced surveillance framework for Greece after the conclusion of the European Stability Mechanism (ESM) stability support program, and on 23 September 2020, the Commission adopted the seventh enhanced surveillance report for Greece. Numerous aspects of this crisis have already been the object of in-depth analysis,[2] from the European tax governance and the legal challenges that it poses to member states, including the impact of financial austerity on national autonomy or the protection of fundamental rights, to the role of independent tax institutions in

1 Greece followed two economic adjustment programs and an ESM stability support program.

2 Panayotis Glavinis, *The Memorandum of Greece* (Sakkoulas Publishing 2010); Panayotis Mantzoufas, *Financial Crisis and the Constitution* (Sakkoulas Publishing 2014).

DOI: 10.4324/9781315181882-13

the restoration of the sustainability of public debt. Public law, especially the Constitution conceived as a framework and limit to the power of the state, has never been more fashionable.

However, we cannot help but notice that an eminently legal analysis of the concept of balanced budget, outside the economic background of the crisis, is a complex matter. Can we identify permanent legal norms for the allocation, management and control of public funds? Essentially, what is a balanced budget from a legal point of view, and why has it become indispensable as a constitutional principle for contemporary public finance? Is there a real need for legal standards in order to regulate public debt? It is certain that the requirement of a balanced budget is posed at constitutional level precisely to have an impact on the way in which the state exercises its functions. The vertical and the horizontal separation of powers are equally affected by it, whereas the multilateral supervision of public finance has become necessary from the bottom (at local level) to the top (at supranational level), in addition to the more traditional one exercised at state level. The above are supplemented by the financial autonomy of independent public authorities as an additional challenge for the democratic control of the budget process. Are all these requirements and challenges set to enhance or reduce the profoundly political nature of the budget process?

The 21st century has witnessed a new form of the balanced budget principle applied to states. Therefore, the basic normative question is what the impact of budgetary discipline is and what are its effects in the contemporary state.

Budgetary rules and their impact on national legal systems

Budgetary rules are included in European law and apply in the national legal orders. The impact of these rules on national legal orders is important, as shown more specifically through the transposition of the Treaty on Stability, Coordination and Governance (TSCG).

Thus, agreed upon on 30 January 2012 between the heads of state and government, and signed by 25 of the then 27 member states of the European Union[3] on 2 March 2012, the TSCG binds only its contracting parties – that is, a reduced number of states. Because it implements a differentiated integration, the TSCG cannot be properly perceived as a treaty of the European Union.[4] This is,

3 In December 2011, the United Kingdom was the first country of the EU to refuse to adhere to this Treaty. At the euro summit held in Brussels on December 9, 2011, Prime Minister David Cameron threatened to exercise a veto against an agreement of 27 member states which did not sufficiently support British interests. Subsequently, the Czech Republic, which had indicated 'constitutional reasons', created a real surprise when it announced on January 30, 2012, its refusal to adhere to this Treaty. In February 2015 the Czech government introduced bills which would enact some provisions of the Fiscal Compact into Czech law. The bills, but not a constitutional amendment, were approved by the Chamber of Deputies in October 2016.

4 Anne Levade, 'TSCG and the French Constitution: When Interpretation Leads to Compatibility' (2012) 4 *Constitutions* 575, 576.

however, an international treaty. In addition, this treaty provides a 'balanced budget rule' which should be transposed, according to the provisions of the Treaty, into national legal systems by means of binding, permanent and, preferably, constitutional provisions. This second particularity revolves around the fact that this has been the first time a treaty has encouraged the contracting states to introduce a rule of constitutional status, following a constitutional review.

Despite the provision of Art 3 (2) of the TSCG for the transposition of the balanced budget rule, commonly called the 'golden rule', 'by provisions of binding force and permanent character, preferably constitutional', the revision of the Constitution follows a specific procedure in each member state and so the balanced budget rule was not transposed by constitutional provisions in all EU member states. Moreover, a number of additional budgetary rules were set for countries under economic adjustment programs, such as Greece. These rules, introduced in connection to the economic adjustment plan, considerably limit national sovereignty.

The constituent power facing the requirements of the Treaty on Stability, Coordination and Governance

The 'golden rule', as part of the framework for the consolidation of budgetary supervision within the EU, provides that the mid-term structural objective of a state should be below –0.5% of the gross domestic product.[5] The Treaty suggests a transposition of this rule into the national Constitution. Nevertheless, since the revision of the Constitution follows a specific and lengthy procedure, in some member states the ratification can only happen by law.

The 'Golden Rule' provided in TSCG

Before the economic crisis, which started in Europe with the financial instability of Greece in 2010, European economic governance had been based on two pillars: the budgetary supervision established by the Stability and Growth Pact,[6] and the social and economic coordination provided by the Lisbon Treaty. Nonetheless, economic imperatives require the coordination of the Union's policy for the purpose of ensuring the management of the euro crisis,[7] and, in this context, a

5 Art 3.1(b), Treaty on Stability, Coordination and Governance in the Economic and Monetary Union (hereinafter TSCG), signed on 2 March 2012 (not published in the Official Journal). However, the limit of the medium-term objective is –1% of the GDP if the state holds debt below 60% of the GDP and presents low-level risks for long-term sustainability of public finance, art 3.1(d).

6 Council Regulation (EC) 1466/97 of 7 July 1997, amended by the Council Regulation (EC) No 1055/2005 of 27 June 2005, Council Regulation (EC) 1467/97 of 7 July 1997, amended by the Council Regulation (EC) 1056/2005 of 27 June 2005, and the Resolution of the European Council of 17 June 1997 on the Stability and Growth Pact.

7 See Olivier Clerc, *La gouvernance économique de l'Union européenne* (Bruylant 2012) for a study on the evolution of the European economic governance since the

European economic government capable of reinvigorating the existing European requirements.[8] As a first step, the Treaty of Maastricht proposed a reference value which should have been observed as a rule of budgetary discipline. According to this rule, the relationship between the planned or actual public deficit and the gross domestic product should be limited to 3%.[9]

Consequently, in terms of budgetary discipline, the TFEU materializes the action policy in Art 121, which provides that 'Member States shall regard their economic policies as a matter of common concern'. It has also restated the rule provided in the Treaty of Maastricht concerning the nominal or actual deficit, which should be lower than 3% of the GDP,[10] in its Art 126 (2): 'Member States shall avoid excessive government deficits [...]'. Furthermore, Art 136 of the TFEU provides the adoption of measures to reinforce the coordination and supervision of the budgetary discipline of member states. Therefore, the aim was to establish a commitment by states to observe in the medium term the objective of a budgetary balance position.[11]

Considering the extent of the economic crisis, the need for budgetary discipline and stability measures has become imperative. The Council of the Member States of the euro area convened on 11 March 2011 has indicated in its conclusions that 'the Member States of the euro area undertake to translate into their national legislation the budgetary rules of the EU that appear in the Stability and Growth Pact. The Member States shall keep the choice of the legal instrument to use nationally but shall ensure that it is by its nature sufficiently binding and sustainable (for example, the Constitution or framework legislation)'. The Council has then added that

> the exact formulation of this rule shall be agreed upon by each separate country (this could be, for example, a 'debt brake', a rule connected to the primary balance, or a rule on expenditure), but it should guarantee budgetary discipline both at national level and at lower levels.[12]

creation of the Economic and Monetary Union in 1992 following the Treaty of Maastricht.

8 Jürgen Habermas, Christian Bouchindhomme, *La Constitution de l'Europe* (Gallimard 2012), 70 and 84.

9 Art 104C (2) of the Treaty of Maastricht and Art 1 of the Protocol on the excessive deficit procedure, according to which 'The reference values referred to in art 104 C para 2 of the treaty are as follows: –3% for the relationship between the planned or actual public deficit and the gross domestic product at market prices'.

10 Art 126, (2) TFEU and art 1 of Protocol No 12 on the excessive deficit procedure, according to which 'The reference values referred to in art 126 para 2 of the Treaty on the Functioning of the European Union are as follows: –3% for the relationship between the planned or actual public deficit and the gross domestic product at market prices'.

11 Gilbert Orsoni, 'Should We Legalize the Budgetary Balance?' in Nathalie de Grove-Valdeyron, Marc Blanquet, Vincent Dussart (eds), *Mélanges en l'honneur du Professeur Joël Molinier* (LGDJ 2012), 483, 490.

12 Conclusions of the Heads of State or Government in the Euro area of 11 March 2011, 10, national budgetary rules.

Then the need to enforce budgetary rules was expressed in the same manner by the European Council in its Decision of 25 March 2011,[13] which came to partially amend Art 136 of the TFEU.[14]

Finally, the new budgetary 'golden rule'[15] was introduced in the TSCG.[16] According to the treaty, the budgetary status of the public administrations of a contracting party is balanced or in surplus if the annual structural balance of the public administrations corresponds to the mid-term objective specific to each country, as defined in the revised Stability and Growth Pact. It provides that the mid-term structural objective of a state must be below –0.5% of the gross domestic product. The TSCG invites member states to enforce the rules established within their national law 'one year after this treaty becomes effective, at the latest, by means of binding and permanent provisions, of constitutional preference, or the full compliance and strict observance of which throughout national budget processes are guaranteed otherwise'.

This 'constitutionalization of a financial standard'[17] meets, above all, the demands of Germany for the fortification of the budgetary discipline by binding rules.[18] It must be noted that this treaty, whose negotiations were rather similar to those of a classic European treaty, thus allowing the key players to display their positions, contains in its first two versions[19] a different provision

13 Conclusions of the European Council of 24 and 25 March 2011, 20, national budgetary rules.

14 European Council Decision 2011/199/EU of 25 March 2011, amending Art 136 of the Treaty on the Functioning of the European Union with regard to a stability mechanism for Member States whose currency is the euro [2011] OJ L91/1. According to this decision, 'The following para shall be added to art 136 of the Treaty on the Functioning of the European Union: '3. The Member States whose currency is the euro may establish a stability mechanism to be activated if indispensable to safeguard the stability of the euro area as a whole. The granting of any required financial assistance under the mechanism will be made subject to strict conditionality.'

15 See, for illustrative purposes, Jean-Claude Zarka, 'Treaty on Stability, Coordination and Governance in the Economic and Monetary Union (TSCG)' (2012) 14 *Dalloz* 893.

16 As stated by Philippe Manin, 'The situation created by the financial crisis has determined the Member States of the Union to engage in the review of art 136 and the Member States of the euro area to conclude on a treaty based on this reviewed provision. (ESM) In two other cases, namely the EFSM and the Treaty on Stability and Governance, procedures for adaptation that are not based on the treaties are encountered.' Philip Manin, 'A Consequence of the Financial Crisis: Review and Adaptation of Constituent Treaties of the European Union' in Chahira Boutayeb (ed.), *La Constitution, l'Europe et le droit, mélanges en l'honneur de Jean-Claude Masclet* (Publication de la Sorbonne 2013).

17 See Philippe Marini, Michel Bouvier, Jean-Raphaël Alventosa, 'The Introduction of the Budgetary "Golden Rule" in the Constitution' (2011) 1 *Constitutions* 23, 24.

18 Jean-Claude Zarka, 'Agreement on the Draft Treaty on European Budgetary Discipline' (2012) 1 *Dalloz* 16.

19 The first version of the Treaty (dated 16 December 2011) and the final version (dated 30 January 2012), see Valentin Kreilingers, 'The "Making-of" a New Treaty: Six Stages of Political Negotiations' (2012) 52 *Notre Europe, Les brefs* 1, 1.

regarding the 'golden rule'. More precisely, the treaty had provided that the transposition of the 'golden rule' should be made by means of 'provisions of binding force and permanent character, preferably constitutional, or otherwise guaranteed to be fully respected and adhered to throughout the national budgetary processes'.[20] Nevertheless, faced with considerable opposition, Germany was forced to accept that several countries included the 'golden rule' in a simple statutory law. The new Treaty provides that the transposition of the 'golden rule' shall be made by means of binding and permanent provisions, preferably of a constitutional nature.[21] There are also measures of verification, across Europe, of the 'golden rule' at national level.[22]

This rule, and especially the suggestion to transpose it at constitutional level, generates an entire series of problems in the national legal system that derive notably from the fact that these matters concern the state budget which, like all other matters related to financial and budgetary measures, *a priori* falls under the competence of the Parliament, as a guarantee of the social state.[23] Finally, it should be emphasized that, for the first time, a Treaty invites the states to attribute to a European standard a specific rank and, when applicable, a constitutional rank.[24]

The 'golden rule' in the national legal systems

The ratification of the TSCG is currently completed by all signatory states plus Croatia, which acceded to the EU in 2013, and the Czech Republic.[25] Also, the

20 TSCG art 3 (2).

21 Zarka (n 15) 896.

22 This power is conferred solely to member states under Art 8 of the TSCG, which has been decided against the opinion expressed by Germany who argued for the direct involvement of the European Commission. See ibid. 897.

23 Dimitra Kontogeorga-Theocharopoulou and Loukas Theocharopoulos, '"Under the Sign" of Crises: Public Administration and Budget Management' (2010) 3 *EfimDD* 274, 288.

24 It should be noted that the economic governance in the euro area is constantly strengthened. On 12 March 2013, the European Parliament adopted with a large majority a set of two draft regulations, known as the "two-pack", aiming at strengthening the economic governance within the euro area. See Jean-Claude Zarka, 'European Union (Economic Governance): Agreement on the "Two-pack"' (2013) 11 *Dalloz*, 709. The first regulation further consolidates budgetary supervision by expanding the powers of control of the Commission and of the Council with regard to national budget policies (Regulation No 473/2013 of the European Parliament and of the Council of 21 May 2013). The second regulation organizes the supervision of the member states that present risks of financial instability and, in case of financial assistance, anchor in the European law the negotiation of the terms of this aid provided by the macroeconomic adjustment program (Regulation No 472/2013 of the European Parliament and of the Council of 21 May 2013). See Alexandre de Streel, 'The Reformed European Economic Governance' (2013) 3 *RTDE* 455, 459.

25 The countries that ratified the TSCG are: Germany on 13 September 2012, Austria on 17 July 2012, Cyprus on 29 June 2012, Denmark on 18 June 2012, Spain on 25 July 2012, Estonia on 5 November 2012, Finland on 21 December 2012,

'golden rule' has by now been introduced in the internal legal system of all EU member states which are also parties to the TSCG and bound by the Fiscal Compact. In the Greek system, the TSCG was introduced in compliance with the constitutional procedure of ratification of treaties. Later, during discussions for the amendment of the Constitution which took place in November 2019, the introduction of the golden rule in the Constitution was proposed but has not been adopted.

Indeed, the 'golden rule' is introduced at constitutional level only in a limited number of states. Switzerland, which is not a member of the EU, was the first state to introduce the 'golden rule' in its Constitution in 2003. As such, Art 126 of the Swiss Constitution establishes the rule of a balanced national budget in terms of expenses and revenues. However, exceptional financial needs, connected to the economic recession or to natural disasters, may justify an appropriate increase of the expenditure limit, which will be decided by an absolute majority of the Federal Assembly.[26]

Poland[27] is a member state where the 'golden rule' existed in the Constitution before the signing of the TSCG. This is also the case of the Federal Republic of Germany. In Germany, following the constitutional review of 1

France on 22 October 2012, the law authorizing the ratification of the TSCG and the organic law no. 2012-1403 of 17 December 2012, referring to the planning and governance of public finance, Greece on 28 March 2012, Hungary on 29 March 2013, Ireland on 27 June 2012, Italy on 23 July 2012, Latvia on 13 June 2012, Lithuania on 4 July 2012, Luxembourg on 29 March 2013, Malta on 11 June 2013, the Netherlands on 26 June 2013, Poland on 24 July 2013, Portugal on 27 June 2012, Romania on 13 June 2012, Slovakia on 11 January 2013, Slovenia on 30 April 2012, Sweden on 7 March 2013, Belgium on 20 December 2013, Bulgaria on 3 December 2013, Sweden on 3 March 2013, Croatia on 31 January 2018 and the Czech Republic on 3 March 2019.

26 See art 126 of the Federal Constitution of the Swiss Confederation accepted by a referendum on 2 December 2001 (AF of 22 June 2001, ACF of 4 February 2002; RO 2002 241; FF 2000 4295, 2001 2255 2741, 2002 1156) with a transitional provision. 'The Confederation shall maintain its income and expenditure in balance over time. 2. The ceiling for total expenditure that is to be approved in the budget is based on the expected income after taking account of the economic situation. 3. Exceptional financial requirements may justify an appropriate increase in the ceiling in terms of para 2. The Federal Assembly shall decide on any increase in accordance with Art 159 para 3 letter c. 4. If the total expenditure in the federal accounts exceeds the ceiling in terms of paras 2 or 3, compensation for this additional expenditure must be made in subsequent years. 5. The details are regulated by law.' Stephan Danniger, 'A new rule "the Swiss debt brake"' (2002) *IMF working paper* 1, Vasilis Tzemos, 'Democratic Rule of Law, Difficult Economic Data and Debt Brake Clause' (2011) 4–5 *ThPDD* 496, 500, and Panayotis Mantzoufas, 'The Golden Rule in the Constitution. Problem Solving or Yet Another Obstacle to Economic Adaptation and the Protection of Rights' in Christina Akrivopoulou, Nikos Papachristos (eds) *The Challenge of Revising the Constitution* (Sakkoulas Publishing 2013).

27 Art 216 para 5 of the Constitution of Poland: 'It shall be neither permissible to contract loans nor provide guarantees and financial sureties which would engender a national public debt exceeding three-fifths of the value of the annual gross

August 2009, the provisions on fiscal policy were reinforced through the introduction of stricter rules concerning the general clause relating to public deficit.[28] Similarly to Switzerland, the federal state of Germany adopted the principle of a balanced state budget over time.[29] However, exceptions were also stipulated in order to counter any disruption of the economic balance as a result of an abnormal development of the economic conditions, in the event of natural disasters or exceptional emergency situations outside the control of the state.[30] As far as the exceptional rules are concerned, subsequent reimbursement rules must be provided. A constitutional provision especially states that 'for the federal budget, Art 115 sets the means of enforcement of such rules, on the understanding that it is fulfilled in phrase 1 when the revenues originating from loans do not exceed 0.35 per cent of the gross domestic product'.[31] This rule puts a brake on public debt and is, in fact, stricter than the 'golden rule' enforced under the TSCG.[32] In Germany, a country which reveals itself to be 'more rigorous than ever',[33] the golden rule inserted in the German Constitution of 2009 is set to apply from 2016 at federal level[34] and from 2020[35] at *Länder* [36] level.

In addition, Spain approved a 'golden rule' of budgetary stability on 7 September 2011, becoming the second country after Germany to introduce this

domestic product. The method for calculating the value of the annual gross domestic product and national public debt shall be specified by statute.'

28 See arts 109, 115 and 143 of the Fundamental Law of Germany.

29 Tzemos (n 26) 501.

30 Art 109 para 3 of the German Basic Law, constitutional reform of 29 July 2009 states: 'The budgets of the Federation and the Länder shall in principle be balanced without revenue from credits. The Federation and the Länder may introduce rules intended to take into account, symmetrically in times of upswing and downswing, the effects of market developments that deviate from normal conditions, as well as exceptions for natural disasters or unusual emergency situations beyond governmental control and substantially harmful to the state's financial capacity. For such exceptional regimes, a corresponding amortization plan must be adopted. Details for the budget of the Federation shall be governed by Art 115 with the proviso that the first sentence shall be deemed to be satisfied if revenue from credits does not exceed 0.35 percent in relation to the nominal gross domestic product. The Länder themselves shall regulate details for the budgets within the framework of their constitutional powers, the proviso being that the first sentence shall only be deemed to be satisfied if no revenue from credits is admitted.' See on this subject Stéphanie Flizot, 'Constitutional Rules for the Limitation of Public Debt: the German Example' (2009) 8 *Jus politicum*.

31 Art 109 para 3 bullet 3 of the German Basic Law.

32 Zarka (n 15) 897 and Zarka (n 18) 16.

33 Sophie Cazaillet, 'Is Revival Possible Without Rigor?' (2011) 452 *Hebdo fiscal* 4 of the electronic version. Germany was among the first states to announce in June 2010 an austerity plan aimed at saving 86 billion euros over the course of 4 years.

34 Art 143d para 1 bullet 2 of the German Basic Law.

35 Art 143d para 1 bullet 5 of the German Basic Law.

36 Frédéric Rueda, '"Golden Rule" or Golden Rules. On Budgetary Discipline in the Comparative European Law' in de Grove-Valdeyron and others (n 11).

rule in its Constitution. Spain also imposes. by organic law, a limit of 0.4% of the budgetary deficit until 2020.[37] Finally, in Italy the 'golden rule' was introduced in the new draft austerity plan in the form of a constitutional amendment.[38] On 17 April 2012, Italy adopted its budgetary 'golden rule'[39] as an amendment to Art 81 of the Constitution and the introduction of an obligation to balance the budget which would become effective in 2014.[40]

Beside these examples, where the introduction of the 'golden rule' into the Constitution is achieved, there are cases where its more general constitutionalization cannot be achieved, primarily due to institutional constraints. For instance, the Austrian Constitution is rigid as its revision is subject, under certain conditions, to a referendum.[41] Similarly, in Ireland constitutional

37 Art 135 of the Spanish Constitution: '1. All public administrations will conform to the principle of budgetary stability. 2. The State and the Self-governing Communities may not incur a structural deficit that exceeds the limits established by the European Union for their member states. An Organic Act shall determine the maximum structural deficit the state and the Self-governing Communities may have, in relation to its gross domestic product. Local authorities must submit a balanced budget. [...] Additional provision. 1. The organic law provided in art 135 of the Constitution must be adopted before June 30, 2012. 2. This law shall provide the mechanisms that will allow the observance of the indebtedness limit considered in art 135, para 3 of the Constitution. 3. The structural deficit limits established in art 135, para 2 of the Constitution shall become effective as of 2020.' [Text amended by the constitutional law of 27 September 2011, B.O.E., issue 233, September 27, 2011].

38 Cazaillet (n 33) 3.

39 The Chamber of Deputies had voted, first of all, the draft law on the "golden rule" on 30 November 2011, followed on 15 December by the Senate. The lower chamber had adopted the draft for the third and second to last time on 6 March. Therefore, the last time was on 17 April 2012.

40 Art 81 of the Italian Constitution amended by the review law no 1 of 20 April 2012, where art 6 mentions that these provisions shall apply starting from the 2014 financial year: 'The State ensures the balances of state revenue and expenditure in its budget whilst taking account of the adverse and favorable phases of economic cycle. No additional loans or credits may be contracted except for the purpose of taking account of the effects of the economic cycle or, subject to authorization by the two Houses approved by an absolute majority of their Members, in exceptional circumstances. Any law implying new or increased expenditures must define the means to cover them. Each year the chambers pass a law on approving the budget and the accounts submitted by the Government. Provisional implantation of the budget is not allowed except by specific legislation and only for periods not exceeding four months in total. The content of the budget law, the fundamental rules and the criteria adopted to ensure balance between revenue and expenditure and the sustainability of general government debt must be established by a law approved by an absolute majority of the Members of each House, in accordance with the principles established by constitutional law.'

41 Art 44, para 3 of the Federal Constitutional Law of October 1, 1920: '(3) Every total revision (Gesamtänderung) of the Federal Constitution, a partial revision, only this is demanded by one-third of the members f the National Council or the Federal Council, upon completion of the procedure in accordance with Art 42, but before the authentication by the Federal President, is to be submitted to a referendum

revision must be validated by a referendum and each act of ratification of an international Treaty is mandatorily submitted to a referendum.[42] The organization of a referendum is considered by the highest court of Ireland[43] as a condition for transferring the rights from the Irish democracy to the European Union.[44] In this context, a referendum on the TSCG was held in Ireland on 31 May 2012 and approved with a majority of 60.3%. This adoption was welcomed by the European Union and considered to be 'an important step towards recovery and stability'.[45]

Hungary has also undertaken, in the provisions of its Fundamental Law, to introduce the 'golden rule' at constitutional level, but the rule is set out in a rather vague manner. Art 36 of the Fundamental Law[46] prohibits the Parliament from adopting a budget 'that will lead to an increase in public debt to the extent to which it exceeds half of the total domestic product'.[47] Provided that the level of indebtedness is superior to this level, the MPs can only 'adopt a national budget law that will provide a reduction of the extent of public debt in relationship to the total domestic product'.[48] As such, Hungary cannot 'diverge' from these two obligations unless this is necessary to mitigate the effects caused by exceptional circumstances, or, in the case of a persistent and material relapse of the national economy, to the extent to which this is

(Abstimmung) by the entire nation (Bundesvolk).' As far as the accession of Austria to the European Union is concerned, it was submitted to a referendum since it was seen as a complete amendment to the Constitution. This could equally be the case for the TSCG if this treaty is considered to be another complete amendment to the Constitution, or if a third of the Members of the National Council or Federal Council equally demand that it be submitted to a referendum. See Manfred Stelzer, *The Constitution of the Republic of Austria* (Hart 2011) 27, 134–136.

42 Lina Papadopoulou, 'The Codification of the Government at Multiple Levels in the Constitutions of Former Europe' in Xenophon Kontiadis (ed.), *5 Years after the Constitutional Amendment, Assessment and Proposals for a New Constitutional Amendment* (Sakkoulas Publishing 2006) 187.

43 See the judgment on Crotty v. An Taoiseach, 1987, IR 713. This judgment required the ratification of the Single European Act by referendum. A referendum had also taken place before the entry into the European communities, in June 1972.

44 See art 29 para 4 bullet 10 of the Constitution of Ireland: '10. The State may ratify the Treaty on Stability, Coordination and Governance in the Economic and Monetary Union done at Brussels on the 2nd day of March 2012. No provision of this Constitution invalidates laws enacted, acts done or measures adopted by the State that are necessitated by the obligations of the State under that Treaty or prevents laws enacted, acts done or measures adopted by bodies competent under that Treaty from having the force of law in the State. [Bullet 10 supplemented by the 30th amendment 2012].'

45 Statement of Herman Van Rompuy, President of the European Council, www.consilium.europa.eu/uedocs/cms_Data/docs/pressdata/en/ec/130582.pdf, accessed 26 November 2020

46 Fundamental Law of Hungary of 25 April 2011.

47 Ibid. art 36, para 4.

48 Ibid. art 36, para 5.

necessary to restore the national economic balance.[49] Finally, Luxembourg announced that the 'golden rule' will not be introduced in its constitutional text, but it was introduced by a legislative provision.[50]

However, the basic problem that the constitutionalization of the 'golden rule' poses is related not only to the process of the revision of the Constitution, but also to a fundamental, substantive question concerning the democratic principle: to what extent is it democratically legitimate to introduce a single economic orthodoxy excluding other political alternatives open to the electorate? Moreover, to what extent is the 'golden rule' compatible with the social state principle? A possible constitutionalization of the 'golden rule' would lead to a new form of public interest which would affect the protection of social rights.[51] Finally, as already noted, the success of the 'golden rule' depends not on its constitutionalization but on the political will to implement it based on the dynamics of the social and financial needs.[52]

The budgetary rules derived from the rescue plan in countries under 'adjustment programs': the case of Greece

Consecutive financial adjustment programs have placed Greece in a situation of financial dependence on its creditor,[53] a condition that creates tensions between state sovereignty, which is tightly linked to economic independence,[54] and budgetary stability, which is an essential aim of the legal system of the Economic and Monteryar Union (EMU).[55] While Greece has followed three financial adjustment programs over the last decade, it has to be stressed that the commitments of the first adjustment program were challenged especially because of the procedure followed in order for these measures to be adopted.[56]

The context of the economic policies of Greece during the first economic package

The agreement on a joint euro area and the IMF financing package signed in May 2010 provided financial support under strong policy conditionality regarding the framework of the economic policy that Greece should observe.[57]

49 Ibid. art 36, para 6.
50 Zarka (n 15) 896.
51 Mantzoufas (n 2) 57.
52 Ibid 53.
53 Apostolos Gerontas, *Public Economic Law* (Sakkoulas Publishing House 2011) 593.
54 Bertrand Mathieu, *Constitution: rien ne bouge et tout change* (Lextenso 2013) 81.
55 Konstantinos Gogos, '"Crime" and Punishment: The Excessive Deficit Procedure in the Economic and Monetary Union between Law and Politics' (2010) 4 *EfimDD* 426.
56 It should be noted that the rescue plan, which enforces a financial support mechanism, is often invoked in the internal system by the term 'memorandum'. This term refers to all documents signed (memoranda of understanding and loan agreements) in this context. This is why the title 'memorandum' is often used in the more recent Greek works.
57 Andreas Dimitropoulos, 'The Constitution and the Pre-determination of the Government Policy' (2014) 1 *EDDD* 5.

The aim was to regulate the economic policies of Greece by relying on the Memorandum of Understanding, signed at the same time, and by subsequently assessing the measures taken.

In addition, at the same time, with the signature of the Memorandum of Understanding, the Council of the European Union presented Greece with Council Decision No. 2010/320/EU,[58] in order to strengthen and consolidate budgetary supervision and for the purpose of requiring Greece to implement measures that would contribute to the reduction of its deficit, measures that were deemed necessary for economic recovery. This decision mentions two articles of the TFEU. On the one hand, Art 136 para 1 of the TFEU provides the possibility of adopting specific measures for the member states where the currency is the euro, in order to strengthen the coordination and supervision of their budgetary discipline. On the other hand, it was based on Art 126 of the TFEU, which requires that the member states must avoid excessive public deficits and defines, for this purpose, the excessive deficit procedure. The undertakings provided in the financial agreement were incorporated into this decision, so that the rescue plan could be implemented. Furthermore, it should be noted that this decision explicitly provides that the funders deliver their aid according to the terms of this decision. Greece should have especially adopted the measures described in this decision, according to the specified schedule. In this context, the financial solidarity, a guiding principle of the EU for overcoming the sovereign debt crisis, remains rather hypothetical in the case of Greece, with respect to the importance of the transformations required.[59]

Therefore, this decision represents a legally binding text for Greece, introducing measures for the enforcement of the rules provided in the Memorandum of Understanding. This decision seems to be at the limit of constitutional legitimacy, and of the legitimacy of EU law.[60] This national budgetary autonomy is only partially transferred to the EU to ensure the proper functioning of the euro area.[61] Thus, the German Constitutional Court, the *Bundesverfassungericht*, in its decision on the mechanism of financial support[62]

58 Decision 2010/320 of the Council was amended three times by the decisions 2010/486 of 7 September 2010, 2011/57 of 20 December 2010, and 2011/257 of 7 March 2011. On 12 July 2011, decision 2010/320 was repealed and then replaced by decision 2011/734 of 19 July 2011, which was also amended by decision 2011/791 of the Council of 8 November 2011.

59 Francette Fines, 'The European Construction Despite the Sovereign Debt Crisis in the Euro Area' in de Grove-Valdeyron and others (eds) (n 11) 222.

60 Stylianos Mavridis, *The Criteria of Financial Discipline in the Construction of the Euro Zone: The Case of Greece* (Sakkoulas Publishing 2011) 328–329.

61 For the evolution of the principle of autonomy and financial sovereignty, see the Art of Claus Zimmerman, 'The Concept of Monetary Sovereignty Revisited' (2013) 2 *EJIL* 797.

62 BVerfGE 1390/12 of 12 September 2012, application for an interim injunction in order to prevent the ratification of the Treaty on the European Stability Mechanism (ESM) and the Treaty on Stability, Coordination and Governance (TSCG). See Emmanuelle Saulnier-Cassia, 'The Treaty Establishing the European Stability

signaled the importance of national budgetary autonomy, as a constitutive element of the democratic order. This autonomy is especially weakened in the case of Greece, not just due to the obligation to adopt specific measures to reduce the excessive deficit, as stipulated in the above-mentioned decision, but also due to the close supervision of the implementation of these measures by the European institutions and the International Monetary Fund.

Issues of legitimacy raised

It should be noted that this decision was not adopted as a result of a democratic debate in the European Parliament. In addition, the financial assistance agreed by euro-area EU countries and the IMF was not ratified by the Greek Parliament, as required by the Constitution.

In this context, the EU imposes the implementation of legislative measures which restrict the initiative of the legislative function and the democratic competencies of the national Parliament. In addition, the invocation of Arts 126.9 and 136 of the TFEU with respect to the adoption of this decision does not solve the issues of legitimacy of such plans of action. This reasoning limits itself to underlining the legal rules that have already been adopted at a generally binding level, thus trying to legitimize the procedure followed. The undertaking of the Hellenic Republic,[63] in accordance with decision 2010/320 of the Council, as amended, to enforce these measures does not resolve in any way the issue of the incompatibility of these acts with EU law. The aspect of imposing legislative measures on a member state cannot be connected to the principle of the primacy of EU law or to the powers of the EU with regard to the construction of the euro area. The European Union may set out quantitative criteria for the fight against an excessive deficit and suggest the measures to be adopted, but cannot bind the financial policy of a member state to such measures.

The EU Council's choice to determine in as much detail as possible the legislative measures that Greece should adopt, in compliance with the provisions of the Memorandum of Understanding, demonstrates the commitment of the EU to guide Greece in this direction, even though the Union did not have at the time the institutional framework appropriate for this endeavor.[64] As is

Mechanism and the Treaty on Stability, Coordination and Governance within Europe, under Constitutional Control' (2013) 1 *RTDE* 160–163. See also decision BVerfGE 1390/12 of 18 March 2014, finally rejecting the requests submitted on this issue.

63 Always subject to the compliance of the loan agreement with art 125(1) of the TFEU.

64 In trying to overcome the risks arising in the euro area, the European Union tends to underestimate the legitimacy of the integration project (the Union's attempt to 'save' the Eurozone risks undermining the substantive balance that sustains the legitimacy of the integration project); Mark Dawson, Floris de Witte, 'Constitutional balance in the EU after the Euro-Crisis' (2013) 76 MLR 817, 826.

cogently noted, such lack of institutional framework shows that 'we are not in the presence of a democratic government of Europe, but a government of Europe based on economy'.[65]

In fact, the Greek crisis has led to the exposure of the deficiencies in the economic governance of the Union,[66] both regarding its democratic legitimacy and its efficacy. In this sense, the mechanisms provided for the management of the Greek crisis have been shaped by the economic reality and by political pragmatism.[67] Nevertheless, the legal framework of the EU, particularly the legal framework of Art 136 of the TFEU, was not adequate for the acts adopted by the EU. Therefore, in the context of the meeting of the European Council on 16 and 17 December 2010, and in order to legitimize all the measures agreed upon, it was decided to introduce a new paragraph in Art 136 of the TFEU, subsequently necessary for providing a 'structural response to a crisis situation'[68] and in respect of the measures already adopted.[69]

Finally, the examples described above show how balanced budget policies reflect the dominance of technocracy and the parallel restriction of means of political dialogue, and initiatives undertaken by the national and the EU Parliament.

The effects of the budgetary rules on the national and European legal systems

European and domestic case law show that, during the early years of the financial crisis, both the Greek and the European judges sought to legitimize, from a constitutional and a European point of view, the restrictions on human rights adopted by the rules addressing the financial crisis. In this context, the Greek judge had initially shown restraint in reviewing the constitutionality and compatibility with European law of the measures adopted. Yet the case law of

65 Francisco Balaguer Callejon, 'Economic Crisis and Constitutional Crisis in Europe' (2013) 2 *Constitutions* 133, 142.

66 Renaud Dehousse, Laurie Boussaguet, 'The Impact of the Crisis on European Governance' (2014) 2 *RFDC* 7, 10.

67 Constantin Yannakopoulos, 'A State Faced with Bankruptcy: between Law and Non-law', intervention at the colloquium 'The End of Law?' organized by the Versailles Saint-Quentin Political Institutions Research Center, on Thursday and Friday, 5 and 6 December 2013, at the Faculty of Law and Political Science of the Université de Versailles Saint-Quentin, published on www.constitutionalism.gr/site/wp-content/uploads/2013/12/2013.12_Fin-du-droit_intervention_Yannakopoulos.pdf

68 Francis Querol, 'The Global Financial Crisis and the Governance within the Euro Area: Between Intergovernmental Logic and Federal Logic' in N. de Grove and others (eds) (n 11) 558.

69 Art 136 (3): 'The Member States whose currency is the euro may establish a stability mechanism to be activated if indispensable to safeguard the stability of the euro area as a whole. The granting of any required financial assistance under the mechanism will be made subject to strict conditionality.'

the two European courts seems to be in line with the Greek case law, contrary to the view of the European Committee of Social Rights.

The influence of the financial crisis on compatibility with the ECHR

It is often the case in Greece that a national legislative provision is legally examined in terms both of the Constitution and of the provisions of either the European Convention on Human Rights (ECHR) or of European Union law, especially in the field of human rights. However, during the first period of financial crisis, the European human rights protection was not always invoked in the jurisprudence of the Greek Council of State. Moreover, the case law of constitutional courts seems to diverge from the initial Greek case law during the early years of financial crisis.

The compatibility control weakened by the measures adopted in accordance with the first financial aid plan

The example of Greece is significant in that the application of the readjustment programs almost rendered its constitutional autonomy nominal.[70] The most sensitive subject, in addition to the limitation to its constitutional sovereignty, was the adoption of the measures provided in the first Memorandum of Understanding and in the decision of the Council of State regarding the reduction of indemnities, salaries and pensions.[71] All these measures were implemented through statutory laws[72] that were criticized by some scholars[73] as

70 Mathieu (n 54) 81: 'en dehors même du cadre juridique, la souveraineté des États est liée à l'indépendance économique. Un État endetté garde en théorie son autonomie constitutionnelle.'

71 George Kasimatis, 'The Incompatibility of the Essential Terms of the Loan Agreements with the Constitution' (2011) 49 *DtA* 11, 19 (in Greek).

72 By way of example: two laws that ratified the signed memoranda no 3845/2010 and 4046/2012, as well as the law that ratified the mid-term program with its update (law 4127/2013). See also: law 3863/2010: new social security system and other provisions, regulations of the labor relations; law 3833/2010: reduction of the salaries of public servants, exceptional financial contribution, restrictions of employment, VAT and other measures; law 3896/2011: measures of the mid-term program, labor legislation, tax legislation, etc.; law 4024/2011: retirement, public servants put in reserve, etc.; law 4051/2012: reduction of pensions and other provisions for the enforcement of the memorandum rules; law 4021/2011: establishment of credit, additional special tax on immovable property; law 4172/2013 on putting public servants in reserve.

73 George Katrougalos, '"Memoranda": Greek Exceptionalism or the Mirror of Europe's Future?' in A. Triandafyllidiou and others (eds), *The Greek Crisis and European Modernity* (Palgrave Macmillan 2013); George Katrougalos, 'Memoranda sunt Servanda? The constitutionality of the Treaties with IMF and EU for the implementation of the stabilization measures' (2010) 2 *Journal of Administrative Law* 151; George Kasimatis, *The Loan Treaties with the EU and the IMF* (Athens Bar Association 2010); Kasimatis (n 72); Panos Lazaratos, 'The Constitutionality of the Exceptions from Securities by the "PSI" Procedure' (2012) 1 *EfimDD* 139;

innately contrary to the fundamental principle of a social state. More precisely, the legitimacy of such measures has been challenged as regards their compliance with the Greek constitutional principles and rules, and with European law.

The first legal issue concerns the social *acquis*. This notion does not mean that there is a constitutional framework which binds the legislator in an absolute manner. However, in accordance with the social acquis, it should be admitted that the acquis cannot lead to the abrogation of the social rights already recognized and acquired, or to an erosion of their protection, in a manner that would affect the core of these rights and the principle of legitimate expectations.[74] At the same time, the principle of social acquis binds the legislative, executive and judicial powers to establish a more comprehensive legal framework aimed at social protection, and not to disproportionately restrict it, as in this particular case.[75]

The Greek Constitution establishes a number of social rights, which impose obligations for the state to respect, protect and fulfill them. Such rights include the right to health (Art 21 para 3), full employment (Art 22 para 3), and social security (Art 22 para 5).[76] Moreover, the rights related to the salary of the public and private sector employees, as well as to the pensions of retired persons, are protected not only from the perspective of social rights, but also from the perspective of property rights. These rights equally fall under the protection of Art 1 of the supplementary Protocol no 1 to the ECHR, and of Art 17 of the EU Charter of Fundamental Rights.[77]

In this vein, the measures implemented in order to alleviate the economic crisis should guarantee a fair balance between the envisaged aim and public interest, as well as the respect of social rights and of the *social acquis* as an expression of the principle of legitimate expectations. However, the Greek jurisprudence relied on the principle of public interest, especially under the financial dimension and the aim of long-term economic sustainability. As such, the need to reduce the deficit, combined with the efforts to avoid state bankruptcy and to take measures for budgetary consolidation,[78] were considered to justify, under the exceptional circumstances of the crisis, the restrictions

Georgios Agapitos, 'The PSI Reduces Public Debt but Increase Unemployment Rates' [2012] *DEN* 481; Athina Petroglou, 'The Memorandum of Understanding of Law 4046/2012 and the Reforms Adopted for Social Security' [2012] *EDKA* 75; Kostas Chrysogonos, Aktitas Kaidatzis, 'The Futile Sacrifice of Iphigenia. Preliminary Reflections on the Unconstitutionality of Law 4093/2012' [2012] *NoV* 2682–2708 (in Greek).

74 For the general framework of the protection of the right to work, see George Katrougalos, *Social Rights* (Sakkoulas Publishing 2006) 133–142.

75 Dimitra Kavvada and Michael Oikonomou, 'The Economic Crisis: A New Aspect of the Role Played by the State and the Economic Constitution' (2011) 10–11 *ThPDD* 918, 922.

76 Stavroula Ktistaki, 'The Influence of the Economic Crisis on Social Rights' [2012] *EDKA* 481, 482.

77 Kasimatis (n 73) 40–41.

78 Mavridis (n 60) 310–311.

imposed on social rights. In other words, a *sui generis* state of emergency related to the financial crisis was considered to legitimize restrictions to human rights which would not be tolerated under normal circumstances.[79]

More specifically, the decision of the Plenary Assembly of the Council of State 668/2012[80] addressed the compatibility with the Constitution and the ECHR of the legislative provisions adopted in compliance with the measures provided in the first program of economic adjustment, which conditioned the first financial aid package to Greece and were validated by Law 3485/2010. The judicial control referred to the measures for the reduction of salaries, pensions and social benefits in relation to the violation of property stipulated in Art 17 of the Constitution and in Art 1 of the Protocol no 1 to the ECHR, as well to the principles of proportionality, equal contributions to public charges, and respect for human dignity.

The Council of State considered that the right to property does not guarantee a right to a specific amount of salary or pension and that restrictions may be provided by the law for reasons of public interest. The Court hesitated to rely on the principle of legitimate expectations, guaranteed at national level but also at European level by the well-established case law of the European Court of Human Rights.[81] It is important to mention that the Court did not proceed to a simple invocation of exceptional circumstances for the satisfaction of the budgetary interest of the state. On the contrary, the measures implemented were controlled in terms of their relevance and their necessity with respect to the proportionality control *stricto sensu* – that is to say, mainly in relationship to the need to protect the economic and budgetary interests against the backdrop of a crisis situation.[82]

Nonetheless, and despite the constitutionality of the measures reviewed, the highest administrative court has reserved the right to change its position in the future,[83] should new measures be adopted that would infringe upon the social nature of the state and the protection of human rights. In fact, the Court has confirmed that the restrictions imposed on fundamental rights in order to manage the financial crisis must have a limited duration, taking into account the impact on the material condition of the persons concerned.[84]

Therefore, in subsequent decisions related to pensions and salary rights, the Council of State abandoned the judicial self-restraint and considered that the

79 Ktistaki (n 76) 500–501.

80 Council of State, Plenary Assembly, 668/2012, commentary by Ioannis Mathioudakis, *Armenopoulos* [2012] *EDKA* 580–582, 634-636; (2012) 1 *EfimDD* 85–87 (synthesis).

81 Frédéric SUDRE, *Droit européen et international des droits de l'homme* (11th ed., PUF 2012) 659ff.

82 Constantin Yannakopoulos, 'Public Interest under the Aspect of the Economic Crisis' (2012) 1 *EfimDD* 100, 112.

83 Julia Iliopoulos-Strangas, 'Constitutional Judges and Parliaments: Greece' (2011) XXVII *AIJC* 278.

84 Didier Ribes, 'Financial Implications of the Constitutional Judge's Decisions' (2008) 24 *Cahiers du Conseil Constitutionnel* 104.

accumulative effect of restrictive measures violated the relevant constitutional guarantees.[85] The change of focus in the jurisprudence of the Council of State shows that the state of emergency which Greece entered because of its financial situation could justify a continuous infringement on the protection of rights.

The jurisprudence of other European constitutional courts

The initial reluctance of the Greek jurisprudence regarding the intensity of judicial review of the measures implemented seems to be in contrast with the judgments delivered by three other constitutional courts with regard to national measures, similar to those voted on in Greece. First, the constitutional courts of Latvia[86] and Romania[87] ruled unconstitutional the reductions imposed on pensions according to a loan agreement signed between these countries and the IMF. The above-mentioned constitutional courts concluded that such measures were unconstitutional, by invoking the constitutional guarantees related to social rights.

It should be noted that the Latvian Constitutional Court actually concluded on the unconstitutionality of these measures by enforcing Arts 1 and 109 of the Latvian Constitution that guarantee the democratic regime, as well as the right to the protection of social rights.[88] In the same manner, the Constitutional Court of Romania concluded on the unconstitutionality of pension cuts by invoking arts 41 and 47(2) of the Romanian Constitution, which guarantee the right to work and the right to social security, as well as to social protection.[89]

Second, a similar reasoning is found in two judgments delivered by the Portuguese Constitutional Court with regard to the suspension of the payment

85 Council of State, Plenary Assembly, 2287/2015, 2288/2015.

86 Latvian constitutional Court, 21 December 2009, no 2009-43-1. Constantin Yannakopoulos, 'The Rule of Law and National Sovereignty before the IMF' (2010) 1 *EfimDD* 2.

87 Constitutional Court of Romania, 25 June 2010, no 872/2010.

88 Art 1 of the Latvian Constitution: 'Latvia is an independent democratic republic.' Art 109: 'Everyone has the right to social security in old age, for work disability, for unemployment and in other cases as provided by law.'

89 Art 41 of the Romanian Constitution: '(1) The right to work shall not be restricted. Everyone has a free choice of his/her profession, trade or occupation, as well as work place. (2) All employees have the right to measures of social protection. These concern employees' safety and health, working conditions for women and young people, the setting up of a minimum gross salary per economy, weekends, paid rest leave, work performed under difficult and special conditions, as well as other specific conditions, as stipulated by the law. (3) The normal duration of a working day is of maximum eight hours, on the average. (4) On equal work with men, women shall get equal wages. (5) The right to collective labor bargaining and the binding force of collective agreements shall be guaranteed.' Art 47 §2 (2): 'Citizens have the right to pensions, paid maternity leave, medical care in public health centers, unemployment benefits, and other forms of public or private social securities, as stipulated by the law. Citizens have the right to social assistance, according to the law.'

of Christmas and summer holiday bonuses, as well as to other benefits granted to public sector civil servants and pensioners, corresponding to a 13th or 14th month's salary. All these measures were declared as contrary to the principle of equity in the distribution of public charges as provided by Art 13 of the Portuguese Constitution.[90] Nevertheless, the same judgment accepted that the emergency circumstances caused by the country's insolvency required the execution of the external financial aid program, and that the inability to observe the annual budget by other equivalent measures, imposed pursuant to Art 282 paragraph 4[91] of the Portuguese Constitution, required accepting the suspension of bonuses during the 2012 budget implementation.

However, it should be noted that, contrary to the judgment mentioned above, the Portuguese Constitutional Court declared in Decision 187/2013 that the unconstitutionality of the equivalent provisions included in the budget of the Portuguese state for the year 2013 was immediately enforceable (with retroactive effect as of 1 January 2013).[92] It should also be mentioned that the IMF warned Portugal that if the Constitutional Court continued to reject the measures adopted according to the object of the budgetary adjustment program, the government would be obliged to adopt alternative measures, according to the program signed, while focusing at the same time on any issues caused in the case of another rejection by the Portuguese judiciary of the measures adopted.[93] However, the same

90 Art 13 of the Portuguese Constitution: 'Principle of Equality 1. All citizens possess the same social dignity and are equal before the law. 2. No one may be privileged, favoured, prejudiced, deprived of any right or exempted from any duty for reasons of ancestry, sex, race, language, territory of origin, religion, political or ideological beliefs, education, economic situation, social circumstances or sexual orientation.' Christina Akrivopoulou, 'Constitution and Suspension of the Payment of the 13th and 14th Salaries in Portugal, judgment 353/2012' (2012) 5 *EfimDD* 628; see also in the same vein the judgment of the Italian Constitutional Court, of 11 October 2012, no 223/2012, in which the Italian Constitutional Court declared as unconstitutional the reductions imposed on judges' indemnities with the decretto-legge 78/2010 (misure urgenti di stabilizzazione finanziaria e di competitivita economica). Christina Akrivopoulou, ibid. 651, and the judgment 116/2013 of the Italian constitutional Court of 3 June 2013, ruling on the unconstitutionality of the legislative measures that imposed on pensioners a solidarity contribution in view of the financial crisis (art. 18, c. 22° bis, del decreto legge 06/07/2011 n. 98, convertito, con modificazioni, dalla legge 15/07/2011 n. 111, come modificato dall'art. 24, c. 31° bis, del decreto legge 06/12/2011, n. 201, convertito con modificazioni dalla legge 22/12/2011, n. 214).

91 Art 282 (4) of the Portuguese Constitution: 'Art 282 Effects of declarations of unconstitutionality or illegality 4. When required for the purposes of legal security, reasons of fairness or an exceptionally important public interest, the grounds for which must be given, the Constitutional Court may determine a scope for the effects of the unconstitutionality or illegality that is more restricted than that provided for in paras (1) and (2).'

92 Portuguese Constitutional Court, 5 April 2013, no 187/2013, Constantin Yannakopoulos, *The Influence of European Union Law on the Judicial Review of the Constitutionality of Laws* (Sakkoulas Publishing 2013) 328.

93 See *IMF Country Report No. 13/324 Portugal: eighth and ninth reviews under the extended arrangement and request for waivers of applicability of end-September performance criteria*

solution has been reiterated in relation to the judgment of the Portuguese Constitutional Tribunal on the unconstitutionality of other austerity measures aiming to reduce the pensions of civil servants by 10%.[94]

These judgments, issued in countries that have concluded loan agreements with the EU and the IMF, show the divergence regarding the depth of the judicial review and the guarantee of rights. Constitutional courts also reflect the development of a feeling of mistrust of national judges vis-à-vis the constitutional actors of the European Union and initiate a movement of increasing dissent that could be emulated by others.[95] Moreover, another issue should be taken into account. The *time* of the judicial review seems to play a significant role in the depth of the review undertaken. In fact, constitutional review seems to be more intense when a Constitutional Court is involved since measures are in principle controlled before their implementation and therefore, if judged unconstitutional, the legislature is required to adopt other policies. In case of Greece, judicial review is exercised only *a posteriori*, at the stage of implementation of a law voted by the Parliament. Therefore, a Greek national judge seems to appear more reluctant to find contrary to the Constitution measures with financial impact and already in force. However, during the financial crisis, which lasted almost a decade, judicial review became more intense.

The case law at supranational European level

In ruling on the compatibility of measures adopted in accordance with the financial aid plan with the ECHR, the European Court of Human Rights seems to confirm the case law of the Greek Council of State. Moreover, the case law of the Court of Justice of the European Union has upheld the measures taken in order to consider the financial crisis at European level. On the contrary, the European Committee of Social Rights, which supervises the European Social Charter, in a series of collective complaints, considers these measures to violate the Charter.

The case law of the European Court of Human Rights

The decision 668/2012 of the Council of State was subject to scientific analysis and debate in Greece.[96] Despite the criticism raised, the ECHR seems to have

(November 2013), as well as *Portugal - Transcript of a Conference Call on the Release of the Staff Report* on the 8th and 9th Review under the EFF (13 November 2013).

94 Portuguese constitutional Court, 19 December 2013, no 862/2013.

95 Guillaume Tusseau, 'European Constitutionalism Grappling with the "Institutional Disobedience" of National Judges' (2013) 1 *RFDA* 149, and Guillaume Tusseau, 'Austerity Budgets in Relation to Constitutional Principles' (2013) 3 *RFDA* 672.

96 See e.g. Xenophon Kontiadis and Alkmini Fotiadou, 'Social Rights, Proportionality and Financial Crisis: Remarks on Judgment 668/2012 of the Council of State Plenary Assembly' (2012) 53 *DtA* 27; Theodora Antoniou, 'Judgment of the Council of State for the Memorandum, a European Affair without European Approach' [2012] *ToS* 197; George Kasimatis, 'Unconstitutional Measures of Loan Agreements: Positions Adopted by Judgment 668/2012 of the Council of State

confirmed it in relation to two petitions submitted by the Confederation of Public Servants' Trade Unions (ADEDY).[97] More precisely, the ECHR examined the compatibility of the national measures for the reduction of salaries and pensions enforced under the laws for the enforcement of memoranda on the basis of the first Protocol of the ECHR. The requests were rejected as manifestly ill-founded pursuant to Art 35 (3a) and (4) of the Convention.[98]

The Court reiterates that states benefit from a rather extended margin of appreciation in terms of determining their social policy. Moreover, it considers that, in principle, national authorities are in a better position than an international tribunal to choose the most appropriate means for achieving the balance

Plenary Assembly' (2012) *NoV* 2648, and Ifigeneia Kamtsidou, 'Public Interest in Times of Crisis', www.constitutionalism.gr/wp-content/uploads/2013/08/2013_Kamtsidou_Linteret-general-et-la-crise-final.pdf

97 ECHR, 7 May 2013, *Koufaki and Adedy versus Grèce*, no 57665/12, 57657/12 (decision), (2013) 7 *ThPDD* 656–663, with commentary by S. Trekli 663–666; see also the decision regarding the case of Portugal by the ECHR, 8 October 2013, *Da Conceição Mateus and Santos Januário versus Portugal*, (no 62235/12 and 57725/12, decision) where the Court rejected by delivering a similar judgment the requests against the reduction of pensions, adopted after the signature of the Portuguese memorandum. See also the referral of the preliminary issues by the Tribunal do Trabalho de Porto, (CJEU, C-128/12, *Sindicato dos Bancários do Norte e.a.*, 7 March 2013, not yet published (order of the Court); CJEU, C-264/12, *Sindicato Nacional dos Profissionais de Seguros e Afins*, June 26, 2014, (order of the Court)). Relating to case C-128/12, the Court demands the CJEU rule on the compliance of the reduction of the salaries of public sector servants, provided under law 55-A/2010, on the adoption of the finance law for 2011 with a view to consolidating public finance in the situation of serious economic and financial crisis with the Charter of Fundamental Rights. The CJEU considered that its jurisdiction is not established in order to address the application for a preliminary ruling given that the order for referral does not contain any specific evidence to enable it to consider that said law is intended to implement the law of the Union. The questions referred to in Case C-264/12 deal with the same matters. Contrary to this judgment are Decisions 65 and 66/2011 of the European Committee of Social Rights of 18 June 2012, ruling on the violation of the Charter of Social Rights by measures introduced in accordance with memoranda of understanding. See Christina Deligianni-Dimitrakou, 'The Decisions of the European Committee of Social Rights on Greek Austerity Measures and Their Effectiveness' (2013) *EErgD* 135. These decisions are not binding because the Committee is not a court. However, the Committee of Ministers adopted two Resolutions CM / ResChS (2013) No. 2 and 3 on 5 February 2013, ruling on the violation of art 4 (4) of the 1961 Charter under Art 17 (5) of Law 3899 of 17 December 2010, which does not provide for periods of notice or termination indemnity in the event of an interruption of a contract of employment qualified by it as 'indefinite' for a probationary period that it extends to one year.

98 Art 35 (3) (a) and art 4 of the ECvHR: '3. The Court shall declare inadmissible any individual application submitted under art 34 if it considers that: a) the application is incompatible with the provisions of the Convention or the Protocols thereto, manifestly ill-founded, or an abuse of the right of individual application; [...] 4. The Court shall reject any application which it considers inadmissible under this article. It may do so at any stage of the proceedings.'

of economic sustainability and human rights, and it respects their choice unless they prove to be clearly unreasonable or the level of interference is so high that there is a risk of exposing the claimants to hardship that is incompatible with Art 1 of Protocol No. 1.[99]

In this case, the European Court seems to adhere to decision 668/2012 of the Council of State by focusing on the fact that the restrictions introduced by related laws would not be considered a 'deprivation of property', as the claimants pretended, but more like limitations in the exercise of this right, as stipulated Art 1 para 1 of Protocol No.1.[100] The Court also attached specific importance to the reasoning of the Council of State which, in its judgment of 20 February 2012, rejected several pleas related to the alleged violation of the principle of proportionality by the impugned measures, on the one hand in order to remedy the acute budgetary crisis and, on the other, in order to restore the public finances of the state in a sustainable manner.

Consequently, the Court stressed the fact that the notion of 'public utility' is vast by its nature. According to its reasoning, it turns out that the decision to adopt laws concerning the balance between the budget expenses and revenues of the state usually involves the examination of the political, economic and social issues, and the legislator benefits, to this end, from an ample margin of discretion in conducting the economic and social policy.

Finally, it should be mentioned that this judgment was also reiterated in relation to the measures adopted by Portugal with regard to the budget crisis.[101] As such, the European Court shows considerable self-restraint and refuses to proceed to an abstract review of the measures adopted.[102] This reticence is partly explained by the fact that the ECHR does not include a list of social rights. For this reason, the European Committee of Social Rights has adopted a diametrically opposed position.

The case law of the Court of Justice of the European Union

Art 136 of the TFEU was amended following the accelerated procedure of review of the treaties. As such, it was supplemented with a third paragraph, providing that

> The Member States whose currency is the euro may establish a stability mechanism to be activated if indispensable to safeguard the stability of the euro area as a whole. The granting of any required financial assistance under the mechanism will be made subject to strict conditionality.[103]

99 Point no 31.

100 ECHR, *Koufaki and Adedy* (n 98), point no 34.

101 ECHR, October 8, 2013, *Da Conceição Mateus and Santos Januário v. Portugal*, no 62235/12 57725/12 (decisions).

102 Mantzoufas (n 2) 139–140.

103 Decision 2011/199 of the Council of 25 March 2011, amending art 136 of the TFEU in terms of a stability mechanism for the member states whose currency is the euro. It became effective on 1 May 2013.

This amendment was deemed necessary in order to guarantee the validity of the Treaty Establishing the European Stability Mechanism (ESM)[104] with respect to European law.[105] However, the issue of validation of Decision 2011/199 of the European Council, which amends this article, as well as that of compliance of the ESM with European Union law, was submitted to the CJEU by the Supreme Court of Ireland for a preliminary ruling.[106]

The Court of Justice decided that the contested amendment did not infringe upon the acknowledged exclusive competence of the Union in the field of monetary policy for those member states whose currency is the euro. Second, it decided that the contested amendment did not affect in any way the acknowledged competence of the Union in the field of coordination of the economic policies of member states.

Furthermore, the Court found that the attribution, under the ESM treaty, of new functions to the Commission to the European Central Ban (ECB) and to

104 This Treaty creates a permanent international financial institution and replaces the European Financial Stabilization Mechanism (EFSM) and the European Financial Stability Facility (EFSF), which were adopted in 2010 when Greece's financial instability was at its critical point. See Jacques Bourrinet, 'Towards a Rebuilding of the Economic Governance of the Euro Area?' in Christian Philip et al. (eds), *Réalisations et défis de l'Union européenne: droit, politique, économie. Mélanges en hommage à Panayotis Soldatos* (Bruylant 2012) 144–148.

105 The TMES was concluded on 11 July 2011, by the 17 Member States of the euro area and an amended version was concluded on 2 February 2012, to widen the scope for ESM intervention by allowing assistance granted as a precautionary measure, and the purchase of government securities on the primary and secondary markets. See Alexandre de Streel, 'The Reformed European Economic Governance', (2013) 3 *RTDE* 458. Currently, all the countries that signed the MES have approved it, Austria on 17 July 2012, Belgium on 14 June 2012, Cyprus on 22 June 2012, Estonia on 30 August 2012, Finland on 3 July 2012, France on 8 March 2012, Germany on 29 June 2012, Greece on 30 March 2012, Ireland on 3 July 2012, Italy on 19 July 2012, Luxembourg on 5 July 2012, Malta on 17 July 2012, the Netherlands on 12 July 2012, Portugal on 19 June 2012, Slovakia on 28 June 2012, Slovenia on 14 May 2012, Spain on 6 June 2012. As non-members of the euro area, the following countries ratified only the amendment of Art 136TFEU: Bulgaria on 27 July 2012, Czech Republic on 3 March 2013, Hungary on 6 March 2012, Latvia on 9 May 2012, Lithuania on 21 June 2012, Poland on 2 July 2012, Romania on 22 June 2012, Sweden on 19 June 2012, the United Kingdom on 10 September 2012.

106 Case C-370/12 *Pringle* [2012] (ECJ, 27 November 2012), published in Recueil numérique. Manolis Perrakis, 'Presentation and Commentary on the Judgment of the Court of Justice of the European Union Pringle (C-370/12) on the European Stability Mechanism' [2013] *NoV* 572–594; Jean-Paul Jacqué, 'The Contribution of the Court of Justice to the Implementation and Interpretation of the Treaty of Lisbon', (2013) 3 *RTDE* 610–19; Marcus Kerber, 'An Endless Teleological Apology (Pringle Decision of the CJEU as an *ultra vires* Legal Act), or Voluntary Blindness to any Economic Reason' (2013) 211 *LPA* 7–11. In addition, the TMES was also appealed before the Karlsruhe Court. In a ruling handed down on 12 September 2012 (BvR 1390/12), the German Constitutional Court authorized the ratification of this treaty by Germany. See BVerfGE, 12 September 2012, 2BVR 1390/12, finally rejecting the requests submitted on this subject.

the Court was compatible with their powers as defined under the treaties.[107] The Court especially emphasized that the functions entrusted to the Commission and to the ECB within the ESM treaty did not include any decision-making authority and that the activities exercised by these two institutions under the same treaty bound only the ESM. Finally, as far as it is concerned, the Court shows that it is competent to rule on any dispute between member states in relation to the object of the treaties, if this dispute is submitted thereto following a compromise[108] and that nothing prevents such approval from being given beforehand by reference to a category of predefined disputes. The CJEU, directly confronted with the jurisdictional control of the exercise of the European-derived constituent power, did not wish to emphasize the extraordinary nature of the crisis,[109] or the eventual infringement of social rights.

The case law of the European Committee of Social Rights

In a series of collective complaints against Greece[110] with regard to the level of pension benefits under the European Social Charter, the European Committee of Social Rights referred to Art 12.3 in conjunction with Art 4.1(a) of the 1988 Additional Protocol, which also appears with identical wording in Art 23,1(a) of the 1996 Revised Charter, stipulating the right of the elderly to adequate resources in order to enable them to lead a decent life. Basing its evaluation on the entirety of the above criteria, the Committee considered that the cumulative effect of these restrictions brought about a significant degradation of the standard of living of the pensioners concerned, which results in a violation of the Charter.

The Committee held that, despite the later international obligations of Greece associated with the Loan Treaties and 'Memoranda', there is nothing to absolve the state party from fulfilling its obligations under the 1961 Charter and that the Committee is competent to examine whether the claims made in the complaint establish that the measures taken by Greece with regard to old-age benefits are not in conformity with Art 12 of the 1961 Charter. The Committee has readopted the aforementioned analysis and specified that

> doing away with such guarantees would not only force employees to shoulder an excessively large share of the consequences of the crisis but

107 See for this purpose art 13 TFEU.

108 Art 273 TFEU.

109 Florence Giorgi, 'The European Constituent Power, the "Holy Grail" of European Constitutionalism? Reflections on the Pringle Judgment' in Vincent Kornenberger, Maria Teresa D'Alessio, Valerio Placco (eds), *De Rome à Lisbonne: les juridictions de l'Union européenne à la croisée des chemins, Mélanges en l'honneur de Paolo Mengozzi* (Bruylant 2013) 277.

110 See George Katrougalos, 'Social security in the "case law" of the Social Rights Committee' in Frans Pennings and Gijsbert Vonk (eds) *Handbook on European Social Security Law* (Edward Elgar 2015).

> also accept pro-cyclical effects liable to make the crisis worse and to increase the burden on welfare systems, particularly social assistance, unless it was decided at the same time to stop fulfilling the obligations of the Charter in the area of social protection.[111]

Moreover, the European Committee of Social Rights (ESRC) considers that the economic crisis accentuates, rather than alleviates, the respective obligations of the states. It notes that, by acceding to the 1961 Charter, the state parties

> have accepted to pursue by all appropriate means the attainment of conditions in which, inter alia, the right to health, the right to social security, the right to social and medical assistance and the right to benefit from social welfare services may be effectively realised.

Accordingly,

> the economic crisis should not have as a consequence the reduction of the protection of the rights recognised by the Charter. Hence, the governments are bound to take all necessary steps to ensure *that the rights of the Charter are effectively guaranteed at a period of time when beneficiaries need protection the most.* [112]

Under this light the ESRC concluded:

> Even taking into account the particular context in Greece created by the economic crisis and the fact that the Government was required to take urgent decisions, the Committee furthermore considers that the Government has not conducted the minimum level of research and analysis into the effects of such far-reaching measures that is necessary to assess in a meaningful manner their full impact on vulnerable groups in society. Neither has it discussed the available studies with the organisations concerned, despite the fact that they represent the interests of many of the groups most affected by the measures at issue. [...] In general, the Committee thus concludes that the Government has not established, as is required by Art 12§3, that efforts have been made to maintain a sufficient level of protection for the benefit of the most vulnerable members of society, even though the effects of the adopted measures risk bringing about a large scale pauperisation of a significant segment of the population, as has been observed by various international organizations.[113]

111 General Federation of employees of the national electric power corporation (GENOP-DEI)/Confederation of Greek Civil Servants' Trade Unions (ADEDY) v. Greece, Complaint No. 65/2011, decision on the merits of 23 May 2012, para 18. See also Complaints 78–80/2012.

112 General introduction to Conclusions XIX-2, 2009, emphasis added.

113 Collective Complaint 80/2012 Pensioners' Union of the Agricultural Bank of Greece (ATE) v. Greece, paras 75–76. See also ibid. paras 36 and 47. The Committee consequently held that, due to the cumulative effect of the restrictive

Finally, the Committee has more recently concluded in the case of another violation of the Charter by taking into account the scale and severity of the economic and financial crisis in Greece but also by reiterating that the aim of the Charter and its own role under the terms of the Protocol on the collective complaints system are not to defend abstract values but to protect practical and effective rights. The Committee underlined that the situation over the years has been worse because of the legislature's inaction which was contrary to the obligation of state parties to undertake both legal and practical measures that will allow the full exercise of the rights recognized by the Charter. The Committee insists that violations of the Charter in the present case 'pose a challenge to the interests of the wider community and to the shared fundamental standards of all Council of Europe's member states, namely those related to human rights, democracy and the rule of law'.[114]

Conclusion

Our analysis focused on the protection of human rights during times of crisis and financial destabilization. The real issue for Europe, however, is to find the necessary balance between the protection of rights and the objectives of the EMU. Speaking in 2010 about the policies confronting the crisis in the euro area, Christine Lagarde admitted that in order to rescue the latter 'we violated all the rules'.[115] Still, the new rules that followed the financial crisis are present today through numerous supranational provisions regarding budgetary discipline which is currently strongly influenced by the COVID-19 pandemic. A new balance between the economic and social dimensions in Europe is necessary in order to safeguard the protection of rights in times of multidimensional, health and economic crisis.

Bibliography

Clerc O, *La gouvernance économique de l'Union européenne* (Bruylant 2012)

Dawson, M, de Witte, F, 'Constitutional balance in the EU after the Euro-Crisis' (2013) 76 *MLR* 817

measures and the procedures adopted to put them into place, contained in the laws Nos. 3845 of 6 May 2010, Act No. 3847 of 11 May 2010, Act No. 3863 of 15 July 2010, Act No. 3865 of 21 July 2010, Act No. 3896 of 1 July 2011, Act No. 4024 of 27 October 2011, Act No. 3833 of 15 March 2010, Act No. 3866 of 26 May 2010, Act No. 3986 of 1 July 2011, Act No. 4002 of 22 August 2011, Act No. 4051 of 28 February 2012 and Act No. 4093/2012 of 12 November 2012, this statutory legislation constitutes a violation of art 12(3) of the 1961 Charter.

114 Collective Complaint 111/2014 Greek General Confederation of Labour (GSEE) v. Greece, decision on the merits, paras 246–251.

115 Christine Lagarde's words in English: 'We violated all the rules because we wanted to close ranks and really rescue the euro zone' in Brian M. Carney and Anne Jolis, 'Toward a United States of Europe', *Wall Street Journal* (17 December 2010). http://online.wsj.com/articles/SB10001424052748704034804576025681087342502, accessed 26 November 2020.

Dehousse R, Boussaguet L, 'The Impact of the Crisis on European Governance' (2014) 2 *RFDC* 7

Gerontas A, *Public Economic Law* (Sakkoulas Publishing 2011)

Glavinis P, *The Memorandum of Greece* (Sakkoulas Publishing 2011)

Gogos K, '"Crime" and Punishment: The Excessive Deficit Procedure in the Economic and Monetary Union between Law and Politics' (2010) 4 *EfimDD* 426

Habermas J, Bouchindhomme C, *La Constitution de l'Europe* (Gallimard 2012)

Kasimatis G, *The Loan Treaties with the EU and the IMF* (Athens Bar Association 2010)

Katrougalos G, *Social Rights* (Sakkoulas Publishing 2006)

Katrougalos G, 'Memoranda sunt Servanda? The constitutionality of the Treaties with IMF and EU for the implementation of the stabilization measures' (2010) 2 *EfimDD* 151

Katrougalos G, '"Memoranda": Greek exceptionalism or the Mirror of Europe's Future?' in A Triandafyllidou and others (eds) *The Greek Crisis and European Modernity* (Palgrave Macmillan 2013)

Katrougalos G, 'Social security in the "case law" of the Social Rights Committee' in Frans Pennings, Gijsbert Vonk (eds), *Handbook on European Social Security Law* (Edwar Elgar 2015)

Kontiadis X, Fotiadou A, 'Social Rights, Proportionality and Financial Crisis, Remarks on Judgment 668/2012 of the Council of State Plenary Assembly' (2012) 53*DtA* 27

Ktistaki S, 'The Influence of the Economic Crisis on Social Rights' [2012] *EDKA* 481

Manin P, 'A Consequence of the Financial Crisis: Review and Adaptation of Constituent Treaties of the European Union' in Chahira Boutayeb (ed.), *La Constitution, l'Europe et le droit, mélanges en l'honneur de Jean-Claude Masclet* (Publication de la Sorbonne 2013)

Mantzoufas P, *Financial Crisis and the Constitution* (Sakkoulas Publishing 2014)

Marini P, Bouvier M, Alventosa JR, 'The Introduction of the Budgetary "Golden Rule" in the Constitution' (2011) 1 *Constitutions* 23

Mathieu B, *Constitution: rien ne bouge et tout change* (Lextenso 2013)

Mavridis S, *The Criteria of Financial Discipline in the Construction of The Euro Zone: The Case of Greece* (Sakkoulas Publishing 2011)

Rueda F, '"Golden Rule" or Golden Rules. On Budgetary Discipline in the Comparative European Law' in Nathalie de Grove-Valdeyron, Marc Blanquet, Vincent Dussart (eds), *Mélanges en l'honneur du Professeur Joël Molinier* (LGDJ 2012)

Saulnier-Cassia E, 'The Treaty Establishing the European Stability Mechanism and the Treaty on Stability, Coordination and Governance within Europe, under Constitutional Control' (2013) 1 *RTDE* 160

Streel (De) A, 'The Reformed European Economic Governance' (2013) 3 *RTDE* 455

Tusseau G, 'Austerity Budgets in Relation to Constitutional Principles' (2013) 3 *RFDA* 672

Yannakopoulos C, 'The Rule of Law and National Sovereignty before the IMF' (2010) 1 *EfimDD* 2

Yannakopoulos C, 'Public Interest under the Aspect of the Economic Crisis' (2012) 1 *EfimDD* 100

Yannakopoulos C, 'The Rule of Law and National Sovereignty before the IMF' in *The Influence of European Union Law on the Judicial Review of the Constitutionality of Laws* (Sakkoulas Publishing 2013)

Zarka JC, 'Treaty on Stability, Coordination and Governance in the Economic and Monetary Union (TSCG)' (2012) 14 *Dalloz* 893

Zimmerman C, 'The concept of Monetary Sovereignty Revisited' (2013) 2 *EJIL* 797

9 The organizational foundations of the IMF's doctrinal turn on fiscal policy after the Great Recession

Cornel Ban

Introduction

In 2008 the International Monetary Fund endorsed a wider array of fiscal tools for a broader spectrum of countries to overcome the greatest crisis that capitalism had known since the Great Depression. Moreover, when most European policymakers stated that austerity was not just necessary to lower debt, but could even lead to growth, the IMF begged to differ.[1] The evolving views of the Fund on fiscal policy were also clear to emerging and developing economy policy elites surveyed by the Fund's Internal Evaluation Office. A common view among them was that 'the IMF has tempered its emphasis on fiscal adjustment and is now more attuned to the social and economic development needs'.[2] As one critic of the IMF put it, this unorthodox thinking was part of an '*interregnum* pregnant with development opportunities'.[3]

This chapter argues that this interregnum in the realm of economic ideas at the IMF has spawned a fiscal policy hybrid of pre-crisis orthodoxy and the more 'Keynesian' overtures that the Lehman crisis brought.

For clarification, neo-Keynesian economics was developed during the early postwar period by macroeconomists who translated Keynes' *General Theory* into the language of neo-classical economic models (hence the use of the term 'neo-classical synthesis' as an alternative to neo-Keynesianism). Their methodological workhorse was the so-called IS/IM model (investment saving liquidity preference money supply), a scientific tool that was used to generally endorse fiscal policy activism. During the 1980s neo-Keynesianism became 'old' Keynesianism and was replaced in mainstream economics by New Keynesianism, a school of thought that

1 Oddný Helgadóttir, 'The Bocconi boys go to Brussels: Italian economic ideas, professional networks and European austerity' (2016) 23 (3) *Journal of European Public Policy* 392.

2 Independent Evaluation Office, 'The Role of the IMF as Trusted Advisor' (IMF 2013), www.elibrary.imf.org/doc/IMF017/20195-9781475573091/20195-9781475573091/Other_formats/Source_PDF/20195-9781475543919.pdf, accessed 28 January 2021.

3 Ilene Grabel, 'Not Your Grandfather's IMF: Global Crisis, "Productive Incoherence" and Developmental Policy Space' (2011) 35 (5) *Cambridge Journal of Economics* 805.

DOI: 10.4324/9781315181882-14

strove to incorporate New Classical microfoundations into the broad Keynesian tradition by using dynamic general stochastic equilibrium models (DGSE). In so doing, New Keynesians became more skeptical of fiscal policy activism than 'old' Keynesians, unless recessions were accompanied by conditions that weakened the effectiveness of monetary policy.[4]

The extent to which this hybrid traveled into IMF loan conditionalities remains to be explored in future research. As such, care must be taken not to understand the conclusions of this chapter as generalizable to IMF policies 'on the ground' in the practice of IMF negotiators and/or article IV writers. Furthermore, this study does not have implications for the IMF loan programs, where the IMF doctrine is heavily filtered.[5] As a recent study shows, the IMF's Keynesian openings in research and official reports had little to do with the loan programs themselves in the case of a large category of countries.[6]

Opening up the IMF black box

In order to understand this 'revisionist' doctrine it is important to look more closely at debates inside the IMF. The chapter's focus is on the Fund's most influential policy and research milieus: the Fiscal Affairs Department (FAD) and the Research Department (RED). Bi-annual IMF departmental reports such as the *World Economic Outlook* (*WEO*) published by RED, and the *Global Fiscal Monitor* (*GFM*) published by FAD, reflect the IMF's official views on fiscal policy.[7] Moreover, because both these departments have prolific and prestigious researchers who often occupy senior positions in the Fund, they are also ideal sites in which to study the role of economic ideas in policy change.

4 See Oddný Helgadóttir and Cornel Ban, 'Managing Macroeconomic Neoliberalism: Capital and the Resilience of the Rational Expectations Assumption since the Great Recession' (2021) *New Political Economy* 1, on new Keynesian theory, and Ben Clift, 'Contingent Keynesianism: the IMF's model answer to the post-crash fiscal policy efficacy question in advanced economies' (2019) 26 (6) *Review of International Political Economy* 1211 for an overview of the policy implications.

5 Parts of this study are based extensively on Cornel Ban, 'From designers to doctrinaires: Staff research and fiscal policy change at the IMF' (2015) 43 *Elites on Trial. Research in the Sociology of Organizations* 337; Cornel Ban, 'Austerity versus stimulus? Understanding fiscal policy change at the International Monetary Fund since the great recession' (2015) 28 (2) *Governance* 167; Cornel Ban, 'Ben Clift's *The IMF and the Politics of Austerity*' (2020) 18 (1) *Comparative European Politics* 78.

6 Alexander E. Kentikelenis, Thomas H. Stubbs, Lawrence P. King, 'IMF conditionality and development policy space, 1985–2014' (2016) 23 (4) *Review of International Political Economy* 543; Kevin P. Gallagher, William Kring, Rebecca Ray, 'IMF austerity since the global financial crisis: new data, same trend, and similar determinants' (2020) Global Development Policy Center GEGI Working Paper 11/2020, www.bu.edu/gdp/files/2020/11/IMF-Austerity-Since-the-Global-Financial-Crisis-WP.pdf, accessed 16 December 2020.

7 Author interview with staff at the IMF Institute for Capacity Development, 11 November 2013; author interview with Joint Vienna Institute graduate and Romanian central banker, 23 October 2013.

The main argument of the chapter stresses the importance of agency: a new managing director whose views had already been favorable to the use of a larger than usual fiscal stimulus hired sympathetic interlocutors in the top management of RED and FAD, who in turn encouraged staff to recalibrate the Fund's fiscal policy orthodoxy. To ensure the internal and external legitimacy of the revised doctrine, the staff research used to support the claims made in WEOs and GFMs was framed in the languages and calculative devices of mainstream macroeconomic models.

The analysis begins with a critical overview of the state of the art and introduces the analytical and methodological apparatus this chapter proposes. Next, it compares the fiscal policy status quo before 2008 with the official policy advice emanating from RED and FAD during and after the Lehman crisis. The rest of the chapter aims to explain the patterns of stability and change in fiscal policy that the 'before and after' comparison brings into relief. Before the concluding section, the paper probes the importance of this doctrinal turn for the concrete management of the European debt crisis.

Analytical framework

The state of the art

Many scholars have examined the internal sources of change in the IMF's policy doctrines and found that staff research plays an important role.[8] The chapter's findings resonate with scholarship that shows international economic organizations derive both legitimacy and authority from claiming that they have the required scientific authority to settle debates on the underpinnings of economic policy.[9] For some, internal change takes place when new senior management arrives and brings with them new economic ideas.[10] For others, however, change originates from insider ideational entrepreneurs who seek change and to that effect enroll sympathetic interlocutors from the broader economic profession. In Chwieroth's work this strategic enrollment comes in the form of hiring new recruits from US-based economics departments where graduate training socializes PhDs in some economic ideas and not others.[11]

8 See Ban, 'From designers to doctrinaires' (n 5) for an overview.

9 Michael Barnett and Martha Finnemore, *Rules for the World: International Organizations in Global Politics* (Cornell University Press 2004); André Broome and Leonard Seabrooke, 'Seeing like the IMF: Institutional change in small open economies' (2007) 14 (4) *Review of international political economy* 576; Jeffrey M. Chwieroth, *Capital Ideas: The IMF and the Rise of Financial Liberalization* (Princeton University Press 2009).

10 Rawi Abdelal, 'The IMF and the capital account' (2006) 19 *Reforming the IMF for the 21st Century* 185.

11 Chwieroth (n 9).

The limits of the state of the art

These are path-breaking contributions, but the distinctive empirical reality of fiscal policy during the Great Recession invites further theoretical and methodological development that builds on these foundational insights. The state of the art focuses on situations when Fund staff initiated a change of the goals, instruments and settings of policy – that is, a 'paradigm shift'.[12] Fiscal policy during the Great Recession, however, falls short of a paradigmatic shift. The Fund did not experience the kind of generational change it experienced during the 1980s when postwar neo-Keynesians retired and made room for a generation of economists who had been shaped by the New Classical revolution of the 1970s. Furthermore, a paradigm shift in macroeconomics in the universities that supply the Fund with staff has not occurred. Finally, it is only as a result of the very recent boom in online professional information services such as *LinkedIn* that researchers can begin to study more systematically the political sociology of the staff via the accretion of biographical information about IMF economists and their collaborators.

Bringing in the sociology of economic organizations and professions

Sociological work on science and organizations suggests that mobilizing large numbers of supporters with respectable scientific credentials and/or powerful institutional positions is critical in scientific transformations; this is even truer in a field such as economics where the discipline's identity has been increasingly invested in a scientific ethos.[13] Like other experts making claims to scientific status, economists are motivated less by meritocratic competition than by the enlistment of other economists in their particular professional networks. As Bruno Latour puts it, in this strategic process of expansion 'the rules are simple enough: weaken your enemies, paralyze those you cannot weaken, help your allies if attacked, ensure safe communication with those who supply you with indisputable instruments, oblige your enemies to fight one another'.[14]

While the possibility of exploring all the tactics of scientific struggle evoked by Latour is not within the ambit of this chapter, one could at least find evidence of ideational entrepreneurs in senior management using their administrative power in the Fund's hierarchy to influence doctrinal debates. One of the effects of the hierarchical nature of international organizations like the IMF[15] is that senior management can use the authority conveyed by their positions to

12 Peter A. Hall, 'Policy paradigms, social learning, and the state: The case of economic policymaking in Britain' [1993] *Comparative Politics* 275.

13 Marion Fourcade, *Economists and Societies: Discipline and Profession in the United States, Britain, and France, 1890s to 1990s* (Princeton University Press 2009).

14 Bruno Latour, *Science in Action: How to Follow Scientists and Engineers through Society* (Harvard University Press 1987) 37.

15 Ngaire Woods, *The Globalizers: The IMF, the World Bank, and Their Borrowers* (Cornell University Press 2006).

influence hiring and promotion decisions in order to increase the number of supporters for a particular economic doctrine. But since promotions follow set performance targets and seniority rules that cannot be overridden by fiat,[16] the only way in which senior management can use their administrative power to shape internal policy debates is through new hires. It is therefore possible to hypothesize that the rise and consolidation of the revisionist doctrine was subsequent or at least contemporaneous with the hiring of a significant number of new economists. Senior management can shape the direction of change through the power to cite, ignore, or reject staff research in WEOs and GFMs. Finally, department directors can highlight the work of junior staff by co-authoring papers with them and then citing the findings in the department reports.

Given the rigors of the Fund's commitment to a scientific culture,[17] new ideas should be formulated using methodological languages that are widely accepted in epistemic ecologies inside and outside the Fund. The IMF's scientific legitimacy depends on the perceived scientific respectability of its policy advice so an intellectual opening in mainstream macroeconomics accompanied by methodological breakthroughs is an important asset for ideational entrepreneurs inside the Fund. Indeed, since the boundaries of contemporary macroeconomics are shaped as much by what is considered theoretically appropriate as by what passes for methodologically rigorous[18] and the epistemic culture of the IMF is methodology-centric,[19] the struggle of building, defending, and legitimizing revisionism should take place on familiar methodological ground.

Methodology

In addition to contributing these new theoretical developments, the chapter proposes a new methodological algorithm to study doctrinal change at the Fund on a more systematic basis. First, to establish the extent of change the chapter compares the Fund's pre-crisis fiscal orthodoxy with the Fund's statements from 2008 to 2013 in WEOs and GFMs.[20] Then, all arguments from IMF studies on fiscal policy (working papers, staff papers) cited in GFMs and WEOs were coded using two categories: revisionist and orthodox. The studies that reproduced the pre-2008 fiscal policy line were coded as 'orthodox'. Those that deviated from the pre-2008 fiscal policy line were coded as 'revisionist'. This enabled the production of visually suggestive descriptive statistics about the positions of IMF staff who authored IMF studies on fiscal policy.

To find how important these voices were in the Fund, the research used *LinkedIn* (a biographical database) as well as the IMF website to code the

16 Author interview with FAD economist, January 2013.
17 Barnett and Finnemore (n 9); Chwieroth (n 9).
18 Fourcade (n 13).
19 Abdelal (n 10); Chwieroth (n 9).
20 While *World Economic Outlooks* can be found in the IMF archive as early as 1969, the *Global Fiscal Monitors* were published only starting in 2009.

professional trajectories of all these IMF authors and matched their positions on doctrine change to their hierarchical position in the Fund. Since some authors (co)authored revisionist papers on some topics of fiscal policy and orthodox ones on other topics, they were coded as 'mixed'. Interviews with staff at the IMF headquarters conducted in 2013 helped refine the findings by providing insight into the perceptions of the staff on select issues. The remaining gaps were covered through research on media sources.

In order to establish the post-crisis evolution of fiscal policy advice at the IMF the research analyzed a special issue of the *World Economic Outlook* from 1998 as well as the WEOs covering the three years in between the East Asia crisis and the recession triggered by the dotcom bust (1999–2001). The findings were then compared with an IMF internal review on the Fund's country advice.[21] Next, the paper examined all WEOs and GFMs published between 2009 and 2013 and then checked the results against an internal IMF review article.[22] The analysis was guided by four themes: the main goals of fiscal policy, the basic options for countries with fiscal/without fiscal space, the pace of fiscal consolidation, and the composition of fiscal stimulus and consolidation.

The results differentiate between different categories of countries and are summarized in Table 9.1. The text in italics indicates post-crisis changes that capture the revisionist (rather than paradigmatic) transformation of fiscal policy doctrine. Overall, the table shows there to be no dichotomy between a pre-crisis 'neoliberal' line and a post-crisis 'Keynesian' one, the former emphasizing balanced budgets at all times and the latter centered on countercyclical fiscal stimulus packages in the event of recession. Instead, before 2008 the Fund was already open to selective Keynesian insights such as the countercyclical use of automatic stabilizers and even discretionary spending in countries like Japan, the US, or China. It is clear, however, that the applicability of these insights became significantly broader after 2008. Such broadening happens in parallel with changes in advice about the timing and composition of fiscal consolidation that generally reduce a recession's pro-cyclical effects and spread the social costs more broadly than before. Although these findings do not necessarily point towards a paradigm shift, the apparent 'edits' are quite extensive when compared with the pre-crisis doctrinal script.

To illustrate, here is an example of a revisionist claim made by the IMF in its October 2012 *WEO* where the Fund's staffers cite supporting evidence on the expansionary effects of countercyclical fiscal multipliers (the smaller the multipliers, the less costly the fiscal consolidation) produced by authors we consequently coded as revisionist after having read the cited papers for consistency:

21 Peter S. Heller, 'Considering the IMF's perspective on a "sound fiscal policy"' [2002] *FinanzArchiv/Public Finance Analysis* 141.

22 Olivier Blanchard and Daniel Leigh, 'Growth forecast errors and fiscal multipliers' (2013) IMF Working Paper 13/1.

Table 9.1 Pre- and Post-Crisis Themes in IMF Analyses

Pre-crisis	*Post-crisis*
The main goals of fiscal policy are growth and the reassurance of sovereign bond markets through credible fiscal sustainability policies.	The main goals of fiscal policy are growth and the reassurance of sovereign bond markets through credible fiscal sustainability policies.
Only high-income economies with fiscal space (stronger fiscal positions, lower public debt) should let automatic stabilizers operate in full, even at the cost of deficits.	*All economies* with fiscal space (stronger fiscal positions, public debt) should let automatic stabilizers operate in full, even at the cost of deficits. *Given the smaller increase in their debts, most developing countries are less likely than wealthy countries to experience substantial increases in debt service over the medium term as a result of their fiscal expansions.*
Only high-income countries with fiscal space but weak welfare states (US, Japan) should also use discretionary spending to stimulate the economy even at the cost of deficits. This spending should be directed at tax cuts.	*All economies* with fiscal space should also use discretionary spending to stimulate the economy even at the cost of deficits. This spending should be directed *at public investment in infrastructure and should avoid tax cuts.*
All expansionary measures should be accompanied by medium-term frameworks that reassure bond markets that debt and deficits will be cut after the recession ends. The credibility of these measures is supported by commitment to public debt thresholds, fiscal rules, and expenditure ceilings.	All expansionary measures should be accompanied by medium-term frameworks meant to reassure bond markets that debt and deficits will be cut after the recession ends. The credibility of these measures is supported by commitment to public debt thresholds, fiscal rules and expenditure ceilings, *independent fiscal councils, financial transaction taxes, carbon taxes, higher taxes on wealth, and the curbing of off-shore tax opportunities.*
Countries for whom fiscal consolidation is the only option should prefer spending cuts over revenue increases.	Countries for whom fiscal consolidation is the only option should *balance spending cuts and revenue increases. Fiscal consolidations based solely on spending cuts are less likely to be sustainable.*
The cuts should be targeted at public job programs, social transfers, public sector wages, employment, housing and agricultural subsidies. Public investments should not be adopted because they crowd out private investments.	The spending cuts should be targeted at public job programs, social transfers, public sector wages, employment, housing and agricultural subsidies. *Public investments should be prioritized, as they do not crowd out private investments in the conditions of the Great Recession.*
If fiscal consolidation is in order, it should always be introduced immediately (frontloading). Fiscal consolidation is likely to have expansionary effects on output.	If fiscal consolidation is in order, it should be introduced *gradually (backloading), unless the country faces collapse in confidence on sovereign bond markets.* Fiscal consolidation is *unlikely* to have expansionary effects on output.

Pre-crisis	*Post-crisis*
The best tax policy package reduces marginal income taxes, expands the tax base, increases reliance on flat consumption taxes, enforces the neutrality of the tax system.	The best tax policy package reduces marginal income taxes, expands the tax base, enforces the neutrality of the tax system, *increases taxes on dividends and the estates of the wealthy, adopts financial transaction and environmental taxes, aggressively pursues offshore wealth.*
Low-income countries for whom fiscal consolidation is the only option should prefer revenue increases over spending cuts, particularly cuts of health and education outlays.	Low-income countries for whom fiscal consolidation is the only option should prefer revenue increases over spending cuts, particularly cuts of health and education outlays.

> If the multipliers underlying the growth forecasts were about 0.5, as this informal evidence suggests, our results indicate that multipliers have actually been in the 0.9 to 1.7 range since the Great Recession, this finding is consistent with research suggesting that in today's environment of substantial economic slack, monetary policy constrained by the zero lower bound, and synchronized scale adjustment across numerous economies, multipliers may be well above.[23]

All three positions share the view that the main goals of fiscal policy are growth and the reassurance of sovereign bond markets through credible fiscal sustainability policies. Yet, as Table 9.1 shows, when it comes to the means of getting there, divergences are quite significant.

Mapping out doctrinal change and stability over time

These are important revisions but their depth and span vary over time. There was a great deal of fiscal policy optimism in 2008 and 2009, but by 2010 the tone changed in favor of an earlier exit from stimulus. The 2010 GFM report applauds the unwinding of the discretionary stimulus in all countries with fiscal space and turn to consolidation. Yet the 2010 report also reflects support for continued stimulus in fast-growing emerging markets with excessive external surpluses and low debt. The bumper sticker is: 'a down payment on consolidation now with continued gradual tightening over the medium term'. This advice is based on optimistic projections that consolidation has a low fiscal multiplier that is less than 1 and on the assumption that medium- and long-

23 Alan J Auerbach and Yuriy Gorodnichenko. 'Output spillovers from fiscal policy' (2013) 103 (3) *American Economic Review* 141; Nicoletta Batini, Giovanni Callegari, Giovanni Melina, 'Successful Austerity in the United States, Europe, and Japan' (2012) IMF Working Paper No. 12/190; Michael Woodford, 'Inflation Targeting and Financial Stability' (2011) conference paper, www.columbia.edu/~mw2230/ITFinStab.pdf, accessed 28 January 2021.

term fiscal measures are not sufficient to reassure markets. Nevertheless, the departmental reports leave the door open to expansion in wealthy countries with fiscal space, should economic activity fall short of WEO projections. The reports also caution against an 'abrupt fiscal withdrawal' (a cut in the deficit greater than 1% a year) and state that the output cost of a 1% of GDP fiscal consolidation can double to 2% for a small open economy where the interest rate is at the zero lower bound and consolidation is done by almost all countries at the same time.

In 2011 the reports swing to a more orthodox line. The IMF documents praise Europe's strong frontloading of austerity and make optimistic projections of its effects on credibility. Moreover, based on a FAD study showing that bond yields in emerging markets are very sensitive to global risk aversion, they counseled for low- and middle-income economies to rebuild fiscal buffers and cut spending despite the fact that they were facing less market pressure than developed countries. The report contains an unambiguous denunciation of the expansionary austerity thesis.

Subsequent reports qualify this doctrinal retrenchment. The 2012 GFM and WEOs acknowledge that fiscal multipliers of consolidation were much larger than the Fund realized and therefore advised slower adjustment in countries with low credibility. The reports also stress the importance of expansion in countries with credibility and criticize the harsh spending cuts in the US and the Eurozone. Critically, both reports warn that austerity could be self-defeating as its negative effects on output have already increased public debt in countries that implemented the most aggressive spending cuts. Also in 2012 and 2013 in the GFMs and WEOs there emerges a call for tax reforms that shift some of the burden of consolidation onto the wealthy.

One wonders, however, whether the intellectual hybridity unearthed by the book is a form of bricolage or whether it is the mere translation of the old neoliberal fiscal paradigm into a new, revisionist neoliberal fiscal paradigm. It can be argued that not all forms of ideational hybridization are bricolage and that intellectually heterogenous and temporally contingent policy paradigms can survive changes as long as their core goals remain stable no matter how baroque the results of hybridization with elements of competing paradigms looks like. To be bricoleurs and not mere paradigm translators, the IMF reformers would have to do their recombination/layering of macroeconomic ideas unconstrained by the core of some paradigm (let's call it 'neoliberalism').

Yet for all its boldness relative to the pre-2008 status quo or, say, the 2010 fiscal philosophy of the German government, the IMF's interventions into the austerity debate did not challenge the three-faceted core of this neoliberal paradigm: institutionalized trade/financial openness, public finances benchmarked by financial market credibility, and growth strategies based on the relative competitiveness of the national economy.[24] As Ben Clift's 2018 book

24 Cornel Ban, *Ruling Ideas. How Global Neoliberalism Goes Local* (Oxford University Press 2016). The only emergency deviation was the Fund's heavily circumscribed agreement with capital controls for a handful of program countries on a temporary basis.

stresses, by maintaining control of the concept of 'fiscal space' the IMF reformers managed not only to circumvent internal opposition to revisionism, but also explicitly linked the size of this fiscal space to the perception and appetites of the markets, as interpreted by the Fund.

This triad of goals is central to the wide variety of neoliberal translations – from the economics of the old Washington Consensus to the open-minded reformism of Olivier Blanchard's tenure at the Fund – because when all is said and done, it continues to discipline the limits of recombination/layering work with market-based devices. As long as translators stick to these goals, they subject the epicenter of local tax-and-spend decisions to the perceptions of financial investors. For all the Keynesian 'edits' accurately captured by the book, adherence to these goals ultimately pushed states and societies to adjust through market-based competitive strategies even as the Fund's new doctrine invited more demand-side policies and less frontloaded fiscal consolidation when the fiscal space allowed by the markets was judged to be there. Rather than do bricolage, then, the IMF reformers worked to cobble together a more reformist, flexible, and pragmatic neoliberal policy paradigm for the age of financialization, secular stagnation, and political turbulence in societies riveted by growing inequality. Indeed, it is precisely this flexible co-option of competing frameworks that we see with the Fund today that has made neoliberalism more resilient to challenges than classical liberalism ever was.

Explaining stability and change

As I showed in earlier work,[25] change was facilitated by a stronger Keynesian turn in mainstream macro. But, in a complex organization like the Fund, doctrinal change takes more than a wind of change in academic macro so organizational dynamics is of critical importance.

Specifically, the Great Recession coincided with changes at the top of the IMF's bureaucratic pyramid. There was a new managing director who hired a new chief economist and a new director of the Research Department. There was little in the professional history of the newly appointed managing director Dominique Strauss-Kahn (DSK) that would suggest substantial commitment to a 'Keynesian' drift in fiscal policy. His past as a technocrat for the Socialist government of Lionel Jospin (1997–2001) predicted instead that he would be an enforcer of the fiscal orthodoxy embedded in the constitutional norms of the European monetary union.[26] DSK was also known in the French Socialist Party as closer to the fiscal rigueur of the Third Way.[27] But during the late 2000s his thinking evolved and seven months before Lehman unleashed the

25 Ban, 'Austerity versus stimulus' (n 5).

26 David Scott Bell, 'France: The Left in 2002 – The End of the Mitterrand Strategy' (2003) 56 (1) *Parliamentary Affairs* 24.

27 Ludivine Bantigny, 'Looking for the Left: Left-Wing Groups and Nicolas Sarkozy' (2012) 16 (3) *Contemporary French and Francophone Studies* 371; Ludivine Bantigny, *La France À L'heure Du Monde: De 1981 À Nos Jours* (Seuil 2013).

havoc of the Great Recession, DSK stunned the participants at the World Economic Forum in Davos by calling for 'a new fiscal policy [as] … an accurate way to answer the crisis'.[28] The *Financial Times* saw in the speech the sign of 'the undeniable shift to Keynes'.[29]

DSK reaffirmed this position at the G20 summit in Washington in November 2008 and called on the participants to launch a coordinated fiscal stimulus to the tune of 2% of global GDP. DSK stressed that 'anyone with the most clearly sustainable debt should take the lead'.[30] A skilled politician, he ironed out a consensus around a coordinated stimulus and when countries announced much weaker measures than he expected, he warned that the IMF's forecast for 2009, 'already very dark … will be even darker if not enough fiscal stimulus is implemented'.[31] The managing director then chastised the EU, indicating that the size of the stimulus there (1.5%) was too low. According to Jack Boorman, a former special adviser to the IMF managing director, DSK was 'a brilliantly gifted politician and a very good economist' and that allowed him to insert himself into the G20 process in November 2008. He seized the moment in a brilliant fashion. Any decisions that were going to be taken, the IMF was moved right into the center of them.

DSK's appointment was a game changer but at the end of the day much of the Fund's authority comes from the scientific credibility of its economists. His opinions therefore needed their imprimatur. To this end, soon after his Davos speech, DSK worked to secure the appointment of Frenchman Olivier Blanchard as chief economist of the Fund and director of the Research Department beginning in September 2008.

DSK and Blanchard knew each other from the small circles of French politics and technocracy where both carried a great deal of professional prestige. An academic celebrity at MIT, Blanchard was known for prolific, innovative, and diverse contributions to economics. It was one particular contribution that would prove to be critical after 2008, however. In a co-authored study written six years before Lehman,[32] the MIT scholar defended countercyclical fiscal policy by using one of the most advanced mainstream macroeconomic models around, thus challenging

28 Dominique Strauss-Kahn, 'Making the Most of an Historic Opportunity: Three Principles for Reshaping the Global Economic and Financial Framework Istanbul' (2 October 2009) speech at Çırağan Palace.

29 Ralph Atkins, Chris Giles, Krishna Guha, 'The undeniable shift to Keynes', *Financial Times* (29 December 2008), www.ft.com/content/8a3d8122-d5da-11dd-a9cc-000077b07658, accessed 21 December 2020.

30 'IMF Managing Director Dominique Strauss-Kahn Calls G-20 Action Plan Significant Step toward Stronger International Cooperation' (15 November 2008) IMF Press Release 08/286.

31 Statement for Reuters, 'IMF head worried about lack of fiscal stimulus' (21 December 2008), www.reuters.com/article/us-imf-stimulus/imf-head-worried-about-lack-of-fiscal-stimulus-idUSTRE4BK0FM20081221, accessed 28 January 2021.

32 Olivier Blanchard and Roberto Perotti, 'An Empirical Characterization of the Dynamic Effects of Changes in Government Spending and Taxes on Output' (2002) 117(4) *The Quarterly Journal of Economics* 1329.

the professional mainstream that had long ceased to take fiscal activism seriously. Soon after his appointment to the IMF, Blanchard advocated for a large fiscal stimulus totaling 2% of global GDP.[33]

It was also in September 2008 that Carlo Cottarelli took over the IMF's influential Fiscal Affairs Department. Unlike Blanchard, Cotarelli was a career IMF economist whose research published before 2008 did not engage the macroeconomic fiscal multiplier debate. Nevertheless, Cotarelli's publications in late 2008 signaled he was on board with DSK and Blanchard.[34] With new senior staff at the helm of two critical departments, DSK could facilitate an internal intellectual transformation that could lend scientific pedigree to a new fiscal policy stance at the Fund.

The defining moment of this intellectual evolution was the publication on 29 December 2008 of a joint RED-FAD staff position paper.[35] The paper was co-authored by Blanchard and Cotarelli among others and laid down the groundwork for macroeconomic policy during recessions: '[a] timely, large, lasting, diversified, and sustainable fiscal stimulus that is coordinated across countries with a commitment to do more if the crisis deepens'.[36]

Its reasoning went as follows: given the collapse in private demand, states should not only let automatic stabilizers run, but also ramp up public investments and expand the reach of income transfers to those who were more likely to spend (the unemployed and poor households). Against the Fund's pre-2008 policy line, the authors stressed the role of public investments and downplayed the expansionary virtues of tax cuts. To this end they deployed the Keynesian argument that tax cuts are more likely to be saved. The authors also dismissed the two macroeconomic policies often used to support demand, namely exclusive reliance on activist monetary policy and export-led recovery. They also spurned as irrelevant the well-worn orthodox objection that spending increases have long time lags. Given the Fund's mission to ensure relative stability in the sovereign bond market, there were also big caveats. The paper stressed that only countries with fiscal space could afford a stimulus and that expansionary measures should be reversible. Expansionary measures should also be announced in parallel with measures that ensure fiscal sustainability such as permanent cuts in healthcare and pension budgets in the medium and long term.

Such changes had far-reaching consequences. In 2009, WEO used staff research to call for a fiscal stimulus.[37] The GFM did too and added that in the

33 Interview with Olivier Blanchard, in Camilla Andersen, 'IMF Spells Out Need for Global Fiscal Stimulus' (29 December 2008) *IMF Survey Online*, www.imf.org/external/pubs/ft/survey/so/2008/INT122908A.htm?mod=article_inline, accessed 28 January 2021.

34 Antonio Spilimbergo, Steve Symansky, Olivier Blanchard, Carlo Cottarelli, 'Fiscal Policy for the Crisis' (2008) IMF Staff Position Note SNP 08/01.

35 Ibid.

36 Ibid (n 34) 2.

37 Spilimbergo et al. (n 34); Jörg Decressin and Douglas Laxton, 'Gauging risks for deflation' (2009) IMF Staff Position Notes 2009 (01), www.elibrary.imf.org/view/

context of the lower tax collection rates in a crisis-ridden environment, governments should strengthen tax institutions rather than cut taxes.[38] The report also renounced the claim that policies that make income taxes more progressive lead to a decline in revenues.[39]

In 2010, the year of the turn to austerity in Europe, a more qualified endorsement of fiscal stimulus is apparent. WEO cites studies warning of high debt and the negative effects of deficits on output and market credibility,[40] while the GFM reiterates arguments against extensive debt restructuring. Yet most of the cited studies contain anti-austerity implications. WEO asks countries to refrain from frontloading consolidation based on IMF research that finds high risks of deflation.[41] The studies cited in GFM find that beyond a certain threshold of adjustment spending cuts are no longer effective.[42] Critically, WEO debunks an iconic study of the austerity camp[43] and uses Blanchard's 2002 methodological innovations to show that fiscal stimulus packages have higher multipliers than consolidation and that the latter is contractionary and increases unemployment during recessions.[44] The 2010 GFM's citations echo the 28 December 2008 paper[45] and suggest that financial transaction taxes are an appropriate contribution to the fiscal sustainability effort.

The 2011 WEOs and GFMs cite IMF studies that try to balance austerity and stimulus while starting a discussion about how the costs of consolidation should be distributed. The WEO critiques existing medium-term adjustment

38 John Brondolo, 'Collecting Taxes During an Economic Crisis' (2009) IMF Staff Position Note 09/23.

39 Thomas Baunsgaard and Steven A. Symansky, 'Automatic Fiscal Stabilizers' (2009) IMF Staff Position Note 09/23.

40 Emanuele Baldacci and Manmohan S. Kumar, 'Fiscal Deficits, Public Debt, and Sovereign Bond Yields' (2010) IMF Working Paper 10/184, www.imf.org/en/Publications/WP/Issues/2016/12/31/Fiscal-Deficits-Public-Debt-and-Sovereign-Bond-Yields-24130, accessed 21 December 2020; Manmohan S. Kumar and Jaejoon Woo, 'Public Debt and Growth' (2010) IMF Working Paper 10/174, www.imf.org/external/pubs/ft/wp/2010/wp10174.pdf, accessed 21 December 2020.

41 Decressin and Laxton (n 37)

42 Baldacci and Kumar (n 40); Spilimbergo et al. (n 34); Olivier Blanchard and Carlo Cottarelli, 'Ten Commandments for Fiscal Adjustment in Advanced Economies' (2010) IMF Blog 24 June 2010.

43 Alberto Alesina and Roberto Perotti. 'Income distribution, political instability, and investment' (1996) 40 (6) *European Economic Review* 1203.

44 Charles Freedman, Michael Kumhof, Douglas Laxton, Jaewoo Lee, 'The Case for Global Fiscal Stimulus' (2009) IMF Staff Position Note SPN 09/03.

45 Spilimbergo et al. (n 34).

plans for vagueness and renders them consequently incredible.[46] The 2011 report at the same time endorses frontloaded fiscal consolidation on the spending side in Southern Europe and Ireland.[47] But other quotes are less hawkish. The report cites research that stresses the importance of current account deficit reduction in debtor countries and expansion in surplus countries.[48] It also warns that countercyclical budget rules are better for fiscal sustainability than balanced budgets.[49] The report is also ambivalent about the effects of fiscal consolidation on reducing the external deficit.[50] The studies cited by GFM emphasize the importance of pairing fiscal consolidation and structural reforms[51] and warn about the fiscal risks of declining credit ratings.[52] WEO inveighs – yet again – against the expansionary austerity thesis of Alberto Alesina and colleagues at the time his followers were shaping fiscal policy in Europe.[53] The 2011 WEO finally endorses IMF research that calls for a more progressive distribution of income and reproduces research that indicates that financialization boosts inequality and inequality contributes to unsustainable growth trends such as those that predated the Great Recession.[54]

While still alert to sustainability issues, the 2012 report indicates an interest in IMF studies that warn about the risk of self-defeating austerity. One of the studies cited in WEO deplores growing inequality and unemployment and layers demands for more income redistribution on top of old IMF recipes (retraining, better education, increased productivity in the service sector) as the price that may be needed to avert a protectionist backlash.[55] The emphasis on the inequality–unsustainable growth nexus is reaffirmed[56] and the cited studies

46 Fabian Bornhorst, Nina Budina, Giovanni Callegari, Asmaa ElGanainy, Raquel Gomez Sirera, Andrea Lemgruber, Andrea Schaechter, Joong Beom Shin, 'A Status Update on Fiscal Exit Strategies' (2010) IMF Working Paper 10/272, www.imf.org/external/pubs/ft/wp/2010/wp10272.pdf, accessed 15 January 2021.

47 Ibid.

48 Olivier Blanchard and Gian Maria Milesi-Ferretti, 'Global Imbalances: In Midstream?' (2009) IMF Staff Position Note SPN/09/29; Philip R. Lane and Gian Maria Milesi-Ferretti, 'External Adjustment and the Global Crisis' (2011) IMF Working Paper 11/197.

49 Michael Kumhof and Douglas Laxton, 'Simple, Implementable Fiscal Policy Rules' (2009) IMF Working Paper 09/76.

50 Chen et al. (n 37).

51 Cline Allard and Luc Everaert, 'Lifting euro area growth: Priorities for structural reforms and governance' (2010) IMF Staff Position Note SNP 10/09.

52 Laura Jaramillo and Michelle Tejada, 'Sovereign credit ratings and spreads in emerging markets: Does investment grade matter?' (2011) IMF Working Paper 11/44.

53 Mark Blyth, *Austerity: The History of a Dangerous Idea* (Oxford University Press 2013).

54 Andrew Berg and Jonathan Ostry, 'Inequality and Unsustainable Growth: Two Sides of the Same Coin?' (2011) IMF Staff Discussion Note 11/08.

55 Mai Chi Dao and Prakash Loungani, 'The Tragedy of Unemployment' (2010) 47 (4) *Finance and Development* 22.

56 Berg and Ostri (n 54).

go beyond conventional recipes to endorse more redistribution and to boost aggregate demand in the short term to help labor markets recover.[57]

Most importantly, although more research warns about the importance of medium-term fiscal frameworks for keeping debt in check,[58] there is a turn against frontloaded austerity in the 2012 WEO. There are warnings about the risk of deflation,[59] but two new lines of attack appear. The most important is the finding that since 2008 the economic slack was so large, interest rates so low, and fiscal adjustment so synchronized that fiscal multipliers were constantly well over 1. This meant that the IMF underestimated the negative effects austerity had on output because it assumed values of the fiscal multiplier that were too low.[60] This concern is echoed in IMF studies cited in the year's GFM.[61] Second, even as another cited study encouraged spending cuts in health, pensions, and public employment in wealthy countries like Italy, its findings also stressed that fiscal consolidation had been ultimately self-defeating in the past because it increased public debt levels.[62] This is echoed in studies cited in GFM that argue that consolidation when the multiplier is high erodes some of the gains in market credibility as a result of a higher debt ratio and lower short-term growth, which causes an increase borrowing costs.[63]

IMF research cited in the 2013 reports makes similar points but unprecedentedly emphasizes raising more revenue via more taxation of the wealthy. In WEO, deflation warnings from a 2002 paper are sounded yet again[64] and the need for stimulus in countries that enjoy fiscal space is reaffirmed. Such ideas cohabit in the report with warnings about the growth-depleting effects of high debt.[65] In turn, the GFM cites studies that establish the ineffectiveness of default[66] and inflation[67] as debt reduction strategies, while stressing the importance of reducing debt. But the GFM cites studies that seem to represent a new taxation philosophy at the Fund. They continue to endorse a few old recipes (the reduction of income taxes while increasing consumption, the scrapping of loopholes in personal and corporate income tax, the elimination of differential

57 Laurence Ball, Daniel Leigh, Prakash Loungani, 'Painful Medicine' (2011) 48 (3) *Finance & Development* 20.
58 Berg and Ostri (n 54); Kumar and Woo (n 40).
59 Decressin and Laxton (n 37).
60 Batini et al. (n 22).
61 Anja Baum, Marcos Poplawski-Ribeiro, Anke Weber, 'Fiscal Multipliers and the State of the Economy' (2021) IMF Working Paper 12/286.
62 Ball et al. (n 57).
63 C. Cotarelli, L. Forni, J. Gottschalk and P. Mauro, 'Default in Today's Advanced Economies' (2010) IMF Staff Position Note 10/12.
64 Decressin and Laxton (n 37).
65 Kumar and Woo (n 40).
66 Udaibir Das, Michael Papaioannou, David Grigorian, Samar Maziad, 'A Survey of Experiences with Emerging Market Sovereign Debt Restructurings' (2012) IMF Working Paper; Eduardo Borensztein and Ugo Panizza, 'The costs of sovereign default' (2009) IMF Staff Papers 56(4).
67 Bernardin Akitoby, Takuji Komatsuzaki, Ariel Binder, 'Inflation and Public Debt Reversals in the G7 Countries' (2014) IMF Working Paper 14/96.

VAT rates, resistance to high marginal income tax, reduced employers' social contributions) yet also advocate greater reliance on taxes targeted at the wealthy: property taxes targeted at the top 1% (a measure estimated to raise between 2–3% of global GDP in new tax revenue), financial transactions tax, and a coordinated taxation of off-shore incomes.[68]

Are there any patterns in the profile of the economists involved in this doctrinal transformation? To address this question, the findings of the textual analysis are connected to the professional trajectories of the individual authors using three coding categories: *orthodox* (authors defending some aspect of the pre-2008 status quo), *revisionist* (authors proposing a significant change), and, in between the first two, the *mixed* group (authors making revisionist arguments in some studies and orthodox arguments in others). To better compare the forces of change with the forces of stability, the descriptive statistics contain a fourth category that merges the revisionist and mixed groups because both showed various degrees of willingness to depart from orthodoxy and engineer the Fund's own doctrinal *perestroika*. To present the results of the before and after comparison in a legible way, the orthodox positions were then relabeled 'stability' and the fourth category as 'change'.

In total, the paper examined the biographies and the work of 144 economists who authored studies cited in WEOs and GFMs. Of these, 84 (58%) supported some kind of doctrinal change and 60 (41%) defended stability. In the 'change' group, 11 were based outside the Fund and 8 were visiting scholars. In the doctrinal 'stability' group, only one was a visiting scholar and 5 were based outside the Fund.

Several detailed findings emerge. First, Figure 9.1 shows that most of the participants in the fiscal policy debate were from the RED and FAD, followed by the European Department. The percentage of economists doing mixed research was significantly higher than that of orthodox researchers in both RED and FAD. When the mixed group is disaggregated, it becomes clear that the resistance of the orthodox was a lot stronger in FAD and that RED was truly the professional realm where the boldest advocates of change (the revisionist) dominated.

Second, the top of the bureaucratic pyramid as well as its base came heavily on the side of change. As Figure 9.2 shows, department directors supported change and economists in entry-level positions and visiting fellows were overwhelmingly in the group with 'pure' revisionist papers. It was only among assistant directors and senior economists that the percentage of orthodox (co)authors was as high as that of economists willing to stick to a strict orthodox line.

68 Jose L. Torres, 'Revenue and Expenditure Gaps and Fiscal Consolidation: a Cross-Country Analysis' (2013) IMF Working Paper 05/xx; Santiago Acosta-Ormaechea and Jiae Yoo, 'Tax Composition and Economic Growth' (2012) IMF Working Paper 12/257; John Norregaard, 'Taxing Immovable Property. Revenue Potential and Implementation Challenges' (2013) IMF Working Paper 13/129.

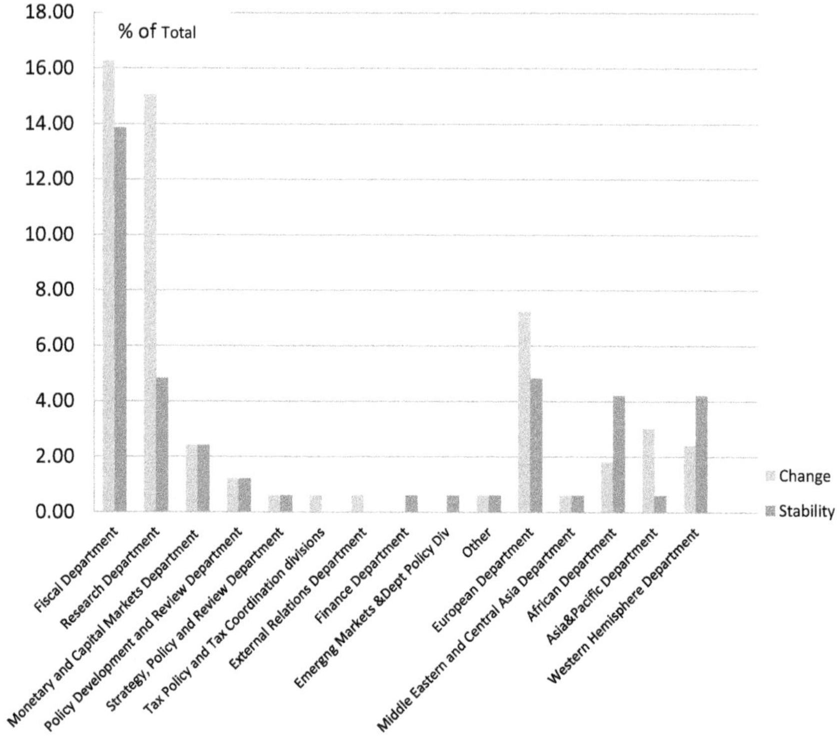

Figure 9.1 Group distribution by department (out of N=144)

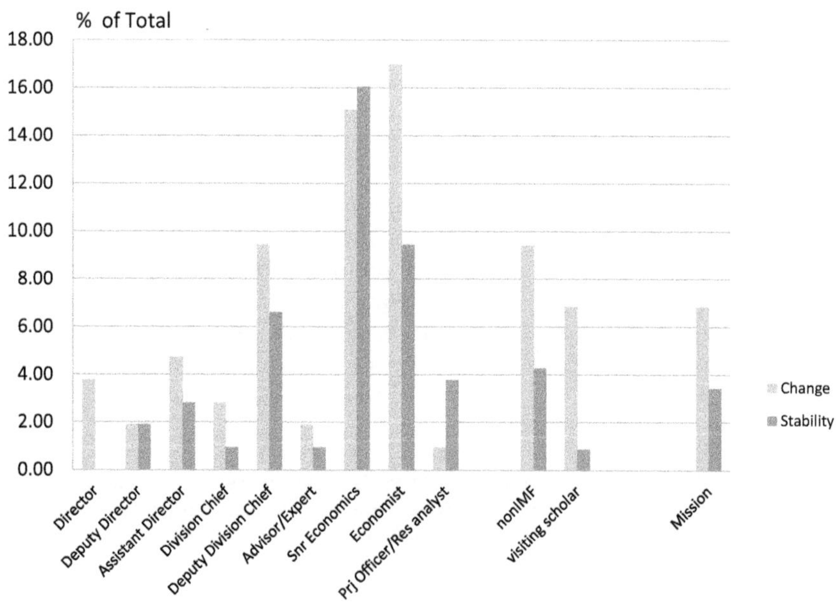

Figure 9.2 Group distribution by position (out of N=144)

Third, the hiring of a significant number of 'young Turks' facilitated doctrinal change. Below follows a systematic analysis of the CVs of the IMF staff from the revisionist, orthodox, and mixed groups through a look at whether they were promoted, newly hired, or experienced no change in their career in the 2007–2013 period. An IMF economist was considered promoted if (s)he moved higher on the pay scale or from a regional department to departments with higher status like FAD or RED. The label 'new hire' was applied to all economists who joined the Fund after 2007. The results (Figure 9.3) show a pattern in line with the hypothesis. While the number of economists who were promoted was equal between the pro-change and pro-stability camps, the new hires joined the former in much greater numbers than the latter.

Future researchers could take up the task of clarifying whether the tendency of the early career staff to support change on fiscal policy reflected a strategy of senior management to pad their departments with intellectually sympathetic 'young Turks' or whether it was the adaptability of these junior economists to the views of their superiors that accounted for the observed outcomes.

All of this was facilitated by the calibration of mainstream macromodels so that they fit the doctrinal shift, with methodological innovations in academia and the Fund facilitating organizational support for high multipliers.[69]

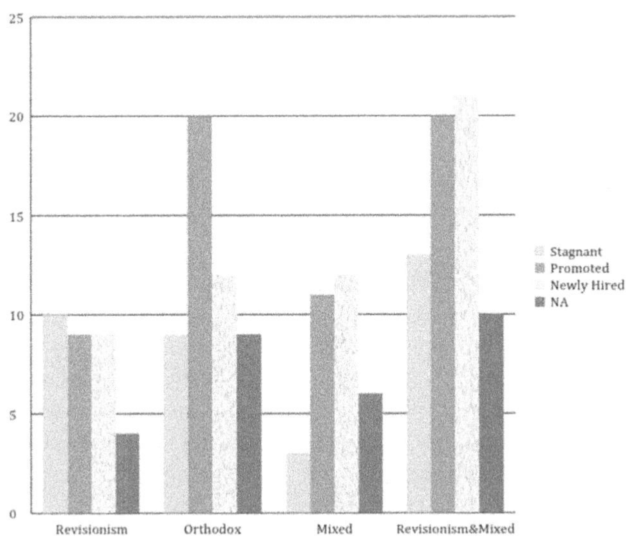

Figure 9.3 Group distribution by career dynamics (2007–2013)

69 Ban, 'From designers to doctrinaires' (n 5).

How does this all matter for the management of the European debt crisis?

The European crisis looms large in Ben Clift's 2018 book on the IMF in non-program European countries[70] and the author delivers a sophisticated account of how the Fund uses its authority to move Paris or London towards a more Keynesian policy status quo or of how the IMF navigated the complex archipelago of EU institutions designed to play crisis management roles. As such, the matter is well covered.

Yet if there is one place that needs more development in Clift's excellent analysis, it is the Fund's local competition. For unlike any other world region Europe has a full-fledged and crisis-tested international lender of last resort: the European Stability Mechanism (ESM). In Clift's book, the ESM figures only as an object of the Fund's positions rather than as an actor in its own right that has posed important challenges to the IMF's 'business as usual' in the European context. Or, the ESM also challenged the Fund on two critical pillars of sovereign debt management: loan conditions and debt restructuring. Given the systemic importance of the ESM regarding the IMF's main mandate (international lending of last resort), the tensions between the two are worth bringing out into relief for the task of mapping out the Fund's policy space and actual authority in one of the largest sovereign debt crises in economic history. Since the ESM is controlled by the Eurogroup (the ministers of finance of the Eurozone) and the Eurogroup is shaped by the authority of non-borrowing countries whose relationship with the Fund is the subject of about half of Clift's book, the comparison of the ESM and the IMF as international lenders of last resort becomes even more important.

Specifically, on loan margins and maturities, the ESM appears to give debtor countries more room for maneuvering. It abandoned the stricter, high-margin, relatively short-maturity (5–12 years) terms specific to IMF loans in favor of low-margins, long-maturity loans (32 years) that lend it a very distinctive outlook as an international lender of last resort. Of course, this competitive edge should be seen in context. This creative take on what is effectively a form of debt restructuring spread over an inordinately long period of time came in the same package as the burden of a fiscal policy orthodoxy that, as the book shows, the IMF had extensively edited with Keynesian insights since 2008.

But even if one goes beyond the IMF's fiscal policy revisionism and sticks to its traditional line on austerity in countries with no fiscal space to stimulate the economy, one finds ESM versions of austerity being much harsher and deflation-prone. To give but one example, the IMF was reluctant to agree to the ESM view on the size of the primary surplus expected in exchange for this long-term financial assistance that acted as a de facto debt restructuring. In December 2016, Maurice Obstfeld, IMF Chief Economist, and Poul Thomsen,

70 Ben Clift, *The IMF and the Politics of Austerity in the Wake of the Global Financial Crisis* (Oxford University Press 2018).

Director of the IMF's European Department, took the unusual step of disagreeing in public (on the IMF's blog) with this long-term view of the ESM in December 2016. The two senior economists insisted that the primary fiscal surplus of 3.5% Greece had to achieve by 2018 'would generate a degree of austerity that could prevent the nascent recovery from taking hold', proposing instead a lower primary surplus of 1.5% in 2018.

Most importantly, however, the ESM used its generous (in relative terms) margins and maturities to block the IMF's pleas that debt restructuring is a prerequisite for the success of the Greek program in particular. Thus, in October 2015 the ESM's Managing Director gave a long interview to *Financial Times* [71] in which he defended the case against a nominal debt haircut for Greece that would be on the scale that the IMF (in their June and July debt sustainability analyses) and the Greek government preferred. The Managing Director clarified that the difference was a different timescale for looking at Greek debt, with the IMF asking for their money back within ten years on average and the ESM reducing the burden of debt thorough agreeing to much longer maturities (32 years) and lower interest rates that the Fund. The IMF's prioritization of the overall debt burden ('stock') in their debt sustainability reports was not applicable to Greece, he argued, because Greek's annual debt payments ('flows') were low relative to almost all other European countries. In effect, the argument went, over the long-term horizon, the ESM member states gave Greece debt restructuring without reducing the nominal value of Greek debt.

According to IMF chief economist Maurice Obstfeld, this higher bar set by the European institutions entailed the adoption of austerity measures additional to those agreed initially, with the Greek government agreeing with the European institutions (and against the advice of the IMF) to cut spending further. Furthermore,

> these cuts have already gone too far, but the ESM program assumes even more of them, with an increase in the primary surplus to 3.5 percent of GDP achieved through further cuts in investment and discretionary spending [...] [I]f Greece agrees with its European partners on ambitious fiscal targets, don't criticize the IMF for being the ones insisting on austerity when we ask to see the measures required to make such targets credible.[72]

ESM representatives expressed dismay at this unorthodox practice and hope for a 'return to the practice of conducting program negotiations with the Greek government in private'.

71 'Klaus Regling interview: the annotated transcript', www.ft.com/content/f5de7464-8d83-3ee8-83bc-8a749c9f479a, accessed 6 July 2021.

72 Maurice Obstfeld and Poul M. Thomsen, 'The IMF is Not Asking Greece for More Austerity' (IMFBlog, 12 December 2016), https://blog-imfdirect.imf.org/2016/12/12/the-imf-is-not-asking-greece-for-more-austerity/#more-15842, accessed 28 January 2021.

Such ideas reflected a dramatic shift on fiscal policy that had started with Dominique Strauss-Kahn and Olivier Blanchard and had become the norm with Lagarde and Obstfeld. An older emphasis on maintaining states' credibility with financial markets remained the primary goal of policy, but this goal now had to cohabit with greater acceptance of discretionary fiscal stimulus programs and an emphasis on gradual fiscal consolidation where fiscal space for stimulus was limited. Also, unlike the pre-2008 period, the IMF now advocates more balance between revenue and spending measures in the approach to fiscal consolidation.[73] After some initial resistance to reconsider the Fund's traditional hostility to debt restructuring, by 2014 change was underway and it became part of the Fund's doctrinal revisionism, affecting areas as wide as capital account regulation and financial regulation.[74]

This open conflict between the two institutions brings to the fore questions about the different fiscal philosophies of the world lender of last resort and its European counterpart while highlighting the more conservative fiscal theory of the latter. At any rate, the fact that the ESM attributes strict adherence to rules-based fiscal consolidation to the preferences of the sovereign bond market is puzzling in the light of the fact that 'the alleged preference of financial market participants for stricter fiscal rules is based on a handful of articles whose generalizability and validity can be questioned'.[75] In that sense, the ESM seems to have been a rescue operation for a version of the Washington Consensus that the Fund has grown out of since the Great Recession. Indeed, it was only the European Investment Bank and the Juncker Commission that somewhat compensated for this 'austerian' face of Europe with a countercyclical lending fund: the European Fund for Strategic Investments.

Furthermore, to better place the Fund into the European crisis management, research building on Clift's book could clarify that it is the ESM and not the Commission and the European Central Bank (ECB) that is at the very core of the Troika. Much of the current analysis misses on the fact that Article 6 (g) of the ESM Treaty stipulates that the Board of Governors of the ESM 'gives a mandate to the European Commission to negotiate, in liaison with the ECB, the economic policy conditionality attached to each financial assistance'. In effect, by creating the ESM the EU member states created a public financial company controlled by the informal consensus of the ministers of finance of the Eurozone but which leaves the adjustment program design (the Memoranda of Understanding) and their enforcement to the Commission, the ECB and the IMF (the so-called Troika/the Institutions).

73 Ban, 'Austerity versus stimulus' (n 5).

74 Cornel Ban, Leonard Seabrooke, Sarah Freitas, 'Grey matter in shadow banking: International organizations and expert strategies in global financial governance' (2016) 23 (6) *Review of International Political Economy* 1001.

75 Charlotte Rommerskirchen, 'Debt and punishment: Market discipline in the Eurozone' (2015) 20 (5) *New Political Economy* 752

Conclusions

How big was the doctrinal shift on fiscal policy at the IMF between 2008 and 2012 and what explains it? This chapter argues that Fund made significant adaptive (rated than paradigmatic) changes to its pre-crisis policy status quo. An older emphasis on maintaining states' credibility with financial markets remained the primary goal of policy but this goal now had to cohabit with greater acceptance of discretionary fiscal stimulus programs and an emphasis on *gradual* fiscal consolidation where fiscal space for stimulus was limited. Also, unlike the pre-2008 period, the IMF now advocates more balance between revenue and spending measures in the approach to fiscal consolidation.

This recalibration can be explained in part by looking at the intellectual dynamics of academic macroeconomics, staff politics and their framing tactics, with this chapter emphasizing staff politics. Changes at the managing and department director levels, the hiring of many new economists, and the strategy to wrap their tinkering activities in the cocoon of generally accepted macroeconomic models facilitated the Fund's intriguing doctrinal evolution

Bibliography

Alesina A, Perotti R, 'Income distribution, political instability, and investment' (1996) 40 (6) *European Economic Review* 1203

Abdelal R, 'The IMF and the capital account' (2006) 19 *Reforming the IMF for the 21st Century* 185

Auerbach AJ, Gorodnichenko Y, 'Output spillovers from fiscal policy' (2013) 103 (3) *American Economic Review* 141

Baum A, Poplawski-Ribeiro M, Weber A, 'Fiscal Multipliers and the State of the Economy' (2012) IMF Working Paper 12/286

Baldacci E, Kumar MS, 'Fiscal Deficits, Public Debt, and Sovereign Bond Yields' (2010) IMF Working Paper 10/184

Ban C, *Ruling Ideas: How Global Neoliberalism Goes Local* (Oxford University Press 2016)

Ban C, 'From designers to doctrinaires: Staff research and fiscal policy change at the IMF' (2015) 43 *Elites on Trial. Research in the Sociology of Organizations* 337

Ban C, 'Austerity versus stimulus? Understanding fiscal policy change at the International Monetary Fund since the great recession' (2015) 28 (2) *Governance* 167

Ban C, 'Ben Clift's *The IMF and the Politics of Austerity*' (2020) 18 (1) *Comparative European Politics* 78

Ban C, Seabrooke L, Freitas S, 'Grey matter in shadow banking: international organizations and expert strategies in global financial governance' (2016) 23 (6) *Review of International Political Economy* 1001

Batini N, Callegari G, Melina G, 'Successful Austerity in the United States, Europe, and Japan' (2012) IMF Working Paper 12/190

Barnett M, Finnemore M, *Rules for the World: International Organizations in Global Politics* (Cornell University Press 2004)

Bell DS, 'France: The Left in 2002 - The End of the Mitterrand Strategy' (2003) 56 (1) *Parliamentary Affairs* 24

Blanchard O, Perotti R, 'An Empirical Characterization of the Dynamic Effects of Changes in Government Spending and Taxes on Output' (2002) 117 (4) *The Quarterly Journal of Economics* 1329

Blanchard O, Cottarelli C, Spilimbergo A, Symansky S, 'Fiscal Policy for the Crisis' (2008) IMF Staff Position Note SNP 08/01

Blanchard O, Cottarelli C, 'Ten commandments for fiscal adjustment in advanced economies' (2010) IMF Direct Blog, 24 June 2010

Blanchard O, Milesi-Ferretti GM, 'Global Imbalances: In Midstream?' (2009) IMF Staff Position Note 09/29

Blanchard O, Leigh D, 'Growth Forecast Errors and Fiscal Multipliers' (2013) IMF Working Paper 13/1

Blyth M, *Austerity: The History of a Dangerous Idea* (Oxford University Press 2013)

Borensztein E, Panizza U, 'The costs of sovereign default' (2009) IMF Staff Papers 56(4)

Brondolo J, 'Collecting Taxes During an Economic Crisis' (2009) IMF Staff Position Note 09/23

Bockman J, Eyal G, 'Eastern Europe as a Laboratory for Economic Knowledge: The Transnational Roots of Neoliberalism' (2002) 108 (2) *American Journal of Sociology* 310

Bornhorst F, Budina N, Callegari G, ElGanainy A, Gomez Sirera R, Lemgruber A, Schaechter A, Beom Shin J, 'A Status Update on Fiscal Exit Strategies' (2010) IMF Working Paper 10/272

Broome A, Seabrooke L, 'Seeing like the IMF: Institutional Change in Small Open Economies' (2007) 14 (4) *Review of International Political Economy* 576

Chen H, Clinton K, Johnson M, Kamenik O, Laxton D, 'Constructing Forecast Confidence Bands During the Financial Crisis' (2009) IMF Working Paper 09/214

Chwieroth JM, *Capital Ideas: The IMF and the Rise of Financial Liberalization* (Princeton University Press 2009)

Clift B, *The IMF and the Politics of Austerity in the Wake of the Global Financial Crisis* (Oxford University Press 2018)

Clift B, 'Contingent Keynesianism: the IMF's model answer to the post-crash fiscal policy efficacy question in advanced economies' (2019) 26 (6) *Review of International Political Economy* 1211

Cotarelli C, Forni L, Gottschalk J, Mauro P, 'Default in Today's Advanced Economies' (2010) IMF Staff Position Note 10/12

Das U, Papaioannou M, Grigorian D, Maziad S, 'A Survey of Experiences with Emerging Market Sovereign Debt Restructurings' (2012) IMF Working Paper

Dao M, Loungani P, 'The Human Cost of Recessions: Assessing It, Reducing It' (2010) IMF Staff Position Note 10/17

Decressin J, Laxton D, 'Gauging Risks for Deflation' (2009) IMF Staff Position Note 09/01

Fourcade M, *Economists and Societies: Discipline and Profession in the United States, Britain, and France, 1890s to 1990s* (Princeton University Press 2009)

Freedman C, Kumhof M, Laxton D, Lee J, 'The Case for Global Fiscal Stimulus' (2009) IMF Staff Position Note SPN 09/03

Grabel I, 'Not Your Grandfather's IMF: Global Crisis, "Productive Incoherence" and Developmental Policy Space' (2011) 35 (5) *Cambridge Journal of Economics* 805

Hall PA, 'Policy paradigms, social learning, and the state: the case of economic policymaking in Britain' [1993] *Comparative Politics* 275

Helgadóttir O, 'The Bocconi boys go to Brussels: Italian economic ideas, professional networks and European austerity' (2016) 23 (3) *Journal of European Public Policy* 392

Helgadóttir O, Ban C, 'Managing Macroeconomic Neoliberalism: Capital and the Resilience of the Rational Expectations Assumption since the Great Recession' (2021) *New Political Economy* 1

Jaramillo L, Tejada M, 'Sovereign credit ratings and spreads in emerging markets: does investment grade matter?' (2011) IMF Working Paper 1/44

Kentikelenis AE, Stubbs TH, King LP, 'IMF conditionality and development policy space, 1985–2014' (2016) 23 (4) *Review of International Political Economy* 543

Kumar MS, Woo J, 'Public Debt and Growth' (2010) IMF Working Paper 10/174

Kumhof M, Laxton D, 'Simple, Implementable Fiscal Policy Rules' (2009) IMF Working Paper 09/76

Lane PR, Milesi-Ferretti GM, 'The cross-country incidence of the global crisis' (2011) 59 (1) *IMF Economic Review* 77

Laeven L, Valencia F, 'Resolution of Banking Crises: The Good, the Bad and the Ugly' (2010) IMF Working Paper 10/146

Latour B, *Science in Action: How to Follow Scientists and Engineers through Society* (Harvard University Press 1987)

Norregard J, 'Taxing Immovable property: revenue Potential and Implementation Challenges' (2013) IMF Working Paper 13/129

Woods N, *The Globalizers: The IMF, the World Bank, and Their Borrowers* (Cornell University Press 2006)

Balanced budgets – the vanity of a principle

Michel Bouvier

Until recently, a balanced budget, or even a surplus, was considered the "holy grail" that was essential to achieve. Conversely, debt was seen as the evil that had to be definitely avoided or controlled. However, since the onset of the coronavirus crisis, the policies pursued by the European Union as well as by the member states in an attempt to curb the pandemic have made the "whatever the cost" logic predominant. So much so that the balanced budget has been thrown out of the window and, as far as the debt is concerned, the criticisms it was subjected to have been forgotten. For the public sector, but also for the private sector, borrowing appears to be the only way to overcome both the health crisis and the economic crisis it engenders. Such oblivion of the balanced budget principle, this essential totem of what has been called "the new public management", is not only the product of a wave of panic caused by a cataclysm whose catastrophic effects to come can be imagined. Even if it is surprising, this oblivion is also indicative of the conceit/vanity of what is, above all, an ideal laid in principle that has found its strength by rooting itself in extra-financial ground.

The notion of balance, which is part of an ancestral background, of shared knowledge, of a common sense that plays an interpretive as well as a reassuring role in social phenomena, goes far beyond the realm of finance. Explanatory and securing, the principle of balance in itself has always been understood as a source of stabilization of an environment perceived as fragile, changing, secret, and ultimately troublesome. Originating in antiquity, in philosophy as well as technology, equilibrium is one of the essential principles needed to establish a stable functioning of the universe. Hence, the cosmos is conceived as a harmonious whole with the Earth forming the motionless pivot around which the stars keep their balance.

Speculative at first, this vision of the world would merge in the 17th century with the discoveries prompted by the "mechanics" that had developed itself on the basis of the notion of balance since antiquity.[1] The associated physical and

1 The first treatise on mechanics, by an unknown author, dates from Greek antiquity and reveals the theory of scale. Archimedes' theory of floating bodies and its mechanics would later serve as the basis for the thinking of Renaissance scholars.

DOI: 10.4324/9781315181882-15

natural sciences would thus carry a perennial image, that of natural balance. This approach was reinforced in the 18th century when mathematics spread to social sciences and we even came to consider, with Melon, that "everything is reducible to calculation".[2] It is also through natural sciences that economic and political phenomena would come to be apprehended and, from the observation of nature, we would seek to identify rules transposable to social relations. "What politics must do, then, is to give in to nature"[3], Turgot wrote, emulating Quesnay, the leader of the Physiocratic[4] school.

From this certainty that fueled the first liberal economic theories it was inferred that the state and its finances must be neutral. Public intervention was considered to be a form of artificial regulation, contrary to natural laws of the economy. The neutrality of the state thus finds its legitimacy in a science that marvels at the perfect balance prevailing within a natural order presented as providential. It was soon inferred that revenues and public expenditures must be exactly adjusted to ensure this neutrality. Thus, the balance of the state's budget was seen as the condition of economic balance and, more broadly, of the general balance of society. Its essence is the order – in other words, the safety of goods and people. Everyone must pay the right price – that is, taxes – for that security. In the end, the state occupies a seemingly paradoxical position because it plays a stabilizing role while being itself subject to the laws of the market.

Indeed, the balance discussed so far remains a static balance that is not in line with a society which, since the 18th century, has been presenting itself as evolutionary and dynamic. During the Enlightenment, the movement was even recognized as one of the characteristics of progress. But it was not until the 19th century that a reasoning combining staticity and movement, order and progress, began to be forged. This reasoning, always rooted in a naturalistic metaphor, then developed the idea of a dynamic balance.[5] However, the notion of balanced budgets did not follow this view, which was nevertheless carried by scientists. In terms of the budget, we remain attached to an arithmetic balance.

Balanced budgets continue to be presented as a stabilizing principle for society. This mathematical and static vision of balance is also reinforced by a family-minded conception of public management, which was perfectly expressed by F.D. Roosevelt in a 1932 speech: "Any government like any family can, for a year, spend a little

See also René François Dugas, *La mécanique au 17ème siècle* (Editions du Griffon 1954).

2 Jean François Melon, *Essai politique sur le commerce* (1736).

3 Anne Robert Jacques Turgot, baron de l'Aulne, Lettre au Contrôleur général du 4 décembre 1773.

4 The Physiocratic school was born in France at the end of the 1750s. It made a decisive contribution to forging modern concepts of economics and placing the reflection and practice of economy in an autonomous frame of reference.

5 Michel Bouvier, *L'Etat sans politique* (LGDJ 1986, avec une préface du doyen Georges Vedel).

more than it earns. But you and I know that continuing in this direction means poverty in the home."[6] The approach is decisive in the choice of financial means to be used. Tax must be the main resource, but it must not "encroach on the area reserved for individual initiative",[7] while borrowing must be limited or even outlawed. As A. Johnson writes, "The road to excessive debt is for a state the way of the devil."[8]

The idea conveyed by a new thinking, that the imbalance can be positive if it is controlled because it is a generator of movement, of energy, has not immediately changed the conception of the balanced budget carried by lawyers and economists specializing in public finances.

It is only when the weight of public spending began to increase, especially during the First World War, and even more so during the 1929 crisis, that we began to recognize that an unbalanced state budget can lead to a rebalancing of the economy. It is well known that J.M. Keynes strongly supported the idea that a global and dynamic budgetary rationale should be adopted, and that imbalance can fulfill a positive function. In other words, public finances are not comparable to private finances. Whereas the period after the Second World War might have suggested that Keynesian conceptions were firmly established, the welfare state crisis caused by the two oil shocks of the 1970s was followed by a return to an arithmetic representation of budgetary balance. This return, however, may seem perfectly anachronistic in view of the diversification of contemporary societies into a multitude of decision-making centers that sometimes make it difficult to accurately define what the public purse is.

In the end, the current complexity of public financial circuits, such as the need to respond to vagaries of all kinds and even disasters that can occur in an increasingly unpredictable and dangerous environment, leads to the question of whether this kind of balance still makes sense. This does not mean, however, that it would be appropriate to rely on an interventionist approach by the state. Apart from the fact that such a direction would run counter to a well-established liberalization of the economy, the contemporary nation-state no longer has the capacity to act as it could have during the 30-year post-war boom.

Nor is it a question of letting fiscal policies sink into blind confidence in management techniques that sometimes reach particularly high levels of sophistication at the risk of leading to financial cybernetics. Such a drift, which

6 This idea has been present since antiquity and is found in Plato's *The Republic.* It can be found at different times in history – for example, in Antoine de Montchrestien, *Treaty of Political Economy* (1615), which states: "Good domestic government, to take it well, is a patron, a public model." The same view is also present in the writings of the Nobel Prize in Economics winner, J. Buchanan ('The economic consequence of deficit' (1986) 3 *Economia delle scelte pubbliche* at 149): "My ideas are very similar to those that stand out from the common sense of the ordinary citizen… The economic consequences of financing the budget deficit through borrowing are the same […] in the conceptions of any economic unit, be it a person, a family…"

7 Rene Stourm, *Systèmes généraux d'impôts* (Editions Guillaumin et Cie 1905).

8 Alvin Johnson, 'Debt and the Devil' (1933) XXII (Spring) *Yale Review* 450.

calls into question the power of political decision-making, not only poses a threat to democracy but can also lead to serious errors in terms of public policy choices and their implementation.

Even better. The notion of balanced budget, in its various conceptions, is a source of misunderstandings and even endangerment of society. In fact, if there can be a "golden rule" in the management of public finances, it should be the authority to return their power to policy makers who are constantly aware that the budget of a public community expresses, beyond its obvious quantitative aspect and proper management, qualitative choices based on the current and future well-being of its citizens. In other words, one cannot limit themselves to assessing only by the yardstick of numerical indicators actions that concern sectors as sensitive to human well-being and to the future of society as those pertaining to health, education or the environment.

From this perspective, it is important that the political representation defines a strategy for public finances. This does not mean, it has been said, that the state would return to an interventionist attitude which, if it may have been effective in its time, is now only a sublimated imagery.

Such a strategy must take shape within an international framework and, in the immediate future, within the European framework. From this point of view, if the suspension of European rules on limiting public deficits and borrowing becomes necessary, this decision should not become the signal for a breakdown of the public financial policies of the member states of the Euro area and, more broadly, of the European Union states.

A mechanism that structures and strengthens the financial relations of states is therefore essential. Furthermore, we need to underline the importance of the decision taken by the European Commission to propose the "Next Generation EU" recovery plan, which was announced on 27 May 2020. It was the subject of heated debates from 17 to 21 July 2020 and was subsequently amended by the European Council. The plan involves issuing an EU disbursement of funds worth €750 billion and distributing it among member states, of which €390 billion would be earmarked for grants and the remaining €360 billion for loans.

However, the plan is founded on the notion that European states create a system and that, as a result, when one of them fails to function, all of them suffer, as Angela Merkel pointed out. The realization of this plan faces a number of obstacles, some of which have been eliminated. The first obstacle would require a favorable decision from all 27 member states, which is no small task. The second was just as daunting because passing such a plan meant convincing Europe's "frugal four" (Austria, Denmark, the Netherlands, and Sweden), which have their doubts when it comes to the "budgetary discipline" of certain southern European countries. The European Council initially held a video conference on 18 July 2020 to debate the recovery plan and the multiyear financial framework for 2021–2027. Despite the will to succeed in the face of the considerable danger they are all facing, significant rifts remained among the EU's member states. Nonetheless, following the video conference Charles Michel gave a speech during which he emphasized: "It was the occasion to observe that on different points there is an emerging consensus, which is very positive. But, at the same time, we don't underestimate the difficulties." Europe's southern member states were opposed to reducing the amount of EU subsidies. As to the "frugal four", they remain resolute, insisting the aid cannot be given without implementing reforms that aim at achieving the Commission's primary objectives and making investments for the climate and digital transition. Eastern European countries came out largely in favor of the plan. It was then decided that the members of the Council would meet in person during a conference in mid-July and, despite some hesitation, an agreement was reached. Concessions were made on both sides and we believe that a new step has been taken towards strengthening the institutionalized solidarity between the European Union's member states.

It must also be noted that the funding for the recovery plan has led the Commission to look into creating new taxes. The Council decided to create a "national contribution calculated on the basis of the amount of packing waste from non-recycled plastics". This tax comes into force on 1 January 2021. Furthermore, the Commission must present, during the first half of 2021, a number of proposals concerning a carbon border adjustment mechanism as well as a digital tax, with a tax on financial transaction also on the table. If the European Parliament goes on and approves, we speculate that such a proposal, together with a shared debt at the EU level, could represent the beginning of a new European budgetary model.

More. Beyond the borrowing facilities that would result for some states, or even beyond problems that might arise, it is a political issue that is at stake. This would be a step towards more solidarity and, perhaps, even towards a form of financial federalism – that is, much more than the necessary economic, budgetary or monetary coordination.

If the implementation of such a development seems difficult today, in view of the opposition of many states, the subject is of such importance that it should be pursued not only in the field of financial negotiations, but also in that of the theoretical debate. It is indeed urgent, and even crucial, to develop and implement a doctrine of public financial governance that does not stop at the gates of states.

It is crucial to build a European doctrine that clearly raises the question of financial federalism – in other words, of political federalism. Now is not the time for improvisations or perfunctory quick fixes in today's interconnected world. It is the time to create strong and appropriate political institutions for this world.

Bibliography

Bouvier M, *L'Etat sans politique* (LGDJ 1986)

Bouvier M, Esclassan C, Lassale J-P, *Manuel de Finances publiques* (*Handbook of Public Finance*) (19th ed. LGDJ-Lextenso 2020)

Buchanan JM, 'The economic consequence of deficit' (1986) 3 *Economia delle scelte pubbliche* 149–156

Dugas RF, *La mécanique au XVIIe siècle (Des antécédents scolastiques à la pensée classique)* (Editions du Griffon 1954)
Johnson A, 'Debt and the Devil' (1933) XXII (Spring) *Yale Review* 450–464
Melon JF, *Essai politique sur le commerce* (1736)
Montchrestien (de) A, *Treaty of Political Economy* (1615)
Stourm R, *Systèmes généraux d'impôts: Impôts sur le capital* (Editions Guillaumin et Cie 1905)
Turgot ARJ, baron de l'Aulne, Lettre au Contrôleur général du 4 décembre 1773

Index

Note: Locators in *italic* and **bold** refer figures and tables respectively, and locators followed by "n" refer footnotes.